D0968523

The Future of Our Religious Past

Essays
in Honour of Rudolf Bultmann

The Future of Our
Religious Past

Edited by James M. Robinson

Translated by Charles E. Carlston
and Robert P. Scharlemann

HARPER & ROW, PUBLISHERS
NEW YORK, EVANSTON, SAN FRANCISCO,
LONDON

200.9
R563

Translated from the German,
Zeit und Geschichte, Dankesgabe an Rudolf Bultmann zum 80. Geburtstag,
im Auftrage der Alten Marburger und in Zusammenarbeit mit Hartwig Thyen
herausgegeben von Erich Dinkler,
copyright J C B Mohr (Paul Siebeck), Tübingen, 1964

First published in the United States of America 1971
by Harper & Row, Publishers, Incorporated
49 East 33rd Street, New York, N.Y. 10016

Copyright © 1971 James M. Robinson
All rights reserved

Library of Congress Catalog Card No. 70–148440
Printed in Great Britain

CONTENTS

60359

TRANSLATORS' PREFACE

THE translations for a few of the essays offered here in English dress have not been provided by the co-translators of this volume. Professors Robinson and Jonas revised and translated their own essays. That of Professor Koester was revised by the author and translated by Mr Bentley Layton, a doctoral candidate at Harvard Divinity School. Professor Heidegger's essay was translated by Professor John Macquarrie. For the other essays the present translators bear sole responsibility, Professor Carlston in the exegetical portion of the work and Professor Scharlemann in the theological and philosophical section. They wish to express their thanks to Professor James M. Robinson and Professor George W. Forell for various suggestions on particular points of translation. A word of thanks is due also to Mr Hans-Dieter Knigge of Göttingen for several suggestions in connection with Professor Conzelmann's contribution.

Quotations from the Bible, including the Apocrypha, are ordinarily cited according to the Revised Standard Version, copyrighted 1946 and 1952, though in several instances a slightly different translation has been used in order to conform to the German original in the essays. The translators wish to express their appreciation to the National Council of the Churches of Christ in the USA for permission to quote from this translation.

Every effort has been made to cite corresponding pages in English translations of the German works where such translations exist. For this tedious work the translators are indebted to Dr Paul D. Meyer and Mr Fred Layman, former research assistants at the University of Iowa, who located these works and prepared the list of English works cited which is printed here as an appendix. Existing English translations have sometimes been used for citation when they seemed adequate, but a considerable freedom in retranslation has been exercised.

The translators join with the contributors to this volume in expressing their best wishes to the distinguished scholar in whose honour it is presented. May this new garb encourage a wider concern for those issues to which he has devoted his learning and his life.

Charles E. Carlston
Robert P. Scharlemann

ABBREVIATIONS

AAL	Abhandlungen der Sächsischen Akademie der Wissenschaften in Leipzig
ADAIK	Abhandlungen des Deutschen Archäologischen Instituts Kairo
AJSL	*American Journal of Semitic Languages and Literatures*
APAW	Abhandlungen der Preussischen Akademie der Wissenschaften
ASNU	Acta Seminarii Neotestamentici Upsaliensis
AThANT	Abhandlungen zur Theologie des Alten und Neuen Testaments
ATR	*Anglican Theological Review*
BevTh	Beiträge zur evangelischen Theologie
BhTh	Beiträge zur historischen Theologie
Bill.	H. L. Strack and P. Billerbeck, *Kommentar zum Neuen Testament aus Talmud und Midrasch*, 1922–56
BWANT	Beiträge zur Wissenschaft vom Alten und Neuen Testament
BZ	*Biblische Zeitschrift*
BZNW	*Beiheft zur Zeitschrift für die neutestamentliche Wissenschaft*
CBQ	*Catholic Biblical Quarterly*
CIL	*Corpus Inscriptionum Latinarum*
CN	Coniectanea Neotestamentica
DtPfrBl	*Deutsches Pfarrerblatt*
EKL	*Evangelisches Kirchenlexikon*, ed. H. Brunotte and O. Weber, 1955ff.
EvTh	*Evangelische Theologie*
ExpT	*Expository Times*
FRLANT	Forschungen zur Religion und Literatur des Alten und Neuen Testaments
GCS	Die griechischen christlichen Schriftsteller der ersten Jahrhunderte
HNT	Handbuch zum Neuen Testament, ed. H. Lietzmann
HThR	*Harvard Theological Review*
HUCA	*Hebrew Union College Annual*
HUTh	Hermeneutische Untersuchungen zur Theologie
IEJ	*Israel Exploration Journal*
JAC	*Jahrbuch für Antike und Christentum*

JBL	*Journal of Biblical Literature*
JBR	*Journal of Bible and Religion*
JR	*Journal of Religion*
JTS	*Journal of Theological Studies*
KuD	*Kerygma und Dogma*
KuM	*Kerygma und Mythos,* ed. H.-W. Bartsch
LXX	Septuagint
MDAIK	*Mitteilungen des Deutsches Archäologischen Instituts, Abteilung Kairo*
NovTest	*Novum Testamentum*
NT	New Testament
NTAbh	Neutestamentliche Abhandlungen
NTD	Das Neue Testament Deutsch, ed. P. Althaus and J. Behm
NTS	*New Testament Studies*
OT	Old Testament
*PRE*³	*Realencyclopädie für protestantische Theologie und Kirche,* ed. A. Hauck, 1896–1913
RB	*Revue Biblique*
*RGG*³	*Die Religion in Geschichte und Gegenwart,* 1957ff.³
RHPhR	*Revue d'Histoire et de Philosophie Religieuses*
RQ	*Revue de Qumran*
RSV	Revised Standard Version of the Bible
SAB	Sitzungsberichte der Deutschen Akademie der Wissenschaften zu Berlin
SAH	Sitzungsberichte der Heidelberger Akademie der Wissenschaften
SBT	Studies in Biblical Theology
SEG	*Supplementum Epigraphicum Graecum*
SHVL	Skrifter utgivna av Kungl. Humanistiska Vetenskapssamfundet i Lund
SJTh	*Scottish Journal of Theology*
StTh	*Studia Theologica*
ThBl	*Theologische Blätter*
ThEx	Theologische Existenz heute
ThLZ	*Theologische Literaturzeitung*
ThR	*Theologische Rundschau*
ThSt	*Theologische Studien*
ThViat	*Theologia Viatorum*
TU	Texte und Untersuchungen
TWNT	*Theologisches Wörterbuch zum Neuen Testament,* ed. G. Kittel and G. Friedrich
VT	*Vetus Testamentum*

VuF	*Verkündigung und Forschung*
WMANT	Wissenschaftliche Monographien zum Alten und Neuen Testament
ZAW	*Zeitschrift für die alttestamentliche Wissenschaft*
ZNW	*Zeitschrift für die neutestamentliche Wissenschaft*
ZThK	*Zeitschrift für Theologie und Kirche*

Introduction

James M. Robinson

THIS volume consists of a selection of essays from the *Festschrift* presented to Rudolf Bultmann on the occasion of his eightieth birthday, August 20, 1964. Significant volumes had already been published in honour of his sixtieth and seventieth birthdays. Yet the 1964 volume is unequalled, not only in the breadth of contributions, embracing exegesis, systematic theology, philosophy, and current events, but also in the distinction of the contributors. Especially impressive is the roster of those from outside Bultmann's own New Testament field. One need only mention such contemporary theologians as Friedrich Gogarten and Gerhard Ebeling, and philosophers such as Hans Jonas and Martin Heidegger.

In sheer size, the German volume is impressive, and can be compared with the volume of 1956 in honour of Karl Barth's seventieth birthday. To whatever extent a *Festschrift* reflects the significance of the person honoured through the visages of those who pay him homage, a comparison would seem to indicate that Barthianism has entered the twilight of the gods, whereas Bultmannianism has enjoyed a rich harvest season, including an American Indian summer. Although Barthianism has been the ecumenical theology *par excellence*, and a third of the Barthian collection comes from outside Germany, the English language world is represented very sparsely (Arthur C. Cochrane). On the other hand the Bultmannian collection not only includes the British theologian Ronald Gregor Smith and the Americans

Amos N. Wilder, Kendrick Grobel, Schubert M. Ogden and James M. Robinson; it also includes, perhaps most significantly, an impressive list of Europeans-become-American: Nils Alstrup Dahl, Dieter Georgi, Hans Jonas, Helmut Koester, Gabriel Vahanian, Eric Voegelin (and Bultmann's daughter Antje Bultmann-Lemke), as well as such a temporary American as the German editor, Erich Dinkler.

The very magnitude of the German volume has made a selection indispensable, if the English version is not to be beyond the financial reach of the public for which it is intended. Yet the remarkable *niveau* of the contents has meant that the essays which could not be included would alone compose a volume of more than usual distinction. In some cases, an omission could partly be justified in that the material was already available in English in the original volume. In general, priority was given to the New Testament and the Contemporary Theology/Philosophy contributions, in view of the envisaged reading public. Yet it was unavoidable that much material was omitted that any person competent to judge would wish to see included. The only consolation that can be offered for the omissions is the great significance of the material that has in fact been made available in English in the present volume.

The full title of the German edition reads: *Time and History: Gift of Gratitude to Rudolf Bultmann on his Eightieth Birthday, Commissioned by the Old Marburgers*. The annual October meetings of 'Old Marburgers' are well-known to English-language theology, in view of the germinal role they have played in launching some of the post-Bultmannian trends active in current theology. The new quest of the historical Jesus was launched by Käsemann at the 1953 meeting, and the debate resumed at the 1961 meeting; the debate about the later Heidegger and theology was carried on at the 1959, 1960, and 1962 meetings.

These meetings of 'Old Marburgers' have a long pre-history, as well as an American postscript. In the early 1920s the regular meetings of 'The Friends of *Die Christliche Welt*' provided an occasion for Bultmann to meet with Barth (1920), and for both to meet with Gogarten and make common cause publicly (1922).

From 1922 on Barth was in Göttingen near Marburg; his personal contacts with Bultmann tended to become small theological conferences, in that each was accompanied by his students. Such was Barth's visit to Marburg in February, 1922, during the semester when Bultmann was lecturing on Barth's *Romans*; and such was Bultmann's programmatic lecture of 1924 in Marburg on 'Liberal Theology and the Latest Theological Movement', in which he openly repudiated liberalism in favour of dialectic theology.

In the period when Heidegger taught in Marburg (1923–28), Bultmann participated in Heidegger's seminar on the philosophy of history, and Heidegger attended Bultmann's seminar on Paul. At the first annual meeting of the newly created German Theologians' Conference (1927), Bultmann presented to the New Testament section an address on the relation of dialectic theology to New Testament scholarship, which, according to the published minutes, 'by far attracted the strongest interest of all; it was like a plenary session – all other sections suspended their programmes to listen to him'. From around 1930 Bultmann led a 'theological study group' of pastors and teachers of religion from the public schools, meeting monthly in Marburg to debate current theological literature.

The most decisive meeting of Bultmann and his pupils was no doubt the one held on the occasion of the visit from Emanuel Hirsch, pro-Nazi Dean of the Theological Faculty of Göttingen, to present to the Theological Faculty of Marburg the party-line objectives for Marburg and also to reorganize them, in the summer of 1933. After his address, there was the customary adjournment to a *Weinstube* to discuss the presentation – but Bultmann conspicuously withdrew to a side room, followed by his pupils, as a blunt act of rejection of the proposal.

After the war, the annual meetings of 'Old Marburgers' were organized to pull together the scattered members of Bultmann's circle, as they returned to academic pursuits and sought to update themselves after the years of often forced separation from university life. The attendance gradually broadened to include a number of Americans as well as many who had not studied under Bultmann and were theologically not Bultmannian. The Hermeneutical Consultations at Drew University in 1962, 1964, and 1966, continued in Vanderbilt conferences organized by the *Journal for Theology and the Church* in 1968 and 1969, reflected much of the atmosphere of the more recent larger meetings of Old Marburgers, just as the meetings of the New Testament Colloquium in America and Germany reflect its more modest beginnings.

Erich Dinkler, for years the convener of the meetings of Old Marburgers, described the ethos of this sequence of Bultmannian meetings as follows: They were not 'meetings oriented to Bultmann's theology, much less to his person, as can be attested by the participants in the debates, which often were extremely lively, and the discussions, which were both rigorous and friendly. Rather it is evident . . . how Bultmann takes satisfaction in intellectual give-and-take, and responds to a "party-line" repetition of his own views with easily discernible boredom; that his desire is to push on with the work; and that he emphasized the basic open-endedness of every science, and thus of theology. The call to freedom is rooted in this basic approach, and in his view of the essence of Christian faith. To be sure it is freedom bound to the kerygma, which however, precisely in its theological explication, is to be grasped anew in freedom by each generation.'[1] This openness of the Old Marburger tradition is ultimately responsible for the quality of the essays collected in this volume.

The essays here presented are not to be read primarily as documentation of Old Marburger theology, or even as hints of further 'post-Bultmannian' trends to come. To be sure, they are more than externally called forth by Bultmann's theology, to which they do, each in its respective way, respond. But this responsiveness to Bultmann's impressive achievement is more than a concern to be responsible for carrying forward his intellectual legacy. Bultmann himself, beyond his own solutions and positions, exemplified responsiveness and responsibility as the only possible ethos for theology, indeed for humanity, in our day:

[1] Erich Dinkler, 'Rudolf Bultmann als Lehrer und Mensch', *Kirche in der Zeit* 14 (1959), pp. 257–61, esp. p. 259.

With regard to history, one is to be responsive to what the past really has to say, and responsible for representing the valid claim of the past to be heard in the present situation; and with regard to our own time, one is to be responsive to what is calling out on all sides to be heard, and responsible for the adequacy of today's response. In this sense theology that is responsive and responsible is the ultimate legacy of Bultmann, a stance that he exemplified but that far transcends in its inescapable validity the significance of any one person.

Bultmann was able to penetrate through the layers of the establishment's interpretation of the New Testament to hear and to bring to expression primitive Christianity as the radical movement it originally was. Moreover he was able to correlate that past with what has been called for in his own time. In this way he gave a religious past (that for many seemed irretrievably lost) a future with promise in our otherwise so chaotic world.

I would like to express my appreciation to the translators, who shared many of the editorial duties involved in preparing this volume for publication, and to Professor Edward Hobbs, who provided a photograph of Bultmann that has well caught the sensitivity, the humaneness, the fineness of his personality and character.

I

EXEGESIS

I

Eschatology and History
in the Light of the Dead Sea Scrolls*

Nils Alstrup Dahl

IN THIS essay[1] I understand 'eschatology' to refer to the doctrine of the last things or to statements which relate to events and persons of the end-time. I understand 'history' to refer to any human, socially relevant event in so far as it is a subject about which records exist and to which research may be directed, the object of historical study in the Greek sense.

This usage is somewhat antiquated. It comes from the period before Karl Barth had formulated the famous sentence: 'A Christianity that is not purely and simply eschatology has purely and simply nothing to do with Christ.'[2] Since that time many theologians have been inclined to designate as eschatological everything that has anything to do with Christ. By this process the meaning of the word 'eschatology' has become so polychromatic that one whose native language is not German may perhaps be given the privilege of harking back to the older usage.

Rudolf Bultmann, to be sure, uses the word 'eschatology' in such a way as to maintain the connection with its use in *religionsgeschichtliche* research. But it is obvious from these remarks

---

* Translated from *Zeit und Geschichte*, pp. 3–18.
[1] This essay is a revised form of a guest lecture given at the universities of Utrecht and Heidelberg.
[2] *Der Römerbrief*, 1922², p. 298 (ET: p. 314).

about terminology that it is not my intention to enter into the whole complex of questions surrounding 'History and Eschatology'. As this problem is posed in Bultmann's Gifford lectures[3] it has comprehensive hermeneutical, philosophical, and theological aspects. At the same time, however, a distinct picture of the history of primitive Christianity and its environment lies at the root of Bultmann's existentialist interpretation.

At many points Bultmann has taken over, probably too uncritically, the results attained by men like Wrede, Heitmüller, and Bousset in order to continue building on this foundation.[4] As far as the understanding of eschatology is concerned, a connection with Albert Schweitzer seems to me to be perfectly clear. For Bultmann, eschatology is that salvation 'which ends everything earthly'.[5] 'It is the doctrine of the end of the world, of its destruction.'[6] Jesus Christ, correspondingly, is '*the eschatological event*, the action of God by which God has set an end to the old world . . . The old world has reached its end for the believer.' The stance of faith can be characterized as 'de-secularization', and Christian existence means paradoxically 'that the believer is taken out of the world and exists, so to speak, as unworldly and that at the same time he remains within the world, within his historicity'.[7] But as early as Albert Schweitzer the word 'eschatology' had been stamped with a new meaning; it meant not merely the doctrine of the last things but rather an orientation of existence determined by the nearness of the end of the world: 'The term eschatology ought to be applied only when reference is made to the end of the world as expected in the immediate future, and the events, hopes, and fears connected therewith.'[8] Behind Paul's expectation stands the conception 'that Jesus

[3] *History and Eschatology*, 1957 (Germ., 1958, 1964²).

[4] On this see my review of Bultmann's *Theologie des NT* in *ThR* 22 (1954), pp. 21–49.

[5] *Jesus*, 1926, pp. 34f. (ET: *Jesus and the Word*, p. 35).

[6] *History and Eschatology*, p. 23 (Germ.: p. 24).

[7] *Ibid.*, pp. 151, 152f. (Germ.: pp. 180, 183f.); cf. *Theologie* . . . , 1961⁴, p. 307 (ET: I, pp. 311f.). *KuM* I, 1951, p. 29 (ET: I, pp. 17ff.).

[8] *Geschichte der paulinischen Forschung*, 1911, p. 178 (ET: *Paul and His Interpreters*, p. 228). Cf. *Geschichte der Leben-Jesu-Forschung*, 1913², p. 23 n. 2 [omitted in ET – tr.].

Christ has made an end of the natural world'.[9] When statements like these are placed alongside one another, one may be permitted to say that Rudolf Bultmann has interpreted Albert Schweitzer's concept of eschatology in an existentialist fashion.

Naturally establishing this does not in any way minimize the many and far-reaching differences between Bultmann and Schweitzer. Schweitzer was never really a good exegete. But before him Johannes Weiss had set forth with exegetical sobriety the eschatological nature of Jesus' preaching of the Kingdom of God. Albert Schweitzer, building on this basis, ingeniously and one-sidedly made eschatology the principal key to an historical reconstruction of the life of Jesus and the history of primitive Christianity. But the presuppositions of the new understanding of eschatology lay further back; they were implicit in the fact that about the middle of the previous century the world of Jewish apocalyptic had first been rendered accessible to scholarship.[10] To this extent one may say, rather crudely and one-sidedly, that Bultmann's works on the theme 'Eschatology and History' stand at the end of a period in the history of research that began with the accessibility of the literature of apocalyptic.

Today research is in one respect in a situation like that of about a century ago. New source material for the history of Judaism and its eschatology has become accessible to us, but the scientific and theological study of it is still only partial. If the new material from the caves of Qumran is to be rightly assessed and evaluated it seems appropriate to me to work with a terminology burdened as little as possible with contemporary issues. Hence my old-fashioned usage.

The new materials cannot be fitted easily into our current picture of late-Jewish eschatology. From Baldensperger to Mowinckel,[11] to cite only two names, it is common to distinguish

[9] *Die Mystik des Apostels Paulus*, 1930, p. 56 (ET: p. 54).

[10] Cf., e.g., A. Dillmann, *Liber Henoch*, 1851 or his *Das Buch Henoch*, 1853; A. Hilgenfeld, *Jüdische Apokalyptik*, 1857.

[11] W. Baldensperger, *Das Selbstbewusstsein Jesu im Lichte der messianischen Hoffnungen seiner Zeit*, 1888; S. Mowinckel, *Han som kommer*, 1951 (ET: *He That Cometh*, 1956); cf. also W. Bousset (and H. Gressmann), *Die Religion des Judentums*, 1902, 1926[3].

between a national, this-worldly future hope and a universalistic and transcendental apocalyptic. The Davidic Messiah is supposed to belong to the first strand, which is purely Jewish, while the heavenly Son of Man is supposed to belong to the second, which has been influenced by Parseeism. In the Qumran writings we find a dualistic doctrine of two spirits, the Prince of Light and the Angel of Darkness, who stand opposed to one another from the creation until the end of the world. But an apocalyptic, superhuman Messiah-figure does not correspond to this speculative doctrine by any means. Not a trace of the Son of Man is to be found. Instead, the eschatological personages named in the Qumran writings are office-holders within the Israel of the last days.

But the two strands of thought, the dualistic and the messianic, do not simply stand side by side. The dualism appears concretely as a dualism between the sons of light and the sons of darkness, i.e., for all practical purposes, between the members of the sect and their opponents. In the foreordained, eschatological conflict between the two groups, the eschatological office-bearers have their functions. Hence it is permissible to elaborate the relationship between eschatology and history on the basis of what is predicated of these persons. This is all the more appropriate in view of the fact that in the New Testament eschatology and history meet primarily in christology.

Scholarly views of the significance of the Qumran materials for the historical understanding of christological origins diverge widely. A. Dupont-Sommer has conceived the so-called 'Teacher of Righteousness' as a Christ-figure before Christ. Others have thought rather to explain the christology of Hebrews or the use of the title 'Christ' in the Synoptics on the basis of Qumran's doctrine of a priestly Messiah.[12] But on the other hand a diametrically opposed assertion is also made: some assert that we

[12] A. Dupont-Sommer, *Aperçus préliminaires sur les manuscrits de la mer Morte*, 1950 (ET: *The Dead Sea Scrolls: A Preliminary Survey*, 1952); and *Les Écrits ésséniens*, 1959 (ET: *The Essene Writings from Qumran*, 1962); H. Kosmala, *Hebräer—Essener—Christen*, 1959; G. Friedrich, 'Beobachtungen zur messianischen Hohepriestererwartung in den Synoptikern', *ZThK* 53 (1956), 265–311.

may say flatly and apodictically that the Qumran texts are totally without significance for the christology of the primitive church.[13] In my opinion, this latter judgment rests on a soberer exegesis and on a sharper ability to make critical distinctions. Yet this purely negative assertion is not the last word on the question. Our task now is to go beyond the direct comparison of isolated texts and concepts to a more structural way of looking at the matter. Krister Stendahl in particular has emphasized this.[14] But Bultmann has also seen it, in that he finds the most significant analogy between the primitive Christian community and the sect of Qumran in the fact that both understood themselves as the True Israel of the last days.[15]

Until recently we had, on the one hand, a body of late-Jewish eschatological literature that was in varying degrees difficult to date; we had little information about the historical and socio-logical background of its expressions and concepts. On the other hand we had, especially in Josephus, a whole series of reports and notices about freedom fighters and charismatics of the period between Judas Maccabaeus and Simon bar Kochba. But how the eschatological expectations and the claims of the leading figures were grounded and how by the interpretation of the Promises they were elaborated ideologically – on this the sources were almost completely silent.

The Qumran materials have now put us in a new situation. The picture of the messianic conceptions of pre-Christian Juda-ism has been expanded and corrected. The necessity of collating and comparing the Qumran materials with Jewish thought as attested elsewhere frees us from the innate tendency to inter-rogate Jewish messianic conceptions too quickly and too un-critically about their positive and negative relationships to christology. It is of great importance that we have now been rather precisely instructed about not only the eschatological doctrines but also the sociological structure and history of one

---

[13] G. Jeremias, *Der Lehrer der Gerechtigkeit* (Studien zur Umwelt des NT 2), 1963, p. 321.

[14] *The Scrolls and the New Testament*, 1957, pp. 1–17.

[15] *Theologie*, 1958³, Vorwort [not in ET of 1954 – tr.].

and the same movement. In other words: it has now become possible to study the relationship between eschatology and history within a community that is temporally and spatially close to Jesus and the primitive church. Such a study will show quite clearly how history was interpreted in the light of eschatology and conversely how the traditional eschatology was transformed by history.

At the end of a series of regulations in the Manual of Discipline it says: 'You shall judge according to the earlier laws, by which the men of the community from the very beginning have been disciplined, until a Prophet and the Anointed of Aaron and Israel come.'[16] The regulations were accordingly understood as interim laws which were not to be changed during the pre-eschatological period. A corresponding expression occurs frequently in the Damascus Document.[17] But this kind of expression is also known from other writings:

'Until a trustworthy prophet should arise' (I Macc. 14.41; cf. 4.46).

'Until there should arise a (the) priest with Urim and Thummim' (Ezra 2.63; Neh. 7.65).

'Until he comes to whom right belongs' (Ezek. 21.32).

So also the messianically interpreted saying about Judah in Gen. 49.10: (or שׁילה) עד כי יבא שׁילה. In the exegesis of the men of Qumran still another passage is added, Hos. 10.12: עד יבוא וירה צדק לכם. This may be understood as 'until he comes and teaches you righteousness' or 'until the Teacher of Righteousness comes for you' (cf. CD vi. 11). In the Talmudic and post-Talmudic literature this text was related to the return of Elijah.[18]

The eschatological interpretation of these biblical passages must have belonged to the common Jewish exegetical tradition. But in the text from the Manual of Discipline (1QS 9.10f.), Prophet, royal Messiah, and priestly Messiah are mentioned side

[16] 1QS 9.10f., according to the very free rendering in H. Bardtke, *Handschriftenfunde am Toten Meer*, 1953.

[17] CD vi.10f.; xii.23f.; xx.l. Cf. 4QPB 3f.

[18] L. Ginzberg, *Eine unbekannte jüdische Sekte*, 1922, pp. 303ff.

by side. That these three are the figures intended has been known
for a long time, and the fact has been confirmed by the citation
of Deut. 18.18ff.;[19] Num. 24.15–17; and Deut. 33.8–11 in a collection of testimonies.[20] We ought not to interpret these texts
on the basis of a Christian concept of messianic precursors; the
texts speak of three simultaneous eschatological office-bearers.[21]
In the emphasis on distinguishing the three offices we may well
see a polemical point directed against the uniting of them that
took place under the Hasmonean priest-kings. It is said of John
Hyrcanus, in fact, that he combined prophetic gifts with regal
and high-priestly dignity.[22]

The expectation of all three figures was grounded in the sacred
scriptures; but the scriptural basis was utilized quite differently
in each case. As far as the Prophet is concerned, we really know
nothing beyond the fact that the prediction of the 'Prophet like
Moses' was referred to him.[23] Among the Samaritans and perhaps in wider circles as well he stood in the centre of expectation.

[19] More precisely, Ex. 20.21b in a text that agrees with the Samaritan
recension. Cf. Skehan's observations in J. T. Milik, *Ten Years of Discovery in
the Wilderness of Judaea* (SBT 26), 1959, p. 124 n. 1.

[20] 4QT. R. Meyer would refer all three testimonies to the 'Teacher of
Righteousness'. (' "Eliah" und "Ahab" ', *Abraham unser Vater: Festschrift für
O. Michel* [Arbeiten zur Geschichte des Spätjudentums und Urchristentums
5], 1963, pp. 356–68.) But the general structure of the sect and its teaching
make it unlikely that the Teacher was viewed as the bearer of this threefold
office. Cf. G. Jeremias, *op. cit.*, and A. S. van der Woude, *Die messianischen
Vorstellungen der Gemeinde von Qumran* (Studia semitica Nederlandica 3), 1957.

[21] That these figures are essentially contemporaneous is not to be questioned, even if one conceives of the high priest (Elijah) as already present
upon the Messiah's arrival. Cf., e.g., 4QFlor 1.11 and Justin, Dial. 8. In
John 1.20f. Messiah, Elijah, and the Prophet are similarly mentioned side
by side, perhaps as bearers of the three offices. The conception of Elijah as
eschatological high priest is pre-Christian, attested for the time of John
Hyrcanus by Targum Pseudo-Jon. on Deut. 32.11. On this see in the
Festschrift für O. Michel (note 20 above), R. Meyer (pp. 356ff.) and S.
Schulz (pp. 434f., following Geiger).

[22] Josephus, *Antiq.* xiii.299; *Bill* i.68. Cf., e.g., R. Meyer, *Der Prophet aus
Galiläa*, 1940, pp. 6off.; *TWNT* VI, pp. 825f. (ET: pp. 825f.).

[23] In a still unpublished text from Cave 4 the true Prophet is said to be
known by the anointed Priest. Cf. Milik, *op. cit.*, p. 126. On the Prophet, cf.,
inter alia, H. M. Teeple, *The Mosaic Eschatological Prophet* (*JBL* Monograph
Series 10), 1957.

In later 'normative' Judaism, on the other hand, the Prophet as a separate eschatological figure dies out. Perhaps enthusiasts were too readily tempted to play the Prophet.

What is said in the Qumran texts about the Davidic Messiah, the Anointed of Israel, is almost entirely paraphrase and exegesis of well-known messianic predictions: Gen. 49.8–12; Num. 24.15–17; Isa. 11; etc.[24] Of special interest is the unambiguous evidence that in pre-Christian Judaism the promise given through Nathan in II Sam. 7 was interpreted messianically. This text must have been of very great significance for the beginnings of christology and for the emergence and development of the whole complex of messianic expectation. The rabbis, on the other hand, avoid the text, apparently because it could be made to serve as the basis of the doctrine of Christ's divine sonship.[25]

The portrait of the Messiah in the Qumran writings is in essential agreement with that of Jewish tradition, as, e.g., in Ps. Sol. 17. But it has been modified. In its connection with the priestly-theocratic ideals of an Ezekiel the Branch of David is called not king but 'Prince of the community' (נשיא). In the congregational meeting, at the sacred meal, and even in the eschatological war he is ranged alongside and subordinated to the eschatological high priest.[26] In this the structure of the community is reflected.

[24] 1QSb 5.20–29; 1QM 11.6f.; 4QPB; 4QT; 4QpIs^a; CD vii.19f. Also van der Woude, *op. cit.*, *passim*, though he does not go systematically into the question of the scriptural basis of the messianic teaching.

[25] Cf. esp. 4QFl; in addition, 4QPB 2–4. From pre-Christian Judaism the following may be mentioned: Sir. 45.25; Ps. Sol. 17.4. From the NT: Heb. 1.5; 3.2, 6; Rom. 1.3f.; Luke 1.32f.; 22.28–30; Acts 2.30; 13.22, 32ff.; Rev. 22.16; probably also Matt. 16.16ff. (ὁ χριστὸς ὁ υἱὸς τοῦ θεοῦ . . . οἰκοδομήσω); 22.41–44 (τίνος υἱός ἐστιν); Mark 14.57–62 (οἰκοδομήσω . . . ὁ χριστὸς ὁ υἱὸς τοῦ εὐλογητοῦ); John 8.35 (οἰκία . . . ὁ υἱὸς μένει εἰς τὸν αἰῶνα). Cf. A. van Iersel, *'Der Sohn' in den synoptischen Jesusworten* (Suppl. to *NovTest* 3), 1961, 1964²; E. Lövestam, *Son and Saviour* (CN 18), 1961; S. Aalen, ' "Reign" and "House" ', *NTS* 8(1961/2), pp. 215–40, esp. pp. 233–40. For the OT: G. von Rad, *Theologie des AT*, I⁴, 1962, pp. 53f., 322ff., etc; II³, 1962, p. 58 (ET: I, pp. 40f., 318ff.; II, pp. 45f.). The questions of the age and original form of Nathan's prophecy may remain open, as may the question of the relationship to Pss. 89 and 132.

[26] 1QSa 2.11f. and 2.17ff.; 1QM 5.1 compared with 15.4ff., etc. So also, probably, the mutilated texts, 4QPB 4f. and 4QpIs^a frag. D.

The expectation of an eschatological Aaronitic high priest will also have belonged to the constituent elements of the older eschatology. From Zechariah (chs. 3, 4 and 6) as well as Jeremiah (33.17–22) one could learn that in the eschatological era a Levitical priest would stand alongside the Davidic ruler. Several texts could be related to the eschatological high priest: the saying of Levi in Deut. 33.8–11, the promise to Phineas of an eternal priesthood (Num. 25.11–13), and the word of God's covenant with Levi in Mal. 2.4–8. This may be confirmed from rabbinic sources, even though in them the eschatological high priest (כהן צדק) remains an extremely stereotyped figure.[27] Yet in the Qumran writings these OT texts remain remarkably little used. Instead the functions of the high priest are described in great detail.[28] But in the process the cultic service proper, with sacrifices and expiatory rites, is emphasized less than the mandate of the coming high priest to offer prayers and blessings in the congregation of the community, at the common meal, and in the holy war and to instruct the community about God's will as set forth in the scriptures. In other words: the picture of the messianic prince is traditional, while that of the high priest is largely projected into the future. For this future high priest the activity of a practising priest within the Qumran community has served as a model.

In the case of the historical Teacher of Righteousness the relationship to the words of scripture is a still different one. His name, מורה צדק, comes from the passage already cited, Hos. 10.12 (cf. also Joel 2.23: נתן לכם את המורה לצדקה). But these texts are not cited in the extant Qumran corpus. Instead a whole series of words from the prophets and the Psalms are related to the מורה צדק and his opponents. Obviously these texts were not understood in advance as statements of the coming Teacher of Righteousness. They were rather cited because they were patient of an *ex eventu* interpretation as predictions of the appearance and eventual fate of the community's founder, designated by the

[27] Material in Bill. IV, pp. 462ff., pp. 789ff.; Ginzberg, *op. cit.*, pp. 340ff.
[28] 1QSa 2.12ff., 19f.; 1QSb 2.24–3.21; 1QM 2.1ff.; 10.1–12.15; 15.4ff.; 16.3–17.9; 18.5ff.; 19.11ff.

title of מורה צדק.[29] The historical Teacher was understood as
fulfilling the hope of a coming מורה צדק, and on the basis of his
eventual fate many texts were reinterpreted as predictions.

A critical examination of the texts yields no convincing evidence for the hypothesis that the return of the historical Teacher
in the form of a priestly Messiah was expected.[30] But it does
produce a considerable body of evidence connecting him with
the Aaronic Messiah. Both bear the same names: 'the priest',
'Interpreter of the Torah', 'Teacher of Righteousness'.[31] In
large measure they also have the same functions: teaching, exposition of scripture, prayer, praise, and leadership of the community.[32] Of course one may speak only of an identity of office,
not an identity of persons.[33] The distinction springs from the fact
that the historical מורה צדק exercised his function at the time of
the eschatological tribulation, while the messianic high priest is
to take office only at the time of the eschatological war and final
salvation. From this it may be concluded that the picture of the
historical Teacher and that of the eschatological high priest have
mutually influenced one another.

It is occasionally asserted that the מורה צדק was identified
with the eschatological prophet.[34] But there is no basis in the

[29] Numerous examples in 1QpHab and the other commentaries, e.g., on
Hab. 1.4, 13; 2.2, 4, 8, 15; Ps. 37.23, 32; also on Num. 21.18 and Isa. 54.6
in CD vi.3–8. The analogy with the christological exegesis of primitive
Christianity is obvious.

[30] Cf. J. Carmignac, 'Le retour du Docteur de Justice à la fin des jours?'
RQ 1(1958/59), pp. 235–48; G. Jeremias, *op. cit.*, pp. 275ff.

[31] הכוהן, eschatological: 1QSa 2.19; 1QM 10.2 (Deut. 20.2); possibly
also 1Q22 4.8; 1Q29 5.2. Historical: 1QpHab 2.8; 4QpPs 37.2, 15.

דורש התורה, eschatological: 4QFl 1.11; possibly 4QPB 6. Historical:
CD vi.7. Uncertain: CD vii.18.

מורה הצדק, historical: 1QpHab 1.13, etc.; cf. CD i.11; xx.32.
יורה הצדק, eschatological: CD vi.11.

[32] This becomes especially clear if one may trace the Hodayoth back to the
community's Teacher – whether in whole or in part is in this respect a
matter of indifference.

[33] G. Jeremias has already done this (*op. cit.*, pp. 283ff.), but only with
relation to the title מורה צדק and without drawing the full consequences of
it.

[34] So, e.g., van der Woude, *op. cit.*, pp. 186f.; *per contra* (rightly), G.
Jeremias, *op. cit.*, pp. 296ff.

text for this hypothesis. Yet it is quite understandable that the expectation of the Prophet became untenable, since there was really no special function left for him. The task of a prophet in this environment must have been primarily the inspired exegesis of scripture and legal pronouncements, and these tasks were actually assumed by the historical Teacher and the eschatological priest.

Another hypothesis, however, is very much worthy of mention, namely that the Teacher was thought of during his lifetime as a candidate for high priestly dignity and to this extent as an Aaronitic *Messias designatus*.[35] This would explain many things. Yet many questions still remain, difficult historical questions – was the מורה צדק a legitimate Zadokite? – and exegetical problems, especially in the interpretation of the Damascus Document.[36]

Within the movement which we may characterize as Essene, eschatological concepts underwent a change. In Judaism what bound the communities' members together and marked them off from other groups was much more the legal ordering of life than theological teachings.[37] In the Damascus Document a single Messiah of Aaron and Israel has come from the two figures,

[35] Cf. D. Flusser, 'Two Notes on the Midrash on II Samuel 7', *IEJ* 9(1959), pp.99–109. According to 4QFl 1.11 the Branch of David will appear at the end of days with the Interpreter of the Law. But it is questionable whether one may date the content of the collection of testimonies back to the lifetime of the Interpreter of the Law/Teacher of Righteousness.

[36] Most hotly contested is the interpretation of CD vii.18–21. In the interpretation of Num.24.17, 'Sceptre' is related to the 'Prince of the Community', 'Star' to the 'Interpreter of the Law'. This seems to reflect the doctrine of the two Anointed Ones. But in what precedes Amos 5.26 has been related to the historical beginnings of the sect. Hence the question is whether the sentence 'And the Star is the Interpreter of the Law who comes to Damascus' is to be understood as a future or a perfect. Linguistically both are possible. In favour of a relationship to the past is not only the context but also the fact that in CD vi.7 'Interpreter of the Law' is an unambiguous designation of the historical Teacher. The difficulties are most readily resolved by the hypothesis that in CD vii.10ff. traditional testimonies are used which go back to a time when it was still believed that the Teacher of the community would become high priest in the messianic era.

[37] Cf. M. Smith, 'What Is Implied by the Variety of Messianic Figures?', *JBL* 78 (1959), pp.66–72.

the Anointed One of Aaron and the Anointed One of Israel. The
singular in the medieval manuscript from the Cairo Genizah
may now no longer be viewed as a scribal error, since it is also
said to be attested in a fragment from Cave 4.[38] The transformation of the eschatology may be connected with a change
in the sociological structure. In the Damascus Document the
twofold division seems to be missing within the community
leadership as well. The designations 'Priests', 'Levites', and 'sons
of Zadok' were spiritualized in Essene exegesis and related to
the first generation of this penitential movement, its adherents
and the elect at the end of days.[39] In its messianic doctrine the
duality of priestly and princely office is given up; a much greater
emphasis is given instead to the chronologically conditioned duality between the sometime מורה צדק and the coming Anointed
One of Aaron and Israel, who is apparently known as 'the Prince
of the whole community' and 'he who teaches righteousness' as
well.[40] This transformation may also be connected with the fact
that in the particular branch of the movement reflected in the
Damascus Document the animosity towards the Hasmonean
princes has died out. Nothing is said here about the opponent
of the righteous Teacher.

Naturally we could discuss at great length the interpretations
of individual texts and historical details. But my concern is really
only with what the individual details show, namely the correlation between the sociological structure and history of the com-

---

[38] Milik, *op. cit.*, p. 125, with n. 3. A plausible explanation of the data is
given by J. F. Priest, 'Mebaqqer, Paqid, and the Messiah', *JBL* 81 (1962),
pp. 55–61.

[39] CD iii.21–iv.4. Elsewhere, to be sure, the distinction between priests,
Levites, and laymen is maintained: CD x.5f.; xiv.3ff.

[40] Cf. CD vi.7–11; xix.35–xx.1. CD vii.18–21 may also have to be interpreted in agreement with these texts (cf. above, note 36). The hypothesis of
a re-working of older traditions also makes it relatively easy to explain the
apparently complicated teaching of the Damascus Document: Only one
Messiah is expected, who will exercise teaching (CD vi.10f.; xii.23), ruling
(CD vii.20f.; xix.10ff.) and – apparently – also priestly functions (CD xiv.19).
In this context, then, 'Aaron and Israel' no longer means priesthood and
laity; it means rather a priestly-Israelitic community of the New Covenant.
Cf. F. F. Hvidberg, *Menigheden af den nye Pagt i Damascus*, 1928, pp. 28of.

munity and its eschatological interpretation of scripture and messianic doctrine. Persons and events are understood in the light of eschatological prophecies, and texts and concepts handed down in the tradition have been re-ordered on the basis of events. In this process interpretation and re-interpretation are not only things added subsequently to the events; in the events themselves eschatological meanings and revisions of meanings must have acted as constitutive factors.

The process of interpretation and re-interpretation, of historicizing and eschatologizing, was certainly not something peculiar to the Essenes. Something similar had happened again and again. At the very beginning of messianic doctrine, there are both an already extant ideology of kingship and the particular history of David. It must have been hoped in the case of many a king of Judah that he would become a new David and by the grace of God be a redemptive king. But the hopes proved illusory and were projected into the more distant future. Deutero-Isaiah rendered the eschatological hopes concrete. In part his predictions were fulfilled; yet they remained important as promises for a more distant future. What Haggai and Zechariah prophesied of the Davidic Zerubbabel and the high priest Joshua became the basis of the teaching of the two Anointed Ones. In the book of Daniel old traditions were related to the present and the immediate future; later Daniel formed the basis of all apocalyptic. One cannot properly speak of eschatology in Maccabean times, if one associates the concept of the end of the world with the word. Yet they surely thought they were living in a time when the fulfilment of the promises was taking place.[41] The Hasmonean priest-kings seem to have compensated for their lack of legitimacy by the assertion that their generation was on account of their zeal for God the true spiritual posterity of Phineas.[42] In widely varied forms the same pattern must have been repeated in the Zealot movements. The expectation of a Messiah ben Ephraim, falling in war, is of course anchored in

[41] Cf. esp. I Macc. 14.4–15.
[42] I Macc. 2.26, 54. Cf. W. R. Farmer, *Maccabees, Zealots, and Josephus*, 1956, pp. 178f. and M. Hengel, *Die Zeloten*, 1961, pp. 168ff.

the scripture, but it none the less must reflect the fate of the leaders in the wars of liberation, above all that of Bar Cochba.[43]

The extent to which the eschatological exegesis of scripture could become distorted on the basis of the factual event becomes frighteningly clear in Josephus, who was capable of referring the saying about the coming world-ruler from Judea (Gen. 49.10) to Vespasian.[44] An example from a very much later period is the story of Sabbatai Zewi, who was converted to Islam in prison. This led to the elaboration of a doctrine of the divine necessity of the apostasy of the Messiah. Gerschom Scholem has seen this as the most interesting parallel to the Christian teaching of the crucified Messiah – quite correctly, from the Jewish standpoint.[45]

The Qumran writings are thus peculiarly suited to sharpening our awareness of the diversity and possibilities of variation in the Jewish teaching regarding eschatological figures. Our rapid survey has yielded the conclusion that the correlation of eschatology and history is by no means an exclusively Christian or New Testament phenomenon. On the contrary, the expectations for the future are always related to the situation in the present, and the eschatological texts and conceptions are always correspondingly re-interpreted. Expectations of fulfilment in the immediate future, the near future, or the distant future; realized eschatology, eschatology in the process of realization, proleptic eschatology, inaugurated eschatology – all of this, *mutatis mutandis*, can be found in Judaism, too. The problem of the delay of the anticipated time of fulfilment was only too well known.[46]

What is new and unique in the teaching of Jesus is not the mere belief that the End, the time of salvation, has come near or already entered the present. The key here is not the simple fact; it is most decisively the What, the How, and the Who of the fact. Historical event, scriptural exegesis, and eschatology are

[43] Cf., e.g., R. Meyer, *Der Prophet aus Galiläa*, pp. 76–82.

[44] *Bell.* vi.312f.; cf. iii.351–4, 400ff. J. Blenkinsopp, 'The Oracle of Judah and the Messianic Entry', *JBL* 80 (1961), pp. 55–64.

[45] *Major Trends in Jewish Mysticism*, 1941, 1961⁴, pp. 307–10.

[46] Cf. A. Strobel, *Untersuchungen zum eschatologischen Verzögerungsproblem* (Suppl. to *NovTest* 2), 1961.

combined with one another in primitive Christianity in about the same way as in the Qumran writings and elsewhere in Judaism. Only in the New Testament everything has changed because of its connection with other and different events – in other words, with the name 'Jesus Christ', which is at once an historical and an eschatological name.

Just how the relationship between the historical event, eschatological teaching, and re-interpretation of the scripture is structured in the New Testament could only be made clear in comprehensive detailed investigations on several levels. But I take the liberty of pointing out several aspects of this relationship which strike me as working hypotheses:

1. The carrying over and applying to Jesus of the title, Messiah, and the new meaning which it acquires as the name of Jesus, are not to be explained on the basis of either the Jewish concept of the Messiah or the proclamation of Jesus, nor on the basis of the resurrection faith as such. What was decisive was the historical fact that Jesus was accused as a messianic pretender and executed as 'King of the Jews'.[47] This brute fact led to the christological re-interpretation of the messianic texts and concepts; it also explains the fact that texts which were not related to the Messiah in Judaism were read as messianic predictions in the primitive church.

2. The Easter events were for the disciples primarily something which were not anticipated but which none the less had taken place, an *interpretandum* rather than an *interpretation* of the meaning of Jesus and his death.[48] The events were interpreted in connection with the eschatological hope of resurrection and the scriptural witness, and the interpretations were extremely varied. On the basis of the resurrection of Christ, which had

---

[47] Cf. my essay, 'Der gekreuzigte Messias', in *Der historische Jesus und der kerygmatische Christus*, ed. H. Ristow and K. Matthiae, 1960, 1961², pp. 149–69. F. Hahn comes to essentially the same conclusion: *Christologische Hoheitstitel* (FRLANT 83), 1963, pp. 193–218.

[48] I would still hold this statement to be correct even if the story of the empty tomb were purely legendary. I doubt, however, that it is, with H. Fr. von Campenhausen, *Der Ablauf der Osterereignisse und das leere Grab* (SAH, 1952, 1958²).

already happened, the entire eschatology had to be rearranged, and this was done in a way never anticipated in Judaism.

3. The events of the death and resurrection of Jesus led to a heightening of the eschatological anticipation.[49] The changed use of the formula 'until so-and-so comes' in Paul may serve as an illustration of this. The one who is to come is identified with him who died for us. In the interim between the present and his coming more is involved than merely holding fast to the legal pronouncements of a particular teacher: with thanksgiving the bread is broken and the cup blessed in remembrance of Jesus and thus the Lord's death is proclaimed 'until he comes' (I Cor. 11.26). But the language of the eschatological formula can also be related to the earthly coming of Jesus, so related, in fact, that the Mosaic Law itself is conceived of as an interim ordinance: It was added because of transgressions, 'until the seed should come to whom the Promise has been made' (Gal 3.19).[50]

4. The growth of the expectation of the Parousia in the primitive Christian church also belongs here, as an example of the revising of eschatology on the basis of historical events. In Judaism what was awaited was the coming of the eschatological office-bearer and, in association with it, the messianic assumption of power; in many circles this hope may have taken the form of hoping for the heavenly enthronement of the Son of Man.[51] But the conception of a Parousia of the Messiah in the sense of his coming from heaven to earth at the end of time is unattested in Jewish sources. The primitive Christian expecta-

[49] Cf. Stendahl, op. cit., pp. 13ff.

[50] This text may be understood as an interpretive paraphrase of Gen. 49.10 (Heb.): 'Until (the seed) comes, to whom (the Promise refers).' Similar interpretive citations are to be found, e.g., in Rom. 3.20; I Cor. 15.45. The fact that in Gal. 3.16, 19 the word 'seed' (Gen. 17.7f. or 13.15, 17, etc.) is understood as a designation of the Messiah has an analogy and presupposition in the messianic exegesis of 'seed' in II Sam. 7.12; cf. 4QFl 1.10ff.; 4QPB 4. The messianic understanding of Gen. 3.15 (and 4.25) would also be a possible analogy if it were pre-Christian. (Cf. Billerbeck, op. cit., I, p. 958, n. 1; pp. 26f.)

[51] On the conception in the similitudes of Enoch, cf. E. Sjöberg, *Der Menschensohn im äthiopischen Henochbuch* (SHVL 41), 1946, pp. 61ff. On the terminology, see P. L. Schoonheim, *Een semasiologisch Onderzoek van Parousia*, 1953.

tion of the Parousia, on the other hand, is essentially the hope that he who had already been present on earth would come in power and glory from heaven. It is consequently a mistake to take the expectation of the Parousia and the near end of the world as a starting-point and thus to view the delay of the Parousia as the principal problem of primitive Christian eschatology.[52]

5. Unlike what often happened in Judaism, the eschatological expectations brought into being by Jesus were not subsequently loosened from his person in order to be associated with new historical figures. As far as the *dramatis personae* of salvation were concerned, the ever varying correlation between eschatology and history came to an end with the christological confession. The only thing that could be re-actualized continually on the basis of historical events was the expectation of the Parousia, and this happened in many ways even during the New Testament period. Thus the Christian teaching about the Last Things became, much more radically than in Judaism, a doctrine of the world and the end of history.

6. In many variations in details the New Testament transformation of eschatology is characterized by the tendency to relate all the promises to Jesus (cf. II Cor. 1.20!). Texts and honorific titles which in Judaism were divided among different eschatological – or non-eschatological – figures all served to express the dignity and meaning of the one Christ. This concentration on Jesus and the corresponding cumulation of all titles and testimonia cannot be explained on the basis of the bare facts of Jesus' crucifixion and resurrection. It presupposes rather the person and ministry of the earthly Jesus – even if he

[52] This is done often and much too uncritically in recent German scholarship; cf., e.g., E. Grässer, *Das Problem der Parusieverzögerung* (BZNW 22), 1957. F. Hahn also uncritically accepts the view that statements about the Parousia belong to the oldest stratum of tradition and finds evidence of this even in the Apocalypse and in the Lukan birth-stories (*op. cit.*, pp. 179–89; 288). Over against this tendency English scholars are right at least in so far as they have seen an historical problem even in the genesis of the Christian expectation of the Parousia; Cf. T. F. Glasson, *The Second Advent*, 1945; J. A. T. Robinson, *Jesus and His Coming*, 1957.

himself laid no claim to any messianic title. He did not permit
himself to be thought of in terms of any already extant messianic category; yet he came forth with such authority that all
the disciples' hopes were concentrated on him.

7. The central theme of biblical eschatology is not so much
the end of the world and the end of history as the fulfilment of
the promises.[53] For the New Testament Jesus Christ is an
eschatological figure and the event associated with his name is
an eschatological event primarily because through him the promises of God are brought to fulfilment. Hence in an historical
description of New Testament theology the history of interpretation must be fully taken into account.[54] Of course this does not
mean that the New Testament christology, e.g., is to be understood solely on the basis of the Old Testament. The Old Testament texts, as they lay before primitive Christianity, were already
invested with late-Jewish meanings. And Hellenistic and gnostic
influences are by no means to be excluded. Exegesis was rather
at that time – as always – the means by which current concepts
could be connected with sacred texts and existing traditions.
Above all it must be noted that all the texts, titles, concepts, and
myths that served to interpret Jesus' history were themselves
re-interpreted on the basis of the event.

My attempt to shed new light on the relationship between
eschatology and history on the basis of the Qumran texts has to
some extent reverted from the modern question of time, history

[53] In *Jesus*, p. 28 (ET: *Jesus and the Word*, p. 28) Bultmann wrote: 'The
message of Jesus is an *eschatological gospel* – the proclamation that now the
fulfilment of the promise is at hand, that now the Kingdom of God begins.'
In the abstract conceptual scheme which he uses in his later existentialist
interpretation this thought has assumed much less importance, and the end
of the world and of history has been more one-sidedly emphasized.

[54] This must also be emphasized over against the current (post-Lohmeyer)
tendency to discuss christology in terms of the individual christological titles.
It is common to see each honorific title as the bearer of a unique christological
conception and even to distinguish a 'paidology' or a 'kyriology' or a
'hyiology' from 'christology' proper. Cf. O. Cullmann, *Die Christologie des
NT*, 1957 (ET: 1959); W. Kramer, *Christos Kyrios Gottessohn* (AThANT 44),
1963 (ET: [SBT 50], 1966). On the basis of the extant writings and Jewish
analogies one must rather suppose that the conceptions were very complex
from the beginning and oriented towards events and texts more than ideas.

and eschatology to the old pattern of 'Promise and Fulfilment'. This has hardly simplified the theological problems, for the old teaching of Prophecy and Fulfilment cannot be repristinated today. One thing has become much too clear to us for that: the high degree to which the fulfilment always includes within itself a re-interpretation of the promise; in no other way can it be understood as fulfilment.[55]

Behind Bultmann's studies of the theme 'History and Eschatology' are hidden not only historical learning but also a hermeneutical programme and a theological stance. My goal was indeed very different; I intended only to make some historical remarks on the theme. But if it is correct that Bultmann's view is moulded by a distinct form-critical epoch within NT studies a discussion and debate with him must not be carried on only on the philosophical, hermeneutical, or theological plane. One must start out over and over again to do the exegetical and historical work, in the consciousness that it may yet be a very long time until historical-critical analysis and theological interpretation are so impressively wedded in a synthesis as they are in Bultmann's work.

In the international chorus that gives back an echo to Bultmann's stimuli the voices of those who have learned from him above all the ethos of serious scientific and theological work on the New Testament and its contemporary setting – such voices must not be lacking. I, in any event, have learned something decisive in this regard from him. And I would like to take this opportunity to attest this fact as one of those who, without ever having been a disciple of Bultmann in the narrow sense, attended his lectures in Marburg in the mid-thirties. At that time I learned to value him not only as a scholar and a teacher but also as a man and a Christian. And I can never forget, too, the way in

[55] What G. von Rad in his *Theologie* . . . has shown in the case of the OT is even more true of post-biblical Judaism and Christianity. On the problem, see R. Bultmann, 'Weissagung und Erfüllung', *ZThK* 47 (1950), pp. 360–83 (= *Glauben und Verstehen*, II, 1952, 1961³, pp. 162–86; ET: 'Prophecy and Fulfilment', *Essays Philosophical and Theological*, 1955, pp. 182–208). See further 'Weissagung und Erfüllung,' *RGG*³ VI (1962), 1584–1590 and the literature there cited.

which in the fall of 1945, after a time of enforced silence, he
re-established relationships as scholar and friend. In the little
study offered here I have tried, as always, to find my own way,
without being bound either positively or negatively by Bultmann's way of posing the questions. May this be accepted, however, as a token of my abiding gratitude and devotion.

2

Eschatological Expectation
in the Proclamation of Jesus*

Werner Georg Kümmel

RUDOLF BULTMANN introduces the description of Jesus' proclamation at the beginning of his *Theology of the New Testament*
with the following statements: 'The dominant concept of Jesus'
message is the *Reign of God* (βασιλεία τοῦ Θεοῦ). Jesus proclaims
its immediately impending irruption, now already making itself
felt. Reign of God is an eschatological concept. It means the
regime of God which will destroy the present course of the
world . . .'[1] This basically futuristic-eschatological understanding of Jesus' message, for which J. Weiss and A. Schweitzer
had laid the groundwork, seems to Bultmann so self-evident that
he adduces no proof of it and mentions no contrary opinions.
And yet this view, according to which Jesus proclaimed the
temporal nearness of the coming of the Reign of God, has always
met with serious opposition and in the last few years has again
been energetically disputed.[2] On the one side are those who

---

* Translated from *Zeit und Geschichte*, pp. 31–46.
[1] R. Bultmann, *Theologie des NT*, 1961⁴, p. 3 (ET: I, p. 4).
[2] For a survey of the history of research, cf. G. Lundström, *The Kingdom
of God in the Teaching of Jesus. A History of Interpretation from the Last Decades
of the Nineteenth Century to the Present Day*, 1963; N. Perrin, *The Kingdom of God
in the Teaching of Jesus*, 1963; also the short summaries in W. G. Kümmel,
Verheissung und Erfüllung, 1953² (=1956³) (ET: 1957) and B. Rigaux, 'La
seconde venue de Jésus', *La venue du Messie*, [Recherches Bibliques 6] 1962,
pp. 173ff.

deny that Jesus ever spoke of a future coming of the Reign of
God[3] or attribute to Jesus only a temporally completely indefi-
nite expectation of the eschatological coming of the Son of Man,
which, however, is totally insignificant alongside the basis proclamation of the presence of the Reign of God.[4] On the other
side are those who categorically deny to Jesus any expectation
of a *near* End or of an *imminent* Reign of God[5] and seek to show
that Jesus' proclamation of the nearness of the Reign of God
does not stand in any temporal context, but rather that Jesus
ignores the question of time because the vertical dimension of
the Spirit cannot be temporal.[6] This is not to say that there are

[3] See C. H. Dodd, E. Stauffer, and J. A. T. Robinson in W. G. Kümmel,
'Futurische und präsentische Eschatologie im ältesten Urchristentum', *NTS*
5 (1958/59), pp. 115f. (ET: in *JR* 43 [1963] 304f.) and E. Jüngel, *Paulus and
Jesus*, 1962, pp. 168f.

[4] E. Fuchs, *Zur Frage nach dem historischen Jesus*, 1960, p. 252 (ET: *Studies
of the Historical Jesus*, SBT 42, 1964, pp. 259f.); G. Neville, *The Advent Hope*,
1961, pp. 59f.; J. A. Baird, *The Justice of God in the Teaching of Jesus*, 1963,
p. 100.

[5] Fuchs (see note 4, above), pp. 325, 395 (ET: pp. 122, 182); Jüngel (note
3), pp. 154, 180; Neville (note 4), pp. 42f.; J. A. Baird (note 4), pp. 123,
142ff.; E. Linnemann, *Gleichnisse Jesu*, 1961, pp. 46, 138ff. (ET: 1966, pp. 38,
132–6); J. W. Doeve, 'Parusieverzögerung', *Nederlands Theologisch Tijd-
schrift* 17 (1962/63), pp. 32ff. According to Perrin (note 2), pp. 198f., Jesus
said nothing about the precise moment when the tension between the
eschatological present and the future is to be resolved, and according to
Sherman E. Johnson, *Jesus in His Own Times*, 1957, p. 129, we cannot say
whether or not Jesus believed the end of the world to be near.

[6] Fuchs (note 4), p. 326 (ET: p. 123): ('The *proton pseudos* of our present
research situation might well consist of the fact that from the outset we
accommodate the *nature* of the Basileia within a secondary temporal context
of phenomena'); also his 'Über die Aufgabe einer christlichen Theologie',
ZThK 58 (1961), p. 256. Jüngel (note 3), pp. 139ff., 154, 174, 180: ('The
future as the near future follows *directly* upon the present; it knows no inter-
vening period'); Baird (note 4), pp. 125, 148ff.: ('The nearness of the spiritual
dimension is primarily a spatial, dimensional nearness, and any sense of
temporal immediacy derives from the eternally present nature of God');
H. Conzelmann, 'Gegenwart und Zukunft in der synoptischen Tradition',
ZThK 54 (1957), pp. 287ff.: ('As long as I keep asking about the exact time
I have completely failed to grasp the nature of the demand; Jesus is not
concerned with time'); Linnemann (note 5), p. 47: ('In the teaching of
Jesus . . . the irruption of the Reign of God is . . . not that temporal
borderline which by its imminent nearness qualifies or stamps a special
character on the present. The irruption of God's Reign is itself "enabling

not also numerous recent scholars who hold firmly to the assumption that Jesus counted on a future coming of the Reign of God,[7] and many have held to a very precise form of this, namely the assumption that Jesus expected the appearance of the Reign of God soon, in his own generation.[8] Yet it must be said that this strictly 'eschatological' understanding of Jesus' preaching is at present being very seriously questioned.

Of course the question of the exact meaning of Jesus' preaching

---

time" [*Zeit zu*]'); Perrin (note 2), p. 185: ('We may not interpret the eschatological teaching of Jesus in terms of a linear concept of time'); E. Käsemann, 'Die Anfänge christlicher Theologie', *ZThK* 57 (1960) p. 179 (= *Exegetische Versuche und Besinnungen* II, 1965², p. 99; ET: *New Testament Questions of Today*, 1969, p. 101: 'The situation was this: . . . [Jesus'] own preaching did not bear a fundamentally apocalyptic stamp but proclaimed the immediacy of the God who was near at hand'); and 'Zum Thema der urchristlichen Apokalyptik', *ZThK* 59 (1962), p. 261 (= *Exeg. Versuche* II, p. 109; ET: p. 112: 'Jesus is obviously speaking of the coming of the *basileia* . . . with a reference not only or primarily to an end of the world which can in principle be dated within chronological time'); J. Gnilka, '"Parusieverzögerung" und Naherwartung in den synoptischen Evangelien und in der Apostelgeschichte', *Catholica* 13 (1959), pp. 277ff: ('Not prophecy in the temporal sense. Furthermore biblical man does not conceive of time as a linear entity').

[7] R. H. Fuller, *The Mission and Achievement of Jesus*, 1954, pp. 20ff.; J. Jeremias, *Die Gleichnisse Jesu*, 1962⁶, pp. 48, 170–79 (ET: pp. 51, 169–80); O. Cullmann, *Christus und die Zeit*, 1962³, pp. 86ff. (ET: pp. 83ff.); R. Schnackenburg, *Gottes Herrschaft und Reich*, 1959, pp. 49–56, 110–22 (ET: pp. 77–86, 160–77); E. Grässer, *Das Problem der Parusieverzögerung in den synoptischen Evangelien und in der Apostelgeschichte*, 1960², pp. 3ff.; G. E. Ladd, 'The Kingdom of God – Reign or Realm?', *JBL* 81 (1962), pp. 230ff.; Perrin (note 2), pp. 81ff.; Lundström (note 2), pp. 232f.; P. Vielhauer, 'Gottesreich und Menschensohn in der Verkündigung Jesu', *Festschrift für G. Dehn*, 1957, p. 77; F. Hahn, *Christologische Hoheitstitel*, 1963, p. 28; G. Bornkamm, *Jesus von Nazareth*, 1956, pp. 82ff. (ET: pp. 90ff.); D. Bosch, *Die Heidenmission in der Zukunftsschau Jesu*, 1959, pp. 73f.

[8] D. Selby, 'Changing Ideas in New Testament Eschatology', *HThR* 50 (1957), pp. 21ff.; O. Knoch, 'Die eschatologische Frage, ihre Entwicklung und ihr gegenwärtiger Stand', *BZ*, n.F. 6 (1962), pp. 112ff.; G. R. Beasley-Murray, *A Commentary on Mark Thirteen*, 1957, pp. 9, 99ff.; H. P. Owen, 'The Parousia of Christ in the Synoptic Gospels', *SJTh* 12 (1959), pp. 173ff.; M. S. Enslin, *The Prophet from Nazareth*, 1961, pp. 72, 87ff.; G. Gloege, *Aller Tage Tag*, 1960, pp. 135, 138f. (ET: *The Day of His Coming*, 1963, pp. 141f., 144f.); U. Wilckens, 'Das Offenbarungsverständnis in der Geschichte des Urchristentums', *Offenbarung als Geschichte* (*KuD*, Beih. 1, 1961), pp. 58, 61; Rigaux (note 2), p. 212; Grässer (note 7), p. 16.

of the Reign of God cannot be raised in all its details here;
and neither can we here demonstrate again the fact that the
presence *and* the futurity of the Reign of God are both equally
certainly attested as Jesus' view.[9] But in view of the many-sided
denial of the futuristic and temporal sense of Jesus' proclamation
of the coming of the Reign of God it has become a very pressing
question whether we really have no sufficient evidence that Jesus
counted on a coming of God's Reign and a concomitant end of
this world in a temporally limited near future, and also whether
it is true that the assumption of Jesus' expectation of an imminent End 'has no sufficient support in the texts'.[10] In other
words, if it can be shown that Jesus preached a *temporally* near
coming of the Reign of God this would provide a firmer point
of departure for the whole understanding of Jesus' preaching
of the nearness of that Reign. We shall consequently limit our
discussion here to those words of Jesus that speak expressly of the
temporal nearness of the eschatological event.[11]

This question could, of course, be quickly answered if the
declarations ἤγγικεν ἡ βασιλεία τοῦ θεοῦ (Mark 1.15 par. Matt.
4.17; Matt. 10.7 par. Luke 10.9, 11) and ὅταν ἴδητε ταῦτα γινόμενα
γινώσκετε ὅτι ἐγγύς ἐστιν ἐπὶ θύραις (Mark 13.29 par. Matt. 24.33,
Luke 21.31) unequivocally attested the near coming of the Reign
of God or the events of the End as the opinion of Jesus. But
against this a twofold objection has been raised: (*a*) Mark 1.15
is a summary statement by the evangelist that does not go back
to Jesus, and Matt. 10.7 as a doublet of this statement can similarly be a formulation of the primitive church;[12] (*b*) in the case
of ἐγγίζειν and ἐγγύς the meaning 'near' is as well attested as
'present', and besides ἐγγίζειν describes temporal as well as spatial

---

[9] See Kümmel (note 2). Cf. further Cullmann (note 7); Schnackenburg
(note 7), pp. 77ff. (ET: pp. 114–17); Perrin (note 2), pp. 79ff., 159; Lundström (note 2), pp. 234; Bornkamm (note 7); Bosch (note 7); Knoch (note 8).

[10] Linnemann (note 5), p. 138 (ET: p. 132).

[11] It is not my purpose to enter once more into a discussion of the literature
criticized in detail in the second edition of my book, *Verheissung und Erfüllung*,
1953 (ET: 1957).

[12] Linnemann (note 5), p. 138 (ET: p. 132); Perrin (note 2), pp. 200f.;
Fuchs (note 4), p. 325 (ET: p. 122).

nearness, so ἤγγικεν says nothing about the coming of the Reign of God soon.[13] Now it cannot be denied that Mark 1.15 is a summarizing formulation of Jesus' preaching that at least partially contains community formulations[14] and hence cannot be used unqualifiedly as evidence of Jesus' own view. On the other hand, Matt. 10.7 par. Luke 10.9 is surely 'no independent logion',[15] yet the whole missionary address in Mark 6.8ff. and Luke 10.4ff. par. Matt. 10.7ff. is the end-result of a very complicated development based on extremely diverse materials;[16] hence a judgment about the age of the individual elements making up this complex of tradition can only be made in the individual case. And since there is no adequate reason to doubt the sending out of the disciples by Jesus[17] there is methodologically no justification for denying the authenticity of Matt. 10.7 unless it can be shown on other grounds that this saying is contrary to Jesus' own view.[18]

But does ἤγγικεν have the meaning 'has come near' and is it used in a temporal sense? W. R. Hutton tries to show that in

[13] W. R. Hutton, 'The Kingdom of God Has Come', *ExpT* 64 (1952/53), pp. 89ff.; F. Rehkopf, *Die lukanische Sonderquelle*, 1959, pp. 44ff.; R. F. Berkey, '*Ἐγγίζειν, φθάνειν* and Realized Eschatology', *JBL* 82 (1963), pp. 177ff.; Jüngel (note 3), pp. 174f.; Baird (note 4), pp. 148f.

[14] Perrin (note 2), pp. 200f.

[15] Linnemann (note 5), p. 138 (ET: p. 132).

[16] Cf. the bibliography in Grässer (note 7), pp. 18f.

[17] W. G. Kümmel, *Kirchenbegriff und Geschichtsbewusstsein in der Urgemeinde und bei Jesus*, 1943, p. 31; J. Jeremias, *Jesu Verheissung für die Völker*, 1959², pp. 16ff. (ET: pp. 27f.); B. Rigaux, 'Die "Zwölf" in Geschichte und Kerygma', *Der historische Jesus und der kerygmatische Christus*, 1960 (= 1961²), pp. 475f.

[18] That *both* words (Mark 1.15 and Matt. 10.7) were formulated in the primitive church is an unproved assertion; and it is truly misleading to adduce in support of this assertion R. Otto, *Reich Gottes und Menschensohn*, 1933, pp. 113–17 (ET: pp. 150–4), since he offers reasons for the *eclipse* of the fact that Jesus proclaimed the imminent appearing of the Kingdom (so Linnemann [note 5], p. 138 [ET: p. 132]). What Otto really tries to show is that the awareness of Jesus' strictly eschatological understanding of the Reign of God as the future kingdom at the end of time did not die out – not that this conception was a secondary importation. Furthermore what Otto adduces in support of his thesis are generalizations devoid of exegetical basis. Fuchs (note 4), p. 325 (ET: p. 122), also gives no sufficient exegetical reason for his assertion that 'the proclamation of the nearness of the Basileia more probably belongs to the Baptist and the early community (than to Jesus)'.

most NT passages ἐγγίζειν must be translated by 'arrive' and that consequently in Mark 1.15 par. the translation 'has come' is appropriate.[19] Now in a few cases the translation 'arrive' in the sense of 'to *have* come near' is possible,[20] but the perfect ἤγγικεν in *all* NT passages means unambiguously 'has come near' (Mark 26.45; Mark 14.42 par. Matt. 26.46; Luke 21.8, 20; Rom. 13.12; James 5.8; I Peter 4.7);[21] so there is no reason not to translate Matt. 10.7 as 'the Reign of God has come near'. And R. F. Berkey's evidence that ἐγγίζειν (like φθάνειν) is ambiguous and may designate 'arrival' as well as 'coming near'[22] overlooks the fact that ἐγγίζειν can have the sense of 'arrive' only in special cases and always involves the addition of the goal to which one has come so close.

That the proclamation, 'the Reign of God has come near', has a *temporal* sense is shown unambiguously by the parable of the fig tree, Mark 13.28f. par. Since this parable is isolated in its context and hence must be explained by itself,[23] the subjects of ταῦτα γινόμενα and ἐγγύς ἐστιν ἐπὶ θύραις are hard to determine. But the picture of the fig tree, whose branches herald the nearness of the coming summer, can hardly be intended to set side by side anything except certain anticipatory signs and the coming of the eschatological consummation. Now there is no reason whatever to interpret the reference to the connection between unspecified anticipatory signs and the End as 'justification of the

[19] See note 13. (See also the addendum by M. A. Simpson, *ExpT* 64 [1952/53], p. 188.)

[20] An examination of the passages adduced by W. R. Hutton in support of the translation 'arrive' yields the following result: only in Luke 12.33; Acts 21.33; Heb. 7.19 is this meaning of ἐγγίζειν more probable than 'draw near'; and even in these cases this translation is not necessary. Rehkopf (note 13) has also succeeded in showing only that ἤγγισεν in Luke 22.47 approaches the sense of προσέρχεσθαι.

[21] P. Staples, 'The Kingdom of God Has Come', *ExpT* 71 (1959/60), pp. 87f., has shown, against Hutton, that in Matt. 26.45; Luke 18.35 ἐγγίζειν *must* mean 'draw near'. Cf. also Kümmel (note 2), pp. 16f. (ET: pp. 22ff.) and F. Blass-A. Debrunner, *A Greek Grammar of the New Testament and Other Early Christian Literature*, tr. by R. W. Funk, 1961, p. 176.

[22] See note 13.

[23] Kümmel (note 2), pp. 14f. (ET: pp. 20f.); Beasley-Murray (note 8), pp. 95ff.; Jeremias (note 7), pp. 119f. (ET: pp. 119f.).

Delay' and hence to deny the authenticity of the parable;[24] and it is equally groundless to suggest that the parable originally formed the conclusion of the Jewish apocalypse which has been reworked in Mark 13.[25] For the very fragmentary nature of the text shows that an old piece of tradition is involved, one that is formulated on the basis of the presupposition that the final consummation is soon to come regardless of whether one refers ταῦτα γινόμενα to yet future anticipatory signs or, much more probably, to present events which the hearers are to *think of* as anticipatory signs. So in any case this ἐγγύς ἐστιν ἐπὶ θύραις shows that Jesus' proclamation of the nearness of the coming of the Reign of God can only have been meant in the temporal sense that God's unqualified Rule is soon to be actualized.

This conclusion is strengthened by the parable of the Unjust Judge, Luke 18.2–8. The assumption that in this parable we are dealing with a product of the community[26] is hardly convincing. E. Linnemann is able to object against the originality of the parable proper (vv. 2–5) only that neither a general admonition to perseverance in prayer nor a particular admonition to persevering prayer for the coming of the Reign of God is fitting on the lips of Jesus, and neither is a promise that such a persevering request will be fulfilled. But Jesus did promise that faithful prayer would be heard (Mark 11.24), and he urged prayer for the coming of the Reign of God (Matt.6.10); though neither the Lord's Prayer nor Luke 18.2–5 led to the notion that man could or should 'bring the Reign of God by persevering prayer'. If,

[24] Grässer (note 7), pp. 164f.; W. Grundmann, *Das Evangelium nach Markus*, 1959[2], p. 270, apparently ascribes this meaning only to the evangelist.

[25] So Linnemann (note 5), p. 140 (ET: p. 135). It is by no means 'a methodological mistake to combine Mark 13.28f. with Luke 12.54–56 and on that basis to interpret Luke 12.54–56 as referring to imminent expectation and to claim priority for Mark 13.28f.'. For both texts ground their demand in the same way on the ordinary consequences of the observation of concrete natural events. So it is immaterial that in Luke 12.56 the *premonitory* character of the figure is not expressly pointed out, since the hearer will do this by himself in the application of it (so R.H.Fuller [note 7], p. 46). The combination of Mark 13.28f. and Luke 12.54–56 is thus exegetically completely appropriate.

[26] Fuchs (note 4), p. 70; Linnemann (note 5), pp. 140, 180f. (ET: pp. 135, 186–9).

then, it can hardly be doubted that this parable comes from
Jesus, the objections to the authenticity of the explanation
(18.6ff.) are more important.[27] The primary objections to the
explanation are that the applications of the parables are often
secondary, that ἐκλεκτοί does not occur in any genuine saying of
Jesus, and that the explanation transforms the parable's general
admonition to continual prayer into a specific admonition to
pray for the coming of the Kingdom. But of course the broad
assertion that the applications of the parables are often secondary does not prove anything, and if the term ἐκλεκτοί does not
occur in any genuine word of Jesus the concept of election does
(Luke 12.32; Matt. 11.25f. par. Luke 10.21). Finally, the interpretation does not disturb the meaning of the parable in any way;
the emphasis in the parable is on the judge, not the widow, and
the explanation corresponds exactly in that it promises God's
certain fulfilling of the request for eschatological redemption.[28]
Hence there is good ground for holding that Luke 18.2–8a belongs to the Jesus-tradition. Then Jesus promises to the disciples
who pray for the coming of God's Reign that God will soon
vindicate them.[29] It has been objected against this understand-

[27] The authenticity of the explanation is rejected not only by those
mentioned in Kümmel (note 2), p. 52 (ET: p. 59) n. 126, but also by Grässer
(note 7), pp. 36f.; Linnemann (note 5), p. 180 (ET: pp. 187ff.); W. Grundmann, *Das Evangelium nach Lukas*, 1961, p. 346; A. R. C. Leaney, *A Commentary on the Gospel According to St Luke*, 1958, p. 235.

[28] Cf. Jeremias (note 7), p. 156 (ET: p. 156). The originality of the
explanation is rightly defended not only by Jeremias but also by C. Spicq,
'La parabole de la veuve obstinée et du juge inerte, aux décisions im-
promptues', *RB* 68 (1961), pp. 68ff. and G. Delling, 'Das Gleichnis vom
gottlosen Richter', *ZNW* 53 (1962), pp. 1ff. Verse 8b is, to be sure (against
Spicq and Delling), to be viewed as a Lukan addition to this explanation, as
is shown by the substitution of the Son of Man for God and the appearing
of the concept of faith. (So also, rightly, Linnemann [note 5], p. 181 [ET:
p. 189]; Baird [note 4], p. 145). We are dealing here with an addition even
if Jeremias is right that v. 8b is a pre-Lukan Son of Man saying; H. E. Tödt,
on the other hand, considers v. 8b a formulation by the evangelist (*Der
Menschensohn in der synoptischen Überlieferung*, 1959, p. 92 [ET: p. 99]).

[29] The *crux interpretum* καὶ μακροθυμεῖ ἐπ' αὐτοῖς (v. 7, end) is possibly to be
understood like Sir. 35.19 and translated 'even though he lets them wait for
him'. (So H. Riesenfeld, 'Zu μακροθυμεῖν [Luke 18.7]', *Neutestamentliche
Aufsätze* [*Festschrift für J. Schmid*], 1963, pp. 214ff.).

ing of the text that ἐν τάχει can mean 'suddenly, momentarily' and that since this is the meaning in most instances it must also be the meaning here, so that Luke 18.8a consequently says nothing about the interval before the Parousia.[30] But even though ταχύς occasionally can have the meaning 'without warning, suddenly' (e.g., in I Tim. 5.22), there is no passage in the New Testament in which ἐν τάχει occurs (Acts 2.7; 22.18; 25.4; Rom. 16.20; Rev. 1.1; 22.6) where any translation except 'quickly', 'soon' is called for. There is thus no reason to abandon this most common meaning in the case of Luke 18.6.[31] In summary, everything points towards the fact that Jesus, even according to Luke 18.2–8a, proclaimed an imminent coming of the final consummation.

But this assumption becomes completely certain only when we investigate the three much-discussed texts in which an interval before the coming of the final consummation is expressly mentioned (Mark 9.1; 13.30; Matt. 10.23). It is quite characteristic to find repeated admonitions about 'centring the discussion on texts that seem to contain a specific indication of a date'[32] or even to find these texts suspect and rejected simply *because* they contain such specific indications,[33] or to hear it said that these are 'awkward fragments of tradition' that even the earliest Christian communities did not know how to fit smoothly into the overall structure of Jesus' eschatological message.[34] Yet of these texts, too, the question can only properly be what they

[30] Spicq (note 28), pp. 81ff.; Jeremias (note 7), p. 155 (ET: p. 155); Delling (note 28), pp. 19f.; Grundmann (note 27), p. 348; as a possibility: Grässer (note 7), p. 38.

[31] So also Linnemann (note 5), p. 181 (ET: pp. 188f.). This is the way the old versions understand it: *cito* vet. lat., vg.; *celeriter* a; ba'gal Pesh; d alone differs: *confestim*; cf. the edition of the *Itala* by A. Jülicher and W. Matzkow, 3, 1954, p. 202. If the translation mentioned in note 29 above is correct it is a further confirmation of the temporal significance of ἐν τάχει.

[32] Schnackenburg (note 7), p. 138 (ET: p. 199); Neville (note 4), p. 60; Gnilka (note 6), p. 31.

[33] Jüngel (note 3), pp. 237f.; Baird (note 4), p. 142; Doeve (note 5), p. 32, n. 2; Fuchs (note 4), p. 70 [not in ET – tr.].

[34] Schnackenburg (note 7), p. 146 (ET: p. 212).

really say and whether or not there are weighty considerations
against dominical provenance in the case of each individual text.
Mark 13.30 presents the fewest problems: 'Truly, I say to you,
this generation will not pass away before all these things take
place.' It has often been shown that this was originally an
isolated logion.[35] Furthermore, it is beyond dispute that ἡ γενεὰ
αὕτη can only mean the contemporaries of Jesus.[36] So the only
real question that remains is what ταῦτα πάντα means. In view of
the fact that the logion was originally an isolated saying, the
evangelist's interpretation, that the words refer to the totality of
the eschatological events until the Parousia, is not necessarily
correct. Hence it is repeatedly suggested that ταῦτα πάντα should
be understood to refer to the events up to the destruction of
Jerusalem.[37] But there is no basis for this suggestion (Mark 13.4
speaks only of ταῦτα while Mark 13.30 speaks of ταῦτα πάντα),
and it can only be designated 'une échappatoire'.[38] And the suggestion that Jesus originally spoke only of his death within the coming generation and the evangelist assimilated the saying to
13.4[39] is totally without support in the text. The literal and most
likely reference of ταῦτα πάντα is to the totality of eschatological
events, and 'this statement of our Lord's . . . simply requires
grace to be received'.[40] For 'in itself this verse contains nothing
that is in contradiction to Jesus' message'[41] and unless one starts
from the preconceived notion mentioned above that Jesus *could
not* have given a date for the End or *could not* have been mistaken,

[35] See, e.g., Grässer (note 7), pp. 128f.

[36] So, e.g., Schnackenburg (note 7), pp. 143f. (ET: pp. 207f.); Rigaux
(note 2), p. 197; Beasley-Murray (note 8), pp. 99f.

[37] Cf. those cited in Kümmel (note 2), p. 54 (ET: p. 60) n. 129, and
Grässer (note 7), p. 129, n. 4; hesitantly also Schnackenburg (note 7), p. 144
(ET: p. 208) and Grässer, *loc. cit.*,; C. E. B. Cranfield, *The Gospel According to
Saint Mark*, 1959, p. 409, thinks the most likely explanation is that ταῦτα πάντα
refers to the *premonitory signs* of the end, and H. P. Owen (note 8), pp. 176f.,
would refer it to the destruction of the Temple, but as an omen of the end
within this generation.

[38] Rigaux (note 2), p. 215.

[39] Neville (note 4), pp. 62f.

[40] Beasley-Murray (note 8), p. 99.

[41] Grässer (note 7), p. 130.

everything points towards the authenticity of Mark 13.30 and indicates that it announces the coming of the consummation within the interval designated roughly as 'this generation'.[42] Nothing in the wording points away from this to a 'word of consolation' created by a Christian prophet 'on account of the delay of the Parousia'.[43]

The problem in Mark 9.1 is similar: 'Truly I say to you, there are some standing here who will not taste death before they see the kingdom of God come with power.' It is widely recognized that this saying is also an individual logion which the evangelist has referred to the Parousia and consequently connected with 8.38.[44] Whether by this connection Mark understood it in its original sense, on the other hand, is strongly disputed. C. H. Dodd has interpreted the statement of the future seeing of the Reign of God by those whose lives extend to that point in time to mean that men will recognize at some appropriate time before their death that the Reign of God *has* already come.[45] J. A. Baird has renewed this interpretation[46] in a special form: the men spoken of are those who will not die before they have come to an inward recognition that the Kingdom of God is in the process of coming in their lives or in the life of the church. But that Mark 9.1 speaks of a future *public* manifestation of God's Reign, not a future interior realization of it, has been rightly shown from many sides and need not be demonstrated again here.[47] C. H. Dodd has therefore subsequently explained the promise that many of those present would see God's Reign in power in the future to be an indication by Jesus of his subsequent resurrection and the Kingdom of God on earth in the community; similarly, others have suggested the efficacy of Jesus' death or

[42] Beasley-Murray (note 8), pp. 99ff.; Grundmann (note 24), pp. 270f.; Bosch (note 7), pp. 145f.; Rigaux (note 2), pp. 197, 214f.

[43] Grässer (note 7), p. 131; Linnemann (note 5), p. 138 (ET: p. 132).

[44] Cf., e.g., Grässer (note 7), p. 131.

[45] C. H. Dodd, *The Parables of the Kingdom*, 1936³, pp. 42, 53f. (= Fontana Books, 1961, pp. 35, 43).

[46] Baird (note 4), pp. 142ff.

[47] Cf. Kümmel (note 2), pp. 20f. (ET: pp. 26f.) and the literature cited there in note 26; also Rigaux (note 2), p. 184.

the influence of the Spirit in the church.[48] But the connection of 'seeing' and 'coming in power' points too obviously to a publicly visible and tangible manifestation of the Reign of God to allow for evading the conclusion that this promise refers to the eschatological appearing of that Reign.[49] But then Mark 9.1 indicates that Jesus expected the beginning of the Reign of God, visible to the whole world, within the lifetime of his generation and hence that he viewed the coming of that Reign unambiguously as an event of the near future.

It is commonly held, to be sure, that this promise, which was undoubtedly not fulfilled in this form, cannot be brought within the framework of the message of Jesus. Hence some affirm that the original sense of the saying on the lips of Jesus can no longer be discerned;[50] others would see in the distinction between τινές, who would have this experience, and the larger number who would die first an indication that in this text we are dealing with a primitive Christian prophetic saying which is intended to give an answer to the pressing problem of the delay of the Parousia.[51]

[48] C. H. Dodd, *The Coming of Christ*, 1951, pp. 13f.; Neville (note 4), pp. 6of.; V. Taylor, *The Gospel According to St Mark*, 1952, p. 386; A. Richardson, *An Introduction to the Theology of the New Testament*, 1958, pp. 63f.; J. A. T. Robinson, *Jesus and His Coming*, 1957, p. 89; R. A. Cole, *The Gospel According to St Mark*, 1961, p. 140; P. Carrington, *According to St Mark*, 1960, pp. 188ff.; cf. also the opinions cited in Bosch (note 7), pp. 144f. Cranfield (note 37), pp. 287f., sees Mark 9.1 as a prediction of the Transfiguration, 9.2ff.

[49] Fuller (note 7), pp. 27f., 118; Owen (note 8), p. 181; Gloege (note 8), p. 140 (ET: p. 147); Perrin (note 2), pp. 139f.; Rigaux (note 2), pp. 192, 196f.; Bosch (note 7), pp. 144f.; Grässer (note 7), p. 132.

[50] Gnilka (note 6), p. 289; W. Strawson, *Jesus and the Future Life*, 1959, p. 74; Schnackenburg (note 7), p. 143 (ET: p. 207).

[51] Cf. those cited in Kümmel (note 2), p. 21 (ET: p. 27), n. 28; further, H. A. Guy, *The Origin of the Gospel of Mark*, 1954, pp. 88ff.; Grässer (note 7), pp. 133f.; Linnemann (note 5), p. 138 (ET: p. 132); E. Percy, *Die Botschaft Jesu*, 1953, p. 177; H. Conzelmann, *Die Mitte der Zeit*, 1954, p. 88 (ET: *The Theology of St Luke*, 1960, p. 104). W. Marxsen, *Der Evangelist Markus* (FRLANT 67), 1956, p. 140 n. 1 (ET: p. 205 n. 193) does not wish to put the question of the dominical origin of the saying: Grundmann (note 24), pp. 177f., thinks that the mention of τινές is an addition spawned by the delay of the Parousia, but apparently he would trace back to the earliest community the original saying, which referred to all Christians. The question of authenticity is left open in S. E. Johnson, *A Commentary on the Gospel According to St Mark*, 1960, p. 153.

conclusion that 10.23a did not always belong together with
10.23b and that the interpretation of 10.23b required by 10.23a,
namely the reference to flight from one city to another, is not the
original meaning of the saying in 10.23b.[59] It is also unsatisfactory to unravel the origin of the saying in the history of the
tradition as a means of illuminating the original meaning of
10.23b,[60] so we are left only with the possibility of deciding the
meaning of 10.23b without reference to either its present context or some hypothetical one. But when looked at in this way,
'you will not finish the cities of Israel until . . .' can hardly
mean anything except 'you will not accomplish the mission to
Israel until . . .'; in other words, the disciples will not complete
their missionary task with respect to their own people before the
coming of the Son of Man. Elsewhere in the synoptic tradition
the 'coming of the Son of Man' always designates the eschatological consummation (Mark 8.38 par. Matt. 16.27/Luke 9.26;
Matt. 16.28; 25.31; Mark 13.26 par. Matt. 24.30/Luke 21.27;
Matt. 24.44 par. Luke 12.40; Mark 14.62 par. Matt. 26.64;

(*sy*^c and *Pesh*) are correct but ambiguous. L. Albrecht's translation is also
correct: 'Before the coming of the Son of Man your work with respect to the
cities of Israel will not yet be finished' ('Vor des Menschensohnes Kommen
wird eure Arbeit an den Städten Israels noch nicht vollendet sein').

[59] The original unity of Matt. 10.23 and hence the interpretation of 10.23b
which refers it to the flight from city to city is defended by Schnackenburg
(note 7), p. 142 (ET: p. 205); Vielhauer (note 7), p. 59 n. 43; Tödt (note 28),
p. 56 (ET: p. 60); Linnemann (note 5), p. 139 (ET: p. 133); Feuillet (note
58), p. 186; H. Schürmann, 'Zur Traditionsgeschichte von Mt 10, 23', *BZ*,
n. F. 3 (1959), p. 85; E. Bammel, 'Matthäus 10, 23', *STh* 14 (1960), pp. 79ff.
(he attempts to demonstrate the existence of a concept involving wandering
from place to place and the termination of this wandering by an eschatological event, and hence to establish a Jewish *Vorlage* for the whole verse without the introductory ὅταν-clause; but the attempt is not notably successful).

[60] Schürmann (note 59), pp. 82ff. (in agreement with Feuillet [note 58],
pp. 182ff.), tries to show that Matt. 10.23 was originally the conclusion of the
Q section in Luke 12.8–12 and hence a consolatory word in time of persecution. But proof is lacking that the basis of Matt. 10.17–22 is Q and not Mark
13.9–13; and this hypothesis becomes completely untenable if Matt. 10.23
was not originally a unity. Dupont (note 58), pp. 228ff., thinks that Matt.
10.23b was originally the continuation of 10.5b, 6 and that Matthew placed
it at the end of the mission charge. But this is completely incapable of proof.

Luke 18.8b; cf. ἔσται ἡ παρουσία τοῦ υἱοῦ τοῦ ἀνθρώπου, Matt. 24.27).[61] This meaning is consequently the most natural one in Matt. 10.23b: the Son of Man will appear before the disciples' missionary activity can be completed. If this exegesis is correct, in this word as in Mark 9.1 Jesus predicted a temporally limited period of brief duration before the coming of the Son of Man, and this promise, too, was not fulfilled. Some have sought to avoid this fact by referring the imminent coming of the Son of Man to the establishment of the church through Jesus' death and resurrection,[62] or to the fall of Jerusalem,[63] or by denying that Jesus' original word intended this 'coming' in a futuristic sense.[64] But none of these explanations may be deduced in any natural way from the wording of the saying; they can at best be rendered possible. So it must be considered exegetically certain that Matt. 10.23b speaks of the eschatological coming of the

[61] I cannot enter here into a discussion with those who fundamentally reject this fact. (Cf., e.g., A. Feuillet, 'Le triomphe du Fils de l'Homme d'après la déclaration du Christ aux Sanhédrites', in *La venue du Messie* [Recherches Bibliques 6], 1962, pp. 159ff.).

[62] Neville (note 4), p. 61 (the original reference was to the coming of the Kingdom with power); R. V. G. Tasker, *The Gospel According to St Matthew*, 1961, p. 108; V. Taylor, *The Life and Ministry of Jesus*, 1955, pp. 107f.

[63] Robinson (note 48), p. 80, 91f. (presumably the word was given 'a chronological twist' and thus assimilated to the hope of the Parousia); Feuillet (note 58), pp. 192f. (Feuillet lists on pp. 190ff. other possible interpretations of the saying; older interpretations are given in P. Nepper-Christensen, *Das Matthäusevangelium ein judenchristliches Evangelium?*, 1958, pp. 185ff.).

[64] According to Baird (note 4), p. 145, Matt. 10.23 originally had 'a present, historic meaning', like that in Mark 9.1 (which he also interprets in a present sense). P. Bonnard, *L'Évangile selon Saint Matthieu*, 1963, p. 149, paraphrases: 'jusqu'à mon retour en gloire, à la fin des temps, vous trouverez toujours un lieu où fuir et témoigner de l'Évangile'; he thus eliminates any concrete date. Dupont (note 58), pp. 238ff., confines the prediction to the Galilean mission and refers 'Son of Man' to the earthly Jesus; the evangelist has chosen this language 'simplement marquer son respect pour le Maître, sans cesse de le considérer dans son existence terrestre et dans ses rapports familiers avec ses disciples'. Feuillet (note 58), p. 188, rightly says that in view of the solemnity of the language used this attempted explanation is 'la déclaration la plus banale qui se puisse concevoir'. W. Grundmann, *Die Geschichte Jesu Christi*, 1956, pp. 245ff., and Schnackenburg (note 7), pp. 142f. (ET: pp. 205ff.), leave open the question of the original meaning of the saying.

Son of Man before the completion of the disciples' mission in Israel.[65]

It is sometimes suggested that the saying, which must be thus explained, is impossible on the lips of Jesus: it represents imminent expectation; it equates the appearance of the Son of Man and the coming of the Reign of God; it presupposes a situation of persecution for the disciples. Furthermore, it is improbable that Jesus confined his preaching to the cities of Israel or spelled out the details of his coming. So it is clear, the suggestion goes, that the saying is a word of consolation from the earliest community or a saying from a narrow-minded Jewish-Christian group that rejected the Gentile mission.[66] But these are remarkably weak and quite unconvincing objections. That Jesus *could* not have represented the teaching of imminent expectation is a *petitio principii* which cannot be used as a critical principle. That the identification of the inbreaking of the Reign of God and the appearance of the Son of Man was first comprehensible where the same Jesus who proclaimed the Reign of God was expected as Son of Man (E. Jüngel) is a conception defended most vigorously by P. Vielhauer.[67] But if not only Mark 9.1 (see

---

[65] Schweitzer's exegesis, according to which Jesus expected the coming of the Son of Man before the disciples' return from the Galilean mission, has been taken up again by M. Goguel ('La caractère, à la fois actuel et futur, du salut dans la théologie Paulinienne', in *The Background of the New Testament and its Eschatology, in Honour of C. H. Dodd*, ed. by W. D. Davies and D. Daube, 1956, p.323); but it is now generally recognized that this exegesis is untenable: cf. Kümmel (note 2), pp.55f. (ET: pp.62ff.); and Feuillet (note 58), pp.189f.

[66] This or something quite similar is the view expressed by those named in Kümmel (note 2), p.56 (ET: pp.56f.) n.137, and by Grässer (note 7), pp.137f.; Linnemann (note 5), pp.138f. (ET: pp.132–6); Vielhauer (note 7), pp.58ff.; Tödt (note 28), pp.56f. (ET: pp.60f.); E. Schweizer, *Erniedrigung und Erhöhung bei Jesus und seinen Nachfolgern*, 1962[2], pp.42f. (ET: *Lordship and Discipleship* [SBT 28], 1960, pp.40ff.); Bammel (note 59), p.92; Fuchs (note 4), p.70 [not in ET – tr.]; Jüngel (note 3), pp.239f.; H. Braun, *Spätjüdisch-häretischer und frühchristlicher Radikalismus* II, 1957, p.102, n.4; W. Schmithals, *Paulus und Jakobus* (FRLANT 85), 1963, p.94 (ET: pp.112f.); G. Strecker, *Der Weg der Gerechtigkeit* (FRLANT 82), 1962, p.41.

[67] Vielhauer (note 7), pp.71ff.; and 'Jesus und der Menschensohn', *ZThK* 60 (1963), pp.135ff.

above) but also Mark 8.38[68] go back to Jesus the association of
these two sayings shows that Jesus spoke equally of the Reign of
God and of the future coming of the Son of Man, regardless of
whether one believes that Jesus distinguished between himself
and the coming Son of Man[69] or designated himself as the coming Son of Man.[70] That Jesus did not confine his proclamation
to the region of the cities of Israel (H. E. Tödt) is simply not true
if Matt. 10.5b, 6 genuinely reflects Jesus' view, as all the evidence
suggests.[71] Finally, the view that Matt. 10.23b is consolatory in
nature has as little support in the language of the text as the
judgment that the sentence implies a rejection of the Gentile
mission, which seems rather to lie completely outside the pur-
view of the text. So everything points towards the authenticity
of Matt. 10.23, which in turn shows that Jesus awaited the
eschatological coming of the Son of Man while the disciples were
still occupied with the proclamation of the coming Reign of God
to the Jews.[72] Naturally this saying gives no precise temporal information about the date of the coming of the Reign of God,
while the reference to not being finished with the cities of Israel
can hardly be understood as anything but an indication that the
coming of the Son of Man will occur unexpectedly soon. So this
word, too, shows that Jesus expected the Reign of God, and with
it the Son of Man, to come in the near future.

[68] See Kümmel (note 2), pp. 38ff. (ET: pp. 44–7).

[69] See Tödt (note 28), pp. 37ff. (ET: pp. 40–6); Hahn (note 7), p. 38.

[70] See Kümmel (note 68) and his 'Jesus Christus. Das Christusverständnis
im Wandel der Zeiten', *Marburger Theol. Studien* 1 (1963), pp. 7f. Vielhauer's
objection that 'in contemporary Jewish eschatology the Reign of God and
the Son of Man had nothing to do with each other' and that 'the combining
of them by Jesus is equally improbable on the basis of his presuppositions in
terms of the history of religions' (*ZThK* 60 [1963], p. 136) may be met by
noting that the objection is without force once one grants that Jesus spoke
both of the Reign of God becoming effective in the present in his activity
(Mark 12.28) and of himself as the Son of Man active upon earth (Mark
2.10; Matt. 8.20); for then Jesus was involved in any case in a conscious
revision of the traditional Jewish eschatology.

[71] See Kümmel (note 2), p. 78 (ET: p. 85); Jeremias (note 17), pp. 16ff.
(ET: pp. 19–39).

[72] So Jeremias (note 17), p. 18 (ET: p. 20); Owen (note 8), pp. 175f.;
Bosch (note 7), p. 157; G. R. Beasley-Murray, *Jesus and the Future*, 1954,
p. 185; apparently also Perrin (note 2), p. 83 and Rigaux (note 2), pp. 194f.

We have now fulfilled our intention of examining those words of Jesus which speak expressly of the *temporal* nearness of the Reign of God or the eschatological event. This examination has shown that it is incorrect to assert that Jesus' expectation of the consummation in the near future 'has no sufficient basis in the texts'.[73] On the contrary, an unbiased critical examination of the relevant texts shows unequivocally that Jesus counted on the nearness of the future Reign of God, a future confined to his own generation.[74] It is also beyond dispute, however repeatedly the fact may be set aside or disputed as a 'foolish question',[75] that Jesus was mistaken in this expectation.[76] Of more importance, however, is the fact which this examination establishes once more: Jesus' proclamation of the near Reign of God actually implies a *temporally* near event; hence the many-sided attack on this concrete temporal meaning of Jesus' proclamation[77] is untenable on the basis of the data in the text. In the statements cited at the beginning of this article R. Bultmann has quite correctly interpreted Jesus' proclamation of the near Reign of God. From this two conclusions follow. For one thing, it is unnecessary to seek the reasons for the emergence in the primitive church of an expectation of the Kingdom oriented towards the near future,

[73] Linnemann (note 5), p. 138 (ET: p. 132). Because of the limitations of space it is not possible to discuss here the texts further adduced by Miss Linnemann (Mark 14.25; Luke 12.54, 56), nor the 'general admonitions to wakefulness' nor the so-called Parables of Growth; but an examination of them would not change our results in any way, since these texts acquire significance as evidence of Jesus' expectations for the near future only in connection with the texts discussed above.

[74] See note 8.

[75] Cf., e.g., Fuchs (note 4), p. 375 (ET: p. 165); Jüngel (note 3), p. 237; Schnackenburg (note 7), p. 147 (ET: p. 213); Schürmann (note 59), p. 86, n. 17; Gnilka (note 6), p. 289; Baird (note 4), p. 142; Rigaux (note 2), pp. 190, 198 (Jesus did not teach that the End would come within his generation, so he was not mistaken in this – but he expected it!).

[76] Rightly, Owen (note 8), p. 176; Gloege (note 8), p. 140 (ET: p. 147) ('It should be freely conceded that in this respect Jesus "miscalculated". But the more astonishing thing is that this error did not lessen his credibility in the community and that the non-arrival of the day of glory [more precisely: *his* delay] according to all the NT accounts was not in any way destructive of faith').

[77] See notes 3, 5, and 6.

since this goes back to Jesus himself.[78] And further, the connection, doubtless characteristic for Paul, between this concrete futuristic expectation and eschatological fulfilment in the present has its roots in the proclamation of Jesus,[79] however much the Easter faith of the earliest community may have given a new direction to this basic element in Jesus' thought. This is not the place to elaborate on this.[80] But at any rate it has become clear that the proper understanding of the unity and diversity of the various forms of proclamation in the New Testament is essentially dependent upon an awareness of the concrete temporal sense of Jesus' eschatological proclamation.

[78] See the reference to older attempts at explanation in Kümmel (note 3), pp. 115ff. T. F. Glasson's conception is that the expectation of the *Parousia* arose between the earliest community and Paul because of the transferral to Jesus of Old Testament statements about the eschatological coming of Yahweh and that the expectation of this coming in the *near* future arose as a consequence of many influences, among them the setting up of Caligula's statue in the temple at Jerusalem; this view, originally set forth in his *The Second Advent*, 1947[2], is repeated in the later edition, with the addition that the misunderstanding of several of Jesus' words about his triumph beyond the cross could have contributed to the emergence of the belief in the Parousia, and with the further addition that the Christian expectation of the coming in the near future arose primarily out of the transferral to Christianity of the similar Jewish expectation (see the third, 1963, edition, pp. 176f., 208). On this, see my critique in *ThR*, n.F. 22 (1954), pp. 144ff. Doeve (note 5) would recognize an expectation of a *near* coming as at most *possible* in some circles of primitive Christendom (even I Thess. 4.15 creates no more than this impression!), but he does not discuss the emergence of these isolated conceptions. And J. G. Davies, 'The Genesis of Belief in an Imminent Parousia', *JTS*, n.s. 14 (1963), pp. 104ff., would deduce from I Thess. 4.15 that belief in the *nearness* of the Parousia goes back to the revelation of a Christian prophet.

[79] See note 9.

[80] See W. G. Kümmel, 'Jesus und Paulus', *NTS* 10 (1963/64), pp. 163ff.

3

Some Thoughts on the Theme
'The Doctrine of Reconciliation in the New
Testament'*[1]

Ernst Käsemann

THE Christian doctrine of salvation has again and again been
subsumed under the catchword 'reconciliation', and correspondingly men have spoken unabashedly of a 'New Testament doctrine of reconciliation'. A large number of theological textbooks
treat the whole soteriology of the New Testament under this
theme, and in the Anglo-Saxon theological world in particular
such a way of viewing the matter has become deeply and firmly
rooted. I have been unable to ascertain the precise *Sitz im Leben*
of this tradition, which was widespread at least as early as the
nineteenth century. It may consequently be all the more useful
to examine comprehensively and critically, with the patterns of
New Testament theology especially in view, the justice, the
appropriateness, and the basis of the obviously tempting, even
seductive, use of the term in the New Testament. Just as a very
specific understanding of the Christian message is expressed by
this term, so also rather considerable dangers arise out of this

* Translated from *Zeit und Geschichte*, pp. 47–59.
[1] I can offer my teacher only this revised form of an essay read at an
ecumenical consultation of NT scholars in Montreal on July 29, 1963. But
if the work of Rudolf Bultmann is really the most important German contribution to the theology of our time the ecumenical church cannot overlook
it; rather, it may be profitable to examine its usefulness for the ecumenical
movement.

way of looking at things, dangers about which there appears to have been remarkably little serious reflection. That the New Testament speaks, among other things, of 'reconciliation' cannot, of course, be denied. But when? And where? And how? Do the statements on reconciliation actually form a material unity? What weight do they have in the NT proclamation as a whole? Do they justify the interest shown throughout the history of theology in this complex of motifs? From what standpoint, finally, are they to be satisfactorily interpreted, both historically and systematically? If one puts the question this way he quickly becomes aware of just how problematic our heritage is at this point and how mistrustful we must be over against any kind of over-simplification.

I. *The New Testament Evidence*

1. The exegete can, strictly speaking, find the New Testament speaking of 'reconciliation' only in those passages in which καταλλάσσειν and ἱλάσκεσθαι and their derivatives occur. If this thesis be accepted, one finds to his astonishment that this happens only rather rarely in the New Testament. A concordance, at any rate, does not support the view that reconciliation is a basic and central category of the primitive Christian message. Apart from Matt. 5.24 this motif occurs only in the Pauline and deutero-Pauline writings. It is used in a secular sense in both Matt. 5.24 and in I Cor. 7.11. In Paul it acquires terminological significance in Rom. 5.10f.; 11.15; and – here only with theological emphasis! – II Cor. 5.18ff. Finally, it appears as a catchword in the hymnic fragments in Col. 1.20, 22 and Eph. 2.16.

If one looks, on the basis of this evidence, at the complex of words associated with ἱλάσκεσθαι he must at once ask the question whether and to what extent the translation 'reconciliation' ought to take the place of (the surely more appropriate) 'expiate'. In the case of this word-complex what is envisaged, fundamentally, is an event in the cultic realm, as is shown by Rom. 3.25; Heb. 2.17; 8.12; 9.5; I John 2.2; 4.10, to which may be added the ransom-sayings in Mark 10.45 and I Tim. 2.6. That such a cultic relationship does not necessarily attach to the former word-group is evident from its occasional profane usage. And for the present the question of the circumstances under which the two groups of words can be associated must remain completely open. In my judgment, these factors lead unavoidably to the conclusion that there is no such thing as a doctrine of reconciliation which is regulative for the whole New Testament. It does not exist even in Paul, who only occasionally makes use of the motif, however important it becomes in the context of II Cor. 5.18ff. In the deutero-Paulines it also characterizes only very limited contexts, specifically the liturgical tradition contained in two passages. Thus that doctrine of reconciliation which is familiar to us from dogmatics and which has been carried over from dogmatics into New Testament theology can claim some connection with individual New Testament texts. But it attains importance and comprehensiveness only in the later thought of the church.

2. Yet the question arises as to the cause and purpose of the terminological use of the concept of 'reconciliation' in the NT. It is indeed a remarkable fact that the motif appears only in the general realm of Paulinism, though without having any significant meaning for Pauline theology as a whole, and that it can be used both casually and thematically. The deutero-Pauline passages provide the decisive clue to the explanation of this fact: We are dealing here with a tradition which is originally hymnic and liturgical in character and which comes, therefore, from the doxological tradition of the Hellenistic community. The pointed saying in Rom. 11.15 uses the expression 'reconciliation of the world' without any preparation and obviously as a formula; this can only be explained on the grounds of a fixed tradition. The fact that the following clause speaks, in antithetical parallelism, of $\zeta\omega\grave{\eta}$ $\dot{\epsilon}\kappa$ $\nu\epsilon\kappa\rho\hat{\omega}\nu$ is further evidence that both expressions are intended as paraphrases for eschatological consummation. Romans 5.9–11 confirms this view: v. 10 is parallel to vv. 8b–9 in order to underscore and point up what it says. Since it applies to sinners, God's love is manifested specifically to God's enemies. 'Reconciliation' is used here, as in Matt. 5.24 and I Cor. 7.11, in a non-cultic sense and means bringing hostility to an end;

according to v. 11 it is granted as a gift of the hitherto angry
God. Its end-product and its goal is the 'peace with God' of 5.1,
and its sign is the untrammelled access to God of 5.2. It is
mediated 'by the death of his Son' or, as it is expressed in v. 9,
'by his blood'. Just as both expressions have a liturgical colouring, so both provide clarification by taking up the liturgical ὑπὲρ
ἡμῶν of v. 8. Cultic associations are now – and only now! – possible and apparently also presupposed. Yet it is characteristic
that Paul does not expressly go into these associations and
accentuates only the element of the vicarious death. Eschatological reconciliation does not exist apart from the 'means of
expiation' mentioned in 3.25, which is the dying Christ himself,
or apart from his vicarious mediation. So the motif of reconciliation is introduced here to heighten to the greatest possible degree
the concept of the *justificatio impiorum*, namely, by the assertion of
the *justificatio inimicorum*. It serves, accordingly, to sharpen and
point up the doctrine of justification. Its use, however, immediately implies the christological concept of vicariousness
which is familiar from the primitive Christian liturgy, particularly from the eucharist. But if this is so one must reckon with
the possibility that Paul is here using a tradition that was handed
down to him.

   This is conclusively proved, in my opinion, by II Cor. 5.18–21.
The hymnic solemnity of the passage is undeniable. The many
participial predicates undoubtedly breathe a liturgical spirit.
The form of expression stands in sharp contrast to what we find
elsewhere in Paul. That God does not reckon transgressions
makes the saving event evident in the forgiveness of the accumu-
lated guilt of sin, just as in Rom. 3.25, a Jewish-Christian hymnic
fragment. Paul himself, in contrast, lays the entire emphasis on
liberation from the *power* of sin. One is surprised to read that the
messengers of the gospel, as representatives of the exalted Christ,
bear the call to reconciliation throughout the world, for this
clearly presupposes the conception that the apostle continues the
work of the earthly Jesus, which the exalted Lord is thus no
longer capable of doing. But in this way the otherwise characteristically Pauline motif 'in Christ' is curiously replaced by 'for

Christ'; indeed, it is God himself who is considered as acting through the apostle. Finally, it should be observed that a quotation seems to be introduced with the transitional ὡς and the ὅτι recitative, when the world's reconciliation (not, as in v. 18, our reconciliation) is spoken of in v. 19, a thought that is maintained through to the conclusion of v. 20. Verse 21 would also be easier to understand as a citation: again ἁμαρτία is not a power, but the guilt of sin. Nowhere else is Paul given to reflection about the sinlessness of Jesus. We must give careful thought to the question of whether on the basis of his conception of sin as a power he could say that Jesus was made sin for us, i.e., made the bearer of all earthly guilt. It is no less remarkable that Christians are designated 'the righteousness of God' in him, since such a predicate is meaningful, as in I Cor. 1.30, only in referring to Christ. The matter would be quite different if this passage were the echo of a Jewish-Christian tradition which related such an expression to the covenant people. This method of speaking in abstractions is of course also familiar to us from the Hodayoth of the Qumran sectarians, and it is not accidental that it is reflected in I Cor. 1.30, a verse which is likewise to be judged a liturgical fragment. It is obvious that the pathos of the paradoxical antithesis would fit my suggestion well. In any case, the verse is a solemn proclamation of the basis for the call to reconciliation, in which the motif of vicariousness once again forms the decisive central emphasis. Though all this brings us to the very edge of the conclusion that in vv. 19–21 we have a pre-Pauline hymnic fragment, for my purposes it is sufficient merely to establish the fact that Paul has taken up and used motifs from earlier forms of the Christian proclamation. At least I hope to have made this a probable and discussible option. That those texts which speak of Christ as an expiation for us are determined by liturgical traditions or allusions may, in the present context, be simply asserted. This is less central to our purpose and serves only to round out the picture I have sketched.

3. But now we must inquire more closely into the content of the statements I have in view. It is of crucial importance to note that we are never said to reconcile God with us, which would be

the appropriate form for a sacrificial conception. God is always the sole subject of the reconciling action. This is even true in the case of II Cor. 5.20, where we are called to be ambassadors and mediators of the word of reconciliation; here we remain instruments of the Logos which acts through us. It sets us in motion in its service, which in good Pauline fashion is seen as a manifestation of grace, not of our own ability. It is even more significant that the tradition under consideration lies before us in two different versions. Over against the anthropological variant – God reconciles us with himself – stands the cosmological form in Rom. 11.15; II Cor. 5.19f.; Col. 1.20; Eph. 2.16: God reconciled the world. Still a further distinction must also be made. While II Cor. 5.19f. speaks of the reconciliation of the world with God, in the other passages the emphasis is on the reconciliation *within* the cosmos, which of course presupposes the reconciliation with God. This second cosmological version must reflect the beginning of the tradition. For only on the basis of such an assumption can the material problematic of the differing versions be clarified and, at the same time, set in a proper historical context. I begin with the two deutero-Pauline texts. We have already seen in Rom. 5.10f. the goal and result of the reconciling act to be peace; similarly these texts are clearly concerned with cosmic peace, the revelation of which is dreamed of as early as Vergil's Fourth Eclogue. This peace is thought of as the eschatological state of salvation, not as a psychological attitude, something in which the NT is very rarely interested. In this situation of peace what was formerly separated becomes solidly united, i.e., the heavenly is united with the earthly, just as warring earthly camps are united with one another. Even religious antipathies now become irrelevant, as may be seen in a radical way in the antithesis between Israel and the Gentile world. The world is made peaceful, as under the *pax romana*, in that it is everywhere subjected to its new Lord, Christ, as Cosmocrator. But since in Christ the Kingdom and majesty of God become manifest the earth reverts, under the sign of eschatological peace, from its conditions of general rebellion and mutual animosities. The new Creation, like the old, grows out of the Chaos.

It should be noted that such proclamation utilizes the present and perfect tenses. It makes joy, not hope sound forth. Though the world may not yet know of the transformation that has taken place, the Christian community does. Its message is characterized by the open proclamation of the seizure of power by God and his appointed Saviour and by the verification of that proclamation in the union of both Jews and Gentiles in the Christian church. Heaven is no longer a closed realm hovering above the earth, and the world is no more the battlefield of every man against his neighbour and the arena of mutually exclusive sovereignties. The principalities and powers have been dethroned. If this picture is correct, reconciliation in this instance implies an eschatological, even an apocalyptic, phenomenon which is not primarily connected with, and cannot be appropriately conceived by the use of, either juridical or cultic categories. The eschatological and worldwide *regnum Christi* necessarily breaks the bounds of a community understood along merely juridical or cultic lines.

4. But what is implied by the transition from a cosmological to an anthropological message of reconciliation? This is nicely illustrated by the relationship between Col. 1.20 and 1.22: If the hymn itself still spoke of the All, in the writer's subsequent commentary he addresses the members of the Christian community, who have personally experienced the cosmic transferral of dominion. A transitional phase is still observable in II Cor. 5.19f. The catchword 'reconciliation of the world' is illustrated in this passage, in that emphasis is laid upon that reconciliation with God which characterizes the community and must be spread abroad by it in its missionary activity. The change in outlook reflects a changed historical situation. For the NT hymns are predominantly witnesses of the unbridled enthusiasm which is characteristic of the earliest Hellenistic community and the beginnings of its world mission. This location in space and time provides the explanation of the motifs of the reconciliation of the world and of the All. But the danger of such enthusiasm is that the individual Christian will understand the salvation he experiences as devoid of temptation and consequently cease looking

towards the future and giving himself to the service of others. So it is no accident that the anthropological statements about reconciliation occur in a parenetic context, portraying existence as still hanging in the balance. The message of reconciliation is not an eschatological myth, as in Vergil's Fourth Eclogue. It is actualized between the indicative of the gift of salvation and the imperative of the duties of salvation, i.e. in the historical realm, the realm of concrete daily life and corporal community. Cosmic peace does not settle over the world, as in a fairy tale. It takes root only so far as men in the service of reconciliation confirm that they have themselves found peace with God. The message of the reconciled world demonstrates its truth in the reconciled man, not apart from him or beyond him. This is the reason that we suddenly encounter the second instead of the third person and that the accent now falls primarily upon the relationship to God instead of upon the cosmic realm. It is also the reason that in place of the proclamation of the accomplished reconciliation of the world we now find the admonition to Christians to live as reconciled men and to the heathen to become reconciled. Now world-wide reconciliation becomes the *telos* of an earthly commission, and in this commission is established the reality of the fact that the exalted Christ has begun to exercise lordship. Finally, a christological shift along the same lines takes place, as decisive weight is now placed, not on the Cosmocrator, but on the Crucified One. For the death of Jesus is now no longer merely a transitional stage on the victorious road to exaltation. It is conceived of soteriologically as the basis of the fact that it is specifically as men under temptation that we have peace with God and access to him.

5. In this passage the motifs of world-wide reconciliation and the expiation effected by Jesus' death are now further associated. The limits of this assertion, however, must be carefully noted. In our context the statements about expiation characterize solely the fundamental reconciling event of Jesus' death on the cross, not the whole ministry of Jesus and certainly not the continuing proclamation of the message of reconciliation. The dogmatician may interest himself in the elaboration of this into a comprehen-

sive doctrine of the Reconciler and the work of Reconciliation. But the NT texts as such do not provide the material for such a venture. If this is not observed, a shift of emphasis and a different perspective will result. For doxology is not yet doctrine, though it can become a point of departure for doctrine. Doxology may have parenetic uses. But even then the statements on reconciliation in the NT remain soteriologically oriented. No christology is yet elaborated under the theme of the Reconciler, and the motif of reconciliation is not even predominant in the soteriology of the NT as a whole. Such a conception of the matter can only arise when one tears the statements about expiation away from their function as servants of the message of reconciliation and makes them central.

Another fact is equally important: Although in the NT the death of Jesus is seen as the beginning and basis of the work of reconciliation, this is not explicitly elaborated. Apparently even two different aspects of the matter are here being conflated. In the deutero-Pauline passages the death of Jesus is seen as the initiatory event of the exaltation, which first of all *as* exaltation – i.e. as the enthronement of the Cosmocrator – guarantees cosmic peace. Elsewhere, however, the event of the Cross is understood as a means of expiation, established by God, in which the reconciliation of the previously hostile parties is realized and manifested. But here too we are faced with an embarrassing shortage of detail. A real explication of such statements does not accompany them. For in doxological expressions, which are always highly abbreviated, such explication is not necessary. Theological reflection in the church, to be sure, has repaired the lack of explanation by all kinds of theories. But the NT itself hardly says more than that Jesus, by dying, has stepped into the breach between God and ourselves, and the distinctive nature of the NT teaching is preserved only when one-sided conclusions are not drawn.

This is especially true in the case of the sacrificial and juridical solution to the problematic which is involved here. It can hardly be denied that 'expiation' can be both a cultic and a legal concept or that cult and law may be intimately associated. Nor is it questionable that the various NT conceptions of expiation rest upon the cultic tradition, chiefly that of the OT. But this state of affairs must not be run into the ground, as we can learn from the Epistle to the Hebrews. If this epistle makes use of the full range of the OT cultic tradition, it does so with polemic intent, namely, to set forth (paradoxically) by the comparisons it draws the incomparable nature of the eschatological Saviour and his work. The eschatological reality, in other words, is not here comprehended by nor subsumed under the cultic: it rather stands over against it, like the truth to the darkness. Confessional controversies have arisen time and again because men have understood the comparison, against its intent and its consequences, as a confirmation of what it surpassed. The exegete may, by an observation of this kind, be warned of the need for critical caution and brought to recognize that although the notion of substitution has been inserted into the texts that deal with reconciliation, the sacrificial and juridical conceptions that are associated with the substitutionary concept do not really lie behind what is said about reconciliation. A different result can be obtained only by forcing the entire stream of NT statements on expiation through narrow locks into the complex of ideas connected with reconciliation. But such a course is prohibited, both by the brevity of the passages cited and still more by the total direction of the NT data. For in the NT as a whole the eschatological is not a mere variant of the cultic; it is the shattering of it. In our present context the expiatory death of Jesus is only adduced to show that we can neither supplant nor support the act of God. He alone acts to bring life and oneness. And in this act no legitimizing of a new cultic usage is really implied. Furthermore, the texts do not really speak of satisfaction, either. Juridical terms do occur, it is true, in Rom. 3.25 and II Cor. 5.19f. But they really attest only the sovereignty of God, the eschatological uniqueness of the Christ-event, and the validity of the apostolic message. When salvation is described in Heb. 2.15 as deliverance from bondage to the devil, to death, and to the fear of death, or in Rom. 5.9 as deliverance from the wrath of God, what is meant is not satisfaction but liberation and release by the act of a change of masters. The net result of the discussion to this point, then, is the thesis that we must leave the NT texts in their own context, pointing in their own direction; we must respect their silence with respect to our dogmatic questions and not utilize them as a quarry for modern theories.

II.   *Conclusions*

Without going beyond the bounds set by the proper competence of the exegete we may venture a few generalizations.

1. In connection with the extraordinarily rare, almost casual, occurrences of the term 'reconciliation', always in texts shaped by tradition, one significant fact must be kept clearly in mind, though it has seldom been taken sufficiently into account and indeed has all too often been systematically obscured: There is no unified, overall category for the soteriological terms and motifs of the NT. One might at first imagine σώζειν and its derivatives to provide such a category. But this word-group, apart from the particular context of the moment, yields little more than the fact that reference to eschatological salvation is intended. In itself it neither grounds nor elaborates a specifically Christian soteriology. In the NT a whole host of different conceptions are used to characterize the essence of the eschatological salvation. This is what is reflected in the bewildering variety of such concepts as forgiveness, healing, sealing, justification, sanctification, cleansing, election, redemption, transformation, rebirth, victory, life. To reduce it to a formula: In this case the variety is constitutive of the whole. Hence one must be careful not to isolate any one of these themes or to give it pride of place over the others. It is even difficult, in fact, to show that any one of them is peculiar to any single NT writer. Naturally certain terms and motifs are associated with distinct types of the tradition, and there are many – like 'righteousness' for Paul or 'life' for John – that have special importance for individual writers. Yet no writer follows any single pattern, and only in the case of a few – perhaps again in the case of Paul or John – is any pattern systematically elaborated. Later dogmatic development no doubt differs in this

regard from the NT. It forces the primitive Christian proclamation into fixed patterns which are supposed to comprise and
organize the whole. It forces the kerygma into a theoretical
mould. But does not this state of affairs demonstrate clearly that
in the NT the formulation of soteriological statements is more
dependent than later formulations upon the time and circum-
stance of the witnesses of the moment? Here too tradition affects
the form of the message, because tradition always affects communication. It is not yet, however, a hallowed ecclesiastical
tradition nor a rigidly set prefiguration of Christian dogma.
There are tendencies, to be sure, in this direction. But what is
decisive is that one is still remarkably open to the world and the
history in which he is taking part. This is the reason that he can
work unabashedly with materials and traditions of the widest
possible diversity. This is true only relatively, of course, since the
horizons of every man and every period are limited ones; no
community is entirely free of the temptation and the danger of
creating an artificial language of its own and eventually speaking a mere 'language of Zion'. Apart from motif-research, which
is ordinarily concerned only with the pathway into the NT, almost no preliminary work has yet been done on this problem.
NT concepts and Christian language tend both to become in-
flated and to be worn out – an event of momentous consequence
in all periods of the church, since it tends both to firm up the
church and to imprison its mission and its communication. It is
hardly possible to assess profit and loss in this process. Yet we
must always keep in mind the fact that the Christian mission involves a kind of exodus in the realm of language too and that
ecclesiastical traditions, especially in so far as they have been
rendered 'holy' by Christian history, also always stand in the
way of this mission. The church itself is always the greatest
obstacle to its own mission. And the more it isolates itself and its
sphere from the world, the more it rids itself of its diversities, the
more of an obstacle it becomes.

2. The message of reconciliation was taken up in primitive
Christianity as one soteriological variant among others, and
this occurred in that particular segment of the church which

does not determine the gospel; it cannot, at a pinch, become a substitute for it. It bears witness to the gospel and consequently is understood and used critically by him. This is just what happens to the statements about reconciliation. They are used because they set in sharp relief the radical and universal nature of the message of justification. They bring out the fact that God aids and purposes to aid his enemies (and thus the whole world). But this does not mean that all of this is not already implied in the message of justification as such. On the contrary, it is only because this is exactly what the justification of the ungodly does imply that the statements about reconciliation become possible and important in the Pauline doctrine of justification. Their pathos serves to point up the consequence of this doctrine. For to Paul the doctrine of justification is the heart of the Christian message; it establishes the legitimacy and sets the limits of all varieties and even interpretations of NT teaching. In his view, it is essential that its substance (not its terminology) be preserved. The extent of the variations serves to prevent oversimplifying, restricting, blunting, or misunderstanding the doctrine. Yet the variations, no matter what degree of refraction they may involve, reflect the *one* central concern; they are taken up by the apostle only in so far as they are capable of doing so.

4. It is certainly striking that in the post-Pauline period the pre-Pauline tradition of the reconciliation of the All, uncontrolled by the doctrine of justification, can be taken up precisely by Paul's disciples. We must insist on the fact that the motif is not yet elaborated expressly in their teaching. Yet one may note here the first sign of the development to come. The doxology over that peace which is created by the saving message of Jesus' death and rule over the world and man can easily be replaced by a metaphysics of supernatural factors, structures, and orders. The disappearance of the primitive Christian eschatology, recognizable already in the deutero-Pauline literature, will serve to accelerate this process. For one of the essential functions of this eschatology was to prevent the subordination of christology to ecclesiology. In general, it is not sufficiently recognized that a different theological orientation can no longer remain equally

cognizant of this function. It looks like a mere shift in emphasis
when the statement that Christ is our peace is elaborated by the
statement that the church is the realm of reconciliation. But such
a shift in emphasis may in some circumstances change the whole
structure of theology, make of Christ the Lord of a cult, domesti-
cate the saving Event, define the Message in terms of sacrament
and dogma, and restrict one's view of the new creation to the relationships between the church and the world. The more differentiated theology becomes, the more the nuances are decisive.
Hence the criteria for the proper way to handle the differing
traditions, for accepting, correcting, or abandoning them must
be sought in their respective centres and tendencies. It is not
enough that they can be assimilated to the mass of theological
material. What must be asked is whether and how far from the
perspective of any one of them the heart of the message is
illuminated and set forth. The statements about reconciliation
in the NT are protected from extravagance by primitive Christian eschatology and by the Pauline doctrine of justification.
They proclaim, as the basis of human solidarity, God's solidarity
with men in Christ. Their presupposition is that only when man's
own work has come to an end does he become the recipient and
bearer of the divine work to a world which God has not forsaken, that the earth is only liberated from enmity and chaos
and made a new creation in so far as the service of Christ is
carried on in her. All the church's teaching about reconciliation
must be tested against this touchstone: to what extent does it
safeguard this presupposition, and to what extent does it seek to
supplant it?

4

The Theological Aspects of
Primitive Christian Heresy*

Helmut Koester

I

TIME and time again, students of Rudolf Bultmann find themselves turning to the problem of heresy in primitive Christianity;[1] it seems to be quite a characteristic interest of those
whose work has been associated with that great scholar and
teacher. All their work on this problem has likewise been influenced by Walter Bauer's pioneering monograph that appeared in 1934, *Rechtgläubigkeit und Ketzerei im ältesten Christentum*.[2]

* Translated by Bentley Layton from *Zeit und Geschichte*, pp. 61–76, after
revision by the author.

[1] The following bibliography is by no means exhaustive; it only suggests
the work done in the last few years on our topic by the writers to whom I
have referred. On I and II Corinthians: G. Bornkamm, 'Herrenmahl und
Kirche bei Paulus', *Studien zu Antike und Urchristentum*, 1963², pp. 138–76;
W. Schmithals, *Die Gnosis in Korinth* (FRLANT 66), 1956; U. Wilckens,
Weisheit und Torheit (BhTh 26), 1959. On II Corinthians alone: E.
Käsemann, *Die Legitimität des Apostels*, 1956 = *ZNW* 47 (1942), pp. 33–71;
D. Georgi, *Die Gegner des Paulus im 2. Korintherbrief* (WMANT 11), 1964. On
Colossians: G. Bornkamm, 'Die Häresie des Kolosserbriefes', *Das Ende des
Gesetzes* (BevTh 16), 1958², pp. 139–56. On Philippians: W. Schmithals,
'Die Irrlehrer des Philipperbriefes', *ZThK* 54 (1957), pp. 297–341; H.
Koester, 'The Purpose of the Polemic of a Pauline Fragment', *NTS* 8 (1961/
62), pp. 317–32. On the Johannine epistles: E. Käsemann, 'Ketzer und
Zeuge', *ZThK* 48 (1951), pp. 292–311 (= *Exegetische Versuche und Besinnungen*
I, 1965⁴, pp. 168–86). Generally: H. Koester, 'Häretiker im Urchristentum',
*RGG*³ III, pp. 17–21; W. Schmithals, 'Zur Sammlung und Abfassung der
ältesten Paulusbriefe', *ZNW* 51 (1960), pp. 225–45.

[2] BhTh 10, 1934, 1964².

Walter Bauer tried to refute the long-standing theory that heresy, both in essence and in its historical appearance, was the later adulteration of a more original orthodox belief. In fact (Bauer claimed), we cannot deny that there was 'heresy' in the apostolic age itself, nor can we show that 'orthodox' belief had universal priority. Bauer's theses were developed still further by the scholars to whom we have just referred. Above all, the latter tried to determine more closely the nature of heresies in the NT age and thus to form a clearer conception of the theology expressed in NT literature.

After one has taken stock of the present state of the discussion, a number of problems must be dealt with. One might begin by undertaking detailed studies of more *extra*-canonical writings which are related to the topic at hand – there is certainly a need for this.[3] The most important question, however, concerns the rise of early Christian heresy and the *religionsgeschichtlich* problem. By now Bultmann and his students have received at least their fair share of the blows exchanged over this controversial question – one can only hope that the controversy has not degenerated once and for all into an uncontrollable polemic.[4] Whether or not the discussion will continue at such a level is now simply a question of one's dignity. But without a doubt, we can no longer ignore the need for a new look at the *religionsgeschichtlich* problem, even though such a task will not be undertaken in this paper.[5]

[3] Under Rudolf Bultmann's influence, a few such studies have already been undertaken; cf. H. Schlier, *Religionsgeschichtliche Untersuchungen zu den Ignatiusbriefen* (BZNW 8), 1929; G. Bornkamm, *Mythos und Legende in den apokryphen Thomasakten* (FRLANT 49), 1933.

[4] Cf. the following words, for example: 'The author of this book lacks historical training', 'a striking proof of the decline of exegetic research since the thirties', J. Munck, 'The NT and Gnosticism', *StTh* XV (1961), p. 187; cf. also the rather condescending judgments of R. M. Grant, 'Hermeneutics and Tradition in Ignatius of Antioch', *Archivio di Filosofia* 1–2 (1963), pp. 183–201. It is unfortunate that in this kind of polemic the arguments of one's opponents are rarely reproduced with great accuracy, a fact which makes further discussion all the more difficult.

[5] The reader will observe that within the so-called Bultmann School quite a bit of sharp critical observation has been made in this regard; e.g., D. Georgi's excellent review of W. Schmithals, *Die Gnosis in Korinth*, in *VuF*

My main concern here is to raise once more the *theological* aspects of the heresy problem and *only* its *theological* aspects – since, as I suspect, our problem is very deeply a theological one, and not just the purely descriptive task of the historian of religion. The situation facing us is not simply the fact that on the basis of new research, we must now date the appearance of heresy a few decades earlier than we had previously supposed, and that the beginning of Christian Gnosticism now dates perhaps from the time of Paul and not just from the time of Ignatius or Justin. Were this the only point of our discussion, the critic would be just as short-sighted as his opponents. For the criteria for determining 'right' and 'wrong' belief which were worked out toward the end of the second century by the anti-gnostic fathers have no validity when we consider the theological problems and relationships of the first Christian generations. Therefore the question is not whether we may rightly label the opponents of Paul as Gnostic heretics, or whether in Paul's time there was yet even such a thing as Gnostic heresy.[6] The danger of putting the question this way is clear; for one would only succeed in casting the theological problems of the Pauline age in the categories of second- and third-century controversy. One would make it appear either that Paul was orthodox and had Gnostic opponents, or that he had no Gnostic opponents but only Judaizing ones, or perhaps none at all. In any case, one would assume that he was 'orthodox', and thus naturally he was 'finally' or 'essentially' or 'properly understood' in agreement with the Pastoral Epistles.

Yet we must not forget that Rudolf Bultmann, in his *Theology of the NT*, *preceded* the treatment of Paul with a chapter on 'Gnostic Motifs'. If Paul's thought was already determined by motifs that appeared to be objectionable heresy to the later

---

13 (1960), pp.90–6, or my review of U. Wilckens, *Weisheit und Torheit*, in *Gnomon* 33 (1961), pp.590–5.

[6] The question of when 'Gnosticism' had its beginning is of course open to debate, although in my opinion one simply cannot explain many early Christian and extra-Christian phenomena without accepting the existence of a pre-Christian Gnosis.

church, Paul himself stands in the twilight zone of heresy. In other words we are forced to redefine the traditional standards of 'heretical' and 'orthodox'.[7] So it appears that we cannot base our research upon the expectation that in the end these labels will fit Paul and his contemporary opponents, as previous generations of scholarship argued. The need to redefine the terms 'heretical' and 'orthodox' if we are going to use them of Paul's time is obvious when one notes that although Paul is fighting Gnostic opponents in I Corinthians, it is *Gnostic* arguments which he himself uses in II Corinthians to combat Jewish pneumatics.[8]

II. *A Critique of the Search for New Criteria for Defining Heresy*

Can we attain any new criteria for defining heresy by studying the beginnings of Christianity? How to answer this question is made difficult by the fact that the church later invented such criteria and read them back into its origins, adroitly translating orthodox teaching and its authority back into the time of the very earliest beginnings. This was accomplished not only by the establishment of the NT canon, but also within the canon by three concepts in particular: the authority of the apostles (which, as it was later conceived, had precedence over that of Paul), the early Christian kerygma and, above all, the life and teaching of Jesus.

From the canon *per se*, no *new* standards can be derived – what then should we take as a guide? To what extent does critical investigation open up new points of view? Or does theology in the end have no other alternative than subjecting itself to tradition and the criteria fixed by it?

In its day, the *religionsgeschichtliche Schule* offered a solution which is still widely accepted: namely, that the standard of

---

[7] One cannot simply give them up, even though the technical terminology is not to be found in the NT. The historian must carry out his responsibility to see primitive Christianity for what it actually is, namely a movement struggling over the theological question of the right or wrong understanding of its revelation.

[8] Dieter Georgi, *Die Gegner des Paulus im 2. Korintherbrief*, 1964.

genuine Christianity is piety, religiosity, and intensity, especially of cultic experience. What is opposed to this standard, and hence heretical, is doctrine abstracted from life, whether it appears as Jewish legalism or as Hellenistic speculation. With this presupposition, the conception of F. C. Baur could simply be continued without modification. Consequently there arose the rule of thumb widely current even today, namely, that the two fundamental errors of Christianity were Judaism or Hellenism, legalism or speculation, apocalyptic fanaticism or Gnostic mysticism. It is within such a conceptual framework that much scholarly discussion of this problem still moves – and not only scholarly discussion but its less scholarly counterpart in the church at large as well.

In such a discussion, however, the fact is overlooked that 'orthodoxy', standing midway between legalism and speculation, is defined only in formal terms, as 'religiousness'; as a result a vacuum arises, not defined further, a linguistic void between the two extremes of false doctrine. The source of error is the fact that in establishing a set of propositions which lie outside the realm of theological discourse, one still cannot escape language and the realm of language. Otherwise, one enters upon a fatal path of error: thinking that the thing which has to be expressed in terms of the supposedly 'unexpressible' can be actualized in cultic gesture, sign and symbol. This line of thinking is a complete misunderstanding of the real character of cultic and liturgical actions. For the latter are in their true intention meant to condense and concentrate religious language, not to overcome it (when this is not the case, cultus has been degraded to pure mysticism). Furthermore, to interpret the central criterion of orthodoxy psychologically – as 'the experience of faith' – or to reduce theological standards to ethical attitudes is simply to propose second-rate substitutes for theological discourse.

The *religionsgeschichtlich* approach brought to light yet another thesis, in this case one which must be maintained under all circumstances: primitive Christianity was a totally syncretistic phenomenon – not just those forms which were judged heretical. When this has been recognized, one traditional criterion for the identification of heresy falls by the wayside, namely, tracing the heresies of one's opponents back to the foreign influences of heathen piety and Greek philosophy. The search for extra-Christian origins of heretical views has not yet been freed from the untenable prejudices of the ancient Christian opponents of heresy. Naturally it remains true that the motifs, myths and cultic conceptions noted in *religionsgeschichtlich* studies could and did migrate from place to place. Likewise one religio-cultural milieu can more or less strongly influence another. Yet cognizance of this fact does not explain the phenomenon of early Christian heresy. This has been finally confirmed by the uncontestable fact that Christianity as such is syncretistic, not just those forms which were later condemned as heretical. The Gnostic *Gospel of Truth* that we now possess, thanks to the Nag Hammadi find, is neither more nor less a product of syncretistic religious development than the contemporary Roman document, *The Shepherd of Hermas* or, for that matter, than the theology of Paul. In view of this, it is quite hard to understand the common zeal for attributing to NT writings a greater theological trustworthiness by citing OT, Jewish-apocalyptic and Rabbinic parallels. For it cannot be doubted that Judaism itself was already a product of Oriental syncretism! And indeed the Christian Gnostic writings of the second century are just as strongly rooted in Jewish theology as are their 'orthodox' counterparts!

The thesis of the *religionsgeschichtliche Schule* that primitive Christianity is itself syncretistic may be of great lasting value; nor, as we have said, is sheer piety any longer a satisfactory criterion for distinguishing orthodox belief. For the question of orthodoxy must be decided not by the most ancient witnesses to religious experience, but by the verbal content of the primitive Christian message.

For this reason, the attempt to orient oneself to the language of the NT might seem more promising. Such an attempt presupposes that the unity of the NT is a unity of language. If evidence to support this presupposition could be adduced, then, in fact, an impressive criterion for the distinction of orthodoxy would have been found. Here the names Cremer and Kögel

come to mind, for their work along these lines was widely influential.[9] It is well known that their fundamental distinction
between biblical and secular Greek decisively influenced that
great project, the *Theologisches Wörterbuch zum Neuen Testament,*
edited by G. Kittel and G. Friedrich (and now at last being
translated into English as the *Theological Dictionary of the NT*).[10]
Of course today we no longer have to fight the tendency to make
this distinction, for to a greater and greater extent this work
itself has led us to realize that NT Greek is intimately related to
the secular Greek of NT times.[11] It was precisely philological investigation which showed that the NT cannot be considered *sui
generis* as a linguistic phenomenon. Clearly, the Greek of the NT
is not classical Greek; but there is quite a strong resemblance –
to say the least – between Hellenistic Greek and the Greek of the
NT, both in structure and in vocabulary. If one relies upon the
methods of philology he can only come to the conclusion that the
language of the NT is neither unique nor uniform. However interesting and informative we may find philological investigations
of biblical language and its characteristics, these investigations
cannot provide us with a standard to separate the heretical from
the orthodox.

Another attempt to work out the linguistic characteristics of
orthodox theological discourse pretends to proceed upon certain
philosophical presuppositions about the nature of language. I
should like to indicate how hopeless it is to search for new criteria
through such an endeavour by making a few critical observations on T. Bonhoeffer's article in the third edition of *Religion in
Geschichte und Gegenwart* on theological language.[12] Perhaps we

[9] *Bibl.-Theol. Wörterb.*, 1st ed. 1866, 11th ed. 1923.

[10] Trans. G. Bromiley, *Theological Dictionary of the New Testament*, 1964ff.
Selected articles translated by J. R. Coates *et al.* in *Bible Key Words* (9 vols.,
London: A. & C. Black, 1949–60; 3 vols., New York: Harper, 1951–60).

[11] For this reason the violent attacks of James Barr, *The Semantics of
Biblical Language* (1961), and *Biblical Words for Time* (SBT 33, 1962) are not
really justifiable; decisive though they be, his remarks are aimed at a few
articles of the *Theologisches Wörterbuch* which are hardly convincing anyway;
likewise they attack such authors as T. Boman and T. F. Torrance.

[12] 'Sprache. IV. Theologisch', *RGG*[3] VI, 272–82.

need not spend too much of our time evaluating Bonhoeffer's
surely profound proposition: 'the noun "speech" is derived from
the verb "to speak".'[13] It is quite obvious that Bonhoeffer attempts to make the word 'God' – or more precisely, the use of
the phonetic unit 'god' – into the measuring stick of orthodox
theological discourse. When Judaism replaced the OT word for
'God' (Yahweh) with the substitute 'Adonai', that was plainly
the theological Fall of Judaism in Bonhoeffer's estimation. On
the other hand (he says) in the proclamation of Jesus, 'the word
"God" lays a mighty claim upon the language of justice and
thereby gives "freedom to the word".'[14] Accordingly, it is supposed to be the word 'God' which holds together the various
fundamental theological concepts like 'kingdom' (Jesus), 'justification' (Paul) and 'witness' (John).

But should we not expect God to be the source as well as the
object of discourse in the NT? Is not the problem actually that
except for the word 'God' the theological vocabulary is different
in every case? Hence it is not immediately clear, for example,
how what Paul says about justification is simply the continuation of what Jesus says about the Kingdom of God. If by 'talk of
God' we simply mean the *subject matter* which holds together the
entire NT, we perhaps can agree. But the problem which faces
us is that this subject matter does not appear in one uniform
language, but in a variety of languages. Our conscientiousness as
historians demands that we consider the linguistic diversity of
the NT to be characteristic of all primitive Christian proclamation.[15] We must learn to grasp the nature of this diversity, and
indeed, we must do so through the methods of philology and
Religionsgeschichte. Thus one cannot begin by assuming the unity

[13] *Ibid.*, 272.

[14] *Ibid.*, 278.

[15] Admittedly in asserting this I have plainly (and confidently) allied
myself with those whose 'historische Gewissenhaftigkeit Gottlosigkeit ist'
(Bonhoeffer, *art. cat.*, 279), especially 'die Gottlosigkeit der Sprache derer,
die das Evangelium schon Paradox genannt und als Torheit dogmatisch
stehen gelassen haben'. I will also cheerfully admit that to me the Gospel,
which preaches the foolishness of the Cross, in fact seems to be a paradox;
but in my opinion this confession is a virtue of faith and not a sign of
Gottlosigkeit.

of NT language, but rather with the observation of its syncretistic character. This point now deserves further elaboration.

III. *The Language of the NT as a Syncretistic Phenomenon*

1. The language of the NT is syncretistic inasmuch as there simply is no peculiarly biblical language. There are no words, concepts, forms or sentences which the philologist and historian of religion can consider typical for the 'New Testament' and upon which they can base the pronouncement of orthodoxy. Proof of this was brought to light long ago by exegetical work on the NT – a glance at the critical commentaries, dictionaries and handbooks makes that immediately clear. Parallels between the language of the NT world and the NT itself, discovered by philological and *religionsgeschichtlich* research, are so overwhelmingly convincing that one does not assume there is any sentence in the NT that has not been found – or not yet – or at least could not be found – outside of primitive Christianity.

2. In all the diverse layers of NT tradition there are no exceptions to this rule. The language spoken by Jesus had the same syncretistic nature as the language of the NT; thus it does not precede the latter as 'not yet syncretistic'.[16] There is no support for the assertion that certain forms of discourse used by Jesus, that is, analogy, antithesis and parable, are 'ur-Christian' and so have no parallels. Admittedly there are some striking dissimilarities in the way such forms of discourse are used here and in the language of apocalypticism, but they are significant only because they result from an interpretation of this same apocalyptic language; hence we can see their profile only against the

---

[16] It seems to me that on these grounds Ernst Käsemann's theses must be revised: the assertion that Jesus' proclamation was not yet apocalyptic seems to set off the language of Jesus from that of the rest of the NT – as a phenomenon *sui generis* – unless we understand Käsemann to mean that the language of Jesus was indeed apocalyptic, but that this apocalyptic language was interpreted so radically in the case of Jesus that it lost its apocalyptic implications. Cf. E. Käsemann, 'Zum Thema der urchristliche Apokalyptik', *ZThK* 59 (1962), pp. 257ff. (= *Exegetische Versuche und Besinnungen* II, 1965, pp. 105ff. ET: *New Testament Questions of Today*, 1969, pp. 108ff.

contrast of their historical background – which it is our task to reconstruct. A good illustration of this may be found in the parables of Jesus, which by and large correspond to Rabbinic and apocalyptic parables. To be sure, they are distinguished from them by the complete absence of allegory. Yet there are parallels for this in the OT (cf. Nathan's parable in II Sam. 12).

3. Likewise, there was never an original Christian kerygma not yet subject to the syncretistic nature as it were of the language of the NT. To designate the proclamation of the Resurrection of Jesus as such an 'Ur-kerygma' would be unfortunate.[17] Without question, talk of the Resurrection belongs primarily to late Jewish apocalypticism both from a linguistic and a theological point of view. Through proclamation in the Christian kerygma of Jesus' resurrection, fulfilment of apocalyptic expectation is 'given verbal expression' (*zur Sprache gebracht*) in the figure of Jesus. Only within the linguistic conceptions of apocalyptic expectation does it make sense to put the revelation in Jesus into words in such a way.[18] Outside this realm of discourse, either one cannot understand what is meant by 'the resurrection of Jesus', or one misunderstands the Jewish hope for resurrection, within which context alone talk of the Resurrection of Jesus is meaningful. Persuasive evidence of this fact may be found in I Cor. 15 and II Tim. 2.18. But other Christians, for whom the language of Jewish apocalypticism was incomprehensible, proclaimed Jesus not as the Resurrected One but as the Exalted One (Phil. 2, Hebrews).

4. Nevertheless the possibilities for any historically given language are not simply formal, for the language of Christian proclamation (which the latter did not create) has its own peculiar content as well. In using a traditional language one cannot strip

[17] Still more unfortunate is the desire to treat the Resurrection of Jesus as an historical fact precedeing such a configuration of problems. For the 'Resurrection of Jesus' is by no means an objective historical event; rather it is nothing but a phenomenon of primitive Christian language. First of all one must speak of the kerygma and only then of the Resurrection of Jesus – not *vice versa*.

[18] See T. Bonhoeffer's article (cited above); cf. also J. M. Robinson, *A New Quest of the Historical Jesus* (SBT 25) 1959.

away the old content and substitute a new one. Rather, the alteration of an historically given linguistic complex takes place so that traditional contents are re-understood in a way corresponding to a new situation, that is, so that they are interpreted and demythologized. And on the other hand, the content inherent in a given language contributes to the understanding or misunderstanding of the contemporary historical situation and of the experiences which are determined by it.

This becomes clear in the case of apocalyptic language, which was for Jesus, and to a certain extent for primitive Christianity, the language of proclamation. Jesus did not simply confirm or contest the correctness of certain apocalyptic expectations in his preaching, but rather he announced their fulfilment. In the same way, the primitive Christian proclamation asserted that certain apocalyptic expectations (such as the Resurrection of Jesus and the Gift of the Spirit) had been fulfilled with the coming of Jesus, but that others were still awaited (e.g., the Parousia). Jesus and primitive Christianity were oriented to the given structure of apocalyptic expectation to such an extent that they could define the place in time at which they themselves stood in the course of apocalyptic events. The sect of the Essenes acted in a very similar way.

Yet in both cases there arises a conflict, which has its roots in the mythological content of the given language. Apocalypticism is in essence mythological, since it speaks of a future salvation through which the worldly, historical existence of man is to be abolished. The Coming of the Messiah, the Resurrection, the Gift of the Spirit, the Messianic Banquet and the Last Judgment are completely mythological concepts. All these concepts are now part of Christian preaching though in a somewhat altered form. To be sure, Christian preaching can still relate itself to the future even today, and thus carry on the traditional and mythological language uncritically. But what is original about this preaching is its assertion of the present historical reality of that salvation which was originally conceived of in mythical, futuristic terms. In this way mythical terminology receives a new meaning. It appears in a peculiar relationship to an historical event and is thus lifted outside the realm of history and made non-mythological, sometimes radically (as in John) and sometimes only partially (as in I Peter). The extent to which that happens at any given time, and to what degree *rightly*, are questions which must be asked in interpreting each individual text. The texts themselves pose this problem. For they are first-rate witnesses to the fact that what was at stake in primitive Christianity was the understanding of a given linguistic content within a new historical situation. Has only the first resurrection occurred, or have all men now experienced resurrection? Has the Messiah come, or only a prophet who proclaimed his advent? So far the question of orthodox language apparently revolves only around the announcement of the time, the time within the given apocalyptic timetable. But much more is really at stake. For that which has been fulfilled has become a part of history. The Spirit as an eschatological gift is the real historical possession of a corporate body. Does that mean that this congregation understands itself unhistorically – as the congregation of the eschatological age, already removed from this world – and that it withdraws from its historical, that is, its political and social responsibility? Or is possession of the Spirit the power of a new moral change? In the answer to these questions lies the difference between orthodoxy and heresy.

IV. *The Historical Jesus as Source of the Problem of Orthodoxy and Heresy*

The task of Christian proclamation and theology, then, is not the repetition of a fixed religious content and mode of expression, but the reinterpretation of traditional linguistic contexts. The critical standard for this task is given in the fact that Christian proclamation is intimately related to the historical revelation in Jesus. Without such an intimate relationship to the historical source, there would be no problem of heresy in this sense. The problem of doctrinal differences or the question of orthopraxy can arise in every religious context. But only in Christianity (and in Judaism) must the historical origin continually be reappropriated and presented anew. This task is indispensable for the self-understanding of the Faith, and heresy is the failure to accomplish it.

The question of the historical Jesus is thus a very valid question to raise. But one must not ask this question unhistorically or uncritically. Below the surface of the *unhistorical* way of putting the question lies a fundamental lack of interest in the work and proclamation of Jesus. It amounts to looking merely for an historical support for the content of the faith and the teaching of the church, support in the sense of an historical causality, and in so doing it presupposes that the known content of the Faith can be found once more in the historical Jesus. Such an inquiry is carried on as though a statement of one's theological convictions could in this way become more 'true' (a word that usually has no comparative degree!), more true because one could substantiate it directly or indirectly by knowledge of the historical Jesus. We are adopting an 'unhistorical' procedure when we make Jesus, his life and his preaching – even critically interpreted – the standard of orthodox belief. On this basis heresy would seem to be nothing more than frivolous or malevolent misinterpretation and falsification of the originally unadulterated teaching of Jesus; and it would not make any difference whether one dated such a 'Fall' from the time of Paul or from the time of Marcion.

The reorientation of Christian proclamation towards its historical origin is no mere formal problem, but concerns the subject matter itself. 'Bridges' between the theology of the church and the historical Jesus – all of which are artificially constructed – are finally of no consequence. This holds true of hypothetical linguistic relationships of the reconstruction of an original kerygma or even of talk about the Resurrection, which like a *deus ex machina* subsequently raises Jesus into a sphere from which an orthodox church can directly trace its doctrine. But actually in its historical reality the earliest community found the connection between its faith and its historical origin to be a stumbling block which could be overcome only with difficulty; it was by no means a joyfully welcomed religious advantage. Historically speaking, this problem became a burning issue right at the hour of Christianity's birth, with respect to the death of Jesus on the cross; it is still crucial. That this has been the case historically is demonstrated by the manifold attempts to remove the offence of this historical event and to incorporate the Cross into the traditional systems of religious expectation as a 'necessary element'. The prophetic proof texts exemplify these attempts, as does the Gnostic interpretation of the Cross in the *Gospel of Truth*.[19]

This does not mean that the heretical position is characterized by abandonment of the historical Jesus as the foundation of faith. For indeed this Jesus had a central and leading place in the thinking of Paul's opponents, whether as renewer of the Law, as teacher of wisdom (I Corinthians), as model of the *homo religiosus* (II Corinthians), or as guide to perfection (Philippians). Paul never reproaches his opponents with deliberate ignorance of Christ. His criticism is rather that they do not make the Cross of Christ the critical standard for reinterpreting traditional theological language (including the language of Jesus!). Of course Paul does not think of 'the Cross' as simply an especially powerful religious symbol; for him it is the critical yardstick of the historical event, 'Jesus', by which it is shown whether the believer's existence is understood in a radical historical way, or whether the traditional mythical content of the language ultimately remains the yardstick. In themselves the life and teaching of Jesus alone have no value as such a standard. They have value only as part of the preaching of the Crucifixion of Jesus through which the paradox and offence of the historical revelation of God were first made manifest.

Heresy arises, then, when the radical nature of the historical dimensions of the new existence are not recognized, when the crucifixion of the Revealer is not seriously taken as the shattering – that is, the demythologizing – of that security which is the attempt to escape – through religiosity, piety and theology – from existence within history. True belief never lies in 'overcoming the paradox of the Cross', e.g., through belief in resurrection, but

[19] 20.10ff.; esp. 20.25ff.

rather in the courage to affirm a theology which dares to understand the content of the believer's historical existence on the basis of the proclamation that this historical event was the revelation of God. In orthodoxy the offence of the Cross is not, as it were, theologically overcome, not even through preaching of the Resurrection. As we can see in Pauline theology, the Resurrection of Jesus is the basis for the believer's hope for the future; through that hope it creates a place in the present for an historical understanding of faith which corresponds to the Cross.

Admittedly, once such an understanding of faith has been attained, it cannot be used as a new standard for the further distinction of heresy and orthodoxy. In itself it is valid only in any unrepeatable historical situation in which it arises from the critical confrontation of the preaching of the Cross and the mythological language associated with it. Naturally the historian and the theologian have much to learn from the latter. But Faith remains bound to its source, the historical Cross of Jesus, which from time to time in a new situation and in a different language must be reappropriated as the critical standard of faith. This task may or may not succeed. But appealing to the orthodoxy of an age that is past is no protection against failure; for it gives no guarantee that we can thus rediscover the historical origin of faith in our interpretation of tradition and of the language of our own world.

The Cross of Jesus is not of interest because it offers formal proof for the historical reality of revelation, nor because it once led the disciples into a doubt which they could overcome in some miraculous way for the benefit of all later generations. Rather in the Cross of Jesus theological security is shattered, the security which is implied by the intention of traditional language and thus by the traditional self-understanding (Christian though it may be).[20] The way in which this is done is never certain in advance, because the origin of the proclamation is this historical event which is always bound to the ambiguity of concrete historical phenomena, including even the historical Jesus.

[20] If this is understood as one possible result of the renewed quest of the historical Jesus, then to that extent the quest is justified.

V.   *Primitive Christian Heresy as the Failure to Demythologize*

We cannot now undertake to re-classify Christian writings
according to the criterion of the Cross. The standard of the Cross
is not available to us as a scholarly tool but must be worked out
in each specific case. In his attempt to re-understand Christian
existence within the framework of language, given to him by
tradition, the interpreter does not know in advance how this
criterion will apply to a certain writing. He can decide what the
criterion is only from case to case, in his interpretation of primary
sources. At the same time, once a linguistic manifestation of
heresy or orthodoxy has been identified, it cannot simply be
carried over as a standard from one document to another one
which arose in a different historical situation. What is the
language of heresy in one case can be the language of orthodoxy
in another. While the common predicates 'Jewish', 'apocalyptic',
'Hellenistic' and 'Gnostic' have a certain correctness from the
religionsgeschichtliche viewpoint, they are quite useless for the
identification of heresy, especially when they are used in
opposition to the concept 'Christian'.

One can proceed methodically, however, first investigating
the background[21] behind the mythological intention of the language that was used (since there is indeed a mythological content
in the language of the primitive Christian writings). Then he
can ask whether the demythologization succeeded, or whether
the decisive criteria were taken from the mythological content
of the traditional language instead of being oriented towards the
skandalon of the historical origin of revelation. In fact, apocalyptic
and Gnostic mythology often influenced primitive Christianity
towards the latter, mythological criteria.

Thus, e.g., apocalyptic thought understands the present from
the standpoint of a strictly future (and therefore unhistorical)
divine act of salvation. At most, this salvation is a present pos-

---

[21] As the *religionsgeschichtliche Schule* has done.

sibility only as a kind of enthusiastic anticipation. But as a rule the present is determined by legalistic rigorism as a preparation for the coming salvation. If God's act of revelation in Jesus is uncritically inserted into this apocalyptic framework, then the traditional words of Jesus may be made into law. The idea of the covenant, which is stamped by apocalypticism and thus mythically conceived (since salvation is not identical with the covenant as such but only corresponds to the supposedly future blessing) makes this a necessary consequence.

In such Judaizing heresy the tradition concerning the revelation in Christ, to the extent that it is not of a legalistic nature, is a matter of apocalyptic prophecy; history itself is no longer a problem. For the Law, demanding obedience, is just as unambiguous and leads just as directly to divinely-ordered perfection as that awaited future event which will unambiguously put an end to the realm of history.

Such an understanding can be noted within primitive Christianity in, for example, Paul's opponents at Galatia, who by requiring circumcision attempt to define membership in the chosen people of the End-time on the basis of the Law. A second example is *The Shepherd of Hermas*, where we find that one can attain membership in the People of God (to whom God's promise applies) by simply leading a perfect life after the second and final repentance which has now been made possible.

In Gnosticism, the dissolution of the ambiguities of history likewise arises out of late-Jewish mythology. The expected eschaton, however, is understood here as being radically present, and the corresponding consequences are drawn only for the individual. If events which transcend the realm of history are the possession of the present, the history has been suspended. What the believer needs is a teaching about the 'way' by means of which he can escape from the historical constraints of the here and now.

From this standpoint the essential characteristic of Gnosticism is not a specific redeemer-myth, but rather a teaching concerning the present situation of man and the possibilities of freeing oneself from the constraining powers of this world and of history.

In this way, Christ the Redeemer[22] can simply become the bringer of the message – although naturally he is also the primal model of the Gnostic who not only knows the way personally, but follows it as well.[23]

Within the context of this problem, namely, the unhistorical purposes for which traditional language may be used, orthodoxy is not a teaching formulated once and for all which neatly avoids every danger of either left or right. Nor, considering the possible misunderstanding of the historical dimensions of Christian revelation and in view of the claim within history which it makes upon man, is orthodoxy identical with a theory that stays clear of all those terminologies through which such misunderstandings necessarily emerge. In the case of Paul, e.g., it would seem that his orthodoxy consists in doing two things: he maintains the historical dimensions of the present by holding to the hope of certain mythological apocalyptic events (like Parousia and Resurrection). But he achieves his understanding of the present existence of the believer not directly from this future hope, but from the paradox of the historical act of God – from the foolishness of the Cross.

Of course the point of our reflections has not been to reassign the labels 'heretical' and 'orthodox'. If, on the one hand, 'orthodoxy' is the venture of a theology which has learned from the crucified Jesus and which wants to speak of the latter suitably in a language which it cannot choose for itself, then the real alternative to orthodoxy is not heresy in the traditional sense,

[22] A Christology is certainly not indispensable to Gnosticism. As the new finds from Nag Hammadi show, we can by no means presuppose the existence everywhere in Gnosticism of a redeemer-myth in the traditional sense. Apparently one should also be more careful in treating Paul's opponents in this regard.

[23] This Gnostic understanding, just like the apocalyptic one, corresponds to one aspect of late Judaism. Jewish Wisdom already brought the heavenly message to the wise man, and this message gives the individual the possibility of freeing himself from the adversities of existence within the realm of history and of anticipating eschatological endowments. In Jewish Wisdom speculation, as in Christian Gnosis, the historical revelation is irrelevant. It is knowledge of primeval time, of the *Urzeit*, that is revealed to the wise man, and it is revealed at the end of time and not in God's activity within history.

but heresy as the uncritical continued use of traditional language, whether the latter be of 'Christian' or of 'secular' origin: it is the escape into tradition. Such an escape might seem to be completely safe, since it does not expose one to the possibility of new heresies; for tradition repeats only what earlier generations have already accepted. But merely repeating tradition does not create an 'orthodox' theology, for no orthodoxy originates in tradition. Rather it is only codified and set up as a sign in tradition, indeed as a sign which needs to be interpreted. Here we can find the voices of former debate, now become past history, and their attempts to answer the problem. But these answers have lost their present historical actuality and acuteness the moment they are accepted as valid tradition; indeed tradition as such becomes heresy as soon as one attempts to use it as if the historical context had not changed since it was formulated.

Yet there is something to be learned from the history of orthodoxy and heresy in primitive Christianity. One cannot learn *what* orthodox theology must say. But one can learn that the historical dimensions of revelation demand that he give his own expression to his own theological existence, while he undertakes the venture necessarily proposed anew in every age – that of courageously grappling with the problems offered by the mythologies of his *own* age, even at the risk of heresy.

5

LOGOI SOPHON: on the *Gattung* of Q*

James M. Robinson

THIS essay makes use of early suggestions by Rudolf Bultmann, in whose honour it was originally published, in order to initiate a systematic investigation of the literary *genre* to which 'Q' belongs. The trajectory of this *genre* of 'Sayings of the Sages' is traced from Jewish wisdom literature through Gnosticism, where the esoteric nature of such collections can lead to the supplementary designation of them as 'Secret Sayings'. The essay illustrates the extent to which the Coptic gnostic library from near Nag Hammadi facilitates the tracing of such trajectories, by filling in previously inaccessible stages in the development.

In his *History of the Synoptic Tradition* Rudolf Bultmann drew attention to the affinity between sayings of the Lord and wisdom literature. The '*logia* in the narrower sense' were designated 'wisdom sayings'.[1] A presentation of the basic forms found in wisdom literature, moving beyond Walter Baumgartner's investigation of the forms of wisdom sayings in Sirach,[2] introduced the analysis of this group of sayings of the Lord. Thus Jesus' *logia* were understood in analogy to Jewish *meshalim*.

---

* An English draft of this paper was read at the meeting of the Western Section of the Society of Biblical Literature in Berkeley, California, February 15, 1964. It was published in German original in *Zeit und Geschichte*, pp. 77–96. The English translation presented here represents a considerable enlargement.

[1] *Die Geschichte der synoptischen Tradition*, 6th ed., 1964, p. 73 (ET: p. 69).
[2] *ZAW* 34 (1914), pp. 165–9.

Form criticism was concerned to move beyond the preceding generation's focus on literary units, and hence shifted attention to the smaller oral units of tradition. This meant that the *genre* or *Gattung*[3] of the sayings collection was not as such investigated, although to be sure Bultmann did note in passing 'that the book of Sirach is in a sense analogous to the collection and redaction of the discourse material in the Synoptics'.[4]

Bultmann used his recognition of a connection between sayings of the Lord and wisdom sayings to move in another direction. His original designation '*logia* in the narrower sense, wisdom sayings', corresponds in form rather well to the designations he uses for the other groups of sayings of the Lord ('prophetic and apocalyptic sayings'; 'legal sayings and congregational rules'). Yet his actual title of the section treating the 'wisdom sayings' reads '*Logia* (Jesus as Wisdom Teacher)'.[5] This personal, rather than material, formulation was not itself discussed. Yet, in Matt. 23.34–39, among the 'prophetic and apocalyptic sayings', one finds a significant analogy. For, as the parallel Luke 11.49 still attests, Q here quotes a Jewish saying spoken by personified Wisdom, Sophia. 'For the subject of this reflection about history must be a transhistorical subject, namely Wisdom.'[6] Bultmann

---

[3] Presupposed is the terminological distinction proposed by Hans Conzelmann (*EKL* 1, 1956, 1310) between *Formgeschichte*, dealing with the smallest (normally oral) units of tradition, and *Gattungsgeschichte*, devoted to the study of the subsequent stage of collection into larger (normally literary) compositions. Although this terminological distinction was not current at the time the classical form-critical works were composed, it is not intended to imply a material divergence from those works. It is merely an attempt to render terminology more precise.

[4] Bultmann, *Geschichte*, p. 104 (ET: p. 99). Not only the form-critical works of Bultmann and Dibelius, but especially Karl Ludwig Schmidt's essay 'Die Stellung der Evangelien in der allgemeinen Literaturgeschichte', *EUCHARISTERION* (Gunkel *Festschrift* [FRLANT 36], 1923), II, pp. 50–134, provide the beginnings of such a *Gattungsgeschichte*, although with only passing allusions to Q. On the *Gattung* of P. Oxy. 1 (Gospel of Thomas) cf. already Johannes Weiss. *ThR* 1 (1898), p. 228.

[5] *Geschichte*, p. 73 (ET: p. 69).

[6] *Geschichte*, p. 120 (ET: p. 114). Johannes Weiss, *ThR* 1 (1898), pp. 230f., made a similar suggestion with regard to the 'new *logia*': 'The sayings are suitable only on the tongue of the Resurrected, who looks back in melancholic lament to his earthly pilgrimage and his entry into the world. . . . Perhaps

concludes that this passage is documentation for the 'myth of the
divine Wisdom', which he considers to be parallel to the 'myth
of the Primal Man'.[7]

This suggestion was followed up two years later in an essay
on 'The History-of-Religions Background of the Prologue to the
Gospel of John'.[8] Here an investigation of what has subsequently
become familiar under the designation 'gnostic redeemer myth'
takes its point of departure precisely by drawing a connection
between the saying in Q attributed to Wisdom and the book of
Sirach. Hence it was the Gospel of John, rather than the Synoptics, or Q with its close correlation to the sayings tradition, that
provided Bultmann with what one might call a christological
explication of the connection between sayings of the Lord and
wisdom literature. Just as the further application of form criticism moved from the Synoptics to kerygmatic confessions and
hymns embedded in the letters, and as Bultmann moved from
his *Jesus and the Word* to his *Theology of the New Testament*, just so
in this case what was first seen in Q and came to expression in
the concept 'wisdom teacher' was not further pursued in the
context of sayings of the Lord.

Such passing insights, which Bultmann has not himself followed up, are left for our generation to pick up and work through.
Only when we honour such hints by treating them as topics for
further research are we able to honour a scholar so much more

---

the saying is taken from a source in which the identification of Jesus with
Sophia had already taken place. Cf. Luke 7.35; 11.49; Matt. 23.34ff.' In view
of the fact that the saying in question is P. Oxy. 1, 3 (Gospel of Thomas,
Saying 28), one should not only note in terms of the history of research the
point of departure provided to Bultmann by his teacher; one should also
acknowledge the task posed by the discovery of the Gospel of Thomas to
carry through the clarification of the relation between Q and the 'new *logia*'.

[7] Bultmann, *Geschichte*, pp. 120f. (ET: pp. 114f.).

[8] 'Der religionsgeschichtliche Hintergrund des Prologs zum Johannes-
Evangelium', *EUCHARISTERION* II, pp. 3–26, esp. p. 6 (reprinted in the
collection of his essays, *Exegetica*, 1969, pp. 10–35, esp. pp. 11f.). This first step
in the history-of-religions investigation of the Gospel of John by Bultmann
was carried further in the essay 'Die Bedeutung der neuerschlossenen mandäi-
schen und manichäischen Quellen für das Verständnis des Johannesevangeliums', *ZNW* 24 (1925), pp. 100–46 (*Exegetica*, pp. 55–104).

absorbed in the issues than in himself as is Bultmann. Hence the question of the *Gattung* of the Gospels as whole literary units must, like the question of the historical Jesus, be posed anew. This essay, then, seeks to confirm, clarify, and carry further Bultmann's association of *logia* with *meshalim* under the concept of 'wisdom teacher', by working out a name for the *Gattung* of Q, λόγοι σοφῶν, '*Logoi Sophon*', 'Sayings of the Sages' or 'Words of the Wise',[9] as a reflection in the sources themselves of the tendency constitutive of the *Gattung* to which Q belongs. It does not carry through the further task of tracing structures of the *genre* through the Jewish, Christian, and gnostic literature cited; a more thorough investigation of Greek literature with regard to this *Gattung* is a still further need.

I.   *Logia, Logoi and Gospel in the Coptic Gnostic Library*

The designation of sayings of the Lord as '*logia*' derives from the Papias fragments. For his treatise was not only named Interpretation of the Lord's *Logia* (Eusebius, *HE* III, 39.1). Referring to the Gospel of Mark, he speaks of Peter 'not making what

---

[9] It is difficult to find a single suitable translation for λόγος and its plural λόγοι, for the term covers a wide spectrum of meanings. The English term 'word' should come nearest in providing a comparable breadth. For it not only designates an individual vocable, whose plural then designates a word-by-word sequence of vocables (cf. German *Wörter*); it can also designate a whole statement, as in such expressions as 'a word for today', or 'a word for the wise is sufficient'. This usage corresponds to the use of the term 'word' to designate the self in responsible commitment, in such expressions as: 'to give one's word'; 'to be as good as one's word'; 'one's word is as good as one's bond'. (Cf. in French *parole* in distinction from *mot*, and the German plural *Worte*.) It is an aspect of the superficiality with which the role of language is often grasped today that this usage is recessive, expressing itself primarily in such traditional expressions. Hence it is sometimes preferable to translate the plural as 'sayings', to prevent an unconscious literalistic identification with a plurality of vocables, even though the term 'sayings' tends to lack the deeper, more authentic overtones present in λόγοι; sometimes it is preferable for a further reason to translate the singular as 'saying', namely to make it clear that 'word' is not a disembodied idea, but rather in its basic form is a linguistic reality. Since consistency in translation would in some instances produce an unnatural or inaccurate rendering, the reader's attention should be oriented to the one term in the original language (λόγοι, *logoi*, except where otherwise noted), translated 'words' or 'sayings'.

might be called a collection of the Lord's *logia*' (III, 39.15). Of course there is also his familiar statement about Matthew that has been repeatedly, though never conclusively, related to Q: 'So Matthew collected in the Hebrew language the *logia*, but each person interpreted them as he was able' (III, 39.16).[10] The result has been that a less accentuated term in Papias, *logoi*, whose precise meaning is even more obscure, has not been adequately noted. This term is involved in such phrases as the following: 'the preface of his (*scil.* Papias') *logoi* [sayings? – Lake: treatises]' (Irenaeus, in Eusebius, III, 39.2); 'I investigated the *logoi* of the presbyters' (Papias, in Eusebius, III, 39.4); 'Papias affirms that he had received the *logoi* of the apostles from their followers' (Eusebius, III, 39.7); 'interpretations of the Lord's *logoi*' (by Aristion, mentioned by Papias according to Eusebius, III, 39.14).

If it is already difficult to clarify in terms of *Gattung* the *logia* mentioned by Papias, it is even more difficult to relate to the history of a *Gattung* these passing allusions to the *logoi* of Papias, the presbyters, the apostles, and the Lord.[11] Hence it is not too surprising that the first fragment of a sayings source discovered

[10] An illustration of such translational variants with regard to the term here under consideration is provided by the Greek translation of the Syrian Acts of Thomas, a translation which is not very precise, especially with regard to Semitic formulae. Cf. my study 'Die Hodajot-Formel in Gebet und Hymnus des Frühchristentums', *Apophoreta* (Haenchen *Festschrift*, [BZNW 30], 1964), pp. 194–235, esp. pp. 199f., 233f. Ch. 39 (Lipsius-Bonnet, II, 2, 156, 12–15) speaks of 'Christ's twin, the apostle of the Most High, and fellow-witness of the hidden *logos* of Christ, who received his hidden *logia*.' This is probably an allusion to the *incipit* or opening words of the Gospel of Thomas (P. Oxy. 654), which uses *logoi*, of which *logia* in the Acts of Thomas is apparently a translational variant. Perhaps the presence of the term *logos* as christological title in the same sentence led as a stylistic variant to the term *logia* to refer to Jesus' sayings. Cf. also the same variants in Test. Ben. 9. 1 and Justin, I Apol. 14.5; Dial. 18.1.

[11] On the imprecision of the term *logia* in Papias in matters relevant to *Gattung*, cf. e.g. Karl L. Leimbach, *PRE*[3] 14 (1904), p. 644; further E. Bammel, *RGG*[3] 5 (1961), p. 48: '[Papias'] book contained annotated reports about sayings and deeds of Jesus.' Ernst Haenchen, *Der Weg Jesu*, 1966, p. 8, translates Papias' reference to Matthew as 'stories of Jesus'. The word *logos* is very common, has many meanings, and is often very imprecise. Quite apart from its christological meaning in the *incipit* of the Gospel of John and

at Oxyrhynchus was published under the title *Jesus' Logia*,[12] and that the scholarly discussion was carried on in terms of the loan word *logia*.[13]

This usage was so firmly established that the publication in 1904 of P. Oxy. 654 (the opening of the Gospel of Thomas), whose first line spoke of *logoi*, had no influence at all on the terminology.[14] But now that the Gospel of Thomas has rendered impossible the identification of the Oxyrhynchus fragments with the collection of *logia* referred to by Papias, one can note in the new wave of publications called forth by the discovery of the Coptic Gospel of Thomas a gradual adoption of the term *logoi* to designate the Oxyrhynchus fragments.[15]

This usage seems on first glance hardly applicable to the Coptic version of the Oxyrhynchus sayings, since the Coptic text

---

as a designation for a 'volume' (Acts 1.1) or 'treatise' (e.g. the title at the end of *De resurrectione* from the Jung Codex, 'The Logos concerning Resurrection'), it can refer to deeds as well as sayings. Cf. Henry J. Cadbury, *The Beginnings of Christianity*, 2 (1922), p. 509 on Luke 1.4: 'Perhaps here περὶ λόγων is used for variety much as περὶ πραγμάτων in verse 1, but of course λόγοι are events reported rather than events fulfilled.' Hence one cannot e.g. distinguish clearly between Aristion's 'narrations of the Lord's *logoi*', and Luke 1.1: 'Narration concerning the deeds fulfilled in our midst.' The term ῥήματα can serve as a synonym for λόγοι in some cases, as in Jude 17 of the apostles' sayings. On the comparable Hebrew term in the titles of historical works in the OT see below.

[12] Λόγια 'Ιησοῦ. *Sayings of Our Lord from an Early Greek Papyrus*, ed. by Bernard P. Grenfell and Arthur S. Hunt, 1897. The document is P. Oxy. 1.

[13] Cf. the bibliography by Joseph A. Fitzmyer, S.J., *ThSt* 20 (1959), pp. 556–60.

[14] *New Sayings of Jesus and Fragment of a Lost Gospel from Oxyrhynchus*, ed. by Bernard P. Grenfell and Arthur S. Hunt, 1904. Although they conjectured (p. 10) quite correctly 'that the present text (*sc.* P. Oxy. 654) represents the beginning of a collection which later on included the original "*Logia*"', they did not draw the terminological inference that one should refer to P. Oxy. 1 as *logoi* rather than *logia*.

[15] Joseph A. Fitzmyer, S.J., 'The Oxyrhynchus *Logoi* of Jesus and the Coptic Gospel according to Thomas', *ThSt* 20 (1959), pp. 505–60; Gérard Garitte, 'Les "*Logoi*" d'Oxyrhynque et l'apocryphe copte dit "Évangile de Thomas"', *Le Muséon* 73 (1960), pp. 151–72. Fitzmyer, *ThSt* 20 (1959), p. 513, points out that '*logion*' normally refers to a saying of a deity, and that 'in A. Resch's collection of *Agrapha* (TU 30, 1906) we find the word used only twice, and in each case it refers to the Old Testament'.

bears at its end the title *Peuaggelion pkata Thomas*. The Greek
grammar reflected in this title suggests that the Greek work from
which the Coptic is generally agreed to have been translated
already bore this title.[16] Thus one has, so to speak, two titles
for this work, one the free use of the designation *logoi* in the
opening clause of the text (the '*incipit*'), and another at the end,
written apart as a more formal title after the body of the text
has ended, 'The Gospel according to Thomas'.

To be sure one can conjecture that the title 'Gospel' was
popular in a polemical or apologetic context as a flag under
which various kinds of writings circulated at the time when the
canonical Gospels and hence the title 'Gospel' had gained wide
acceptance in the orthodox church. Thus the *incipit* of a Nag
Hammadi tractate that is not a Gospel in terms of its *Gattung*,
CG I, *2*,[17] reads: 'The gospel of truth is joy for those who have
received grace from the father of truth,' and Irenaeus (III, 11.9)
may have understood this as a polemical title:[18] 'For indeed they

[16] Cf. Hippolytus, *Ref.*, V, 7, 20: 'in the Gospel entitled "according to
Thomas" '. On the relation of this document to the Gospel of Thomas from
Nag Hammadi cf. Puech in Hennecke-Schneemelcher, *Neutestamentliche
Apokryphen* I, 1959³, pp. 203f. (ET: I, 1963, pp. 283f.).

[17] The numeration of the codices proposed by Martin Krause and Pahor
Labib (*Die drei Versionen des Apokryphon des Johannes im koptischen Museum zu
Alt-Kairo* [ADAIK, Koptische Reihe, Vol. 1], 1962), and adopted by both the
Coptic Museum and UNESCO, has now prevailed over those used by
Doresse and Puech. For a catalogue of the Nag Hammadi *codices* including a
conversion table for the divergent numerations cf. my article 'The Coptic
Gnostic Library Today', *NTS* 14 (1967/68), pp. 356–401; 'The Institute for
Antiquity and Christianity', *NTS* 16 (1969/70), pp. 188–90; 'The Coptic
Gnostic Library', *NovTest* 12 (1970), pp. 83–5. The designation of the Nag
Hammadi material as CG (Cairensis gnosticus) is derived from Walter Till,
Die gnostischen Schriften des koptischen Papyrus Berolinensis 8502 (TU 60), 1955,
and is adopted by W. C. van Unnik, *Evangelien aus dem Nilsand*, 1960, p. 23.

[18] Hans-Martin Schenke, *Die Herkunft des sogenannten Evangelium Veritatis*,
1959, questions whether the *incipit* is a title, since the work is a homily. Yet
gnostics would have no reason to limit the designation 'good news' to works
conforming to a *Gattung* defined by orthodox sensitivities. Johannes Munck,
'*Evangelium Veritatis* and Greek Usage as to Book Titles', *StTh* 17 (1963),
pp. 133–8, calls attention in this connection to Ernst Nachmanson, 'Der
griechische Buchtitel: Einige Beobachtungen', *Göteborgs Högskolas Årsskrift*
47 (1941), no. 19. Krause, *Apokryphon des Johannes*, pp. 28f., regards the *incipit*
here (and elsewhere) as the title, indeed as the original title. Later, but before

go on to such great audacity as to entitle what they themselves only recently wrote as "The Gospel of Truth", although it agrees at no point with the Gospels by the apostles, so that not even the gospel can be among them without blasphemy. For if what they publish as of truth is the gospel, but is dissimilar to those handed down to us by the apostles, persons who so wish can learn (as is shown from the writings themselves) that what was handed down from the apostles is not the gospel of truth.'

One may also compare CG IV, *2*, commonly called the Gospel of the Egyptians.[19] After the text ends with Amen at 69.5, and decorative marks confirm this break, the rest of the page is filled with two different titles, the scribe's spiritual and fleshly names, the Christian fish cryptogram, and again titles. Line 6 reads: 'The Egyptian Gospel'. Lines 7–8 give an additional title: 'The Holy Hidden Book Written by God . . .' Lines 15–17 give a variation of this title: 'The Holy God-written Book of the Great Invisible Spirit'. Again there occurs 'Amen', and again lines to mark the end of the text. Then, in lines 18–20, a final title is given: 'The Holy Book of the Great Invisible Spirit. Amen.' This source, which has 'absolutely nothing to do with a Gospel',[20] still received as one of the titles appended at the conclusion of the text the designation 'The Egyptian Gospel'. Though the *incipit* is fragmentary, it clearly begins with 'The holy *book* . . .' The term gospel seems secondary. One may further note the possibility that the title of the Gospel of Philip was not originally present in Codex II, since it is not set off in the usual manner.[21]

---

the copying of the Nag Hammadi *codices*, briefer titles, set apart (and decorated) as subscriptions or super-scriptions, were added.

[19] Jean Doresse, ' "Le livre sacré du grand esprit invisible" ou "l'Évangile des Égyptiens" ', *Journal asiatique* 254 (1966), pp. 317–435; 256 (1968), pp. 290–386.

[20] Puech in Hennecke-Schneemelcher, I, pp. 270f. (ET: I, p. 362).

[21] Johannes Leipoldt and Hans-Martin Schenke, *Koptisch-gnostische Schriften aus den Papyrus-Codices von Nag-Hamadi* (Theologische Forschung 20), 1960, p. 82: Leipoldt argues that when the Nag Hammadi copy was made the tractate had no title. In distinction from the style of Codex II elsewhere, the empty part of the last line of text is not filled out with decorations, but with the beginning of the title ('Gospel'). The rest of the title ('according to Philip') stands somewhat off-centre on the next line, whereas usually the

In general one may sense that the titles appended as subscriptions at the end of tractates may be logically secondary to
the titles implicit in an *incipit*, even in cases when both were
already present when the Nag Hammadi codices were written.
Martin Krause concludes his investigation of the titles of codices
I–VI with the following generalization: 'In terms of literary
historical method we must assume some such procedure as the
following: After a period in which the tractates were transmitted
without title, there came one in which the writings received a
title that we refer to as the "original" one and that is sometimes
designated the "introduction". Still later this long title was shortened and was given the "decorated" form present in the *codices*.'[22]
Puech, to whom Krause refers, assumes that the introduction
to the Gospel of Thomas (including Saying 1) was secondarily
added.[23] Since it is present in both the Coptic and Greek texts
available to us, it is a mere conjecture to assume that this particular collection of sayings existed in writing without its present
introduction. One could more readily assume that generally
such collections may have circulated without such an extensive
introduction, even though they tend to be designated as 'sayings'
collections in quotation formulae and other allusions to them.
In any case, the trend of Krause's analysis is to suggest that the
introduction to the Gospel of Thomas, defining the work as a
collection of sayings, is more primitive than the subscription,
which designates it as a Gospel.

---

title is centred on two independent lines. In the case of this tractate, less
space than usual separates it from the following tractate, which would suggest
that the space originally left blank between tractates had been partially
filled by adding the last part of the title. Yet Schenke remarks that the hand
of the title seems to be the same as that of the rest of the tractate. To be sure
the hand of Codex II is so similar to that of Codex XIII that Krause ascribed
both to the same scribe (*Apokryphon des Johannes*, p. 297), and then later
ascribed each to a different scribe, 'Zum koptischen Handschriftenfund bei
Nag Hammadi', *MDAIK* 19 (1963), p. 111 n. 2.

[22] *Apokryphon des Johannes*, p. 29 n. 6. Whether the tractates ever existed
without their *incipit* may be questioned in specific instances; it would be more
cautious to speak of sources of the present tractates having been enlarged by
various supplements, at times including an *incipit*, where such redactional
activity seems to have taken place.

[23] Hennecke-Schneemelcher, I, 205 (ET: I, p. 285).

In the Gospel of Thomas the term 'gospel', apart from the title appended at the end, is completely lacking (as it is also from Q). But the designation *logoi* is at home in the sayings tradition it uses, and was taken over from that tradition into the introduction.[24] Hence one may seek in the term *logoi* the original designation for the *Gattung*. Not only does Saying 38, discussed below, speak of the desire 'to hear these sayings which I say to you'; Saying 19 also speaks of Jesus' sayings: 'Blessed is he who was, before he came into being. *If you* become my disciples and *hear my sayings*, these stones will minister to you. For you have five trees in Paradise which are unmoved in summer (or) in winter and their leaves do not fall. Whoever knows them *will not taste death*.' Here the idea that knowledge of the sayings brings salvation is secondarily expanded by use of independent conceptualizations.[25] The original concept, which is suggested at

[24] Cf. esp. Saying 13, which refers to 'sayings' of Jesus that only Thomas knows and that the other disciples ask him to divulge, which he fears to do. The fourth line of P. Oxy. 654 reads: ἂν τῶν λόγων τούτ[. This documents the term *logoi* in the Greek *Vorlage* of Saying 1 of the Gospel of Thomas: 'Whoever finds the explanation of these *sayings* will not taste death.' The content of this saying suggests it belongs to the introduction of the collection. This is also suggested by the fact that it is introduced with the aorist tense, 'he said.' For in the Greek text Jesus' name and the present tense, used as a historical present, are so predominantly (though not exclusively) used in the quotation formula for Jesus' sayings that one may even wonder whether the subject of Saying 1 is not found in the nearer antecedent, Thomas. To be sure, in the Testaments of the Twelve Patriarchs, their discourses begin with the aorist, and the subject is not the immediately preceding sons or parents of the patriarch in question, but obviously the patriarch himself, who had been mentioned at the beginning. Yet this aorist does not stand out as an exception to a fairly fixed formula, as is the case with the Gospel of Thomas. None the less the fact that elsewhere (e.g. John 8.52) variants upon this saying are attributed to Jesus, together with the overriding impression that we have to do with a collection of Jesus' sayings (cf. the *incipit*: ' . . Jesus spoke . . . Thomas wrote'), should indicate caution in ascribing the first saying in the author's intention to Thomas. It is inadvisable to base a divergence from the standard numeration of sayings on such a fragile possibility that, as does Johannes Leipoldt, *Das Evangelium nach Thomas* (TU 101), 1967, p.21.

[25] Paul E. Kahle, *Bala'izah: Coptic Texts from Deir el Bala'izah in Upper Egypt*, 1954, I, p.476. Cf. Crum, *JTS* 44 (1943), pp.176–9, 'Lo, I have explained . . . unto thee, O Johannes, concerning Adam and Paradise, . . . and the Five Trees, in an intelligible allegory.' Cf. also 'Bäume' in the index to Carl Schmidt and Walter Till, *Koptische-gnostische Schriften* (GCS) I, 1959³.

various points in the Gospel of John, is especially clear in John 8.52: 'If any one keeps my *logos*, he will never taste death.' It is this original concept which is apparently presupposed in Saying 1, which serves as the conclusion to the introduction of the Gospel of Thomas: 'Whoever finds the explanation of these sayings will not taste death.'[26]

If the term *logoi* is at home in the sayings tradition, and a saying referring to Jesus' *logoi* was taken up into the introduction of the Gospel of Thomas, it would seem to be the logical outcome of this development that the term be taken up into the *incipit* itself: 'These are the secret sayings . . .'

This is not intended to suggest that this designation was taken up into an *incipit* first by the Gospel of Thomas, and only then elevated to the designation for a *Gattung*.[27] The connection between individual sayings referring to themselves as *logoi* and the use of this term to designate collections of sayings has no doubt a longer history. Hence we turn further afield to trace the broader context of this development.

CG II, 7, usually referred to by the title at the end (145.17–19), 'The Book of Thomas the Contender, which he writes to the perfect ones', has as its *incipit*: 'These are the secret sayings that the Saviour spoke to Judas Thomas, which I wrote, I my-

[26] The Gospel of John shows that the matter of the right relation to Jesus' *logoi*, which the first half of Saying 1 puts hermeneutically, can be formulated in various ways. In addition to 'believing', the Fourth Gospel speaks of 'hearing' the *logos* (5.24; 8.43; 14.24) or *logoi* (7.40; cf. 8.47), as well as of 'becoming disciples' (8.32). The last half of Saying 1 uses a formula that occurs elsewhere, e.g. at the end of Saying 18 just before the allusion to Jesus' sayings in Saying 19. A variant to John 8.52 is found in John 8.51: 'If any one keeps my *logos*, he will never see death.'

[27] To be sure some particular affinity of Thomas to sayings of the Lord may be suggested in the scene in Saying 13, which modifies in Thomas' favour the scene we know as 'Peter's confession'. 'And he [sc. Jesus] took him [sc. Thomas], withdrew, and spoke three sayings to him.' Hippolytus takes this to refer to three vocables rather than to three sayings (*Ref.*, V, 8, 4, ed. Wendland, p.89, cited in Walther Völker, *Quellen zur Geschichte der christlichen Gnosis* [Sammlung ausgewählter Kirchen- und dogmengeschichtlichen Quellenschriften, n.s.5], 1932, p.17; ET: Robert M. Grant, *Gnosticism*, 1961, p.107, modified): 'These are the three supremely important *logio*, Kaulakau, Saulasau, Zeear: Kaulakau is of Adamas above; Saulasau, of the mortal below; Zeesar, of the Jordan which flows upward.'

self, Mathaias, as I walked, listening to them speaking with each other.'[28] This provides a further attestation for the designation 'secret sayings', for the Coptic of this term is identical with the Coptic text of the Gospel of Thomas.[29] One would have an instance of this *incipit* functioning as a title, if Thomas the Contender could be identified with the Basilidean source ascribed to Matthias by Hippolytus, *Ref.* VII, 20.1:[30] 'So Basilides and

[28] The word order of the *incipit* varies slightly, in that Thomas the Contender begins, 'The secret sayings are these', whereas the Gospel of Thomas begins, 'These are the secret sayings.' P. Oxy.654 (Fitzmyer) provides the Greek *Vorlage* for the *incipit* of the Gospel of Thomas: οὗτοι οἱ λόγοι οἱ [ἀπόκρυφοι οὓς ἐλάλησεν⁸ Ἰη(σοῦ)ς ὁ ζῶν κ[αὶ ἔγραψεν Ἰούδας ὁ] καὶ Θωμᾶ⟨ς⟩ καὶ εἶπεν. The closest parallel is Luke 24.44, 'These are the words that I spoke to you, while I was still with you.' Other parallels are less oriented to collections of sayings. Fitzmyer (*ThSt* 20, p.513) also compares Bar.1.1, 'These are the words of the book that Baruch wrote.' Much the same *incipit* is used in a martyrdom of James, in which is imbedded a discourse of the resurrected Christ, CG V, *4*, the (Second) Apocalypse of James. The *incipit* reads: 'This is the word that James the Just spoke in Jerusalem, that Marim one of the priests wrote down. He told it to Theuda, the father of this just man, since he was a relative of his, saying: . . .' The reconstructed end of the text reads: '[His] word [s were written?] then [in a] *logos*.' (*Koptisch-gnostische Apokalypsen aus Codex V von Nag Hammadi im Koptischen Museum zu Alt-Kairo*, ed. by Alexander Böhlig and Pahor Labib, a special volume of the *Wissenschaftliche Zeitschrift der Martin-Luther-Universität Halle-Wittenberg*, 1963, pp. 56–85.) One may compare Deut.1.1: 'These are the words that Moses spoke to all Israel beyond the Jordan.' The *incipit* of Deuteronomy does not seem to have been sufficiently noticed to account for the frequency of this *incipit*; for it is not used in a Qumran document so dependent on Deuteronomy that J. T. Milik suggested one might call it 'Little Deuteronomy' (*Discoveries in the Judaean Desert* I, 1955, p.92). According to Milik's reconstruction (pp.91–7), it refers several times to 'words': 'the words of the law' (1.4); 'these words from his mouth' (2.6); 'all the words of the law' (2.9); 'all these words of the covenant' (3.3). Yet the *incipit* reads: 'And God [addressed] Moses . . . saying:' The modern title finally given the document, 'Words of Moses' ('Dires de Moïse', abbreviated 1QDM), does not occur in the document itself.

[29] Cf. Puech in Hennecke-Schneemelcher I, p.223 (ET: I, p.307).

[30] This identification advocated by Jean Doresse, *Les livres secrets des gnostiques d'Égypte: Introduction aux écrits gnostiques coptes découverts à Khénoboskion*, 1958, p.244 (ET: p.226), is given up by Puech in Hennecke-Schneemelcher, I, p.227 (ET: I, p.313), since, contrary to Doresse, he reads 'Matthew' rather than 'Matthias' in the *incipit* of CG II, 7. The identification is held to be 'very probable' by Siegfried Schulz, *ThR*, n.s. 26 (1960), pp.247f. The Coptic itself, in spite of Puech's statement, is indecisive, since

Isidore, the actual son and disciple of Basilides, say Matthias
told them secret *logoi* that he heard from the Saviour as he was
privately taught' (cf. also VII, 20.5: 'one of Matthias' secret
logoi'). In any case the title at the end, naming Thomas the
Contender as the scribe, is put in question by the *incipit*, '. . .
which I have written, I, Mathaias'. For this reason the title
at the end is to be regarded as secondary, and hence hardly an
expression of the *Gattung* under whose influence the document
was originally composed.

The fact that the *incipit* of Thomas the Contender is almost
identical in form with that of the Gospel of Thomas does not
mean that Thomas the Contender is necessarily a further instance of the same *Gattung*. Rather it is more probably in transition to the *Gattung* of dialogues of the resurrected Christ with
his disciples. This *Gattung* of course makes use of sayings ascribed
to Jesus, and can refer to 'sayings', although such a reference
would be less constitutive of this revelation *Gattung*[31] than it is

---

it reads *Mathaias*, i.e. neither exactly Matthew (*Maththaios*) nor Matthias
(*Maththias*). Puech, 'Les nouveaux écrits gnostiques découverts en Haute-
Égypte', *Coptic Studies in Honour of W. E. Crum*, 1950, p. 120, and in Hennecke-
Schneemelcher, I, pp. 224–8 (ET: I, pp. 308–13), discusses the relation
to the 'Gospel' and 'Traditions' of Matthias mentioned in patristic sources.

[31] The Apocryphon of John, CG II, *1*; III, *1*; IV, *1*; BG 8501, *2*, begins
in its longer recension (II, 1. 1–4) with the following reconstructed text: 'The
teaching [and the words] of the Saviour. And he revealed these mysteries]
that are hidden in a silence, [namely Jesus Christ did, and] he taught them
to John [who] hearkened.' After a brief narrative framework there follows
a dialogue that rapidly turns into a discourse, which concludes (31.28–31):
'But I have told you all things, in order that you record them and gived them
to your fellow spirits in secret. For this is the mystery of the race that is not
shaken.' The concluding framework states (31.32–34; 32.4–5): 'And the
Saviour gave him these (mysteries), that he write them and safely leave them
behind. . . . And he went to his fellow disciples and he proclaimed to them
the (words) that the Saviour had said to him.' The title following the end of
the text is 'Apocryphon of John'. Thus it is not certain that to describe itself
this text uses the term 'words', which has been conjectured or added by the
editors. But the conclusion of the shorter recension (III, 40.6–9) does use the
term: '[He] went to his fellow disciples (and) began to speak with them [of
the] words that the Saviour had said to [him].' Compare BG 76, 18–77, 5:
'And he came to his fellow disciples and began to say to them what had been
said to him by the Saviour.' In any case the term 'secret sayings' from the
Gospel of Thomas has been replaced in the Apocryphon of John to a large

of a sayings collection. The allusion to 'words' in the *incipit* of
Thomas the Contender, if not simply coincidental or indicative
of dependence on The Gospel of Thomas, may be due to the
long section at the end of the document, where the dialogue with

---

extent by revelation terminology such as 'mystery' and 'what is secret'
('apocryphon'). For this text cf. Martin Krause and Pahor Labib, *Die drei
Versionen des Apokryphon des Johannes im Koptischen Museum zu Alt-Kairo*,
(ADAIK, Koptische Reihe, 1), 1962; and Walter C. Till, *Die gnostischen
Schriften des koptischen Papyrus Berolinensis 8502* (TU 60), 1955, of which there
is a revised reprint in W. C. van Unnik, *Evangelien aus dem Nilsand*, 1960,
pp. 185–213. Another gnostic 'apocalypse' also entitled 'words' can readily
escape notice, due to an oversight on the part of Jean Doresse. He successfully deciphered the cryptogram at the end of CG VIII, *1* (132, 7–9),
and identified it with the allusion in Porphyry to documents used by
Plotinus' opponents, who cite 'apocalypses of Zoroastros, of Zostrianos,
of Nicotheos, of Allogenes, of Mesos, and of other such ones'. '"Les Apocalypses de Zoroastre, de Zostrien, de Nicothée, . . ." Porphyre (Vie de
Plotin, 16),' *Coptic Studies in Honor of W. E. Crum*, 1950, pp. 255–63. He
argues on the basis of the cryptogram that this usual translation of Porphyry
is inaccurate, in that the first apocalypse was entitled 'Apocalypse of
Zoroaster and Zostrianos'. For he deciphers the cryptogram to read: 'Discourse of Truth of Zostrianos, God of Truth; Discourse of Zoroaster.'
Already Puech pointed out that since Porphyry and Amelius divided the
task of criticizing the gnostic writings, the one addressing himself to the
work of Zostrianos, the other to that of Zoroaster, there must be two distinct
works, not one, as Doresse had argued. 'Les Nouveaux écrits gnostiques
découverts en Haute-Égypte (Premier inventaire et essai d'identification)',
in the same Crum *Festschrift*, pp. 91–154, esp. pp. 107f., 131ff. However, even
Puech failed to note that Doresse has inaccurately deciphered the cryptogram; indeed, he himself repeats Doresse's oversight. For the term '*logos*',
which Doresse translates 'discourse', is both times in the plural. The title
is then '*Logoi* of Truth of Zostrianos; God of Truth; *Logoi* of Zoroastros'.
Martin Krause, 'Der koptische Handschriftenfund bei Nag Hammadi:
Umfang und Inhalt', *MDAIK* 18 (1962), pp. 121–32, esp. p. 128, holds that
this tractate begins at VIII, 1.1, rather than somewhere later (as Doresse
and Puech assume). In that case the fragmentary *incipit* provides some confirmation of this title. For 1.1 includes the expression 'these words', 1.2 the
personal pronoun in the first person singular, and 1.3 the name 'Zos[trianos]'.
This would suggest an *incipit* in which Zostrianos refers to himself as related
to the *logoi*, much as in the case of Thomas the Contender discussed above.
Whether Zoroaster is also mentioned in the *incipit* is unclear because of its
fragmentary nature; and the role of 'God of truth', which is not as obviously
in apposition to 'Zostrianos' in the cryptogram as Doresse would lead one
to assume, remains unclear. The document seems primarily related to
Zostrianos, since in the line just prior to the cryptogram (132.6), his name
appears alone, centred on the line and ornamented, i.e. treated as a title.

Thomas gives way to something more like a sayings collection: a chain of woes (cf. Matt. 23) and beatitudes, and other material similar in form and content to the Sermon on the Mount. It is perhaps indicative of some such original relation between the *incipit* and this concluding section of the document that this concluding section is introduced by a final question of Thomas concerning 'these words' that Jesus speaks. Since Thomas the Contender seems to be a secondary compilation of traditions or sources, such a conjecture is possible; but clarity must await a thorough investigation of this unpublished document.[32]

In its present form Thomas the Contender attests the triumph within Gnosticism of the *Gattung* of dialogues of the resurrected Christ with his disciples over the *Gattung* of sayings collections. This victory was inevitable, as the oral tradition died out and Gnosticism advanced in its speculation increasingly beyond the range of interests that a traditional sayings collection could readily serve.

Pistis Sophia represents in various ways the end point of the development. Here we find the final definition of who the scribes of the words of the Lord were: Philip, Thomas and Matthew. This is less a reflection of the situation in Pistis Sophia, where only Philip functions as scribe, than a retrospective resumé of the whole literature, for which CG II has provided partial documentation.[33] Furthermore Pistis Sophia does not hesitate to put side by side traditional sayings and their interpretive expansion,

[32] Martin Krause, 'Der Stand der Veröffentlichung der Nag Hammadi Texte', *Le origini dello Gnosticismo*, (Studies in the History of Religions 12, Supplements to *Numen*, 1967), p. 76, lists Thomas the Contender among those tractates that have been secondarily reworked to make them Christian. He does so on the basis of inner contradictions within the text, for which he refers to his forthcoming publication of the document, *Gnostische und hermetische Schriften aus Codex II und VI* (ADAIK, Koptische Reihe, 2).

[33] CG II provides among the 'apostolic' works (in addition to the 'Apocryphon of John') sayings of the Lord written by Thomas, Philip and Mathaias: CG II, *2*, 'These are the secret sayings that Jesus the living spoke and Didymus Judas Thomas wrote', i.e. 'The Gospel according to Thomas'; CG II, *3*, 'The Gospel according to Philip', a gnostic tractate partially presented as a dialogue, cf. R. McL. Wilson, *The Gospel of Philip*, 1962, pp. 7–11; CG II, *7*: 'These are the secret sayings that the Saviour spoke to Judas Thomas which I wrote, I myself, Mathaias', i.e. 'The Book of Thomas

so that one can see the dissolution process taking place. The dialogue consists basically in a discourse by the Lord, followed periodically by its 'resolution' or 'analysis' by a disciple (or one of the women). Just at this point, between the discourse and its resolution, a characteristic formula occurs: 'But it came to pass as Jesus stopped speaking these words to his disciples', whereupon a disciple volunteers a 'resolution of the words'. Thus we are carried step by step through the final stage in the procedure that one can only sense from the introduction to the Gospel of Thomas to have begun in some sayings already there. For in the Gospel of Thomas the 'secret sayings' of Jesus that the gnostic is to 'interpret' have in some instances already received a gnosticizing interpretive reformulation, which would then be carried a step further when the gnosticized saying is again interpreted for a still deeper meaning. Yet the saying and its interpretation are not kept distinct, side-by-side, as in Pistis Sophia, but rather are presented in fusion with each other, as a single statement. In Pistis Sophia, the speech of Jesus that the disciple proceeds to resolve is already gnosticized; yet the side-by-side presentation in Pistis Sophia of two advanced stages in the process illustrates what was less visibly happening in the earlier stages as well. Thus the introduction to the Gospel of Thomas points to the outcome in Pistis Sophia, which, in the formula it uses and in the elaboration it presents, is only bringing to unmistakable clarity what one can already sense in the Gospel of Thomas.

the Contender'. Puech, in the Crum *Festschrift*, pp. 117f., refers to Deut. 19.15 and Matt. 18.16. Cf. also Doresse, *Livres secrets*, p. 239 (ET: p. 221). Helmut Koester, '*GNOMAI DIAPHOROI*', in *Trajectories through Early Christianity*, 1971, ch. 4, points out that the double ascription of CG II, 7 to Matthew (?) and Judas Thomas may reflect the association of these two with parallel strands of the sayings tradition, in western and eastern Syria respectively. It is perhaps significant that when the Letter of Eugnostos the Blessed (CG III, *3*; V, *1*) is Christianized as the Sophia of Jesus Christ (BG 8502, *3*; CG III, *4*), the dialogue form superimposed on the original work names only three disciples who (in addition to Mary) pose questions: Matthew (BG 82. 17–83. 4; 93. 12–15), Thomas (87. 8–11; 106. 10–13), and Philip (86. 13–16). Cf. Martin Krause, 'Das literarische Verhältnis des Eugnostosbriefes zur Sophia Jesu Christi: Zur Auseinandersetzung der Gnosis mit dem Christentum', *Mullus* (Klauser *Festschrift*, *JAC* Ergänzungsband 1, 1964), p. 218 n. 36.

We thus arrive in Pistis Sophia at the point in the trajectory
of the sayings collection where it is absorbed into and finally
replaced by the *Gattung* which had no doubt all along been most
typical of Christian Gnosticism, namely the dialogue of the
resurrected Christ with his disciples, a *Gattung* whose trajectory
has most recently been traced by Kurt Rudolph.[34]

II. *Primitive Christian Collections of Jesus' Sayings*

This development ending in Gnosticism also had its prehistory
going back into the primitive church. The expansion of the 'Two
Ways' in the Didache over and above the form attested in the
Epistle of Barnabas is partially under this influence. In distinction to Barn. 19.1a, the introduction to the 'way of life' in Did.
1.2 consists of the saying of the Lord about the greatest
commandment (Matt. 22.37–39). Then, in distinction to Barn.
19.1b, the further expansion in Did. 1.3 is introduced with the
phrase: 'Now these sayings' teaching is as follows',[35] followed by
a series of sayings of the Lord that are absent from Barn. 19.
Thus the given form of the 'Two Ways' is led in the direction
that has already become visible in the gnostic dialogues, where
such a formula connected sayings of the Lord with their exposition in the form of expanded material.[36] To be sure, such a

[34] 'Der gnostische "Dialog" als literarisches Genus', *Probleme der koptischen Literatur* (Wissenschaftliche Beiträge 1968/71, 2, Martin-Luther-
Universität Halle-Wittenberg). Cf. Hennecke-Schneemelcher, I, esp. Section
VI, 'Conversations between Jesus and his Disciples after the Resurrection',
pp. 125–57 (ET: I, pp. 188–230). Cf. for the conflation of these *Gattungen*
with that of the Testament the title of a Syriac work of apocalyptic contents,
retranslated into Greek by de Lagarde: 'First Book of Clement called Testament of our Lord Jesus Christ. The sayings that, after he rose from the dead,
he spoke to his holy apostles.' Adolf von Harnack, *ThLZ* 9 (1884), col. 340,
refers to it, citing de Lagarde, *Reliquiae iuris ecclesiastici antiquissimae*, 1856,
pp. 80–9. Cf. William Wrede, *Das Messiasgeheimnis in den Evangelien*, 1901,
1963³, pp. 246–51.

[35] On Qumran's similar hermeneutical formula 'the interpretation of the
saying is that (or: about)', from which the '*pesharim*' receive their name (e.g.
1QpHab, familiarly known as the Habakkuk Commentary; 4QpIsa, *JBL*
77, 1958, pp. 215–19), cf. already Jean Paul Audet, *La Didaché: Instructions
des Apôtres* (Études bibliques, 1958), pp. 261f.

[36] Cf. also Mark 10.24: 'And the disciples were amazed at his sayings',

comparison also draws attention to the Didache's more conservative relation to the tradition in presenting the interpreting
sayings, which may have been taken over from the Gospel of
Matthew.[37] The other section of the 'Two Ways' that has no
parallel in Barnabas is characterized by a form of address absent
from Barn. 18–20, 'my son' (Did. 3.1, 3, 4, 5, 6; 4.1; the plural
in 5.2), which, however, is common in wisdom literature.[38] There
emerges in this context a piety that is reminiscent of Papias,
in its exhortation to be 'always revering the *logoi* you have
heard' (3.8; cf. Barn. 19.4) and its desire to be with 'the saints,
to find rest in their *logoi*' (4.2).

From here one can move to the NT book most akin to the
Didache, the Gospel of Matthew. It is especially in Matthew
among the Gospels that the term *logoi* seems related to collections
of sayings and thus to point towards *logoi* as a designation for the
Gattung of such collections.[39] For a peculiarity of Matthew is his

---

whereupon the preceding saying is repeated, but enlarged by means of a
comparison, in such a way as to serve as an interpretation of the original
formulation. This repetition of the preceding saying is absent from Matthew
and Luke. Cf. also Luke 9.44–50 discussed below.

[37] Cf. Bentley Layton, 'The Sources, Date and Transmission of *Didache*
1.3b–2.1', *HThR* 61 (1968), pp. 343–83.

[38] Bultmann, *EUCHARISTERION* II, p. 11 n. 3 (= *Exegetica*, p. 19 n. 17),
appeals to Prov. 8.32 ('son') and Sirach 4.11 ('wisdom exalted her sons'),
to speak of a 'form of address current in catechetical terminology'. As roughly
synonymous forms of address one finds, in addition to υἱέ, also παιδίον (e.g.
Tobit 4.12) and τέκνον (Prov. 31.2; Sir. 2.1; 3.12, 17; 4.1; 6.18, 23, 32; 10.28;
11.10; 14.11; 16.24; 18.15; 21.1; 31.22; 37.27; 38.9, 16; 40.28) or the plural
τέκνα (Sir. 3.1; 23.7; 41.14). Especially significant is Sir. 31.22, 'listen to me,
(my) son, and do not scorn me, and in the end you will (approve) my *logoi*.'

[39] Indicative of Matthew's interest in *logoi* is also 10.14, where the term
logoi has been introduced redactionally into Mark 6.11, '. . . nor hear you',
to produce 'nor hear your sayings'. To be sure Matthew reveals traces of a
trend to designate such sayings collections as 'gospel', the same conflation
of terminology characteristic of the title of The Gospel of Thomas. For in
Matt. 4.23 and 9.35 Matthew inserts into summaries derived largely from
Mark, but used by Matthew to introduce the Sermon on the Mount and
the Mission of the Twelve, the term 'gospel'. Cf. Willi Marxsen, *Der Evangelist Markus: Studien zur Redaktionsgeschichte des Evangeliums*, (FRLANT 67),
1956, 1959², p. 81 (ET: p. 123). This terminology is analogous to his com-
positional procedure of imbedding the sayings collection Q in the Marcan
Gospel outline.

composition of five discourses, which are actually collections of sayings, and each of which ends with almost the same formula. This formula designates these collections as *logoi*. For even though in one case the commissioning of the twelve introduces into the formula the variant 'commissioning' (Matt. 11.1), and in the collection of parables the variant 'parables' is used (Matt. 13.53), we still find in the other instances (Matt. 7.28; 19.1; 26.1), representing the basic form of the formula, the term *logoi*: 'and it came to pass when Jesus completed (Matt. 26.1: all) these *logoi*'.

This trend, though clearest in Matthew, leaves some traces in the other gospels as well. One may compare Luke 9.28: 'And it came to pass after these *logoi*', a clause added at the conclusion of a small Marcan collection which itself contained an allusion to Jesus' *logoi* (Luke 9.26; Mark 8.38). This sensitivity on Luke's part towards recognizing small collections of *logoi* in his Gospel is to be seen in the broader context of his (and Matthew's) policy of locating the *Gattung* of the sayings collection within the public ministry, by imbedding Q in the Marcan framework. A somewhat similar trend can perhaps be sensed in the way Luke uses quotation formulae referring to Jesus' *logoi*. Such formulae occur only after the resurrection. Yet the passages in question betray a desire on Luke's part to refer sayings of Jesus current after Easter back to the public ministry as their original location. To be sure, in Acts 20.35 it is unclear whether a saying of the earthly Jesus or of the resurrected Lord is intended; the saying is absent from Luke's Gospel. But the reference in Acts 11.16, which points back to Acts 1.5, does not go back only to the Resurrected, for Acts 1.4 refers it further back to the public ministry. Luke 24.44 not only uses a quotation formula like the *incipit* of the Gospel of Thomas, suggesting he was aware of collections of the resurrected Lord's sayings; for by means of its careful formulation Luke 24.44 makes clear that these are not new sayings, but rather reminiscences of sayings from the public ministry: 'These are my *logoi* that I spoke to you while I was still with you.' Gnostic texts, such as the Letter of Peter to Philip (CG, VIII, *2*), make similar references to the effect that Jesus' (gnostic) teaching is the same as what he previously taught. In both cases one has to do with an apologetic concern to protect the teaching from the suspicion that it is not based on the authority of Jesus. If for the gnostics the effect was a defence of their *Gattung* of resurrection discourses, the effect in Luke's case was to replace it with the biography of the earthly Jesus.

The empty tomb story with which Luke 24 begins does not have the Resurrected appear at all. Yet he is represented by 'two men' (*angeli interpretes*), whose function is to announce the resurrection and quote from the public ministry the standard prediction of the passion. The quotation formula (24.6) is almost identical with 24.44: 'Remember how he spoke to you while he was still in Galilee.' Following the quotation is the affirmation (24.8): 'And they remembered his words' (with *rhemata* as a stylistic variant for *logoi*). Thus the resurrection message becomes the same as that of the public ministry. At 9.44 Luke begins the second prediction of the passion with the clause: 'Let these *logoi* sink into your ears', a clause which seems to function as a superscription for a small sayings collection he composes out of originally disparate dialogues. For he frees the subsequent Marcan material from its changes in scene (Mark 9.33–35) and thus moulds it into a continuous dialogue as an interpretation of the prediction. Thus the prediction becomes a 'secret saying' to be interpreted. This is suggested both by the exhortation to hearken (see below), and by the fact that Luke adds 'hidden . . . word' to the Marcan *Vorlage*. The resolution of the secret saying is a discussion, which is in effect the Lucan preparation for the way of the cross that begins at 9.51. Wrede argued[40] that Luke 24.24f., 44ff. reflects the pattern of the Marcan messianic secret, to the effect that the secrecy of the so-called 'public ministry' would be replaced by public or open or decoded proclamation after Easter. But if this pattern meant for Gnosticism a way to attain higher authority for their teachings as revelations of the resurrected Christ, it meant for Luke only an occasion to validate the teachings of the earthly ministry of Jesus.

[40] *Messiasgeheimnis*, pp. 164ff.

Although Luke is at this point going beyond Mark, the latter seems himself to have proceeded to a similar composition leading up to the third prediction of the passion. The pericope 10.17–22 concluded with the note that the rich man was quite upset by Jesus' *logos* on giving his wealth to the poor. Mark adds another saying about how hard entrance into the kingdom is. Thereupon the disciples are dumbfounded at his *logoi* (10.24). This observation is followed by a repetition of much the same saying, which is then amplified, each time stimulated by further wonder on the part of the disciples. Mark 7.14ff. provide a further instance of such a saying (called in 7.17 a 'parable', i.e. 'riddle') that mystifies and hence has to be repeated with accompanying commentary.

The collection of parables and sayings in Mark 4.1–34 also reflects the hermeneutical problem of how the material in such a collection is to be understood correctly. The first parable is followed by the thematic statement of its mystifying nature, which is expressed in the language of Isa. 6.9 about looking but not seeing and listening but not understanding. This OT text, quoted in Mark 4.12, is in substance integrated into the whole collection of Mark 4, both as the burden of what the parable of the sower means (cf. the contrast between inadequate hearing, 4.15, 16, 18, and 'hearing and receiving', 4.20), and in connection with other exhortations to hearken. Indeed the collection begins, in a way reminiscent of the first saying of the Gospel of Thomas, with Jesus' exhortation 'Hearken!' Mark 4.24 exhorts to 'see to what you hear'. This apparently echoes the OT language about seeing and understanding.

There are other instances of Marcan conflation of Isa. 6.9 with exhortations to hearken. One instance is especially similar to Mark 4. Mark 7.14 introduces a difficult saying with the exhortation: 'Hear me, all of you, and understand.' This saying is called a 'parable' or 'riddle' in 7.17, which the following sayings are intended to clarify. Thus the structure is the same as in ch. 4, and as in other instances of a secret saying to be interpreted through further sayings, such as in the Didache, Pistis Sophia, *pesharim*, Luke 9.44ff., etc.

Mark 8.18 makes use of the same OT passage, but varies the OT language, '. . . and having ears do you not hear?' (Cf. Luke 9.44: 'let these *logoi* sink into your ears.') This variation of Isa.6.9 in Mark 8.18 suggests that the OT passage has been associated with the saying: 'He who has ears to hear let him hear.' This latter saying follows immediately upon the Parable of the Sower in 4.9 as a transition to the hermeneutical discussion in which Isa.6.9 is quoted at 4.12; and it immediately precedes (in 4.23) the exhortation to 'see to what you hear' (4.24). There it follows upon the statement that what is hidden will be revealed (4.22), which in this context may be meant hermeneutically, in analogy to 4.11, 33f.

This same saying about having ears to hear is appended, with only minor variations, to difficult sayings in Matt.11.15; Luke 14.35, and to an interpretation of a parable in Matt.13.43. It is a floating saying that attaches itself readily to other sayings as a hermeneutical warning. In the manuscript tradition it is attached frequently, especially to parables, cf. to Matt. 25.29f.; Mark 7.16; Luke 12.21; 13.9; 21.4. And it is used regularly towards the conclusion of each message from the Lord in the seven letters of Revelation (2.7, 11, 17, 29; 3.6, 13, 22), and at random in the Gospel of Thomas, Sayings 8, 21, 24, 63, 65, 96. When the Letter of the Blessed Eugnostos (CG III, *3*; V, *1*) was christianized into the form of a dialogue between Jesus and his disciples under the title Sophia of Jesus Christ (CG III, *4*; BG 8502.*3*; P. Oxy. 1081), one of the christianizing insertions is this saying (BG 89.4–6; 90.13–15; 100.10–12; 107.13–108.1; P. Oxy. 1081.6–8, 35–36).[41] In Mark 4 the saying's connection with the other material about hearkening reveals its hermeneutical relevance in a collection of obscure sayings, and its presence in other such collections tends to confirm the definition of Mark 4.1–34 as such a collection.

In other respects Mark 4.1–34 betrays the traits of a sayings

[41] Martin Krause, 'Das literarische Verhältnis des Eugnostosbriefes zur Sophia Jesu Christi: Zur Auseinandersetzung der Gnosis mit dem Christentum', *Mullus* (Klauser *Festschrift*; *JAC*, Ergänzungsband 1, 1964), p.219. Cf. *The Oxyrhynchus Papyri Part VIII*, ed. by Arthur S. Hunt, 1911, pp. 16–19.

collection. It uses a rather set quotation formula (reminiscent of
the Gospel of Thomas' regular use of the historical present,
'Jesus said'), with only minor irregularities. The basic form is in
the imperfect tense, 'and he said' (4.9, 26, 30), to which can be
added 'to them' (4.2, 11, 21, 24; cf. 4.34), or in the historical
present 'he said to them' (4.13).[42] One may compare Rev. 2–3,
'thus says' (2.1, 8, 12, 18; 3.1, 7, 14); *Pirke Aboth*, '[Shammai]
says', or 'he used to say' (cf. 6.7f. 'and it says' in a sequence of
scriptural passages); Lucian, Demonax, 'he said',[43] placed post-
positively within the quotation itself. And the concept, already
encountered in Pistis Sophia (cf. also Deut. 1.5), of 'resolving'
sayings, occurs in Mark 4.34, a term used elsewhere of the
allegorical interpretation of parables, e.g. in the Similitudes of
Hermas, 5.3. 1f.; 5.4. 2f.; 5.5. 1; 9.10. 5; 9.11. 9; cf. the noun
'resolution' in 5.5. 1; 5.6. 8; 5.7. 1; 8.11. 1; 9.13. 9; 9.16. 7. In
Mark 4 the interpretation makes use of a formula for identifying
the persons intended by the allegory, 'these are the ones who
. . .', or the like (4.15, 16, 18, 20). This formula is used in Jude
19 to interpret an apostolic saying, and in Jude 12, 16; II Peter
2.17 to interpret Scripture. A somewhat similar style is used by
Matthew in the interpretation of the Parable of the Tares (Matt.
13.37–39).

The collection of Mark 4 refers to itself as 'parables', (4.2, 10,
11, 13, 30, 33, 34; cf. 3.23). Of course it is, strictly speaking, not
quite correct to translate παραβολαί here as 'parables'. For
Jülicher has taught us that the term 'parable' should be restricted to stories that make a point simply and clearly, i.e. what

---

[42] Joachim Jeremias, *The Parables of Jesus*, revised ed., 1963, p. 14,
esp, n. 11, uses these variants as a basis for reconstructing the stages in the
growth of the collection. For 'and he said (imperfect) to them' is typically
Marcan (2.27; 6.10; 7.9; 8.21; 9.1), whereas 'and he said' (imperfect) is not,
and hence may be 'pre-Marcan'. He does not comment on the historical
present 'and he said to them' in 4.13, which he attributes to the pre-Marcan
stage (pp. 13f., 18 n. 31). Yet the use of the historical present tense is as
distinctively Marcan as is the addition of 'to them'. This can be seen by the
frequency of its occurrence in Mark and by the tendency of both Matthew
and Luke to change to a past tense. Of course Mark could also have edited
his source into conformity to his own preferred usage.

[43] ἔφη, rather than λέγει, ἔλεγεν, and εἶπεν in the Christian usage cited above.

we today would call sermon illustration.[44] This distinction was lost on the Evangelists, who had no hesitation in calling an allegory such as the Wicked Husbandman a 'parable' (Mark 12.1, 12). This is due not only to their lack of form-critical concern and the fluidity of the Greek term and its Hebrew equivalent,[45] but also to the fact that they had lost sight of the parable in its own right, and misunderstood it as allegory. In Mark 4 παραβολαί are allegorical 'riddles' intended to obscure the point for the outsiders (4.11f., 33f.). In Mark 7.17 the term occurs in connection with the disciples' question requesting clarification, i.e. it tends to mean 'riddle', as does παροιμία in John 10.6; 16.25, 29.

That is to say, 'parables' are for Mark (with the probable exception of 3.23) approaching what the Gospel of Thomas calls 'secret sayings', i.e. statements whose true meaning is not evident, but is to be established by means of special interpretation. (In Mark 13.28 'parable' seems to refer to this deeper, interpreted meaning.) In such a context, the allegorical interpretation given to the Parable of the Sower, 4.13–20, is quite appropriate (cf. Matthew's *pendant*, the interpretation of the Parable of the Tares, 13.36–43). From Mark's point of view Mark 4 is then not a collection of parables, but rather of riddles, allegories, secret sayings. Between the Parable of the Sower and the two concluding Parables of the Seed Growing Secretly and the

[44] For the discussion of the understanding of the nature of parables since Jülicher cf. my essay 'Jesus' Parables as God Happening', *Jesus and the Historian: Written in Honor of Ernest Cadman Colwell*, ed. by F. Thomas Trotter, 1968, pp. 134–50.

[45] Joachim Jeremias, *Parables*, p. 20, presents the wide spectrum of meanings for the Hebrew *mashal* (Greek παραβολή, 'parable'). On p. 16, n. 22, he presents the material for the meaning 'riddle, dark saying', which seems to have been near the original meaning of 'magical saying' or 'riddle' (so Eissfeldt, *Einleitung in das Alte Testament*, 1956[2], pp. 94, 98 [ET: pp. 82, 86]. Jeremias, *Parables*, pp. 97f., correlates the Marcan pattern of presenting the deeper meaning to the inner circle with the contemporary Rabbinic practice to which David Daube called attention, 'Public Pronouncement and Private Explanation in the Gospels', *The New Testament and Rabbinic Judaism*, 1956, pp. 141–50. The *locus classicus* on this topic is William Wrede, *Messiasgeheimnis*, pp. 51–65, esp. pp. 51–4, 65 on private vs. public, and pp. 54–65 on the Marcan theory of 'parables'.

Mustard Seed (4.26–29, 30–32), Mark inserts a series of sayings (4.21–25). It may well be the case, in view of the framework material at 4.21a, 23–24a, that Mark grouped the sayings into what he would consider a further pair of 'parables' (4.21–22, 24–25), but this should not be taken to imply the corollary 'and not as a collection of sayings'.[46] For to Mark a collection of 'secret sayings' and a collection of 'parables' in the sense of 'riddles, dark sayings', would belong together rather than being mutually exclusive. The Gospel of Thomas would concur in this view. For not only does it contain parables (*less* allegorized than in Mark), but also contains precisely the sayings found in Mark 4.21–25, as Sayings 33. 5. 41. Thus Mark 4 is not simply a collection of parables in our sense, but rather of obscure sayings in need of interpretations, i.e. 'parables' in Mark's sense, quite comparable to a collection of 'secret sayings' such as the Gospel of Thomas.

Yet Mark 4 avoids the term *logoi*. This avoidance may be due not simply to his use of the term 'parables' to convey the concept of 'riddles', which after all could have been expressed with the term 'secret sayings', but also to the fact that he uses the singular *logos* as a synonym for 'gospel' (Mark 1.1, 14f.; 8.35; 10.29; 13.10; 14.9). It is in this sense that *logos* is used in 4.14, 15 *bis*, 16, 17, 18, 19, 20, to designate what the Parable of the Sower is talking about. The parable becomes itself a hermeneutical discussion about right and wrong ways of 'hearing' the 'word'. This hermeneutical problem is then met theoretically by the Marcan method of 'resolving riddles', from which process the 'word' emerges into clarity: 'And with many such riddles he spoke to them the word, . . . but privately to his own disciples he resolved everything' (4.33f.). Thus the same trend that led Mark to the (Pauline) term 'gospel' led him to the

---

[46] Jeremias, *Parables*, p. 41 n. 69, says these '*logia*' were included by Mark here because he regarded them as a pair of parables, but adds, 'and not as a collection of sayings' (p. 91). When Jeremias appeals to the frequent exhortations in Mark 4 to hearken as evidence that this chapter is not a collection of sayings, he has overlooked the evidence presented above that such exhortations are characteristic of such collections of secret sayings as the Gospel of Thomas.

term 'word' as its synonym. It was then more appropriate for him to refer to sayings that were in his view still coded as 'riddles' rather than '*logoi*'; for Jesus 'spoke the word openly' (8.32) when he spoke the kerygma.

None the less Mark may not have been unaware of the tendency to refer to such collections as *logoi*. This may be suggested by the saying, put significantly near the end (v.31) of the collection of apocalyptic sayings and parables in Mark 13: 'Heaven and earth will pass away, but my *logoi* will not pass away.'

If one may discern in Mark 4 traces of a pre-Marcan collection, it is possible that what we know in expanded form as the Sermon on the Mount (or Plain) is the outgrowth of another such early cluster of sayings and parables.[47] It uses as its conclusion a double parable exalting Jesus' *logoi* in much the same way

[47] The cohesion of the collection suggests that the Sermon on the Mount (Plain) is derived from an oral or written collection of its own, and did not first come into being in the context of Q. Cf. W. D. Davies, *The Setting of the Sermon on the Mount*, 1964. The end seems to be the conclusion of a collection, and this not simply because of the occurrence there of the term *logoi*. Rather the eschatological climax is the same concluding motif that one can sense in the Didache (ch. 16), the Gospels (Mark 13 par.), and even in Q (Luke 17.20–37). This develops into what Günther Bornkamm (*Die Vorgeschichte des sogenannten Zweiten Korintherbriefes* [SAH Philos.-hist. Klasse 2. Abh.], 1961, pp.23ff.) has called the 'form-critical law' to the effect that one sign of the end, the emergence of heretics, can become a trait characteristic of the end of a document. In this regard, as in others, the Sermon on the Mount goes beyond the Sermon on the Plain. Matthew seems to have recognized the unity of this collection over against the rest of Q. For he did not compose the Sermon on the Mount simply by scanning the whole of Q for suitable material, as Vincent Taylor has shown to be the regular Matthean practice in composing his other sayings collections, 'The Order of Q', *JTS*, n.s.4 (1953), pp.27–31, and 'The Original Order of Q', T. W. Manson *Festschrift*, 1959, pp.246–69. Rather, as the Lucan Sermon on the Plain shows, Matthew has acknowledged the framework of the collection as the framework of the Sermon on the Mount, merely filling out the given outline with further material gleaned partly from Q (cf. Taylor's tables in *JTS*, pp.29f., and in the Manson *Festschrift*, p.249). Of course one could argue that Matt.3–12 tend to follow the original (Lucan) order of Q (cf. especially Matt.3, 4, 5, 7, 8, 11, 12), and that it is for this reason that Matt.5 and 7 do not follow the 'gleaning' method of the four later Matthean discourses, but prefer the method of the 'rest of Matthew' in retaining the Q order. Yet each of the

as does Mark 13.31. For the double parable Luke 6.47, par.
Matt. 7.24 (cf. v. 26) begins: 'Every one who comes to me and
hears my *logoi* and does them . . .' Hence the term *logoi* may
have functioned as a designation for this early collection. In that
case it would be the trend towards alluding, near its end, to such
a collection as *logoi*, that would have provided Q with the catchword for connecting this collection to the rest of the Q sayings by
means of what is the most prominent exception to its policy of
including only sayings material. For here Q presents the story of
the healing of the centurion's servant, oriented to the centurion's
trust in the authority of Jesus' word (Luke 7.7, par. Matt. 8.8).[48]
It would be this same trend at work in Matthew that leads to the
fixed formula with which he ends his five sayings collections, the
first occurrence of which follows directly upon the double parable
(Matt. 7.28). Thus we seem to be able to trace the beginnings of
a designation for the *Gattung* of collections of sayings back into
the earliest such collections of the primitive church.[49] Somewhat
as in the case of the Gospel of Thomas, the term would seem to
be initially imbedded in the sayings themselves, and to move towards a title first by means of the significant placement of such
sayings, from which it is taken into redactional subscriptions.

---

two small collections from the same period found in I Clem. 13.2 and Did.
1.3–6 (see below) seem to reflect a similar unity. Helmut Koester's research
(*Synoptische Überlieferung bei den apostolischen Vätern*, [TU 65], 1957, pp. 12ff.,
217ff.) leads to the conclusion that in both cases we have to do with small
collections ante-dating their use in the documents we know, collections very
similar in content to the Sermon on the Mount (Plain). In the case of the
Didache, this may in part be due to dependence on Matt. and Luke, as
Bentley Layton, 'The Sources, Date and Transmission of *Didache* 1, 3b–2, 1',
HThR 61 (1968), pp. 343–83, suggests. Yet even in this case the removal
of this block of material from Matt. and Luke to insert it into the 'Two
Ways' and thus into the Didache may be due to a surviving awareness of
the traditional unity of the cluster. Cf. also Justin, I Apologia 14.5; Athena-
goras, Supplicatio 11.1, 3.

[48] Cf. Ernst Haenchen, *ZThK* 56 (1959), pp. 23–31, reprinted in *Gott
und Mensch*, pp. 82–90, and my discussion in 'Kerygma and History in the
New Testament', *Trajectories through Early Christianity*, 1971, ch. 2.

[49] Cf. Helmut Koester, '*GNOMAI DIAPHOROI*', in *Trajectories through
Early Christianity*, ch. 4, for further comments on such primitive collections.

III.   *From the Quotation Formula to the Collection of Sayings*

An analysis of the way in which the individual saying is introduced in the early church will reveal a similar terminological sensitivity. For quotation formulae can be used both with individual sayings and with sayings collections.

A saying that has just been quoted can be referred to with the term *logos* (Mark 9.10; Mark 10.22, par. Matt. 19.22; Mark 14.39, par. Matt. 24.44; Matt. 15.12; 19.11; John 2.22; 4.50; 6.60). Even a saying quoted much earlier can be recalled and repeated with a quotation formula using that term: 'And Peter remembered the *logos* (*rhema*?) of the Lord, how he had said to him' (Luke 22.61);[50] 'Remember the *logos* that I said to you' (John 15.20); or, replacing 'remembrance' with 'fulfilment', 'This was to fulfil the *logos* that he had spoken' (John 18.9).[51] One may also compare Paul's quotation formula in I Thess. 4.15: 'But this we declare to you by the *logos* of the Lord.' It is apparently from this quotation formula that Bultmann derived his favourite designation *Herrenwort*, 'dominical saying', 'word of the Lord'.

In tracing the sensitivity of the sources for the name appropriate to collections of sayings, an odd trait is of particular significance: the plural form *logoi* is so standard in one quotation formula that the plural is even used when introducing a single saying rather than a plurality of sayings. One of the last dissertations under Bultmann, that of Helmut Koester,[52] called attention to this formula. It combines the verb 'remember', already encountered in Luke 22.61 and John 15.20, with the plural *logoi*. The passages where this formula occurs are the

[50] The variant reading with *rhema* has been usually rejected as derived from the parallel in Matt. 26.75 (Mark 14.72); yet the support for the reading provided by P[69] and P[75] may prove decisive (as in *The Greek New Testament* of the Bible Societies). Luke uses the same term in Luke 24.8, 'and they remembered his words', and Acts 11.16, 'and I remembered the word of the Lord, how he said . . . '.

[51] The same variant occurs in John 18.32, 'to fulfil the *logos* that Jesus had spoken'. The reference is apparently to 12.32, to which 12.33 also refers with the simple expression 'he said this'.

[52] *Synoptische Überlieferung bei den apostolischen Vätern* (TU 65), 1957, pp. 4–6.

following: 'To remember the *logoi* of the Lord Jesus, that he said' (Acts 20.35); 'Remember the *logoi* of the Lord Jesus, for he said' (I Clem. 46.7f.); 'Especially remembering the *logoi* of the Lord Jesus that he spoke when he was teaching gentleness and long-suffering, for he spoke thus' (I Clem. 13.1f.).[53] These passages tend to indicate that sayings collections as well as individual sayings were referred to as '*logoi* of the Lord Jesus'. In fact, this quotation formula provides a path for tracing sayings collections down to their final discontinuation in the orthodox church as the canonical Gospels took their place.

In Acts 20.35 the quotation formula is followed by a single saying: 'It is more blessed to give than to receive.' This rule, ascribed in Greek tradition to the Persian court,[54] is also found in I Clem. 2.1: 'giving more gladly than receiving'. Probably this rule is also understood as a saying of Jesus, in view of the remark in the same sentence, 'paying attention to his *logoi* you stored them up carefully in your hearts', even though an explicit quotation formula is lacking here.[55] The exhortation to 'give' is already found in the collection of sayings of Jesus in I Clem. 13.2.[56] Since both Acts and I Clem. are aware of sayings collections such as Q, one can infer that this quotation formula, making use of the plural *logoi*, is derived from a formula alluding to such a collection.[57]

[53] A variant of this formula, again used with an individual saying, occurs in Jude 17: 'Remember the sayings (*rhemata*) foretold by the apostles of our Lord Jesus Christ, that they said to you. . . .' The parallel in II Peter 3.2 adds a reference to the prophets and roots the apostles' authority in the Lord's commandment, although in this secondary setting the saying is less clearly marked as such. For the identification of 'Jude' and 'Thomas' cf. Helmut Koester, '*GNOMAI DIAPHOROI*', *op. cit.* The affinities between the books of Jude and Thomas the Contender call for special investigation.

[54] Ernst Haenchen, *Die Apostelgeschichte* (Meyer Kommentar, 3), 1961[13], pp. 526f.

[55] Contrary to Haenchen, *Apostelgeschichte*, p. 2.

[56] Koester, *Synoptische Überlieferung*, p. 13.

[57] This transition from the singular to the plural could have a parallel in I Thess. 4.15–18, which begins in the quotation formula with the singular, '*logos* of the Lord', and closes with the exhortation: 'Therefore comfort one another with these *logoi*.' For Paul normally speaks in the singular of *logos* in the sense of the 'gospel', and uses the plural only in connection with the wisdom teaching of the Corinthian heretics, I Cor. 2.13, 'in *logoi* not

In I Clem. 46.7f. the quotation formula is followed by a woe and two threats. Comparison with a double tradition in the Synoptics leads Koester to the conclusion: 'There remains only the assumption that I Clem. 46.8 is related to a stage behind the Synoptics, and one doubtless thinks of Q. Indeed all the sayings in I Clem. 46.8 that are related to the Synoptics could have stood in Q.'[58] Thus one may assume that such collections were familiar to Clement, and also that excerpts from such collections were introduced with the quotation formula cited above making use of the plural form *logoi*.

In I Clem. 13.2 the quotation formula is followed by a chain of seven sayings. They are partly attested in the Gospels (mostly in the 'Sermon on the Mount'), partly elsewhere; yet they can be derived from no surviving source. Hence Koester concludes: 'Perhaps the author is making use of some written collection of sayings of the Lord no longer known to us, but perhaps earlier than our Gospels (cf. Saying 3). Perhaps it is the reproduction of an oral, though firmly formulated, local catechism.'[59]

There is a quite similar collection in Polycarp, Phil. 2.3, though varied in details and enlarged by the first saying of the 'Sermon on the Mount'. Here too the collection is introduced with a quite similar quotation formula, though the term *logoi* is lacking: 'but remembering what things the Lord said as he taught.' (Another instance of the quotation formula without the term *logoi* is II Clem. 17.3: 'Let us remember the command-ments of the Lord.') Even if Polycarp is here dependent on I Clem. and the Gospels,[60] the freedom with which he adapts his collection still attests his connection with the free development of such sayings collections; to be sure, his tendency to bring I Clem. 13.2 into line with the Gospels points to the beginning of the end of this freedom in the orthodox church.

---

taught by human wisdom but taught by the Spirit'. In I Cor. 2.4, there occurs the variant reading 'in plausible *logoi* of wisdom', comparable to Corpus Hermeticum, 1, 29: 'I sowed in them the *logoi* of wisdom'. In I Cor. 12.8 one finds in the singular, '*logos* of wisdom'.

[58] Koester, *Synoptische Überlieferung*, p. 18.

[59] *Ibid.*, p. 16.

[60] Koester, *op. cit.*, pp. 115–18.

In the case of Polycarp one can detect what was no doubt generally a major factor in the restriction of that freedom: the misuse of the sayings tradition by gnosticizing heretics. For the other instance of his appeal to sayings of the Lord stands in just that context. In 7.1 he warns against 'whoever perverts the *logia* of the Lord for his own lusts, and says that there is neither resurrection nor judgment'. Over against this heresy Polycarp presents an exhortation exemplifying the right use of such sayings, followed by the language of Matt. 26.41a, par. Mark 14.38a, brought into conformity to that of the Lord's Prayer; then a quotation formula introduces a *verbatim* quotation of Matt. 26.41b, par. Mark 14.38b: 'Wherefore, leaving the foolishness of the crowd, and their false teaching, let us turn back to the *logos* that was delivered to us in the beginning, watching in prayer and persevering in fasting, beseeching the all-seeing God in our supplications to "lead us not into temptation", as the Lord said, "The spirit is willing, but the flesh is weak."'[61]

A somewhat later but quite clear example of the gnostic use of Jesus' *logoi* in their competition with Marcion is found in Ptolemaeus' Letter to Flora. For here a Valentinian tripartite division of the OT law is proven 'from the *logoi* of our Saviour' (Epiphanius, *Haer.* 33.3.7), by means of citing (in 33.4.4. and 33.4.11) Matt. 19.8, 6; 15.4–9.[62]

Justin attests the continuing shadowy existence of collections of sayings at a time when the Gospels have replaced them and the *Gattung* as such is hardly alive any longer in the orthodox church. The term *logoi* usually means something quite different for him, namely Scripture (understood prophetically and hence also called 'prophetic sayings'), or an individual proof text. Hence a frequent quotation formula for introducing an OT quotation is: 'And these are the *logoi*' (Dial. 31.2; 39.4; 62.3; 79.3), or the like. Of course the transfer of such a Scripture

---

[61] For a further investigation of this heresy combatted by Polycarp in its relation to the sayings tradition and to the heresy combatted by Paul in I Cor., cf. 'Kerygma and History in the New Testament', *Trajectories through Early Christianity*, 1971, ch. 2.

[62] Cf. Walther Völker, *Quellen zur Geschichte der christlichen Gnosis*, pp. 87–93; Robert M. Grant, *Gnosticism*, 1961, pp. 184–90.

formula to sayings of Jesus would not be difficult; for Christ already spoke in the OT (I Apol. 49.1; 63.14; Dial. 113f.). Hence revelation is transmitted both 'through the prophetic spirit and through Christ himself' (I Apol. 63.14), just as truth is 'in his *logoi* and those of his prophets' (Dial. 139.5). The common phrase used to mark a transition in a chain of scriptural passages, 'in other *logoi*' (I Apol. 35.5; Dial. 12.1; 56.14; 58.6; 97.3; 126.6; [133.4]), is also used in a sequence of sayings of Jesus, Dial. 76.5 (cf. 76.6). Furthermore in Dial. 17.3–4 (cf. also 18.3) sayings of Jesus are quoted in a chain of scriptural passages with the following comment: 'recalling short *logia* of his together with the prophetic (*logia*)' (18.1), in which case Jesus' sayings, though termed *logia* rather than *logoi*, are described with a term commonly used of scriptural passages.[63] Thus we find ourselves at the stage in the trajectory of Jesus' sayings in which they are not only derived from the Gospels, but are even treated as one would treat passages of Scripture.

Yet Justin also refers to his Second Apology (i.e. the Appendix to his Apology) as *logoi* (12.6). He even refers to the Dialogue (*dialogos*) with Trypho as *logoi* (11.5; 39.8; 45.1; 47.1). One may compare especially Dial. 80.3, 'I shall make a composition of all the *logoi* that have gone on between us', with II Apol. 1.1, 'to make the composition of these *logoi*', and 15.2, 'because of this only have I composed these *logoi*'. Trypho also understands his speeches as *logoi* (38.1). What the two are doing is 'sharing *logoi*' (38.1; 64.2; 112.4; cf. II Apol. 3.5). That is to say, they understand themselves as philosophers, such as those whose *logoi* are mentioned in Dial. 2.2.

Of course it was also the *Logos*, i.e. Christ, who spoke through Socrates (I Apol. 5.3f.; 46.3; II Apol. 10.8). Yet when an individual Socratic saying is quoted (II Apol. 3.6), it is introduced simply with 'the Socratic (thing)', rather than with a quotation formula making use of the term *logoi*. This may be a negative indication that in Justin's usage it would have been inaccurate

---

[63] In Dial. 65.3; 109.1 Justin designates scriptural passages of a few verses as 'short *logoi*'. The designation seems to be almost identical with the term 'section' or '*pericope*', 65.3; 110.1.

to refer here to *logoi*. For a 'Socratic *logos*'[64] was precisely such a
discourse or dialogue as the philosopher Justin himself carried
on, and as he conceives of Plato composing; the term would
hence not fit an individual saying.[65] Yet he does use the term
logoi with regard to Jesus: Dial. 8.2 = 35.8 = 100.3; 113.7 =
113.5. And in one instance he is still able to present a collection
of loosely connected sayings of Jesus, I Apol. 15–17 (cf. also
14.3f.). But when he refers to this collection as *logoi*, he does so
with the apologetic clarification (14.5): 'But short and concise

[64] First attested in Aristotle, cf. *Poetica* 1447ᵇ, 11. From Karl Joel's
investigation, 'Der λόγος Σωκρατικός', *Archiv für Geschichte der Philosophie* 8
(1895), pp. 467ff., one finds 'that the "Socratic dialogue" in Aristotle's time
was a long-since established literary *genre*, and that these *logoi* were regarded
by Aristotle, in agreement with the current view, as "artistic reproductions"'
(so Heinrich Maier, *Sokrates: Sein Werk und seine geschichtliche Stellung*, 1913,
p. 27).

[65] Diognetus 8.2, '*logoi* . . . of philosophers' perhaps means '*sayings* . . .
of philosophers', since the context is a discussion of conflicting doctrines of
God each succinctly put, e.g. 'some say fire to be God, others water'. In the
Gospel of Thomas, Saying 13, Matthew compares Jesus to a 'philosopher',
which occurs as a loan word in the Coptic text. Thus a connection of 'sayings'
with the 'philosopher' is not excluded; indeed the term philosopher, like the
term sophist, is etymologically related to the term sage. On the Platonic
'*Logoi* on the Good' cf. Hans Joachim Krämer, *Arete bei Platon und Aristoteles*,
1959, p. 408, note 53; on the sayings of the Greek sages cf. Ulrich Wilckens,
TWNT VII, (1964), p. 469. On the relation of Greek gnomic sayings to
traditions about Jesus cf. Arnold Ehrhardt, 'Greek Proverbs in the Gospel',
The Framework of the New Testament Stories, 1964, pp. 44–63; Hildebrecht
Hommel, 'Herrenworte im Licht sokratischer Überlieferung', *ZNW* 57
(1966), pp. 1–23. This has been examined in detail in terms of a single saying
by Albrecht Dihle, *Die Goldene Regel: Eine Einführung in die Geschichte der
antiken und frühchristlichen Vulgärethik*, Studienhefte zur Altertumswissenschaft 7,
1962). Cf. my review in the *Journal of the History of Philosophy* 4 (1966), pp.
84–7. The tradition of Greek collections of sayings is Christianized in the
Sentences of Sextus (whose Coptic version has turned up at Nag Hammadi:
CG XII, *1*). In connection with editions of the Sentences of Sextus further
literature is to be found: Josef Kroll in Edgar Hennecke, *Neutestamentliche
Apokryphen*, 1924², pp. 625ff; Henry Chadwick, *The Sentences of Sextus* (Texts
and Studies 5), 1959; Gerhard Delling, 'Zur Hellenisierung des Christentums
in den "Sprüchen des Sextus"', *Studien zum Neuen Testament und zur Patristik*
(Klostermann *Festschrift* [TU 77] 1961), pp. 218–41. On Aesop's Fables cf.
Babrius and Phaedrus (Loeb Classical Library, 1965), ed. and tr. by Ben Edwin
Perry. Johannes Leipoldt, *Das Evangelium nach Thomas* (TU 101), 1967, pp.
4–5, has listed further Greek literature that should be brought into consideration.

logoi came from him. For he was not a sophist; rather his *logos* was the power of God.' This is a good characterization of the *Gattung* of sayings collections in its distinction from discourses, dialogues and tractates. Yet the very fact that it was necessary to make the distinction indicates that the traits constitutive of the *Gattung* had become noticeable as defects;[66] it could be defended only by means of a contrast to the scorned '*logoi* of the sophists'.[67]

The Gospel of Thomas falls within much the same situation of transition as do Clement,[68] Polycarp and Justin, when the sayings collections derived from the oral tradition were becoming dependent on the written Gospels, but have not yet been entirely replaced by Gospels, discourses, dialogues and treatises. For even if it were the case that the Gospel of Thomas derived its sayings in large part from the canonical Gospels, which is far from obvious,[69] in any case it retained the *Gattung* of sayings

[66] A somewhat similar sensitivity is reflected in the covering letter Arrian wrote to accompany Epictetus' 'Discourses'. The letter nowhere refers to them by this accepted title (lit. 'Diatribes'); rather they are introduced as his *logoi*. And Arrian's first concern is to make clear that it is a collection, not a literary composition 'as one might be said to "compose" books of this kind'. They were not written for publication. 'But whatever I heard him say I used to write down, word for word, as best I could, endeavouring to preserve it as a memoir, for my own future use, of his way of thinking and his effective speech. They are, accordingly, as you might expect, such remarks as one man might make off-hand to another, not such as he would compose for posterity.' Thus, though they are more nearly a random collection of informal brief discourses than a collection of sayings, Epictetus' *logoi* are clearly distinguished by Arrian from the formal philosophical discourse. Yet Arrian is concerned to claim for them that they achieve the purpose of 'the *logoi* of the philosophers', namely 'to incite the minds of his hearers to the best things'.

[67] Aristotle, *Sophistici Elenchi*, 165ᵃ, 34. Cf. Justin, Dial. 129.2: 'The sophists (are) able neither to say nor to think the truth.' For a comparison between the *logoi* of the prophets and those of the philosophers cf. Dial. 7.2.

[68] Helmut Koester, *Synoptische Überlieferung*, pp. 12–16, 220–37, and recently '*GNOMAI DIAPHOROI*', in *Trajectories through Early Christianity*, ch. 4, suggests the transition takes place between Clement and Didache.

[69] Ernst Haenchen, *Die Botschaft des Thomas-Evangeliums*, 1961, p. 11, presents a theory making dependence on the Gospels seem conceivable, in spite of the omitted narrative ingredient of the Gospels: 'Gnosticism was . . . only concerned with the redeeming message, not with any miracles of the redeemer or his death for our salvation. Gnosticism, at least in its pure form, was a piety that saw all salvation contained in the *word* that assured the elect of his union with the divine and thus of his eternal salvation. If such a gnostic

collections.[70] With the final discontinuation of the oral transmission of Jesus' sayings, the *Sitz im Leben* of the *Gattung* was

---

read the Gospels, then this gnostic presupposition functioned like a sieve. The
miracle stories that take up considerable room in Mark, Matt., and Luke,
and also are important in John, disappeared on their own accord, so to speak.
Just like the passion narrative, they were unimportant. Hence one need not
presuppose any kind of sayings collection as source of The Gospel of Thomas,
in order to explain its nature as a pure collection of sayings of Jesus.' Yet
other Nag Hammadi tractates indicate that Gnosticism tended not to carry
elimination through consistently, but rather to proceed by means of interpretation of given traditions. The retention, in gnostic reinterpretation, of
the passion narrative in The Second Treatise of the Great Seth (CG VII, *2*)
is a case in point. Johannes Leipoldt in his review of Haenchen's book (*ThLZ*
87, 1962, col. 755), and in his own edition (*Das Evangelium nach Thomas* [TU
101] 1967, p. 16), assumes dependence on the Synoptics, and yet locates The
Gospel of Thomas correctly within the history of the *Gattung* of sayings collections. Wolfhart Schrage, *Das Verhältnis des Thomas-Evangeliums zur synoptischen
Tradition und zu den koptischen Evangelienübersetzungen* ([*BZNW* 29], 1964) is
the first to present a detailed argument to show dependence of the Gospel
of Thomas upon the canonical Gospels. However, as the unpublished dis-
sertation of John Sieber, *A Redactional Analysis of the Synoptic Gospels with Regard
to the Question of the Sources of the Gospel of Thomas*, Claremont Graduate School,
1965, has indicated, his argument is not fully convincing. For he considers a
demonstration of the Coptic translator's dependence on the Coptic New
Testament (if this be chronologically likely) as an argument for an analogous
dependence of the Greek original on the Greek New Testament. Another
alternative, to the effect that the source of those close parallels to the New
Testament that do occur is the Coptic translator's dependence on the Coptic
New Testament, rather than the original Greek author's use of the
Greek New Testament, has not been adequately considered. Schrage's own
investigation of the Greek fragments, 'Evangelienzitate in Oxyrhynchus-
Logien und im koptischen Thomas-Evangelium', *Apophoreta* (Haenchen *Festschrift*, [*BZNW* 30], 1964), pp. 251–68, somewhat contrary to his own pur-
pose, indicates the Greek to be further from the New Testament than the
Coptic. Cf. also the criticism by Helmut Koester, '*GNOMAI DIAPHOROI*',
op. cit., ch. 4.

[70] It is precisely at this point that the position, most recently advocated by
Werner Georg Kümmel, seems to be misleading: 'The document [sc. the
Gospel of Thomas] is as such certainly no late form of the same literary
Gattung as Q, but rather a late stage, different in kind, of the development in
the tradition of Jesus' sayings.' *Einleitung in das Neue Testament*, 12th ed. of the
standard work by Paul Feine and Johannes Behm, 1963, p. 41 (ET: p. 58).
Cf. further literature there. Koester, '*GNOMAI DIAPHOROI*', *op. cit.*, ch.
4, accepts the view presented above and suggests Thomas 'represents the
eastern branch of the *Gattung* "*Logoi*"', the western branch being represented
by the Synoptic *Logoi* of Q'.

gone; hence orthodoxy contented itself with the canonical Gospels, while Gnosticism devoted itself all the more to imaginary dialogues of the Resurrected with his disciples.

The *Gattung* of sayings collections has become comprehensible under the designation *logoi* in light of quotation formulae referring to '*logoi* of the Lord Jesus' or the like. This designation was then taken up into the conclusion or *incipit* of written collections, thus serving to designate the *Gattung*. Thus the *incipit* of the Gospel of Thomas was not to be explained simply in terms of the one document, but required for its explanation a context of usage in early Christianity as part of the history of a *Gattung*. Just so this whole early Christian development is to be seen in a more encompassing trajectory, if the course of this *Gattung* and its cultural *Sitz im Leben*, and thus its history, are to be understood.

IV. *Jewish Wisdom Literature and the* Gattung *LOGOI SOPHON*

The history of the early Christian designation for the 'sayings' *Gattung* came first into view in its gnostic variant, as 'hidden sayings'. This poses the question as to what there may have been in the tendency of the *Gattung* itself that contributed to this outcome. Bultmann has provided a useful suggestion, when he sensed in Matt. 23.34–39 (par. Luke 11.49–51; 13.34–35) a speech by Sophia cited from some lost wisdom document, whose conclusion 'you will not see me again until . . .' was explained in terms of 'the myth of the divine Wisdom . . ., who, after tarrying in vain on earth and calling men to herself, takes departure from earth, so that one now seeks her in vain'.[71] For this myth does seem to be presupposed in the Gospel of Thomas, to judge by Saying 38: 'many times have you desired to hear these sayings that I say to you, and you have no other from whom to hear them. There will be days when you will seek me (and) you will not find me' (cf. Q: Luke 10.24; 13.34f. par.). Thus Bultmann's suggestions of an early Christian association of Jewish wisdom literature's personified Sophia with Jesus and of the

[71] *Geschichte der synoptischen Tradition*, pp. 120f. (ET: p. 115).

absorption of part of a collection of wisdom sayings into a collection of Jesus' sayings may in their way point to the pre-history of a *Gattung* that, though apparently not gnostic in origin, was open to a development in that direction, once a general drift towards Gnosticism had set in.

If the Gospel of Thomas shows the way in which the Sophia tradition used in Q ends in Gnosticism, an early Catholic theologian attests equally clearly its origin in Jewish wisdom literature. 'For All-virtuous Wisdom said thus: "Behold I will bring forth to you the expression of my spirit, and I will teach you my *logos*, since I called and you did not obey, and I put forth *logoi* and you did not attend. . . . For it shall come to pass when you call upon me, I will not hear you. The evil shall seek me and they shall not find me. For they hated wisdom . . ."' (I Clem. 57.3ff.). Here one has much the same content as in the Gospel of Thomas, Saying 38, and in Q (Matt. 23.34–39, par. Luke 11.49–51; 13.34–35), with a quotation formula reminiscent of that in Q (Luke 11.49), 'Therefore the Wisdom of God said.' Yet in fact what we have is a verbal quotation from the LXX of Prov. 1.23–33; the quotation formula is simply making use of the primitive Christian name for the book of Proverbs. Yet the OT origin of the passage neither separates it from Jesus, 'who is also called Sophia . . . in the *logoi* of the prophets' (Justin, Dial. 100.4) nor from the gnostic Gospel of Thomas. For when Bultmann first worked out the gnostic redeemer myth, he appealed to Prov. 1.23–33 as 'the most important passage . . ., in which the whole myth is reflected'.[72] The personified Wisdom of OT wisdom literature developed into the gnostic redeemer myth, especially as it identified Jesus with that redeemer, and thus understood Jesus as bringer of the secret redemptive *gnosis* or *logoi*.

[72] Bultmann, *EUCHARISTERION* II, 9. The unwillingness of Ralph Marcus, 'On Biblical Hypostases of Wisdom', *HUCA*, 23.1 (1950–51), pp. 157–71, to assume a move beyond 'poetic personification' to 'hypostatization' for Sophia in Judaism, in criticism of Helmer Ringgren, *Word and Wisdom: Studies in the Hypostatization of Divine Qualities and Functions in the Ancient Near East*, 1957, seems based on an idealized view of early Judaism (cf. pp. 169–71).

The fact that such a development comes into view especially in the sayings tradition is more comprehensible when one has noted the close connection between sayings collections and the sages, the *sophoi*. It is partly because the *Gattung* was itself associated with the 'wise' that it could easily be swept into the christological development moving from personified Wisdom to the gnostic redeemer. It is this relation with the 'wise' that becomes clear from the antecedent history of the *Gattung* within Judaism, as λόγοι σοφῶν, 'Words of the Wise' or 'Sayings of the Sages'.

Already in *Pirke Aboth* one has to do with a collection of sayings that (especially in its first parts) corresponds formally to this *Gattung*. For one finds here a chain of loosely linked sayings. In distinction from most of the material studied thus far, the sayings are attributed to different rabbis, rather than to a single sage. None the less the common designation *Pirke Aboth* ('Chapters of the Fathers') is misleading. For these six *'perakim'* or 'Chapters' from the Mishnah, when they contain references to themselves, use only the term *devarim*, 'sayings'. The critical edition by Taylor[73] begins with the title 'Sayings of the Ancient Fathers' and ends with the subscription of the title to Chapter 6 as *'Sayings* of Meir', rather than the frequently-heard title *Pirke R. Meir*. Also the oldest[74] Rabbinic reference to *Pirke Aboth*, found in the Gemara, b. B. Kamma 30ª, cites Rabbi Jehudah (died A D 299) as referring to 'the *sayings* of "Nezekin"' and Raba (died A D 352) as referring to 'the *sayings* of the fathers'. Here the Aramaic term translated 'sayings' refers to the Hebrew equivalent that is found in the source itself. For *Pirke Aboth* speaks not only of 'the words of the law' (2.5, 8; 3.3f.; 4.7), but also of the 'sayings' of a given rabbi, i.e. 'the sayings of Eleazar ben Arach' (2.13f.; cf. also 5.10; 6.6).

Furthermore the quotation formulae do not refer to the rabbis as 'fathers', and the title Rabban does not occur there until Gamaliel I (1.16; middle of first century A D); not until Jehudah

---

[73] Charles Taylor, *Sayings of the Jewish Fathers*, 1897².

[74] R. Travers Herford, *Pirke Aboth: The Ethics of the Talmud: Sayings of the Fathers*, 1962⁴, p.4.

(2.1; ca. AD 200) does the title Rabbi enter a quotation formula. In the sayings themselves the title Rab is mentioned in passing in 1.6, 16; 6.3, and 'fathers' are mentioned in 2.2. But the sayings refer to the bearers of the sayings tradition predominantly as 'sages': 'May your house be a meeting place for the sages, and cover yourself with the dust of their feet and drink thirstily their sayings' (1.4). The 'wise' are exhorted to watch their 'words' (1.11). When a person challenges this way of life, he does so with the comment that he has lived his whole life among the 'wise' and has learned to prefer silence to the many 'words' that only give rise to sin (1.17). Hence the bearers of this tradition are called 'sages' in a quotation formula (1.5), and at the opening of the subsequently added sixth Chapter. The inference seems unavoidable that the sayings tradition recorded in *Pirke Aboth* would have considered itself 'words of the wise', 'sayings of the sages', even though this formulation does not occur as such in *Pirke Aboth*.

One also finds elsewhere in the Judaism of this period such an association of 'sayings' with the 'sages'. The Testaments of the Twelve Patriarchs are of course regarded as testaments, as the *incipit* 'Copy of the testament of Naphthali that he gave at the time of his departure', and the like, attest. But in seven of the twelve cases the *incipit* is varied to refer to *logoi*, e.g.: 'Copy of the *logoi* of Dan which he spoke to his sons in his last days.' Then follows the exhortation to hearken to the *logoi* (Dan 1.2; Naph. 1.5; Gad 3.1 *v. l.*; Rub. 3.9; Jud. 13.1); when *logoi* has already been used in the *incipit*, the synonym *rhemata* is used in the exhortation (Iss. 1.1b; Zeb. 1.2; Jos. 1.2). Then the patriarch's experiential wisdom is given in analogy to wisdom literature. One may compare the common form of address 'my sons', the speech in praise of 'the wisdom of the wise' (Levi 13.7), the exhortation 'become then sages in God, my sons' (Naph. 8.10), and the parallels to Ahikar.[75] Thus there seems to be some

[75] R. H. Charles, *The Apocrypha and Pseudepigrapha of the Old Testament* II, 1913, p. 291. The form of address 'my son(s)' fits of course the imagined situation of a testament, where a father addresses his son(s). Yet this situation itself is characteristic of wisdom literature (Ahikar; Prov. 31); and the son-

overlapping between the *Gattung* of the 'Testament' and that of
'Sayings of the Sages'. Just as the *Gattung* 'Sayings Collection'
can gain profile by more thorough correlation with the trajectory of the *Gattung* of revelatory discourses of the Resurrected
with his disciples, both would gain in profile if the course of the
Gattung of Testament in this period were to be fully plotted.

Much the same situation is found in the Apocalypse of Adam.
To be sure this document is from Nag Hammadi's gnostic
library (CG V, 5), and hence could have been treated in Section
I above. Yet it is regarded by the editor Alexander Böhlig[76] and
by Kurt Rudolph[77] as an outgrowth of Syrian-Palestinian baptismal sects, documentation for pre- or non-Christian Jewish
gnosticism.[78] Although the work is designated 'The Apocalypse
of Adam' in the title found both before (64.1) and after (85.32)
the text, and has an *incipit* (64.2–4) using the loan word 'apocalypse' ('The revelation that Adam taught his son Seth in the
700th year'), it is in form much like the Testaments of the
Twelve Patriarchs. For the text continues immediately (64.4f.):
'And he said, "Hear my words, my son Seth."' Adam says
(64.12f.) that Eve taught him 'a word of knowledge of God', and
that he heard 'words' from the three great men (66.9f.), namely
the revelation he gives Seth (67.14–21). When Adam's narration of the future arrives at Noah, the latter's testament is
similarly introduced (72.18f.): 'He [Noah] will say to them,
"My sons, hear my words."' And at the end of the work Adam's
speech closes (85.3–18): 'The words of the God of the aeons that
they (those with gnosis) have preserved did not (of themselves)
come into the book nor are they written (at all). Rather angelic

---

ship is readily spiritualized and thus made generally applicable (*Corpus
Hermeticum* 13). To be sure the Testaments are less collections of transmitted
sayings than invented discourses. Hence these *logoi* are in form more comparable to the gnostic and apologetic *logoi*, where the collector has been replaced by the author and the sayings collection by the dialogue, discourse or
tractate.

[76] Böhlig and Labib, *Apokalypsen*, p. 95.

[77] In his book review, *ThLZ* 90 (1965), cols. 361f.

[78] Cf. my report in 'The Coptic Gnostic Library Today', *NTS* 14 (1967/
68), pp. 377–8.

ones will bring them, whom all generations of men will not recognize. For they will come on a high mountain on a rock of truth. Hence they will be called "the words of incorruption and of truth", of those who know the eternal God with wisdom, gnosis and doctrine from angels for eternity. For he knows everything.' In the concluding framework the concept 'apocalypse' recurs (85.19–29): 'These are the revelations that Adam revealed to Seth his son and that his son taught his seed. This is the hidden *gnosis* of Adam that he gave to Seth, the holy baptism of those who know the eternal *gnosis* through those born of *logos*, (and) the imperishable luminaries who came forth from the holy seed.' Here those 'with wisdom', called 'luminaries',[79] could well be a gnosticized and mythologized development of the concept of the sages as the bearers of the saving 'words'.

The situation is similar with another 'apocalypse', the Ethiopian Enoch, which according to the oldest documentation was called the 'Words of Enoch the Righteous' (Test. Ben. 9.1; cf. Jub. 21.10, 'in the words of Enoch and the words of Noah'). The *incipit* reads: 'Words of the blessing of Enoch', and a superscription in 14.1 reads: 'The Book of the Words of Righteousness' (cf. 14.3: 'words of wisdom'), just as at the end of the parenetic book in chs. 91–105 the terms 'words' and 'wisdom' recur. This relationship of words to wisdom is especially clear in the Similitudes, chs. 37–71, whose origin as an independent work is recognizable by means of the superscription in 37.1f.[80] For here the

---

[79] The gnostic redeemer is named 'luminary' (*phoster*, 76,9f. 28; 77,15; 82,28); so are his parents (82,7), who, according to Böhlig, *Apokalypsen*, p. 93, are the sun and moon (cf. Gen. 1.16 and Rev. 12.1), and the gnostics themselves (75.14f.; 85.28). Cf. also the four 'luminaries' of the Apocryphon of John, CG II, 7. 33ff. (Krause and Labib, *Apokryphon*, pp. 129ff.). This term 'luminaries' (Gen. 1.14–16 LXX) occurs in the title, preserved on a fragment, of a Qumran document, 'Words of the Luminaries' (4Q Dib Ham). Both the meaning of the title and its relation to the liturgical contents are unclear. Maurice Baillet, 'Un Recueil Liturgique de Qumrân, Grotte 4: "Les Parôles des Luminaires"', *RB* 68 (1961), pp. 195–250, esp. p. 249, conjectures that the title does not refer to the contents, but rather to the occasion when the material was used. On this assumption he arrives at the translation 'liturgie d'après les luminaires', i.e. 'office selon les jours de la semaine'. Such a translation seems, however, to be quite strained.

[80] Otto Eissfeldt, *Einleitung*, p. 764 (ET: p. 618).

work is introduced as 'Words of Wisdom', as well as with the
exhortation to listen to the 'words of the holy one' (*v. l.* 'holy
words'), since the Lord of spirits has never before granted such
'wisdom'. Hence it is not surprising to find in ch. 42 the *locus
classicus* for the Sophia myth, attesting the otherwise only 'conjectured view that the hiddenness of wisdom [alluded to in wisdom literature] is the consequence of her rejection by men'.[81]
Thus we are directed a step further back, into the wisdom
literature in the narrower sense.

The term 'wisdom literature' is itself a reflection of an early
Christian title for the book of Proverbs. Eusebius (*HE* IV, 22.9),
in discussing Hegesippus, says: 'And not only he but also
Irenaeus and the whole company of the ancients called the Pro-
verbs of Solomon All-virtuous Wisdom.' The use of this title in
I Clem. 57.3 has already been noted.

The book of Proverbs 'bears on its forehead more clearly than
do other books the traces of its origin. For its individual parts
have special superscriptions, and these show that the section
following each one comprised at some time an independent
collection.'[82] Since the first collection, 1.1–9.18 (like the second,
10.1–22.16, and fifth, chs. 25–29) bears the superscription
'Proverbs of Solomon', the whole book was subsequently given
this name. Hence the term 'proverb' has been the basic term
used in discussing the sayings in wisdom literature. Less
noticed is the term used in other collections in the book of
Proverbs. Chapter 30 bears the superscription 'The Sayings
of Agur Son of Jakeh of Massa', and Ch. 31 the superscription
'The Sayings of Lemuel, King of Massa, which his mother
taught him'. Both superscriptions are less clearly set apart as
superscriptions in the LXX than in the Hebrew, which may
account for their having been less noted than the term
'proverb'.

Already in the Hebrew text the superscription of the collection in Prov. 22.17–24.22 'was taken up into the first verse of the
collection it introduces (22.17); but, as the LXX shows, it be-

81 Bultmann, *EUCHARISTERION* II, p. 9.
82 Eissfeldt, *Einleitung*, p. 579 (ET: p. 471).

longs before this verse'.[83] This superscription reads 'The Sayings
of the Sages'[84] (cf. the *incipit* in the LXX: 'To the *logoi* of the
sages lend your ear and hear my *logos*'). Here the superscription
'Sayings of [a given Sage]' used for Prov. 30 and 31 is generalized
into 'Sayings of the Sages' (LXX: λόγοι σοφῶν, *logoi sophon*), and
so presents itself as the fitting designation for the *Gattung* that the
sources here investigated have tended to put in profile.

The designation 'sayings' occurs in a superscription again in
Eccl. 1.1, 'The Words of the Preacher, the Son of David, King of
Jerusalem', although to be sure the LXX here uses the translational variant *rhemata* in place of *logoi*. Towards the conclusion
(12.10) the book speaks again of the preacher's 'sayings of delight'
and 'sayings of truth'. Then in 12.11 one finds praise of the 'sayings of the sages', the same expression as at Prov. 22.17. Even
though Eccl. 12.11 is not readily translatable[85] (RSV: 'The
sayings of the sages are like goads, and like nails firmly fixed are
the collected sayings which are given by one Shepherd'), we
seem to have to do with the designation for a *Gattung* that is
recognizable as such.

When one inquires behind Jewish wisdom literature, one finds
similar collections in Egypt and Mesopotamia. In Egypt the
common *incipit* of such collections of sayings is 'Beginning of the
instruction'. Hence the expression 'Sayings of the Sages' at the
opening of the sayings collection in Prov. 22.17–24.22, a source
that has been shown to go back to the Book of Wisdom of Amen-

---

[83] Eissfeldt, *Einleitung*, p. 580 (ET: p. 471).

[84] It is unclear whether in the superscription to 24.23–34, 'also these are
of the wise', the term 'proverbs' is to be understood, or, as the preceding
superscription 22.17 (LXX 30.1) would suggest, the term 'sayings'. Cf. RSV:
'These also are sayings of the wise.'

[85] The obscure words could mean 'collected sayings' (RSV), '(Spruch)-
sammlung' (Zimmerli, Altes Testament Deutsch, *ad loc.*), and thus could be
understood as a description of the *Gattung*. Yet the LXX has here a different
reading, and commentators have emended the text in various ways. Further
it is unclear whether the one shepherd to whom the sayings of the sages are
attributed is God (RSV) or Solomon (so Eissfeldt, *Einleitung*, p. 608; ET:
p. 493, who takes the phrase to allude to the book of Proverbs). In the latter
case the use of the plural ('sages') to designate the sayings of an individual
sage would be intelligible best on the assumption that a current designation
for a *Gattung* is simply taken over without adaptation.

em-Opet, cannot itself be attributed to the Egyptian *Vorlage*.[86] Perhaps an antecedent for the title can more nearly be found in Mesopotamia. For the Ahikar collection, from which Prov. 23.13–14 seem to have been borrowed,[87] may have been designated as 'sayings'. To be sure the Ethiopian fragments, preserved in the 'Book of the Wise Philosophers', reflect Egyptian usage in the superscription 'Instruction of Ahikar the Sage'.[88] But Ahikar's collection of sayings in the Syrian version A begins by calling upon his son Nadan to regard Ahikar's 'sayings' as he would God's words.[89] And the Aramaic version (fifth century BC) speaks occasionally of Ahikar's 'counsel and sayings'.[90] The Ahikar collection is also relevant in terms of its contents, in that parallels with various other collections, including Q, occur (Matt. 24.48–51, par. Luke 12.45–46); the Syrian version also shows affinities of style with the 'Sayings of Agur' (Prov. 30).[91]

It should be well known that designations for *Gattungen* are less precisely and consistently used as technical terms in the sources themselves than in modern scholarship. Furthermore we are not obliged to derive our designations for *Gattungen* from the sources. It is enough that the *Gattungen* themselves have been shown to exist there. However, the tendency or direction of a *Gattung* comes more readily to our attention if a movement of language can be found in the sources that names what is constitutive of the *Gattung* and thus brings its tendency to expression. The fact that the sayings collection as a *Gattung* tended to

---

[86] Cf. the section 'Egyptian Instructions' in *Ancient Near Eastern Texts relating to the Old Testament*, ed. by James B. Pritchard, 1955², pp.412–25, esp. 'The Instruction of Amen-em-Opet', pp.421–4.

[87] Cf. Eissfeldt, *Einleitung*, p.584 (ET: p.475).

[88] Cf. *The Story of Ahikar*, ed. by F. C. Conybeare, J. Rendel Harris, and Agnes Smith Lewis, 1913², pp.xxiv–xxv, 128f.

[89] *The Story of Ahikar*, p.103.

[90] To be sure Karl Ludwig Schmidt, *EUCHARISTERION* II, p.63, seems to go too far in claiming that the Aramaic title read: 'Sayings of a wise and instructed scribe named Ahikar, which he taught his son.' For the decisive first word is lacking in the fragmentary text and is not presupposed in the English translation (*The Story of Ahikar*, p.168).

[91] E.g. Prov.30.21: 'three things . . . and four'; 30.24: 'four things are . . . '; cf. *The Story of Ahikar*, p.lvii; Eissfeldt, *Einleitung*, p.98 (ET: pp.85f.).

associate the speaker of the sayings with the sage has become audible in noting the connection between 'sayings', *logoi* and 'sages', *sophoi*, which in substance leads to *logoi sophon*, 'Sayings of the Sages' or 'Words of the Wise', as a designation for the *Gattung*.[92]

The movement of the sayings of Jesus into collections of sayings has already been discussed. There remains only the question as to what effect there would be upon such collections in view of the wisdom implications they bore. It can be presupposed that some wisdom sayings were among Jesus' sayings from the beginning, which could of course have facilitated the collection of his sayings into this *Gattung*. The addition of further wisdom sayings would be facilitated within the *Gattung*, whose proclivities were to be more concerned with the validity or 'truth' of the sayings incorporated than with their human authorship or 'authenticity'. Ulrich Luck[93] has sketched the development from the apocalyptic context that may have predominated in Jesus' sayings to a wisdom context predominating in the sayings in Matthew, who of all the canonical Evangelists retains closest affinities with the *Gattung* of Sayings Collections, in spite of his having imbedded Q in the Gospel *Gattung* of Mark. This movement is made all the more comprehensible in view of the emerging

[92] To be sure the term 'words' seems to occur in the *incipit* of various kinds of Hebrew works, such as Deut. 1.1; 28.69; Amos 1.1; Neh. 1.1; Baruch 1.1. It figures in the superscription of the Ten Commandments (Ex. 20.1; 34.28; cf. 24.3, 4, 8). In the titles of the historical sources of the books of Kings the term '*devarim* of days' occurs, with quite a different meaning from 'words', i.e. the whole phrase means 'history' or (RSV) 'chronicles'. In the case of Solomon, I Kings 11.41, 'The Book of the History (or Chronicles) of Solomon' is a title to which the content, as established by Martin Noth, (*Überlieferungsgeschichtliche Studien*, 1957², pp. 66f.) would be well suited. Yet in this one instance 'of days' has been omitted, either in deference to the usage of *devarim* at the opening of the verse to embrace both action and wisdom, or as a scribal error. Hence the dangling '*devarim* of . . .' could be taken not only to mean 'The Book of the *Acts* of Solomon' (RSV), in analogy to other such historical works. It could also be mistaken as analogous to the other Solomon literature, i.e. wisdom literature. Hence the shortened title could be taken to mean 'Book of the *Sayings* of Solomon'. Such a misunderstanding would be a further reflection of the association of 'words' and 'sages'.

[93] *Die Vollkommenheitsforderung der Bergpredigt* (ThEx 150), 1968.

scholarly awareness that apocalypticism and wisdom, rather than being at almost mutually exclusive extremes within the spectrum of Jewish alternatives, share certain affinities and congruencies that encourage a transition from one to the other.

There are in the Synoptic Gospels peripheral indications of an association of Jesus with personified Wisdom. In Q (Matt. 11.19, par. Luke 7.35) Jesus and John the Baptist seem to function as bearers of or spokesmen for Wisdom; in Luke 11.49 a Q saying is introduced as spoken by Wisdom, which in Matt. 23.34 is spoken by Jesus himself. M. Jack Suggs[94] has worked out this christological development from Q, which regarded Jesus merely as Wisdom's envoy, to Matthew, which identified Jesus directly as Wisdom. Thus, prior to the elimination of the *Gattung* of Sayings Collections completely from emergent orthodoxy, one can sense a development whose more radical correlative and ultimate outcome can be seen only in Gnosticism.[95]

Q's association of Jesus with Wisdom together with its criticism of the sages (Matt. 11.25, par. Luke 10.21) provides a foretaste of the debate to come. The Gospel of Thomas indicates

[94] *Wisdom, Christology and Law in Matthew's Gospel*, 1970. Cf. Koester, 'The Structure and Criteria of Early Christian Beliefs', in *Trajectories through Early Christianity*, 1971, ch. 6.

[95] It is hoped that the English translation has here overcome the ambiguity of the German text responsible for the critical question of Wilhelm Wuellner, *JBL* 84 (1965), p. 302: 'I question the view that the *Gattung* "as such" provoked subsequent association of Jesus with the *sophos/hakam* tradition, and wonder whether it was not the other way round.' The article does not presuppose the absence of such an association prior to the time Jesus' sayings were brought into collections. Wisdom sayings may well have been transmitted as individual sayings of Jesus prior to their incorporation in a collection (just as Matt. 11.19 par. may be older than Q); and there were early christological developments related to Wisdom outside the sayings tradition (cf. my remarks in 'A Formal Analysis of Col. 1.15–20', *JBL* 76, 1957, pp. 270–87, esp. 277–80). The purpose of the present essay is to draw attention to the *Gattung* and the tendency at work in it, and thus to gain some awareness of the influence that would be at work upon the sayings tradition by being transmitted in this *Gattung*. This is intended to help to make intelligible the development from Q to the Gospel of Thomas, as an aspect of the general development from Jewish wisdom to Hellenistic Gnosticism, from God's Sophia to the gnostic redeemer. This scope is well sensed by Helmut Koester, '*GNOMAI DIAPHOROI*', *Trajectories through Early Christianity*, ch. 4.

the gnosticizing distortion of sayings that took place readily within this *Gattung*. Hence the ongoing orthodox criticism of this distortion provides something of a context for understanding the process in which Q[96] is imbedded in the Marcan outline by Matthew and Luke and continues to be acceptable in the orthodox church only in the context of this other *Gattung*, that of 'Gospel'.

The tendency at work in the *Gattung logoi sophon* was coordinated to the trajectory from the hypostasized Sophia to the gnostic redeemer. As 'hidden sayings', the *Gattung* found a place in Gnosticism. But with the dying out of the oral tradition of Jesus' sayings, it fell into disuse even here. For the *Gattung* of dialogues of the Resurrected with his disciples provided a freer context for the imaginary gnostic speculations attributed to Jesus.

[96] Cf. with regard to Q my papers 'Basic Shifts in German Theology', *Interpretation* 16 (1962), pp. 76–97, esp. pp. 82–6, and 'A Critical Inquiry into the Scriptural Bases of Confessional Hermeneutics', *Journal of Ecumenical Studies* 3 (1966), pp. 48–9 (reprinted in *Encounter* 28 [1967], pp. 28–9).

6

ΒΑΠΤΙΣΜΑ ΜΕΤΑΝΟΙΑΣ ΕΙΣ
ΑΦΕΣΙΝ ΑΜΑΡΤΙΩΝ*

Hartwig Thyen

I

THE baptism of John the Baptist[1] is characterized by Mark (Mark 1.4 = Luke 3.3[2]) as βάπτισμα μετανοίας εἰς ἄφεσιν ἁμαρτιῶν.

* Translated from *Zeit und Geschichte*, pp. 97–125.

[1] ὁ βαπτίζων instead of ὁ βαπτιστής only here and 6.12, 24; cf. W. Marxsen, *Der Evangelist Markus* (FRLANT 67) 1959[2], p. 19 (ET: p. 33), contrary to E. Lohmeyer, *Das Evangelium des Markus* (Meyer), 1959[15] *ad loc.* The fixed surname ὁ βαπτιστής, also attested in Josephus (*Antiq.* xviii. 116ff.), shows that *baptism*, not the preaching of repentance, is the essential and characteristic mark of John. See also P. Vielhauer, 'Johannes der Täufer', *RGG*[3], III, cols. 804–808 (bibliog.).

[2] Unlike Matthew (see below, note 31), Luke can follow the Marcan formulation here because for him repentance and forgiveness are merely the preparation for and condition of salvation; they are not salvation itself. This is also the explanation of the fact that he can take over the Johannine birth stories so uninhibitedly. Because John mediates the forgiveness of sins he is for Luke the appropriate precursor of the σωτήρ and his σωτηρία. In Luke's hands repentance and forgiveness are moralized – in contrast to their original sacramental and cultic meaning – and John is thus assimilated to the preacher of social ethics. Cf. the thorough analysis of this matter, in a different connection, in Hans Conzelmann, *Die Mitte der Zeit* (BhTh 17), 1962[4], pp. 198ff. (ET: *The Theology of St Luke*, pp. 225–8). 'For Luke, the content of salvation is ζωή or σωτηρία, and the basis of it is forgiveness, which in turn is conditional upon repentance' (*ibid.*, pp. 200f. [ET: p. 228]). What we have said above about Luke's reception of the Baptist tradition fits exactly with this view.

Vincent Taylor, in *Forgiveness and Reconciliation* (London, 1956[5]), views the whole of the NT materials too one-sidedly through Lucan glasses. Hence he comes out with a quite illegitimate harmonization of the materials, glosses over the sharp and vital individual contours, and finally subsumes the whole under the category 'reconciliation', which is by no means a central NT concept.

Although Mark is concerned solely with the preaching of repentance by John as the lesser forerunner and with his testimony
to the Stronger One who shall follow him,[3] the formulation
βάπτισμα μετανοίας εἰς ἄφεσιν ἁμαρτιῶν, which Mark apparently
took over from the tradition, shows clearly[4] that he is no mere
preacher of repentance. The anarthrous usage clearly reflects
technical theological language[5] and characterizes John's baptism as an eschatological sacrament which effects both repentance and forgiveness.[6] The hendiadys 'repentance and forgive-

[3] It seems to me questionable that κηρύσσων βάπτισμα κτλ. should be taken
as a Johannine testimony to the practice of auto-baptism, in which case the
D reading ἐνώπιον αὐτοῦ in Luke 3.7 would also point in this direction (so,
following others, Dibelius, *Die urchristliche Überlieferung von Johannes dem Täufer*
[1911], p. 135). Kurt Rudolph, *Die Mandäer* I (FRLANT 74), 1960, p. 231,
in dependence on H. V. Martin, 'The Primitive Form of Christian Baptism',
ExpT 59 (1947/48), pp. 160–3, also too quickly assumes that the concept
of auto-baptism is self-evident. It is more probable that one should see a
Christianizing tendency in the use of κηρύσσων in early Christian missionary
language instead of the more primitive βαπτίζων; cf. the expression, βαπτίζειν
βάπτισμα μετανοίας, attested in Acts 19.4 and in the Gospel of the Ebionites
(Epiphanius, *Haer.* 30. 13. 6), the commentaries on the passage, and Oepke
in *TWNT* I, p. 544 (ET: pp. 545f.). Against the concept of auto-baptism see
also Erich Dinkler, 'Taufe', *RGG³* VI, 62 and Vielhauer, *RGG³* III, 805.
The expression 'the Baptist', for which there are no analogies, also clearly
attests the practice of baptism by John; otherwise we should expect κῆρυξ τοῦ
βαπτίσματος or some such expression. The concept of auto-baptism is connected
also with the highly questionable assumption that proselyte baptism is the
model and forerunner of John's baptism; cf. George Foot Moore, *Judaism* I,
pp. 331ff. and Carl H. Kraeling, *John the Baptist* (1951), pp. 95ff. The expression ὑπ' αὐτοῦ in Matt. 3.6 should also be noted.

[4] Because of the tendency, shared by Mark with the entire Christian
tradition, to make John the forerunner of Jesus and because of the story of
the healing of the paralytic, which reaches its high point in the question τίς
δύναται ἀφιέναι ἁμαρτίας εἰ μὴ εἷς ὁ θεός; (Mark 2.7; cf. Bill. *ad loc.*) we must
assume that the expression βάπτισμα μετανοίας εἰς ἄφεσιν ἁμαρτιῶν was so fixed a
designation for John's baptism that it could hardly be suppressed. An indirect
evidence of this is provided by Josephus' explanation (*Antiq.* xviii, 116ff.) that
John's baptism did not effect the forgiveness of sins (see below, note 6).

[5] On this usage cf. the pertinent remarks of L. Köhler, *Kleine Lichter*, 1945,
pp. 84f.

[6] The clearest evidence for this is the apocalyptic context of John's baptism and its typological correspondence with the coming baptism of fire,
which is broken by Mark (1.8) but preserved in Q (Matt. 3.11f. ≒ Luke
3.16f.). Just as the latter is once and finally efficacious, so is the former; just
as the latter destroys, the former rescues. Consequently, in agreement with

ness' implies no less than the final, eschatological salvation.[7]

C. M. Edsman, *La baptême de feu* (ASNU 9) 1940, Kraeling (*op. cit.*) asserts that for John the Jordan represents the fiery river of apocalyptic and that *voluntary* baptism in the former saves from *involuntary* baptism in the latter. 'John's baptism would, therefore, be a rite symbolic of the acceptance of the judgment which he proclaimed' (pp. 117f.).

On the Iranian concept of the river of fire, cf. 1QH 3.14ff., 28ff.; II En. 10.2ff.; 1QH 6.16ff.; 8.17ff.; Sib. Or. III 72f. (here combined with the concept of the Flood), and Pseud. Clem. Hom. 11.26: προσφεύγετε τῷ ὕδατι. τοῦτο γὰρ μόνον τὴν τοῦ πυρὸς ὁμὴν σβέσαι δύναται; on this, see Heinrich Schlier, *Religionsgeschichtliche Untersuchungen zu den Ignatiusbriefen* (BZNW 8), 1929, pp. 146f. See further Karl G. Kuhn, 'Die Sektenschrift und die iranische Religion', *ZThK* 49 (1952), pp. 307ff.

F. Lang, in his article, 'πῦρ κτλ.' (*TWNT* VI, p. 943 [ET: p. 943]) misses the genuine significance of the baptism of fire and hence has John announce the Messiah, who will baptize with Spirit (!) and fire.

Kraeling also rightly notes that John's baptism does not reflect an initiatory rite, for that presupposes the idea of a gathered and exclusive community. The wilderness typology connected with the Baptist also serves to describe the eschatological saving significance of baptism, even though this typology is quickly Christianized into a conception of a wilderness *preacher* and is misunderstood by Matt. and Luke as a geographical item; cf. Marxsen, *op. cit.*, pp. 26f. Kraeling is quite right when he interprets Josephus' statement (note 4, above) as follows: Josephus wishes, as a Jew, to make it clear to his Gentile readers that Judaism possesses no sacraments analogous to the Gentile mysteries (120ff.). It is more questionable, however, when Kraeling appropriates Josephus' view and polemically opposes a sacramental understanding of John's baptism like that vigorously represented, e.g., by Rudolf Otto, *Reich Gottes und Menschensohn*, 1954[3], pp. 73ff. (ET: pp. 76f.). He does this under the influence of John's preaching of repentance without sufficiently taking into account, in my opinion, the fact that the tendency in early Christianity is to make the wilderness baptizer into the wilderness preacher of repentance; hence he does not judge John's preaching more critically.

Bultmann as early as 1926, in his *Jesus* (1951[2], p. 25; ET: *Jesus and the Word*, p. 26), speaks of John's baptism as an 'eschatological sacrament'.

If we may see in John's baptism the saving and efficacious anticipation of the destructive baptism of fire then this would be evidence for an essential element in Paul's understanding of baptism (in Rom. 6), and sayings like Mark 10.38f. and Luke 12.50 should be judged in the same light; cf. Dinkler, *op. cit.*, p. 627 and Martin Dibelius, 'Täufer', *RGG*[2] III, 318. The pre-Pauline Christian contribution to the doctrine of baptism would then be the relating of dying in baptism to the death of Jesus, while Paul's contribution would be the emphasis on the Not Yet, i.e., the characterizing of Christian existence as a new relationship of service (unlike Eph. and Col.!).

Cf. also Pistis Sophia 143 and Sib. Or. IV. 161ff. (In the latter passage, however, Dinkler, *RGG*[3] VI, 628, finds Christian redaction.)

[7] The concept of μετάνοια which is here presupposed and its firm connection

We need not enter here into the yet unresolved question of the *religionsgeschichtlich* significance and origin of John and his baptism. But it would be helpful if we could lay to rest, and not only in our present context, the old alternatives 'Judaism or Hellenism' – still reflected even in the article '*βάπτω κτλ.*' in the *Wörterbuch*[8] – as comprising a sterile polemic category. That this is what it is has been shown by recent studies and the discoveries and excavations at Qumran, which have revealed in even the Palestinian soil heretofore judged completely orthodox the presence of a Hellenistic Judaism apparently long and thoroughly permeated with a peculiar dualism, possibly of Iranian origin.[9]

---

with ἄφεσις are not to be traced solely to the cultic, ritual penitential practice of the OT, nor to the proclamation of the prophets, nor to LXX usage (cf. Würthwein/Behm in *TWNT* IV, pp. 972ff. [ET: pp. 975–1008]); it points rather towards a syncretistic Judaism.

The association of μετάνοια and ἄφεσις in express relationship to σωτηρία occurs in the Prayer of Manasseh (v. 7); this is also the proper context of the conception of the penitential angel, Phanuel (I En. 40.9) and the eschatological *dies paenitentiae* (Ass. Mos. 1.18); cf. further Test. Gad 5.17ff. (the moralistic retouching seems to be secondary); Philo, *De somn.* i. 105ff.; *De Abr.* 17; *Quaest. Gen.* i. 82; *De spec. leg.* i. 187; *De fug.* 157; Corp. Herm. i. 28; I En. 12.5 (εἰρήνη and ἄφεσις, in synonymous parallelism); Luke 1.71 (σωτηρία interpreted by the term ἄφεσις, a Baptist tradition, see below); etc.

Erik Sjöberg, *Gott und die Sünder* (BWANT 4, 27) 1939, is oriented too one-sidedly to the question of the dogma of recompense and its rejection.

[8] A. Oepke, *TWNT* I, pp. 534ff. (ET: pp. 53ff.) would derive John's baptism exclusively from Jewish baptisms. But he overlooks especially the Christian tendencies in the description of John.

On the question of proselytizing and proselyte baptism, cf. K. G. Kuhn, 'Proselyten', in Pauly-Wissowa and the brief bibliography on the whole discussion in Rudolph, *op. cit.*, p. 230 n. 2.

On the question of Mandean relationships see most recently *ibid.*, pp. 66ff., as well as Dinkler and Vielhauer, *op. cit.*

[9] Cf. esp. Hugo Odeberg, *The Fourth Gospel*, 1929; R. Bultmann, *Das Evangelium des Johannes* (Meyer), 1959[16]; Hans Jonas, *Gnosis und spätantiker Geist*, I and II/i (FRLANT 51 and 63), I (1934) 1954[2], II 1954 (see esp. the material on Philo); Hartwig Thyen in *ThR* 23 (1955), pp. 230ff.; Egon Brandenburger, *Adam und Christus* (WMANT 7) 1962; etc.

On Qumran: Herbert Braun, *Spätjüdisch-häretischer und frühchristlicher Radikalismus*, 2 vols., 1957 (BhTh 24). Bibliography on the discussion in J. Maier, *Die Texte vom Toten Meer*, 2 vols., 1960 (see II, pp. 18f.).

On Mandaeanism: Rudolph, *op. cit.*

The question of the origins of such Jewish heterodoxy and the beginnings of a Jewish Gnosis need not be discussed here; cf., *inter alia*, K. G. Kuhn,

As long as no new and unambiguous *religionsgeschichtlich* material *forces* us to revise this judgment, we must therefore follow Vielhauer and Rudolph[10] in judging John's baptism to be the Baptist's 'original creation' on the soil of a heterodox Judaism[11] which differed widely from Talmudic Judaism.[12]

Therefore apart from the *religionsgeschichtlich* question, we see in John the Baptist a man who sees himself as sacramentally effecting the eschatological forgiveness of sins which rightly belongs to God alone.[13] Hence he constructs 'in the wilderness' the sacred highway for the coming of God, the work to which in the call of Second Isaiah the angelic forces summoned one another.[14] There is no room here for any further messianic figure,

---

'Die Sektenschrift und die iranische Religion', *ZThK* 49 (1952), pp. 296–316, and Hans-Joachim Schoeps, *Urgemeinde, Judentum, Gnosis*, 1956, pp. 44–61.

[10] *Op. cit.* In Rudolph, see esp. p. 76, n. 5; cf. further Kraeling, *op. cit.*, pp. 109ff.

[11] In the future we shall increasingly have to recognize the 'domesticated Judaism of the Aboth' (Braun) as only *one* strand in the history of Judaism, on the one hand, and as a restorative counter-process of purification from alien syncretistic tendencies, on the other. The presence of the 'Hellenists' in Jerusalem (Acts 6.3) shows that we must reckon with the existence of a heterodox Judaism even in Judaism's principal city (see below, n. 83). This has important consequences for the dating and evaluating of the Talmudic tradition; cf. Schoeps, *op. cit.*, pp. 44ff.

[12] The greatest possible caution must be exercised in asserting *religionsgeschichtlich* dependence.

[13] Cf. Mark 2.7 and the commentaries *ad loc.*; esp. Bill. I, p. 495.

[14] Karl Ludwig Schmidt (*Rahmen der Geschichte Jesu*, 1919, pp. 21ff.) notes an inconsistency in the gospel's connecting of two originally distinct motifs, namely that of the wilderness preacher, on the one hand, and that of the one who baptizes in the Jordan, on the other; but this misses the mark, in so far as the conception of the wilderness *preacher* is a secondary, even a Christian, motif. On the other hand, the wilderness typology seems to have belonged to the original Baptist tradition, as is evidenced by John's dress, manner of life, and (Elijah's) girdle; see above, note 6 (*Rahmen der Geschichte Jesu* 1919, pp. 21ff.); cf. Marxsen, *op. cit.*, pp. 20ff. (ET: pp. 35ff.); Günther Bornkamm, *Jesus von Nazareth*, 1956, pp. 40ff. (ET: pp. 44–7). On the wilderness motif, see Martin Hengel, *Die Zeloten*, 1956, pp. 255ff.

Marxsen's correct observation that Mark 1.2f. is the only formula quotation in the entire gospel (p. 18 [ET: p. 32]), is evidence, in my view, *against* seeing in this passage the evangelist's work. The syntactical difficulties are more easily explained as resulting from taking over Baptist tradition than as Marcan composition. For a different view, see Ferdinand Hahn, *Christologische Hoheitstitel* (FRLANT 83, 1963), pp. 378f.; but see 1QS 8.12–16.

for either a political Messiah or the apocalyptic Son of Man.[15] The Judge of all the earth will himself ratify in the coming baptism of fire what John's baptism has already decided.[16]

This baptismal forgiveness is the final opportunity for repentance provided by God.[17] Beyond it stands no second repentance, but only the Judgment. This and other factors require us to ask whether the Christendom of the Epistle to the Hebrews and the polemic found there against a second repentance do not arise out of a Christendom influenced by Baptist conceptions.[18] On these grounds the *potestas clavium* and I John are to be judged anti-Baptist documents and emphases, as illustrations of the triumph of grace and thus – though naturally in a sense completely different from what the Baptist intended – of the triumph of the Stronger One.[19]

The Baptist's ethical instruction (Luke 3.10–14) is a late parenetic formulation of Hellenistic Christianity, probably constructed by Luke himself and placed on the lips of John.[20] In the view of the historical John there is neither time nor place for concern with such social teaching or its preservation.[21] Is not

[15] ὁ ἰσχυρότερος (Mark 1.7) is a Jewish circumlocution for the divine name. According to Mal. 3.25 Elijah is the herald of Yahweh himself. Furthermore, any proclamation by John of a Messiah would have left a clearer deposit, extending even to the nomenclature, in the Synoptics and in the Fourth Gospel. Lang's view (*op. cit.*) is surely unsatisfactory. Vielhauer holds that ἰσχυρότερος is the title of a transcendental figure who is to be distinguished from God; on this, see below, n. 162f.

[16] When the Judgment is temporally near the possibility of apostasy is simply not considered.

[17] For the conception of repentance as God's gift rather than his demand alone see the texts adduced in Behm, *TWNT* IV, p. 988 (ET: IV, p. 992) and Rom. 2.4.

[18] Heb. 6.8; 10.26ff.; 12.16f. Cf. Herm. Vis. ii. 2. 5 and see Hans Windisch, *Der Hebräerbrief* (HNT 14) 1931², pp. 52ff.; Otto Michel, *Der Brief an die Hebräer* (Meyer) 1960¹¹, pp. 150ff., who refers to the juridical-sacramental character of the concept of repentance in Hebrews and to its relationship with the concept in Qumran.

[19] It is hardly accidental that the concept of μετάνοια is missing in the Fourth Gospel; cf. Bultmann, *Johannesevang.*, p. 95.

[20] Cf. Rudolf Bultmann, *Die Geschichte der synoptischen Tradition* (FRLANT 29) 1931², pp. 155, 158f. (ET: pp. 145, 147).

[21] See below, pp. 148ff.

this, and not the gnosticizing proclivities of the evangelist,[22] the proper basis for understanding the critical elimination in the Fourth Gospel of the presumably 'primitive' but actually more probably Baptist apocalyptic?[23] In the light of the anti-Baptist stance which can be – and often has been – observed elsewhere in the gospel of John, such an interpretation would not seem to be wide of the mark; it would also provide additional justification for speaking of the evangelist's 'purified concept of revelation'.[24]

Even in Matthew, who is greatly concerned to portray John's baptism as an effective sacrament for the forgiveness of sins, the old characteristic of that baptism as a βάπτισμα μετανοίας is still visible in the saying taken over from Mark (and Q) ἐγὼ μὲν ὑμᾶς βαπτίζω ἐν ὕδατι[25] εἰς μετάνοιαν, where εἰς μετάνοιαν in any case has a more strongly final sense than the genitive μετανοίας, which is epexegetical. But because water baptism (repentance – as Matthew understands it?) saves from the coming baptism of fire it has a definitive and sacramental significance.[26]

There is another possible interpretation, according to which here (and in Rev. 19.4, where John's baptism is also described as βάπτισμα μετανοίας without the εἰς ἄφεσιν ἁμαρτιῶν) the original, more legalistic sense is maintained: baptism is a seal of the

[22] So Ernst Käsemann, in his review of Bultmann's *Johannesevang.*, in *VuF* 1942/46, p. 200.

[23] Cf. Ernst Fuchs, 'Das Zeitverständnis Jesu', *Ges. Aufs.*, II, 1960, pp. 304–76 (ET: pp. 104–66) and see below, note 67.

[24] Cf. the index to Bultmann's *Johannesevang.* under the word 'Offenbarung'.

[25] The phrase ἐν ὕδατι (3.11) does not arise as a Christian interpretation, created to contrast John's baptism as a mere water baptism with the Christian baptism of the Spirit; rather it corresponded originally with the coming baptism of fire, which affords a simple explanation of the elimination of the baptism of fire and the substitution of the baptism of the Spirit for it. Naturally, the baptism of the Spirit is not part of what John promised; cf. Herbert Braun, 'Qumran und das NT', *ThR* 28 (1962), pp. 106f.

[26] Naturally, this is no sufficient reason for denying that John demanded repentance; but this is hardly constitutive for him, and we know nothing of its nature, since what we have of his preaching of repentance (Matt. 3.7–10 = Luke 3.7–9) has at least been very thoroughly retouched by Christian hands, if not (except for the phrase about the baptism of fire) completely formulated by them.

Baptist's message of repentance[27] and only a preliminary step in
salvation. In this case, we would have in the Marcan (and Lucan)
εἰς ἄφεσιν ἁμαρτιῶν a fixed *interpretatio christiana* of John's baptism.[28] But in the light of the tendency, observable throughout
the NT, to demote John to a mere preacher of repentance and
the precursor of Jesus, this interpretation is extremely improbable.[29] In addition, there are specific dogmatic grounds for the
Marcan omission of εἰς ἄφεσιν ἁμαρτιῶν. Just as the mere thought
that Jesus should have allowed himself to be baptized (εἰς μετάνοιαν!) by John, the forerunner, is so repugnant that he is forced
to legitimize this baptism by creating (on the analogy of Gal.
4.4) a conversation between Jesus and John,[30] so also the thought
that the saving gift of the forgiveness of sins, based solely on

---

[27] Dibelius (*Täufer*, pp. 58f.) is much too prone, in my opinion, to begin
with John's preaching of repentance rather than his baptism; he also holds
that John expected a Messiah, so that he even considers the question of John's
disciples (Matt. 11.1ff. par.) authentic (pp. 33ff.) and consequently sees John's
baptism as a purely 'interim' phenomenon. The εἰς ἄφεσιν ἁμαρτιῶν is correspondingly eliminated as a Christian elaboration. Against Dibelius, see
also Hahn, *op. cit.*, p. 371; Herbert Braun, 'Die Täufertaufe und die qumranischen Waschungen', *ThViat* 9 (1964), p. 3.

[28] So many exegetes. See, e.g., Lohmeyer *ad loc.*; Dibelius, *RGG*² III,
315; in the right direction, but still undecided, Julius Schniewind, *Das
Evangelium nach Mk* (NTD 1) 1960⁹, p. 10; cf. Erich Klostermann, *Das
Markusevangelium* (HNT 3), p. 10, etc.

[29] At least two things speak very unambiguously against this view:
Josephus' (mis)interpretive note about the forgiveness of sins (see above,
note 6), and the descriptive comment on John that he would give to the
people the knowledge of salvation through the forgiveness of sins (δοῦναι γνῶσιν
σωτηρίας τῷ λαῷ αὐτοῦ ἐν ἀφέσει ἁμαρτιῶν), in a very ancient fragment of unquestionably Baptist provenance (Luke 1.77; on this, see below, p. 156).
May we also add a third, the silence of the Fourth Gospel about baptismal
forgiveness and the connection of ἄφεσις to the gift of the Spirit by the Exalted
Lord, all of which corresponds closely to the inclusion of βαπτισμοί (plural!)
among the elementary doctrines in Heb. 6.1f. and the inclusion of the
obviously polemic comment that without the shedding of blood there is
no forgiveness in the Λόγος τέλειος? (See below.)

[30] Of course Bornkamm is quite right (*Jesus*, pp. 43f. [ET: p. 48]) in
emphasizing the fact that Matthew's reserve is motivated not by the (later)
dogma of Jesus' sinlessness but by the fact that once the Promised One has
appeared John's baptism has no more meaning. Nevertheless it is apparent
that the way for the former development is already being prepared by the
temptation story, which follows immediately; cf. Kraeling, *op. cit.*, pp. 132ff.

Christ's sacrificial blood, was already available in the forerunner's baptism is completely unacceptable to him.[31] This is
why Matthew, in his description of John's baptism, omits the εἰς
ἄφεσιν ἁμαρτιῶν and consciously and deliberately inserts it into
the words of institution: only Jesus' shed blood grants to his
community the gift of the forgiveness of sins, and (so we may
continue – with Luther – the Matthean thought) 'where the forgiveness of sins is, there is life and blessedness'.[32] In Matthew's
suppression of the sacramental understanding of John's baptism as a means of forgiveness, then, we could also observe an
unconscious (or perhaps conscious?) anti-Baptist emphasis.[33]

If we look at the Fourth Gospel in this way we find our suggestion confirmed. For here the reserve vis-à-vis John is much
greater. It is also, as Bultmann has shown, greater (apparently)
not because of the increased historical and geographical *distance*
from John but rather because of the evangelist's *nearness* to John
and the Baptist's followers.[34] Here John's baptism has no function except to make known the 'Lamb of God, who takes away
the sin of the world' so that John can assume his *heilsgeschichtlich*

---

[31] Georg Strecker, *Der Weg der Gerechtigkeit* (FRLANT 82) 1962, p. 48
interprets matters correctly when he says that for Matthew ἄφεσις ἁμαρτιῶν 'is
not in any event the basis of John's ministry'. But that is precisely the reason
that it is illegitimate for him to add that 'Matthew takes over ἄφεσις and
its derivatives from the tradition but (unlike Mark) does not particularly
emphasize these concepts'. On the contrary, that is just what he does not
do! Cf. Günther Bornkamm, 'Enderwärtung und Kirche im MtEv', in
Bornkamm-Barth-Held, *Überlieferung und Auslegung im Matthäus-Evangelium*
(WMANT 1), 1961², p. 13 (ET: p. 15; cf. also n. 2), and see the following
notes.

[32] Contrary to Taylor, *op. cit.*, the work of salvation, at least for Matthew,
consists in the forgiveness of sins; cf. Matt. 1.21 and see Nils A. Dahl, *NTS*
2 (1955/56), pp. 17ff.

[33] Matthew 'removes this saving effect from John's baptism and attributes it to the eucharist, in agreement with the ideas set forth earlier, in
1.21' (Heinz Schürmann, *Der Einsetzungsbericht Lk 22, 19–20*, NTAbh 20,
1955, p. 6); cf. Lohmeyer, *ThR* 9 (1937), p. 177. Because he does not recognize
Matthew's programmatic intention, Joachim Jeremias, in *Die Abendmahls-
worte Jesu*, 1960³, p. 165 (cf. ET: p. 114) also sees the origin of the expression
εἰς ἄφεσιν ἁμαρτιῶν in the rite of baptism; cf. Conzelmann, *op. cit.*, p. 15, n. 4
(ET: p. 24 n. 3).

[34] See esp. Bultmann, *Johannesevang.*, pp. 5, 76.

role of μαρτύς to Jesus.[35] R. Gyllenberg, in the *Festschrift* for Rudolf Bultmann on his seventieth birthday, sets forth the notion that we must reckon with the possibility that the adherents of Jesus were kept together during his lifetime only by Jesus himself and that disparate elements began to break apart immediately after his death, so that several forms of Christianity sprang into being simultaneously; on this view, we find in the Fourth Gospel one of these primitive forms. The suggestion deserves much more serious scholarly mention than it has received.[36] For there never was any such thing as a *single* primitive Christianity, *the* original confession, or *the* primitive christology, on the basis of which we might be able to judge every development as either a justifiable or heretical elaboration of the *one* legitimate beginning. And consequently we look in vain for it, either in Paul or in the earliest Synoptic strata. The single Credo of the church arises, not out of the deliberate elaboration of the one true origin, but out of the critical (and thus, of course, also tendentious) simplifying of the original diversity.[37]

The Fourth Gospel goes far beyond Matthew in the depreciation of John and his baptism. Here, in fact, one can truly say that the baby has been thrown out with the bath water. For because baptism is seen as the Baptist's activity, several things have happened: All positive relationships to baptism are lack-

[35] Cf. *ibid.*, p. 31.

[36] R. Gyllenberg, 'Die Anfänge der johanneischen Tradition', *Neutestamentliche Studien für R. Bultmann* (BZNW 21) 1954, pp. 144–7; Gyllenberg, rightly in my opinion, believes that the portrait of the Baptist which emerges in the tradition behind the Fourth Gospel (a Gnostic atmosphere!) is more primitive than the secondary conception found in the synoptics – a preacher of repentance sketched in OT colours. The judgment of John A. T. Robinson is similar; '. . . the fourth Gospel, which preserves, I am persuaded, in the Baptist material some very good independent tradition'. ('Elijah, John and Jesus: An Essay in Detection', p. 264; in *NTS* 4 (1957/58), pp. 263–81 (= *Twelve New Testament Studies* [SBT 34], 1962, pp. 28–52); cf. *ibid.*, n. 2.

[37] Cf. Ernst Käsemann, 'Die Anfänge christlicher Theologie', *ZThK* 57 (1960), pp. 162ff. (= *Exegetische Versuche und Besinnungen* II, 1965², pp. 82ff.; ET: *NT Questions of Today*, pp. 82ff.). It has been Bultmann's service to have seen and pointed out clearly Paul's share in the unifying of the churches into one Church; see, e.g., 'Paulus', *RGG*² IV, col. 1025 (ET in: *Existence and Faith*, p. 119).

ing;[38] the report of Jesus' own baptism, understood in the synoptics as instituting Christian baptism, is also missing, and so is the Risen Lord's command to baptize;[39] and even the account of the foot-washing is clearly slanted against the practice of baptism.[40] If for John there was only one (sacramental) forgiveness and then the final judgment, here the Risen Lord's gift to his church, by which it judges the world, is the right of mutual – not sacramental, but verbal – forgiveness of sins[41] as the work of the Holy Spirit.

The actions of the historical Jesus differ from those of his witnesses. He stands by the Baptist's side and defends him as the 'greatest of those born of women'.[42] Under the influence of John's expectation of the *temporal* nearness of the Kingdom, an expectation which he himself adopts, he submits to the eschatological penitential sacrament of baptism.[43]

[38] Contrary to Dibelius, *Täufer*, pp. 109ff.; depreciation not only of John's baptism, but of baptism in general, for the passages cited by Dibelius to show the high value placed on Christian baptism by the author of the Fourth Gospel belong to the ecclesiastical redaction (see Bultmann, *Johannesevang. passim*). The transformation of water (κατὰ τὸν καθαρισμόν) into wine at the marriage in Cana (John 2.1ff.), on the other hand, is fittingly interpreted by Dibelius (p. 112) as an affront to the Baptist sect.

[39] The Word has replaced the sacrament, pointedly and programmatically: see John 20.22f.

[40] John 13.1–17; so Bultmann, *Johannesevang.*, pp. 357ff., vs. Hans von Campenhausen, *ZNW* 33 (1934), pp. 259–71, who sees baptism reflected in the foot-washing. This could be true for the source, but hardly for the evangelist.

[41] See above, note 39. Since the discussion with Nicodemus occurs in the context of controversy with Baptist theology (if, with Dibelius – see note 38, above – we can include the miracle of the wine in the same context) it is possible to glimpse in the concept of rebirth (3.7ff.) the older understanding of John's baptism, though of course critically reinterpreted to refer to his proclamation (*Wortgeschehen*); see above, note 6 and below, notes 153f.

[42] Cf. Ernst Käsemann, 'Das Problem des historischen Jesus', *ZThK* 51 (1954), p. 149 (ET: *Essays*, p. 43); Bultmann, *Syn. Trad.* pp. 177f. (ET: pp. 164f.); Dibelius, *Täufer*, pp. 9ff.; etc. It is important methodologically to observe, with Bultmann (*ibid.*), that the Christian tradition about John is divided: against the Jews he is claimed as the baptizer of and witness to Jesus, while against the Baptist sect he is treated critically. Hence we must not simply trace every positive statement about John back to Jesus himself.

[43] Imminent expectation is not, however, 'constitutive' for Jesus (Käsemann, *ZThK* 57 [1960], p. 179 = *Exeg. Versuche* p. 99 [ET: p. 101]). It is

While it is certain that the 'delivering up' ($\pi\alpha\rho\alpha\delta o\theta\hat{\eta}\nu\alpha\iota$) of the
Baptist is intended by Mark as a theological motif and not a
biographical item,[44] and that this is made possible only by Jesus'
preaching of the nearness of the Kingdom and his appearance as
the 'Son of Man', it may be taken as equally certain that chronologically speaking Jesus really did begin his ministry only after
John.[45] For one thing, the saying about 'men of violence', which
looks back on John's activity as already concluded, points in this
direction.[46] But the strongest evidence for it is the total lack of
any attempt to separate Jesus from John, such as would have
been clearly visible in the sources if Jesus had proclaimed the
near Basileia simultaneously with John, especially in view of the
lively interest Jesus' witnesses took in just such a critical separation, as we have shown above.[47]

Hence what is reflected in John's question from prison,
whether or not Jesus was the Promised One (Matt. 11.2–6 =
Luke 7.18–23), is not the historical relationship between John
and Jesus but rather the relationships between their disciples as
they later came to compete with one another.[48] John's disciples

transcended by Jesus' understanding of time; cf. Fuchs, *Zeitverständnis* (note
23, above). For further discussion, see below.

[44] Cf. Marxsen, *Markus*, pp. 22ff. (ET: pp. 38ff.), who for this reason rejects
the historical alternative Mark (Jesus follows John, chronologically) or John
(simultaneous ministries) and speaks instead of a 'schematic' *Heilsgeschichte*,
in agreement with Schmidt, *op. cit.*, p. 24.

[45] The sources do not permit a judgment on the question of whether John
had already been put to death or merely imprisoned.

[46] The literature on the 'men of violence' saying is enormous (Matt. 11.12
= Luke 16.16). The question of authenticity cannot be answered decisively
(see note 42, above). Possibly Mark 9.11–13 is an early elaboration of the
saying (cf. Dibelius, *Täufer*, p. 30). See also Fuchs, *Ges. Aufs.*, II, p. 366 (ET:
pp. 157f.). The fact that Jesus could be considered John *redivivus* (Mark 6.14)
implies the death of John before the beginning of Jesus' ministry; cf. Bultmann, *Syn. Trad.*, p. 329 (ET: pp. 301f.).

[47] In any event, did John proclaim the imminent 'Reign of God'?

[48] Vs. Dibelius, *Täufer*, p. 37ff., who not only holds to the historicity of
the question but even considers the form of the scene authentic. But it is
quite obvious that Jesus is not the $i\sigma\chi\nu\rho\acute{o}\tau\epsilon\rho o\varsigma$, who baptizes with fire! (So,
rightly, Kraeling, *op. cit.*, pp. 128ff.; 'anti-Baptist polemic' [p. 179]; and Bult-
mann, *Syn. Trad.*, p. 22 and *Erg.-Heft* p. 7 [ET: pp. 23f. and p. 384]) against
Werner G. Kümmel, *Verheissung und Erfüllung*, 1953², pp. 102ff. [ET: pp.
109f.]).

soon after his death made a messianic figure of him and institutionalized his baptism.[49] They transformed his conduct, conditioned by the temporally imminent end of the world, into an orderly ritual of fasting and prayer.[50] The young church disputed these claims by making their own master into a messianic figure, by transforming the Baptist into a mere forerunner of Jesus, and by either completely ignoring his baptism[51] or charging it as 'mere water-baptism' with an incapacity for acting as the vehicle of the Spirit.[52]

Our sources do not allow us to trace Jesus' inner development from his baptism by John to his own ministry and eventual death.[53] Nevertheless it is quite appropriate to set forth briefly,

[49] See below, pp. 153ff. Only through this process of institutionalization does John's baptism become what Christian baptism was from the beginning, namely an initiatory rite; it is, in my view, imprecise for Herbert Braun, in 'Die Täufertaufe und die qumranischen Waschungen', *ThViat* 9 (1964), p. 1 to call John's baptism an 'initiatory rite' (see above, note 6).

[50] Cf. Mark 2.18ff. par. and Luke 11.1. Furthermore, the fasting of John's disciples has an exorcistic, not a moral, significance; cf. W. Heitmüller, *Im Namen Jesu*, 1903, p. 310.

[51] See above, nn. 38ff. The church was able thus to appropriate John for its own because they knew in their own midst the ἰσχυρότερος of whom he had spoken.

[52] Cf. Mark 1.8; Matt. 3.11; Luke 3.16; Acts 2.38; 8.15ff.; 18.24 and 19.1ff. and see the commentaries *ad loc.*; on Acts 18.24ff. and 19.1ff., see esp. Ernst Käsemann, 'Die Johannes-Jünger in Ephesus', (*Exegetische Versuche und Besinnungen* I, 1960, pp. 158–68 [ET: *Essays*, I, pp. 136–48]) and Ethelbert Stauffer, 'Probleme der Priestertradition', *TLZ* 81 (1956), cols. 135–50, esp. col. 145.

Unlike this Christian construct, the historical Johannine baptism was probably a pneumatic phenomenon, since Mark 6.14 and John 10.41 seem to reflect a background containing a knowledge of Johannine miracles; cf. Bultmann, *Syn. Trad.*, pp. 22, 329 (ET: pp. 23f., 301f.) and his *Johannesevang.*, p. 300. See also Luke 3.15.

[53] When such attempts are made, the psychology always is very unjustly subjected to a theological judgment, simply because our sources do not yield the information they might be able to give on the psychological aspect. For obviously the study of psychology and its critical use is a legitimate and important instrument in the hand of the historian, just as it is in the hand of the criminologist. Cf. Gerhard Ebeling, *Theologie und Verkündigung* (HUTh I), 1962, pp. 119ff.; Fuchs, *Ges. Aufs.* II, p. 294 (ET: p. 96); James M. Robinson, *Kerygma und historische Jesus*, 1960, p. 133 (cf. English ed., *The New Quest of the Historical Jesus* [SBT 25], 1959, pp. 67f.). Also relevant here is what Käsemann says in *ZThK* 57 (1960), p. 163 (= *Exeg. Versuche* II, p. 83

along with what has been said about his close relationship and adherence to John, several characteristic differences between the two men which can hardly be understood except as the product of such an inner development.

We select three of the many possible *differentiae*: (1) baptism, (2) eschatological expectation, and (3) John's 'asceticism'.

1. *Baptism.* Jesus himself submitted to John's baptism as a saving seal before the imminent Judgment in which penitence and forgiveness were provided. But after John had been 'delivered up' he can hardly have practised baptism himself. The silence of the synoptic tradition is clear evidence on this point, for it is simply inconceivable that that tradition could have failed to take note of Jesus' having practised himself the baptismal sacrament which from the beginning was understood as the foundation of the Christian life. It is no adequate objection to suggest that Jesus' own baptismal activity was suppressed in order to establish a certain distance and even independence from John. Consequently the assertion that Jesus himself practised baptism with vastly better success than John (John 3.22; 4.1f.) can only be viewed as the evangelist's composition, created to illustrate the Baptist's 'He must increase, but I must decrease'. In spite of John 4.2, no historical value can be ascribed to this assertion.[54]

Naturally, the 'forgiveness of sins' was hardly a subject of theological reflection for Jesus, nor of magical, sacramental transference. What the 'little ones' and the *am ha-aretz* experience in Jesus' concrete ministry is neither 'sacramental' in the magical sense nor 'verbal' in the sense of contemporary Protestant sacramentalism of the Word[55] – it is the power of God's forgiveness

---

[ET: p.83]), about the necessity of historical reconstructions. On the question of methodology see R. G. Collingwood, *The Idea of History*, 1946, pp. 255ff.

[54] Against Maurice Goguel, *Jean-Baptiste*, 1929, pp. 86ff., cf. Bultmann, *Johannesevang.*, pp. 121ff. Is John 4.2 the creation of the evangelist or is it a correction by the ecclesiastical redactor? The source-relationships behind John 3.22ff. are extremely opaque; see Bultmann on 3.25.

[55] This actually very acute danger is seen and cogently described by Fuchs in *Ges. Aufs.*, II, pp. 353f. (ET: p. 146): 'Once transubstantiation has been removed from the sacrament, it should not be allowed promptly to slip back

and the breaking-in of the *Basileia*. The validity of John's baptism stands or falls with his mythical expectation of the imminent
End. Jesus' own conduct,[56] on the other hand, enables Luther
to arrive at an existentialist interpretation of Christian baptism,
which 'signifies[57] that the old Adam, with all his sins and evil
desires, is to be drowned, put to death by daily contrition and
repentance and then come forth again daily, to arise a new man
and live forever in righteousness and purity before God'. No
further repentance can follow John's baptism of repentance, but
only the appearing of the baptizer who annihilates in fire. With
respect to the proclamation and ministry of Jesus, on the other
hand, the case is different: 'Dominus . . . noster . . . dicendo:
Poenitentiam agite etc. *omnem* vitam fidelium poenitentiam esse
voluit.'[58]

---

into the word! We are concerned not with the issue of whether an appeal can
be addressed to us; not with the whole man but wholly with man; with being
which is based on an event, not with the event of being.'

[56] In spite of Bultmann's criticism, *Das Verhältnis der urchristlichen Christusbotschaft zum historischen Jesus* (SAH 1960, Abh. 3), pp. 18ff. (ET: pp. 31ff.),
we utilize this concept from Fuchs' studies (see, *inter alia*, *Ges. Aufs.*, II,
pp. 143–67) even though it is often difficult to know whether Fuchs himself
distinguishes sharply enough between self-understanding (*Selbstverständnis*)
and self-consciousness (*Selbstbewusstsein*). A favourable understanding and
clear delineation of the concept is to be found in Eberhard Jüngel, *Paulus und
Jesus* (HUTh 2) 1964[2], p. 139 and elsewhere. On the substantive issue, see
K. E. Løgstrup, *Die ethische Forderung*, 1959, pp. 240ff. Similarly, Bornkamm,
Jesus, p. 163 (ET: p. 178), speaks of recognizing 'that the Messianic character
of his (Jesus') being is contained in his words and acts and in the immediacy
of his historical ministry'.

[57] Cf. Friedrich Gogarten, *Entmythologisierung und Kirche*, 1953, pp. 65, 83ff.
(cf. ET: pp. 63f.).

[58] C. Mirbt, *Quellen*, 1924[4], p. 253 (Kidd, *Documents*, 1911, p. 21). Wilhelm
Kamlah, *Christentum und Geschichtlichkeit*, 1951[2] (= *Christentum und Selbstbehaup-
tung*, 1940), contests the possibility of existentialist interpretation of NT
concepts apart from the preliminary hermeneutical qualification that the
'marriage' of primitive Christianity's mythical message with Greek reason
in the apologists is an inherent and constitutive aspect of Christianity, because
the very thing the outlook within which the NT was conceived does *not* do
is to understand human existence in its universal and recurrent possibilities,
i.e., 'rationally' (p. 346). But is not the 'marriage' which Kamlah finds
necessary preceded in both Jesus' conduct (*Verhalten*) and Paul's doctrine of
justification by a kind of 'engagement' which renders it simultaneously possible and legitimate? On this, see below, pp. 152f. and cf. Philipp Vielhauer,

Hence from the very beginning there stands alongside the *Christ-kerygma* of, say, the Pauline type the *Jesus-tradition* becoming visible behind the synoptic traditions. It is this tradition alone that keeps the Christ-kerygma from hardening into myth and vanishing into the ancient syncretistic world. For in Jesus' message and work the sacramental world of antiquity and its radical religious legalism are alike transcended and shattered.[59] Here, in the Jesus-tradition, 'the God beyond the God of theism'[60] appears. Here, in a way at once different and more primitive than

'Urchristentum und Christentum in der Sicht Wilhelm Kamlahs', *EvTh* 15 (1955), pp. 307–333.

[59] Cf. Marxsen, *Anfangsprobleme der Christologie*, 1960, pp. 27ff. and his 'Zur Frage nach dem historischen Jesus', *TLZ* 87 (1962), cols. 577ff. In his Heidelberg guest lecture (Jan. 7, 1964), 'Die Auferstehung Jesu – Ereignis oder Interpretament?', Marxsen attempted to spell out precisely an interpretation according to which two potential reactions on the disciples' part to the appearances of the Risen Lord are to be distinguished: on the one hand, a functional concentration on setting forth Jesus' cause as the cause of God (the Jesus-kerygma), and on the other, personal reflection on Jesus' person in the categories of contemporary Messianism and in the thought-forms of apocalyptic (the Christ-kerygma). Naturally neither type ever existed in a pure form, but the distinction does appropriately point up two differing emphases.

On transcending in Jesus the thought-forms of the ancient world, cf. Käsemann, *ZThK* 51 (1954), pp. 144ff. (ET: *Essays*, pp. 37ff.); Fuchs, *Ges. Aufs.*, II, pp. 288, 346, 353f., 367, etc. (ET: pp. 91, 140, 146ff., 158f.); Gerhard Ebeling, 'Jesus und Glaube', *Wort u. Glaube* (*Ges. Aufs.*, 1960, pp. 203–54), pp. 207f. (ET: pp. 201–46, esp. 204ff.); Bornkamm, *Jesus*, p. 163, etc. (ET: p. 178); Løgstrup, *op. cit.*, pp. 231ff; Bultmann, *Jesus* (ET: *Jesus and the Word*).

By taking up the 'historical Jesus' into its kerygma the church proclaims 'that it is not minded to allow myth to take the place of history nor a heavenly being to take the place of the Man of Nazareth . . . Primitive Christianity is obviously of the opinion that the earthly Jesus cannot be understood otherwise than from the far side of Easter, that is, in his majesty as Lord of the community and that, conversely, the event of Easter cannot be adequately comprehended if it is looked at apart from the earthly Jesus. The Gospel is always involved in a war on two fronts' (Käsemann, *ZThK* 51 [1954], p. 134 [ET: *Essays*, p. 25]).

[60] Cf. Paul Tillich, *Der Mut zum Sein*, 1958, pp. 131ff., etc. (ET: pp. 186–90). See particularly Rudolf Bultmann, 'Der Gottesgedanke und der moderne Mensch', *ZThK* 60 (1963), pp. 335–48 and the dialogue initiated there with Gabriel Vahanian, Dietrich Bonhoeffer, John A. T. Robinson, etc.

in the 'Christological encoding', are experienced the inbreaking
of the *Basileia* and the fulfilment of the eschatological promises
as they spark the handing-on and continuation of Jesus' ministry.[61] Jesus' sermon in Nazareth (Luke 4.16–21) is a superb
theological meditation by the third evangelist on this existential
experience. The phrase placed on Jesus' lips (in Mark 2.5 par.
and Luke 7.48), ἀφίενταί σου αἱ ἁμαρτίαι, is a concrete theological
expression of the experience in the presence of Jesus of God's
nearness and God's coming[62] as this experience continues in the
community of Jesus' followers.[63]

Of course it is true that Easter is the 'primary datum of the
church'. But this must not be understood to mean that here
something completely new is beginning. It means rather that
here Jesus, the historical Jesus, is revealed, so to speak, as the
Christ.[64] This is the genuine theological significance of the messianic secret; it does not indicate, as Wrede thought, that Mark
created the device of the commands to silence in order to square
the church's belief in Jesus as the Messiah with an actually non-
messianic ministry and thus to render this non-messianic life

[61] See above, note 59.

[62] See Bultmann's analysis of the pericope in *Syn. Trad.*, pp.12f. (ET:
pp.14ff.); also Ferdinand Hahn, *Christologische Hoheitstitel*, p.43 (n. 1 gives
all the relevant literature on recent discussion of the passage). 'The action
of forgiveness is recorded, for example, in the miracle story about the healing
of the sick of the palsy (Mark 2.5b–10) in just the same way as the Christian
formula is in other instances – "Your faith has made you well" . . . not to
mention the power of the keys granted to Peter or the community after
Easter. . . . Jesus did not forgive sins, but he called sinners and therefore
fearlessly and gladly ate and drank with them . . .' (Fuchs, *Ges. Aufs.*, II,
pp.353f. [ET: pp.146f.]). On Jesus' sermon in Nazareth, cf. the fitting
observations of Fuchs, art. 'σήμερον', *TWNT* VII, p.273.

[63] Cf., e.g., the parallel pericope in Matt. (9.1–8), where the phrase καὶ
ἐδόξασαν τὸν θεὸν τὸν δόντα ἐξουσίαν τοιαύτην τοῖς ἀνθρώποις instead of ὅτι ἐξουσίαν
ἔχει ὁ υἱὸς τοῦ ἀνθρώπου reflects this basic experience in the community.

[64] 'Easter did not render this experience superfluous; on the contrary,
it confirmed it. So far as it is desirable or possible to speak of a variation in
faith before and after Easter, we can only say that out of the isolated encounter with Jesus, limited as it had been by death, came the presence of the
exalted Lord, as described in the Fourth Gospel' (Käsemann, *ZThK* 51
[1954], p.139 [ET: *Essays*, p.31] – a formulation which Bultmann, *Das
Verhältnis der urchristlichen Christusbotschaft*, p.25 [ET: p.40], characterizes as
the solution of the problem).

of Jesus acceptable.[65] The cross and the resurrection as saving events are not something new, serving as the touchstone of Christianity; they are merely a variant of what the disciples had experienced with their Lord on earth. Hence the affirmation of the *theologia crucis*, as over against an incarnational theology – however good in itself such a theology may be – takes up a function which has already become visible in Jesus' earthly life, namely the transcending of the world of religion in both its legalistic and sacramental-metaphysical aspects.

2. *Eschatological expectation*. The situation is similar with respect to the Baptist's eschatological expectation. It is quite certain that Jesus shared the *temporal* eschatological expectation which is so richly attested in the literature of Jesus' day and which for Jesus apparently received its particular form and emphasis in the existence and the preaching of John the Baptist.[66] In the light of the texts it is not possible, it seems to me, to deny this.[67] But at the same time this eschatological expectation is shattered by Jesus' conduct, by his 'understanding of time'.[68] In his presence the fullness of time is experienced; the nearness of God takes place in encounter with him. Because even after his 'ascension' the community in their daily round, with one another and with

[65] So, essentially, H. J. Ebeling, *Das Messiasgeheimnis und die Botschaft des Marcus-Evangelisten* (BZNW 19), 1939, and Hans Conzelmann, 'Gegenwart und Zukunft in der synoptischen Tradition', *ZThK* 54 (1957), pp. 293ff., as against William Wrede, *Das Messiasgeheimnis in den Evangelien* (1901), 1963[2]; cf. G. Ebeling, *Theologie und Verkündigung*, pp. 125f.

[66] Cf. Erich Grässer, *Das Problem der Parusieverzögerung in den synoptischen Evangelien und der Apostelgeschichte* (BZNW 22), 1957, who rightly warns about making the problem of the imminent expectation into something harmless; also Kümmel, *Verheissung und Erfüllung* (AThANT 6), 1953[2] (ET: 1957).

[67] See the essay by Kümmel in this volume.

[68] Fuchs is quite correct when, after conceding that the imminent expectation is the 'psychological form' of Jesus' eschatological hope, he inquires more deeply into the matter and adds, e.g., 'Jesus lays claim to his time as the present before God's coming, in such a way that he contrasts it to every other time'. (*Ges. Aufs.*, II, p. 367 [ET: p. 158]; this is not to be misunderstood psychologically, of course, as the end-product of Jesus' thoughtful reflection on the matter.) Cf. Käsemann, *ZThK* 57 (1960), p. 179 (= *Exeg. Versuche* II, p. 99 [ET: p. 101]); Bornkamm, *Jesus*, p. 99 (ET: p. 108); and Bultmann's terse comment, 'Jesus is indifferent to time' in Hans Conzelmann, *ZThK* 54 (1957), p. 288 n. 1 as well as the whole discussion on pp. 288f.

the 'least brethren', thus experience God's nearness, they know
Jesus as the living and acting Lord in their midst. This experience,
in turn, finds its theological reflection in the reception of words
like Matt. 25.31–46 into the gospel.[69] It is most certainly not
true that Jesus thought or spoke about 'the eternal in the daily'
or 'God's transformations';[70] this is rather the way his own presence was experienced. The community did not hand down his
parables in order to preserve for posterity timeless religious truths
from the mouth of the master or his call to ethical decision. They
did so because those who were originally encountered by them,
because the parables were told by *Jesus*, saw the curtain drawn
back, so to speak; they saw 'the watermark behind the multi-
coloured imprint of time'[71] and experienced the irruption of the
era of salvation. Hence what is central in interpreting the parables of Jesus is not primarily what they say but rather who said
them, not teaching about the Reign of God but its irruption
in the words of Jesus.[72] Here John's temporal eschatological
expectation is transcended by Jesus in precisely the same way as
Luther's rediscovery of the gospel broke through his Catholic
heritage.[73]

3. *The Baptist's 'ascetic' existence.* The matter under considera-

[69] Cf. Bultmann, *Syn. Trad.*, pp. 130f. (ET: pp. 123f.) and Fuchs, *Ges.
Aufs.* II, p. 313 (ET: pp. 111f.). In taking over the traditional material, the
primitive community allows the Son of Man to enter instead of God; but it
does not thereby take over a Jewish-eschatological ethic at the same time.
Rather it expresses in this way what it experienced in its association with the
earthly Jesus, whom they now know to be present in their midst in the proclaimed Word in such a way that they experience in hearing the Word what
the story projects into the apocalyptic Last Judgment. On this, see Bultmann,
ZThK 60 (1963), p. 348.

[70] *Ibid.*, pp. 344f.

[71] H. E. Holthusen, *Acht Variationen über Zeit und Tod* (*Labyrinthische Jahre*,
1952, pp. 9–17), p. 13; in my opinion, a fundamental contribution to the
dialogue with modern poetry in the 'culture of our post-Christian Era'
(Vahanian).

[72] I owe a decisive debt to the stimuli provided on this matter by Prof.
Käsemann's lectures on Mark in the winter semester, 1947, in Mainz. Cf.
Fuchs, *Ges. Aufs.* II, pp. 137ff., 291 (cf. ET: p. 93): 'But the similitude is no
longer a pious address, nor is it toying with irony; it has the effect of a sudden
flash of lightning that illumines the night.' See also Jüngel, *op. cit.*, pp. 87ff.

[73] See above, note 58; cf. Fuchs, *Ges. Aufs.* II, p. 373 (ET: pp. 163f.).

tion here has been set forth so often already that we may confine ourselves to a few lines in elaboration of our brief sketch.[74] We must make it clear at the outset that the Baptist's 'ascetic' mode of life is to some extent a dubious term, since it is not a matter of world-weary cultural pessimism.[75] The 'wilderness' is not, as in modern speech, a lonely place for meditation; it is rather the place of encounter and conflict between opposing heavenly and infernal powers,[76] the place of eschatological decision and consummation.[77] So too John's practice of fasting is not 'a noble external discipline';[78] it has an exorcistic and apotropaic significance.[79] The 'repentance' that he preached and set forth has the same significance.[80] If the data in the Lucan birth-stories about John's priestly provenance are to be trusted,[81] then his

[74] See the commentaries on the texts cited and the monographs on John and Jesus.

[75] What is involved is neither the 'simple life' nor a Spartan ideal; some portrayals of John give this impression.

[76] 'John's wilderness sojourn did not have eremitic seclusion as its sole or dominant purpose' (Kraeling, op. cit., p. 10). A fundamental investigation along religionsgeschichtlich lines of the significance of the wilderness unfortunately does not exist. See, however, Gerhard Kittel, art. 'ἔρημος', TWNT II, pp. 654ff. (ET: pp. 657ff.); Hengel, op. cit., pp. 255ff.; Bill. IV, pp. 939f.; Werner Schmauch, 'In der Wüste', In Memoriam E. Lohmeyer, 1951, pp. 202–23 and his Orte der Offenbarung und der Offenbarungsort im NT, 1956.

[77] The conception is prefigured in the prophets (cf. Kittel, art. cit.) and occurs frequently in late Judaism; see above, note 14.

[78] It is legitimate to say that Luther here 'secularizes' fasting in complete accord with Jesus' intention (Gogarten).

[79] 'Asceticism, however, is concerned neither with autonomous morality nor with religious ethics. For it is an extreme type of celebration – essentially an acquisition of power . . .' (G. v.d. Leeuw, Phänomenologie der Religion, 1956², p. 521 [ET: Religion in Essence and Manifestation, p. 457]); the truth of the statement may be illustrated by Apoc Elijah 22f.: 'Fasting forgives sins and heals diseases; it drives out spirits and has power even unto the throne of God'; cf. J. Behm, 'νῆστις κτλ.', TWNT IV, pp. 925ff [ET: pp. 924–35].

[80] See above, note 7; cf. Adam's repentance in the Jordan (Vita Adae) and Sib. Or. IV. 161ff.

[81] So, rightly, Vielhauer, RGG³ III, 804. Kraeling attempts to provide a psychological motivation for John's sojourn in the wilderness by postulating a disappointment with the rural Jerusalem priesthood in John's early youth (op. cit., pp. 23–32). 'All this is hypothesis, a twentieth-century "legend"' (p. 27); essentially – i.e. apart from all the feelings supposedly moving John – this modern legend could very well be correct; cf. the following notes.

baptism is also a polemic substitute for temple-sacrifice.[82] One may also ask whether the ground was not already prepared for the 'Hellenists' of Acts by the existence of such religious convictions even in pre-Christian Judaism.[83] Certainly the 'romantic constructions' about John's early adherence to Qumran[84] are just as untenable as the view, often suggested or even stated, that he was the ancestor of the Mandeans.[85] It seems to me, however, that we must (with Rudolph) 'reverse Lohmeyer's

[82] On the Qumran withdrawal from the 'profaned' Temple, see P. Kahle, 'Die Gemeinde des Neuen Bundes und die hebräischen Handschriften aus der Höhle', *TLZ* 77 (1952), cols. 401–412; Oscar Cullmann, 'L'Opposition contre le Temple de Jérusalem', *NTS* 5 (1958/59), pp. 157–73; Rudolph, *op. cit.*, pp. 94, 224, 231, n. 3, etc.

[83] The analogy with the animosity towards the Temple among the Qumran sect – which really is a kind of stunted love, to which the heightening of the Torah and the radicalizing of the Law fully correspond – can hardly be a *direct* one! Nor indeed can *eschatological* baptism, which, in spite of a possibly common background, has nothing in common with the sect's *ritual* washings; cf. Herbert Braun, *Spätjüdisch-häretischer und frühchristlicher Radikalismus* (BHTh 24, 2 vols), 1957 and his excellent delineation of the difference between John's baptism and the washings at Qumran in *ThViat* 9, 1; Gert Jeremias, *Der Lehrer der Gerechtigkeit* (Studien zur Umwelt des NT 2), 1963; Millar Burrows, *More Light on the Dead Sea Scrolls*, 1958, pp. 56ff. The note in Acts 6.7 that many *priests* became Christians could bear some relationship to the Baptist community; cf. Kraeling, *op. cit.*, p. 172.

'Hellenists' (Acts 6.3) is not a mere 'innocuously intended description of descent' – even though Luke may have so understood it. The Christianity represented by the term, carefully reconstructed by Bultmann (*NT Theol.*, pp. 64–182 [ET: pp. 63–183]) as the 'kerygma of the Hellenistic church', brought Paul into its wake, first as persecutor and then as follower, and mediated to him (with the problem of the Law) the central theme of his doctrine of justification (vs. Schoeps, *op. cit.*, pp. 6ff.); cf. Ernst Haenchen, *Die Apostelgeschichte* (Meyer) 1959[12], pp. 213ff. and Hans Conzelmann, *Die Apostelgeschichte* (HNT), 1963, pp. 43ff.

[84] Vielhauer, *RGG*[3] III, 806; cf. Millar Burrows' balanced and careful judgment, *op. cit.* The fundamental sorting out of the similarities and differences between John and Qumran by Karl G. Kuhn (e.g., in his articles 'Askese', *RGG*[3] I, 642f. and 'Qumran', *ibid.*, V, 751) naturally has nothing to do with such 'romantic constructions', though the assertion, expressed in both articles, that John had once belonged to the Qumran community is not, in my view, sufficiently well-based; hence we should do better to speak of the two movements as having a common soil or background.

[85] Cf. Rudolph, *op. cit.*, I, pp. 66ff., 230ff., which does not, however, exclude Kraeling's judgment (*op. cit.*, p. 183): '. . . and in the very late Mandean texts there is preserved a tradition about John's baptism which in

judgment[86] and place at the beginning of the development those Baptist sects which flourished around John and were vanquished by him'.[87] This would mean, to draw a conclusion analogous to that set forth in Rudolph's careful and thorough investigations of the Mandean question, that John sprang from proto-gnostic soil.[88] Is there sufficient material to summarize John's ministry thus: His attitude is one of 'secularization' in the sense of a No to the world, a secularization which abandons the world to itself and thus to the Judgment?[89]

Jesus' relationship to the world, on the other hand, may perfectly justly be characterized as essentially 'responsibility for the world' (Gogarten)[90] in the sense of affirming the world in such a way that those who met him – and this applies to the earthly Jesus in his historical contingency as well as to the crucified and risen Lord in the 'once-for-all' word of proclamation[91] – could say, in mythological language, when they came to reflect on what they experienced in this encounter, 'God so loved the world, that he gave his only Son. . . .' Whereas for John the existing world is evil, so that one becomes its master only by fasting,[92] for Jesus it is more like a festive wedding occasion, during which fasting is absurd.[93] Hence Fuchs fittingly says, 'Jesus' preaching does not create so to speak a *theologically* new bridge to the Kingdom of God, but rather an *existential status* which draws those who are

---

large part is independent of Christian sources'. It is highly probable that old Baptist tradition is also preserved in the Pseudo-Clementines.

[86] Ernst Lohmeyer, *Das Urchristentum I; Johannes der Täufer*, 1932.

[87] *Op. cit.*, p. 76.

[88] Cf. Gyllenberg, *op. cit.*, p. 147.

[89] Does a rejection of the Baptist sect lie behind Luke 9.54?

[90] Cf. Friedrich Gogarten, *Die Verkündigung Jesu Christi*, 1948, pp. 39ff.

[91] See above, note 64.

[92] See above, note 79; Mark 9.29 is an excellent example of this.

[93] Cf. Mark 2.18ff. and see the analysis of the passage in Bultmann, *Syn. Trad.*, pp. 17f. (ET: pp. 18ff.). In my view, the original logion ran: μὴ δύνανται οἱ υἱοὶ τοῦ νυμφῶνος νηστεύειν (v. 19), in which surely not the bridegroom but only the eschaton as a nuptial period was in view. Only after Jesus' death, when the Jewish and Johannine custom of fasting began to appear once more, was the phrase ἐν ᾧ ὁ νυμφίος μετ' αὐτῶν ἐστιν added, a step in the direction of allegory, which readily served to found the new practice of fasting (v. 19bf.). Matt. 11.18f. reflects the same state of affairs.

called into the presence of God.'[94] While for John the path *out* of the world *into* the wilderness is characteristic, the gospels rightly portray Jesus' existence as a path *from* the wilderness *into* the world. Must one not, therefore – in spite of the 'lack of harmony in Jesus' teachings'[95] – characterize the extreme imminence of the primitive church's eschatological expectation as a false response to Jesus' life and death?[96] It is not accidental that the account of Jesus' eating with publicans is right next to his basic rejection of fasting, a rejection whose radical nature the later church grasped as little as it grasped his attitude towards the Law.[97]

The saying of the Baptist that God could 'raise up children to Abraham from these stones'[98] does not indicate any overcoming on John's part of the limitations of Israelite particularism;[99] it merely underscores the radical nature of his legalism, though we can hardly attain a clear picture of this, because the 'Stronger One' as he increased so caused that legalism to decrease that the historical phenomenon has grown hazy in the murk of history.[100]

II

We indicated above that John soon after his death was made into a messianic figure by his followers,[101] and we now turn to the question of the categories which were used for this purpose. We must try to ascertain whether this process was, so to speak, only a Baptist reaction to the Christian messianizing of Jesus or whether it arose before the latter development and influenced it

[94] *Ges. Aufs.*, II, p.346 (ET: p.140).

[95] *Ibid.*, p.216 (not in ET – tr.).

[96] *Ibid.*, p.314 (ET: p.112).

[97] Mark 2.13–18; see above, note 83, and cf. Fuchs, *ibid.*, p.288 (ET: pp.90f.).

[98] Matt.3.9.

[99] Cf. Kraeling, *op. cit.*, pp.71ff.

[100] On this, see Günther Bornkamm, 'Der Paraklet im Johannesevang.', *Festschrift R. Bultmann zum 65. Geburtstag*, 1949, pp.12–35; Bornkamm views the relationship between John and Jesus as formed according to the same scheme as that between Jesus and the Paraclete. But note Bultmann's objections, *Johannesevang.*, *Erg.-Heft*, pp.48f.

[101] See above, note 49.

both positively and negatively. And we must ask, finally, whether and to what extent it is rooted in John's own understanding of his mission.

In pursuing this question we take up again the catchword ἄφεσις ἁμαρτιῶν which appears, as we have said, in the so-called Benedictus of Zechariah.[102] The Benedictus in turn occurs in the context of the consciously interwoven legends of the births of John and Jesus.[103] It has long been recognized and may be taken as established that here Christian tradition is intermingled with fragments which come from the Baptist sects. So we can confine ourselves here to noting the careful literary analyses of (above all) Bultmann[104] and Dibelius[105] and to summarizing briefly the results of those basically concurring studies:

1. Luke 1 and Luke 2 are mutually independent and in many essential points competing traditions.[106]

2. The following fragments certainly come from Baptist tradition: 1.5–25 (the description of John's parents and Gabriel's annunciation in the Temple of John's birth);[107] 1.57–66 (John's birth).

3. 1.26–38 (the promise to Mary of Jesus' virgin birth) comes from Christian tradition.[108]

4. The report of the meeting of Elizabeth and Mary (1.39–45) was created only when the two traditions joined; but Luke probably took it from his tradition.[109]

5. Only the two 'eschatological hymns'[110] are left, namely

[102] Luke 1.68–79; forgiveness of sins in v. 77.
[103] On Luke's reception of the Johannine birth-stories, see above, n. 2.
[104] *Syn. Trad.*, pp. 320ff. (ET: pp. 294ff.).
[105] *Die Formgeschichte des Evangeliums* (1919), 1961[4], pp. 120ff. (ET: *From Tradition to Gospel*, pp. 123–26) and *Jungfrauensohn und Krippenkind*, SAH 1931/32, Abh. 4.
[106] According to Luke 1 Jesus is the son of the Virgin, who knows no man (26ff.); Joseph as her fiancé is first brought into the story by Luke at v. 27. According to Luke 2 Jesus is the first son of his parents. In Luke 1 Jesus is the future Son of David. In Luke 2, on the other hand, his birth is a present saving event; cf. Dibelius, SAH.
[107] Cf. the above-mentioned works by Bultmann and Dibelius *ad. loc.*
[108] See Dibelius, SAH.
[109] Cf. Bultmann, *Syn. Trad.*, p. 322 (ET: p. 296).
[110] Cf. H. Gunkel, *Festgabe für A. von Harnack*, 1921, pp. 43–60.

the Magnificat, placed on the lips of Mary,[111] and the Benedictus of Zechariah (1.67–79), as well as v. 80, which forms a link to chapter 3.

That the Benedictus also comes from Baptist circles may, after the illuminating study of Vielhauer,[112] be taken as certain. As for the Magnificat, the possibility of a Baptist origin is worth considering at least, and it could perhaps even be shown as probable;[113] but for our purposes the decision may be left open.

The Baptist tradition in Luke 1 is not itself a unity; it must have arisen at different times and in different places within Baptist circles. But the material is too limited to provide us any insight into the history of this movement. We must remain content with merely establishing the differences.

The first, and longer, part of the Benedictus (1.68–75) is an eschatological hymn, in pure form, which is representative of current Jewish messianology:[114] the 'horn of salvation'[115] prophesied by the prophets is established in the house of Yahweh's servant David; redemption has come,[116] for the Messiah has appeared.

This hymn, which is obviously an older Jewish Psalm, is now interpreted in 1.76–79 by means of the identification of the Baptist with the eschatological bringer of salvation; this corrects its messianology.[117] The bringer of salvation is called προφήτης

---

[111] *Ibid.*

[112] 'Das Benedictus des Zacharias', *ZThK* 49 (1952), pp. 255–72.

[113] Cf. Bultmann, *Syn. Trad.*, pp. 322f. (ET: pp. 296f.) and Vielhauer, *op. cit.*, p. 257.

[114] Cf. Gunkel and Vielhauer, *op. cit.*

[115] Cf. Werner Foerster, art. 'κέρας', *TWNT* III, p. 669 (ET: 669f.); Herbert Braun, *ThR* 28 (1962/63) p. 177.

[116] ἐποίησεν λύτρωσιν (v. 68).

[117] For what follows, see esp. Vielhauer, 'Benedictus'. The compiling of the two sections is, to be sure, Baptist, not Christian (against Braun, *op. cit.*, p. 178). The delineation of the views of the Johannine community in Hahn, *Hoheitstitel*, pp. 371ff., esp. his analysis of the Benedictus (p. 373), is not convincing. Hahn considers Luke 1.68–75, as well as vv. 78, 79a, to be Christian elaboration of the Baptist tradition reflected in vv. 76f. and 79b. But in that case, what is specifically Christian about vv. 68–75 and 78f.? And, on Hahn's grounds, could anyone except Luke himself (from whom we ordinarily expect far better work!) be the compiler? Hahn does not inquire about the

ὑψίστου (v. 76), and as such he is destined to go before the κύριος and prepare his way – a clear reflection of Mal. 3.1.[118] His preparatory work consists in the fact that he gives the knowledge of salvation (γνῶσιν σωτηρίας) to Yahweh's people; this knowledge is the forgiveness of sins.[119] The two following verses (vv. 78f.) we cite verbatim:

διὰ σπλάγχνα ἐλέους θεοῦ ἡμῶν,

ἐν οἷς ἐπισκέψεται ἡμᾶς ἀνατολὴ ἐξ ὕψους,

ἐπιφᾶναι τοῖς ἐν σκότει καὶ σκιᾷ θανάτου καθημένοις,

τοῦ κατευθῦναι τοὺς πόδας ἡμῶν εἰς ὁδὸν εἰρήνης.

Helmut Koester, in his basic study of the history of the term σπλάγχνον,[120] has located in the Testament of the Twelve Patriarchs and the late-Jewish literature closely allied with it a usage which clearly differs from the LXX usage of σπλάγχνα;[121] our passage must be classed with this usage. In Test. Zeb. 8.2, e.g., the text says, 'In the last days God will send τὰ σπλάγχνα αὐτοῦ upon the earth'. Even the Messiah himself can be called σπλάγχνον κυρίου.[122] On this basis Koester rightly concludes that διὰ σπλάγχνα ἐλέους κτλ. in Luke 1.78f. sounds 'almost like a citation from the Test. XII'.[123] The following phrase about the visit of the Light

religionsgeschichtlich background of vv. 77ff., nor does he discuss Vielhauer's view that vv. 76ff. are to be conceived as a Baptist correction of a Jewish Psalm (vv. 67–75) which antedated even John's disciples.

[118] Cf. Gerhard Friedrich, art. 'προφήτης', TWNT VI, pp. 838ff. (ET: pp. 836ff.); Vielhauer, ZThK 49 (1952), p. 266. The clear use of Malachi here and in Luke 1.17 (which is likewise Baptist) shows that John is the messianic Prophet and forerunner of Yahweh himself, not of his Messiah.

[119] This provides almost conclusive proof that the characterizing of John's baptism of repentance as a baptism 'for the remission of sins' (Mark 1.4) is to be seen as Baptist and not as first arising in the Christian community (see above, section I).

[120] TWNT VII, pp. 548–59.

[121] In late Judaism the noun occurs almost exclusively in the plural; cf. Koester, art. cit.

[122] Test. Naph. 4.5; Koester, ibid., p. 551.

[123] Ibid., p. 557. The expression προφήτης ὑψίστου points in the same direction; in Test. Lev. 8.15 it is a messianic title; cf. Gerhard Friedrich, 'Beobachtungen zur messianischen Hohepriestererwartung in den Synoptikern', ZThK 53 (1956), pp. 265–311.

from on high (ἐπισκέψεται ἡμᾶς ἀνατολὴ ἐξ ὕψους) and its epiphany among those who sit in σκότος and the σκιᾳ θανάτου points in the same direction. The relationship with the dualism of the Testament of the Twelve Patriarchs, the Qumran texts, and the Gospel of John is evident.

Philipp Vielhauer has demonstrated that the translation 'offspring of Yahweh' for ἀνατολὴ ἐξ ὕψους is mistaken.[124] It should rather be rendered 'light from on high'. Heinrich Schlier has made clear, in a different connection, the astral-mythical-gnostic background of the Redeemer who appears like a star in the heavens.[125] Ought we then to understand the mediation of the γνῶσις σωτηρίας in a technical gnostic sense? The fact that the concept is interpreted in the context by the phrase ἄφεσις ἁμαρτιῶν does not settle this issue, for we need not necessarily begin with the Jewish usage of this phrase.[126] Is it not simpler to begin instead with the distinctive usage of ἄφεσις in association with μετάνοια which we have seen in the section above on John's baptism? 'That the concept of repentance is present in gnostic texts is shown, e.g., by the passage in Corpus Hermeticum 1.28: Repent, you who have wandered with Error and consorted with Ignorance.'[127]

Thus in the Benedictus the Baptist is described as the Redeemer from heaven, so that we are required on formal grounds to continue: ἦν τὸ φῶς τὸ ἀληθινόν, ὃ φωτίζει πάντα ἄνθρωπον[128]

---

[124] 'Benedictus', pp. 265f.; cf. Friedrich, *art. cit.*; see further Walter Bauer's lexicon s.v. 'ἀνατολή'; Bill. II, p. 113. Test. Zeb. 9.8 reads: καὶ μετὰ ταῦτα ἀνατελεῖ ὑμῖν αὐτὸς ὁ κύριος, φῶς δικαιοσύνης. W. Bousset, *Kyrios Christos*, 1921², p. 12 and W. Bousset and H. Gressmann, *Die Religion des Judentums* (HNT 21), 1926³, p. 265 overlook the specific meaning of the concept in our context. Philo (*De conf. ling.* 14) understands the Logos as ἀνατολή; on this, cf. Heinrich Schlier, art., 'ἀνατέλλω', *TWNT* I, pp. 354f. (ET: pp. 351f.).

[125] *Religionsgeschichtliche Untersuchungen zu den Ignatiusbriefen* (BZNW 8) 1929, pp. 28ff.

[126] Acc. to Test. Lev. 18.3 the Messiah brings the φῶς γνώσεως. On the history of the concept of ἄφεσις, cf. Rudolf Bultmann, *TWNT* I, pp. 506ff. (ET: pp. 509–12).

[127] μετανοήσατε οἱ συνοδεύσαντες τῇ πλάνῃ καὶ συγκοινωνήσαντες τῇ ἀγνοίᾳ. Citation from O. Hofius, 'Das koptische Thomasevangelium und die Oxyrhynchus-Papyri', *EvTh* 20 (1960), p. 184.

[128] John 1.9; cf. Bousset, *Kyrios Christos*, pp. 165ff.

and on this basis to support once more Bultmann's observations on the Johannine prologue – Haenchen's recent criticism notwithstanding.[129] But first we must fill out the portrait of the Baptist by discussing the remaining materials in the Lucan birth stories.

John comes of a priestly family: *both* parents are of priestly descent.[130] On his mother's side he is Aaronic.[131] His birth is miraculous, since he comes from a barren woman ($\sigma\tau\epsilon\acute{\iota}\rho\alpha$ v.7).[132] He will be great before the Lord.[133] The note $\kappa\alpha\grave{\iota}$ $o\mathring{\iota}\nu o\nu$ $\kappa\alpha\grave{\iota}$ $\sigma\acute{\iota}\kappa\epsilon\rho\alpha$ $o\mathring{\upsilon}$ $\mu\grave{\eta}$ $\pi\acute{\iota}\eta$, a conflation of Num. 6.3 and Judg. 13.4 (Luke 1.15), seems to imply that John is a Nazirite.[134] Even in his mother's womb he bears the Spirit (Luke 1.15).[135] He appears 'in the spirit and power of Elijah' to convert the people of God.[136] Hence he serves as precursor and forerunner of God himself; nothing is said of a Messiah, nor is there any place for one.[137]

Here we may include a brief observation on the Johannine prologue. The thorough studies of Käsemann[138] and Haenchen[139] deserve of course a more solid discussion than our present context will permit. So we will omit completely a discussion of the details and set forth alongside of these investigations our own view of the prologue as a working hypothesis (a view, incidentally, that essentially coincides with Bultmann's results.)[140]

[129] 'Probleme des johanneischen "Prologs" ', *ZThK* 60 (1963), pp. 305–34.

[130] Luke 1.5.

[131] Cf. Braun, *ThR* 28 (1962/63), p. 174; on the significance of the Aaronite priest as a bringer of salvation, see below.

[132] Cf. the commentaries *ad loc.*

[133] Cf. Friedrich, *art. cit.*

[134] Cf. Vielhauer, 'Benedictus', p. 259; more critically in *RGG³* III, 805.

[135] Cf. Friedrich, *art. cit.*, and Braun, *ThR* 28 (1962/63), p. 174.

[136] Mal. 3.23f.

[137] See above, notes 15f.

[138] 'Aufbau und Anliegen des johanneischen Prologs', *Libertas Christiana*: *Festschrift für F. Delekat*, 1957, pp. 75–99 (ET: *NT Questions of Today*, pp. 138–67).

[139] See note 129.

[140] Cf. Bultmann, *Johannesevang.*, pp. 1ff. Ethelbert Stauffer, 'Probleme der Priestertradition', *TLZ* 81 (1956), cols. 135–50, accepts the thesis that the prologue of the gospel of John was originally a hymn from the Baptist community.

For a long time now the *crux interpretum* has been vv. 6ff., (12f.), and 15, which are in prose and destroy the hymnic context; it is they which mention the Baptist. Baldensperger[141] years ago rightly observed that these verses not only (positively) proclaim the Baptist's witness to Jesus; they also (negatively) contest polemically John's redemptive authority.[142] The statement οὐκ ἦν ἐκεῖνος τὸ φῶς cannot, in my opinion, reasonably be understood in any way except as a rejection of the Baptist claim that John is the heavenly Light,[143] so that 'the text of the source was a hymn of the Baptist community'.[144] Haenchen has recently attempted to attribute vv. 6ff., 12f., and 15 to the ecclesiastical redactor to whom we owe, among other things, the adjusting of the traditional eschatology, the 'eucharistic' discourse in ch. 6, and ch. 21.[145] But he can adduce no convincing stylistic and linguistic bases for this view.[146] So he is forced to postulate that the redactor no longer understood the meaning of the original hymn, and he is ultimately at a loss to suggest a motivation for the interpolation of vv. 6–8 between v. 5 and v. 9.[147] Furthermore the content of vv. 12 and 13, which according to Haenchen owe their existence in any case to a misunderstanding of the hymn,[148] and in which the redactor does not even succeed in 'setting forth clearly the meaning of these statements'[149] (his own statements!), does not fit well, in my opinion, into the redactor's world. At most, v. 15, which (as Haenchen observes) actually breaks the context (a sequential chain!), may go back to the redactor.

But might not these problems be more simply resolved by assuming that both v. 6 and v. 15 – i.e. both mentions of the Baptist – come from the original hymn, naturally in an altered

---

[141] *Der Prolog des 4. Evangeliums*, 1898.

[142] Cf. Bultmann, *Johannesevang.*, pp. 4f.

[143] Is John 5.35 also to be understood polemically in this sense? Cf. Stauffer, *art. cit.*, p. 146; but see Bultmann *ad. loc.*

[144] Bultmann, *Johannesevang.*, p. 5.

[145] *Op. cit.*, pp. 325ff.

[146] *Ibid.*

[147] *Ibid.*, p. 328.

[148] *Ibid.*, pp. 329ff., 332.

[149] *Ibid.*, p. 332.

form which is hardly to be reconstructed? And is not this view
obscured for us simply by the fact that from the early church
down to our own times it has been customary to see the decisive
turning-point in the prologue at v. 14, the incarnation of the
Logos? On the other hand, many difficulties vanish if we assume
that the description of the pre-existence of the Logos is followed
immediately by his historical appearance in two parallel courses,
namely in vv. 5ff., where the shining of the light in the darkness
is immediately identified with the appearing of John,[150] and in
vv. 14ff., where the incarnation of the Logos is also immediately
referred to the Baptist. In my view, this interpretation is supported by both the emphatic present in v. 5 ('the light *shines* in
the darkness') and a very obvious hiatus between v. 5 and v. 9.[151]
Finally, vv. 12 and 13 might very well have originally contained
a reference to John's baptism as divine birth.[152]

In such a case, then, we would actually have in the prologue
a fragment of Baptist theology, of which the evangelist is making
critical and polemic use.[153] If we presuppose that the gospel
accepts the Baptist conceptuality and enters into polemic controversy with it, however, we must not assume that this is accidental; it is deliberate. What the fourth evangelist is really
concerned with is the mission of the Baptist sects.[154] According
to the prologue, the messianic claims of these sects are explicitly

[150] In this case a motif much like that in Luke 1.76 is reflected; correspondingly, something similar is possible in the hymn itself. The extant
prose form, then, rests on the polemic Christianizing of John.

[151] Haenchen (*op. cit.*, pp. 326f.) bases his view that vv. 6–8 come from the
redactor on (among other things) the fact that here a different view of John
is presupposed from that of the evangelist (which he finds in 5.33f.). The
observation is correct, but in my opinion a better explanation is that the
evangelist is here influenced by a concrete text. In the original hymn v. 9
cannot have been attached to v. 5.

[152] Haenchen's attempt (*ibid.*, p. 330) to ascribe v. 12 to the redactor is not
convincing.

[153] Cf. Bultmann, *Johannesevang.*, pp. 5ff. On this basis the designation
'Prologue' seems to me especially appropriate; for a different view, see
Haenchen, *op. cit.*, p. 308.

[154] So also Stauffer, *art. cit.*, who, however, (certainly wrongly) suggests
the son of Zebedee as a former disciple of John and the author of the Fourth
Gospel.

rejected by John himself.[155] And if, with Dibelius,[156] we may understand the miracle at Cana (2. 1–12) as a rejection of John's water baptism, then it is possible that behind the following pericope (the cleansing of the temple) lies John's hostility to the Temple, which, as criticism, is exceeded by Jesus' saying about the temple.[157] Finally, the Baptist controversy is continued in chs. 3 and 4: The Nicodemus episode rejects the significance of John's baptism as a divine rebirth,[158] repudiates the Baptist eschatology,[159] and stresses the significance of faith.[160] The scene with the Samaritan woman at the well is similarly motivated.[161]

Here we conclude this hasty Johannine excursus. The validity of our hypothesis could only be established or called into question by a more thorough investigation of the Fourth Gospel as a whole. But in any case the picture of John which emerges from this hypothesis corresponds extensively with that of the Benedictus.

Vielhauer says of the picture of John in Luke 1 and the 'historical' John: 'But in the place of the eschatological figure whose precursor John understood himself to be, in both predictions John himself appears; and he appears to prepare the way, not for a "Messiah" but for God himself.'[162] Is this verdict convincing? I believe that it is not. For it seems to me that the historical John also understood himself as the precursor, not of a Messiah, but of God himself.[163] Again, is Vielhauer not right

---

[155] John 1.19–28. Braun (*ThR* 28 [1962/63], pp. 196ff.) engages in critical polemic with the view, often asserted, that the Messianic teaching rejected here is near to or even dependent upon Qumran. In my opinion, he is unduly influenced by the synoptic picture of John as a preacher of repentance; cf. Bultmann, *Johannesevang.*, pp. 57ff.

[156] *Täufer*, p. 112. Naturally this result is attained not by exegesis of individual pericopes but only by the interpretation of the whole complex phenomenon, 'The Baptist in the Fourth Gospel'; cf. *ibid.*, pp. 98–123.

[157] See above, notes 82f.

[158] This takes up again the thought of John 1.12ff.; see above.

[159] See above, note 23.

[160] Once more a polemic antithesis in the Prologue is taken up.

[161] In the concept of 'living water', with which the evangelist toys in this passage (cf. Bultmann, *Johannesevang.*, pp. 131ff.), the saving significance of the baptism in the Jordan would be set aside; cf. Rudolph, *op. cit.*, I, pp. 62ff.

[162] 'Benedictus', p. 267.

[163] See above, note 15.

in saying, 'The theme of these prophecies about John is the
dawning of salvation; the theme of John's own prophetic message
is the dawning of Judgment'?[164] Can this be said so unqualifiedly? Might not this too be a case in which the Christian
community *ad majorem gloriam* of its Lord blurred the precise
contours of the Johannine portrait? Of course John proclaimed
the Judgment towards the outside world in general. But what do
we really know of what he said to those who came to him for
baptism, i.e., of his esoteric teaching to his disciples?[165]

In any case it would be a mistake to go beyond the asking
of such questions to positive assertions about the Baptist's messianology or even to construct a unique messianic consciousness
for him. The texts no more allow this in his case than in the case
of Jesus. But could we put the matter more cautiously and suggest something like this: The historical John's ministry, the
forgiveness of sins[166] he made available, and his message all combined to bring his disciples almost immediately to theological
reflection and thus engendered the messianic-gnostic portrait
which soon emerged?[167] And could not the historical John in
any event have provided his disciples a basis for understanding
him in this particular way, for 'messianizing' him? Whether the
messianizing of John was really post-Christian and represented a
Baptist response to the church's christology is by no means so
certain as Thomas asserts.[168] We can leave this question open.
On the other hand, it seems to me quite probable that the christological interpretation in *gnostic* categories arose in Baptist circles
and that both the Fourth Gospel and Hebrews, in different ways,

[164] 'Benedictus', p. 267.

[165] Cf. Gyllenberg, *op. cit.*

[166] That God alone can forgive sins is also a fixed conviction at Qumran;
cf. A.S. v.d. Woude, *Die messianischen Vorstellungen der Gemeinde von Qumran*,
1957, p. 32 and Herbert Braun, *ThR* 28 (1962/63), p. 159.

[167] It seems to me questionable whether we may, with Stauffer (*op. cit.*,
p. 145) call Alexandria (to whose syncretism Philo bears eloquent witness)
the 'centre' of the Baptist sect; but in any event Acts 18.24ff.; 19.1 shows
how widespread it was.

[168] Joseph Thomas, *Le Mouvement Baptiste en Palestine et Syrie*, 1935, pp.
84ff. So also Hahn, *Hoheitstitel*, p. 374.

attest and reflect polemic against just such an interpretation.[169]

In any event, if the interpretation of John's baptism set forth in the first part of this essay is approximately correct, the question must have been asked as early as John's ministry: 'Who but God alone can forgive sins?'[170] An answer to this pressing question was not to be avoided, and in conclusion it is fitting to try to reconstruct that answer.

The expiation of sins is a priestly prerogative.[171] John was, as we have seen, of Aaronic, priestly descent. According to Test. Levi 18 the work of the eschatological 'priestly Messiah' is 'to shine on the earth like the sun and to take away all darkness from the earth'. He spreads abroad the knowledge of the Lord 'and in the time of his priesthood all sin will vanish'.[172]

The question of whether or not the Qumran texts also speak of the priestly Messiah has been discussed many times.[173] Meanwhile a scholarly consensus seems to have formed to the effect that several passages speak of two – if not three – messianic figures,[174] and that within the sect there was a tendency to re-assimilate this distinctive concept to the traditional Jewish messianic understanding.[175] Probably even those texts that speak

---

[169] See above, note 18, and below, notes 189–92.

[170] Mark 2.7; on this, see above, notes 4, 166.

[171] Cf. Friedrich, *art. cit.*, p. 294. Friedrich's attempt to establish, on the basis of the *religionsgeschichtlich* background of the Test. XII and of Qumran, an early stratum (later displaced) of high-priestly Christology in the synoptics must be reckoned unsuccessful, in spite of valuable isolated observations; cf. the thorough critical evaluation of this attempt in Joachim Gnilka, 'Die Erwartung des messianischen Hohenpriesters in den Schriften von Qumran und im NT', *RQ* 2 (1959/60), pp. 395–426; cf. also Hahn, *Hoheitstitel*, pp. 238ff.

[172] Test. Lev. 18.9; cf. Braun, *ThR* 28 (1962/63), p. 178, who, however, understands Luke 1.77 too one-sidedly on the basis of OT analogies and underestimates the dualistic and astral-mythological background of the Benedictus.

[173] Cf. esp. K. G. Kuhn, 'Die beiden Messias in den Qumrantexten und die Messiasvorstellung in der rabbinischen Literatur', *ZAW* 70 (1958), pp. 200–8 (ET: cf. also Stendahl, *Scrolls*, pp. 54–64) and Gnilka, *art. cit.* (with bibliog.). See also n. 42 of Dinkler's contribution to this volume.

[174] Cf. esp. 1QS 9.11.

[175] See the discussion in Gnilka, *art. cit.*

of several messianic figures reflect an early stage of this process
of assimilation. If so, originally the expectation was not of two
heralds of salvation, the king and the priest, but of only one, the
priestly messiah; to him, under the impact of the tradition, the
Davidic king was then added, though clearly in a subordinate
role. Finally both *offices* were ascribed to the *one* Messiah, a stage
that represented the triumph of the tradition, though (characteristically) in modified form.[176]

The mention of *the* (singular) 'Messiah of Aaron and Israel'
in the Damascus Document (CD) has long been noted.[177] Now,
however, we have also 1QS 9.10f., 'They (namely the men of the
community) shall be judged according to the earlier laws, which
the men of the covenant began to obligate themselves to follow,
until the Prophet and the Messiahs of Aaron and Israel come.'[178]
In other words, until the arrival of these messianic figures the
Manual of Discipline is binding. The oracle of Balaam in Num.
24.17 is given the following allegorical interpretation in CD
7.18f.: 'The "Star" is the Teacher of the Law דורש התורה who
comes (will come[179]) to Damascus, as it is written: a star shall
come forth out of Jacob, a sceptre shall arise out of Israel. The
"sceptre" is the Prince of the whole community, and he breaks
all the sons of Seth in pieces.'[180] Gnilka has shown that both
here and in the other passages in the Qumran literature in which
the Balaam-oracle appears the 'star' and the 'sceptre' are
apparently occasionally intended to denote priestly messiah and
the Davidic messiah-king, respectively.[181] An analogous use of

[176] Whether this development occurred as early as the time of the
Qumran community-order or only much later (in the Middle Ages?) is still
a matter of dispute; cf. Gnilka, *art. cit.*, pp. 395ff.

[177] CD 12.23f.; cf. 14.19; 19.10f.; 20.1.

[178] See above, note 174, and cf. Gnilka, Kuhn, and Stauffer, *art. cit.*

[179] Gnilka, *art. cit.*, p. 399; he wishes – in my opinion, rightly – to translate הבא in a futuristic sense, for the context clearly shows that what it says
of the דרש התורה who is to come to Damascus refers to a messianic
figure.

[180] Following Johann Maier, *Die Texte vom Toten Meer*, 2 vols., 1960, I,
p. 56; cf. II, p. 53; Gnilka, *art. cit.*, p. 399; and G. Jeremias, *Lehrer*, pp. 289ff.

[181] Cf. 4 QT 12f.; 1 QSb 5.20ff.; 1QM 11.6; and see Gnilka, *art. cit.*,
pp. 397ff.

the Balaam-oracle occurs in Test. Jud. 24. 1ff.[182] In 4QT too it appears that 'as in the Manual of Discipline three eschatological figures are distinguished and their future appearing is documented with words of Scripture'.[183] The appendix to the Manual (1 Q Sa) shows 'that the Messiah of Aaron is to be distinguished from the Messiah of David and is superior to him'.[184]

The same subordination of the messianic king to the messianic priest is reflected in the Testament of the Twelve Patriarchs.[185] Finally, it should be pointed out that Billerbeck also demonstrates the existence in rabbinic Judaism of the expectation of a high priestly Messiah of the house of Aaron alongside the Davidic Messiah-king.[186]

Since we have already seen above the close relationship between the Benedictus and the world of the Testament of the Twelve Patriarchs, it is plausible to suggest that the ἀνατολὴ ἐξ ὕψους is nothing but the 'Star out of Jacob', the priestly Messiah, who mediates the saving *gnosis*. If this is so, we have in this kind of late-Jewish literature the reservoir from which the Baptist's disciples drew the raw material for the messianizing of their master.[187]

Is this perhaps the explanation of the fact that the NT shows such severe restraint (except in Hebrews) in the designation of

[182] The nature and extent of the Christian re-working of the Testaments of the Twelve Patriarchs is still disputed; R. H. Charles, *The Greek Versions of the Testament of the Twelve Patriarchs*, 1908 (the original conception was of a Levitical priest-Messiah; all the Judah-Messiah passages are interpolated; pp. xlii f.); M. Philonenko, 'Les Interpolations chrétiennes des Testaments des Douze Patriarchs et les Manuscrits de Quomrân', *RHPhR* 38 (1958), pp. 309–43 and 39 (1959), pp. 14–38 (denies any Christian re-working); M. de Jonge, *The Testaments of the Twelve Patriarchs*, 1953 (considers the Test. XII a Christian writing, using Jewish material). Against de Jonge (convincingly): K. Baltzer, *Das Bundesformular* (WMANT 4), 1960, pp. 146ff. But clear evidence that a doctrine of two Messiahs is characteristic of the Test. XII is provided by its use of the oracle of Balaam, which is analogous to its use at Qumran; cf. Gnilka, *op. cit.*, pp. 400ff.

[183] Gnilka, *op. cit.*, p. 403.

[184] *Ibid.*, the Messiah of Aaron presides at the eschatological meal.

[185] See above, n. 182.

[186] Bill. IV, pp. 462ff.

[187] Cf. the exposition of the Benedictus, above, and Stauffer, *art. cit.*

Jesus as the messianic high priest, in spite of the prevalence of
the conception of this eschatological bringer of salvation in the
surrounding world?[188] The view that the conception was un-
known to the NT writers is, in view of the proximity between
the Baptist sects and both the Lucan birth-stories and the Fourth
Gospel, not really satisfactory. Is it not possible that the reti-
cence of the NT writers is to be explained on the assumption
that the conception was *tabu* because of its association with John
the Baptist? Then among NT writers only the author of Hebrews – boldly taking the bull by the horns – could be said to
enter into direct and polemic controversy with the Baptist sect
by taking up their high priestly christology, going beyond it, and
thus giving expression to the unique dignity of his Lord.[189]

Several indicators of such anti-Baptist polemic appear in
Hebrews: the denial of a second repentance,[190] the pointed
reference to βαπτισμοί (plural) in the elementary doctrines, the
statement in 9.22 – apparently a sharp polemic against baptismal
forgiveness: καὶ χωρὶς αἱματεκχυσίας οὐ γίνεται ἄφεσις,[191] and above
all the elaborate scriptural proof of the high priesthood of Jesus
after the order of Melchisedek, which can hardly be conceived
of as anything other than a rejection of a concrete claim to an
Aaronic, messianic high priesthood.[192]

To summarize my conclusions, as I have elaborated them in
connection with the catchword βάπτισμα μετανοίας εἰς ἄφεσιν ἁμαρτιῶν: Almost everywhere in the NT the forgiveness of sins appears

---

[188] A different view in Friedrich (see above, n. 171); well-founded
criticism of Friedrich in Braun *ThR* 28 (1962/63), *passim*, e.g., pp. 158, 159,
16off.; cf. also Erich Grässer, 'Der Hebräerbrief, 1938–1963', *ThR* 30
(1964/65), pp. 138–236.

[189] On the conception of the priestly Messiah, cf. besides Friedrich, *op.
cit.*: Ernst Käsemann, *Das wandernde Gottesvolk*, 1957², pp. 126ff.; F. J.
Schierse, *Verheissung und Heilsvollendung*, 1955; Otto Michel, *Der Brief an die
Hebräer* (Meyer), 1960¹¹, pp. 374ff.; Hahn, *Hoheitstitel*, pp. 231ff.

[190] See above, note 18.

[191] We have noted similar phenomena in Matthew (note 31).

[192] Heb. 7, anticipated in 5.6, 10; 6.20; see esp. 7.11 and cf. on the
passage C. Spicq, *L'épître aux Hébreux* II, Paris, 1953³, pp. 188f. On
Melchisedek-speculation, see Michel, *Hebr.*, pp. 158ff.; Käsemann, *Gottesvolk*, pp. 129ff.; and Hahn, *Hoheitstitel*, pp. 231ff.

in a close and primary connection with baptism.[193] I think I have shown that the association begins as early as John's baptism. The eschatological forgiveness conveyed sacramentally by John is experienced by those associated with Jesus existentially as forgiveness and as the gift of God himself. In the fact that this experience continues in the community after the death of Jesus that community knows him as the One who lives in their midst. On this basis – and not on account of demonstrable ecstatic phenomena[194] – the community can continue to affirm its possession of the Spirit against John's disciples. The church took over John's baptism as the sign by which they knew themselves sealed to their own Master, while at the same time so bound the gift of the Spirit to him that the Spirit was understood not as a possession but as the realm of the lordship of that κύριος to whom the community owed obedient discipleship.[195] Because of the special affinity created by the historical situation between the Christian community and the Baptist sect the early church was threatened from the outset by a dangerous Baptist submovement against which it had to provide clear and decisive defences.[196] The practice of mutual forgiveness, i.e., the daily association with each other as justified men, is quickly tied to the cultic act and to the 'official' grace mediated by ordination.[197] The high-priestly Christology of Hebrews, originally intended polemically against all earthly priesthood, soon has to bear the responsibility for legitimizing a new priesthood.[198] The gift of the forgiveness of sins, which provides the basis of the community's eschatological freedom, is threatened at a very early stage by an individualistic-moralistic misunderstanding – which

[193] Cf. Bultmann, *TWNT* I, pp. 506ff. (ET: pp. 509–12) and see a concordance on ἄφεσις (ἁμαρτιῶν) or ἀφιέναι. The usage in Barnabas is very instructive in this regard.

[194] Cf. Paul's concern on the matter in I Cor. 12ff.; but see also Acts 18.24ff. and 19.1ff.

[195] Cf., e.g., Rom. 6.4 and Gal. 5.25.

[196] We have tried to show (above) traces of this conflict.

[197] Cf. H. Thyen and J. Heubach, art. 'Schlüsselgewalt', *RGG*³ V, 1449–1453 (bibliography).

[198] Cf. B. Lohse, art. 'Priestertum III', *RGG*³ V, 578–81 (bibliography).

explains why Paul, in order to affirm what it intends, avoids the concept.[199] For forgiveness really does have a 'fundamental significance' in the NT, as Bultmann has repeatedly emphasized.[200] When he concludes his 1926 book on Jesus with a consideration of the concept of forgiveness and says 'In the Word, and not otherwise, does Jesus bring forgiveness',[201] the 'Word' here is naturally not to be understood in the sense of an autonomously efficacious formula 'Your sins are forgiven'! Neither the formula nor the priestly authority to declare it brings it about. Jesus is rather in his *persona* God's Word of forgiveness.[202] Bultmann expresses this clearly by closing *Jesus and the Word* with the exclamation, 'Blessed is he who is not offended at me' (Matt. 11.6).[203]

[199] Cf. Bultmann, *TWNT* I, pp. 506ff. (ET: pp. 509–12).
[200] E.g., *ibid.*, p. 509 (ET: pp. 511f.).
[201] *Jesus*, p. 200 (ET: p. 182).
[202] See above, e.g., note 59.
[203] *Jesus*, p. 200 (ET: p. 182).

7

Peter's Confession and the 'Satan' Saying

The Problem of Jesus' Messiahship*

Erich Dinkler

IN HIS introduction to the Hasidic books Martin Buber writes:[1]
'To claim to be the Messiah is fundamentally incompatible with
Messiahship.' He goes on to discuss the relationship between
Judaism and Jesus of Nazareth and adds:

> Whatever his significance for humanity as a whole (and to my
> mind his appearance is the most profoundly serious event in
> the history of the West), from the viewpoint of Judaism he is
> the first in a series of men who, representing the genuine
> 'messianic secret' in the hiddenness of God's servants, first
> acknowledged their own messianic nature in their words and
> in their souls. That this first in the series – as I discover for
> myself again and again when I am able to visualize the one
> who spoke, as his words commend themselves to me as
> genuine and form a substantial unity – that this one was in-
> comparably the purest, most just, and most genuinely en-
> dowed with messianic gifts of all in the series does not in any
> way alter the fact that he was the first; indeed, it is a central
> characteristic, it belongs to the frightfully impressive reality
> of the whole series of such self-acknowledged Messiahs.

* Translated from *Zeit und Geschichte*, pp. 127–53.
[1] Martin Buber, *Die Chassidischen Bücher*, 1925, p. xxviii; repr. in his
Deutung des Chassidismus (Bücherei des Schocken Verlag Nr. 43), 1935, pp. 6of.
and in his *Werke, Bd. III: Schriften zum Chassidismus*, 1963, p. 755.

As far as the basic judgment on the messianic claim is concerned, on the basis of the eschatological conception of the
messianic reign which informs his judgment and provides the
presupposition of it, Buber is quite right. But what he says is also
very significant for a Christian eschatology. For it would be
disquieting for our traditional Christian understanding of Jesus
because it would mean either that Jesus transcended the category 'Messiah' and was incompatible with it – in which case he
was not the Messiah – or, on the other hand, that he made no
'messianic claim'. In one respect or the other the representation
of Jesus in the canonical gospels would have to be subjected to
criticism. But this in turns leads to a twofold question: What position did Jesus take towards Peter's confession of him as Christ or
Messiah? And, how is the relationship between the Jewish concept of the Messiah and the Christian title Christ to be described,
historically and materially? With these two questions in mind,
we turn to the synoptic pericope of Peter's confession at Caesarea
Philippi.

I.   *Mark 8.27–33: W. Wrede, J. Weiss, and R. Bultmann*

Here, as in so many instances, the modern orientation of the
problems connected with the synoptic pericope Mark 8.27–33
begins with the work of William Wrede. In his book,[2] which
even today must still be judged a classic, he set forth an impressive denial of Jesus' messianic consciousness, though it should be
noted that at first, until the time of W. Bousset,[3] scholars were
generally hesitant about following him in his argument. Naturally Wrede had to contest the historical authenticity of the
messianic confession;[4] but his reasons for doing so were inadequate and had no enduring success. He also mentioned the
possibility that the incident might have had a special occasion

[2] William Wrede, *Das Messiasgeheimnis in den Evangelien*, 1901, pp. 115ff.

[3] Wilhelm Bousset in *ThR* 5 (1902), pp. 307ff. and in his *Jesus*, 1904, pp.
84f., 98. Cf. also the description in Werner G. Kümmel, *Das Neue Testament:
Geschichte der Erforschung seiner Probleme*, 1958, p. 367.

[4] Wrede, *op. cit.*, p. 115, deduces the non-historicity of the Caesarea
Philippi pericope directly from his analysis of the 'secret Messiahship'.

and stimulus in the fact 'that Peter was the first to recognize the Resurrected Jesus'.[5] It is of course no accident that Johannes Weiss in his book, *Das älteste Evangelium*[6] – dedicated in large measure to refuting Wrede – attaches a considerable amount of importance to Peter's confession, seeing in it a kind of *rocher de bronze* for Jesus' messianic consciousness; this way of viewing the matter bound his judgment completely, in the final analysis, to nineteenth-century categories. He does admit that this and other messianic pericopes reflect all too clearly 'how hesitant, hopeful, and vague attitudes and ideas were until the Passion', but for this very reason they 'were not created by the more confident faith of the post-resurrection Church'.[7]

The gaps in Wrede's demonstration – because of his presupposition that the messianic consciousness of Jesus was unhistorical, a satisfactory explanation of the incident at Caesarea Philippi is lacking – were filled in by Rudolf Bultmann in his essay, 'Die Frage nach dem messianischen Bewusstsein Jesu und das Petrusbekenntnis'.[8] He takes for granted the view, mentioned by Wrede only as a possibility, that Mark 8.27–33 comes from the Risen Lord and that the passage represents the faith of the primitive church, whose 'messianic faith grew out of Peter's Easter experience'.[9] In Mark 8.33, Jesus' addressing Peter as 'Satan', Bultmann thinks he can discern a relationship to the preceding verse, to the passion prediction (more precisely, to Peter's rejection of it); he also thinks, since he judges the pericope as a whole to be a post-Easter creation, that the passage reflects the polemic 'of the Hellenistic or even of the Pauline party' against Peter.[10] Post-Bultmannian critical NT scholarship has held widely to the view that Jesus had no 'messianic' self-consciousness and that the Caesarea Philippi pericope grew out of

---

[5] *Ibid.*, p. 238.

[6] Johannes Weiss, *Das älteste Evangelium*, 1903. Cf. also Bousset's review in *TLZ* 29 (1904), cols. 680–5.

[7] *Op. cit.*, p. 358. On p. 50 he suggests that it is 'arbitrary radicalism' to doubt the historicity of Peter's confession.

[8] *ZNW* 19 (1919/20), pp. 165–75; cf. also his *Geschichte der synoptischen Tradition*, 1921, 1964[6], pp. 275ff. (ET: pp. 257ff.).

[9] *ZNW* 19 (1919/20), p. 173.

[10] *Syn. Trad.*, p. 277 (ET: p. 258).

an Easter-story. But this view is also merely a *working hypothesis*, since it presupposes (with the evangelist) in Peter's confession that the Χριστός-title is a *Christian* confession and rejects *a limine* any attempt to give an historical interpretation of the Χριστός-title on the basis of the pre-Easter situation. But it seems to me, particularly in view of the position of the pericope in the structure of Mark as a whole, that this hypothesis is in the pure sense 'question-able', i.e. worth questioning [*frag-würdig*] by means of a *counter-hypothesis*. It is particularly unsatisfactory in answering one question: Where in the literary remains do we find Jesus' own stance?[11]

II. *Elaboration of the Question*

It is no longer necessary to discuss the fact that for the evangelist a high point and a turning-point are intended in the structure of his book in the pericope Mark 8.27–9.1, the messianic confession, or that the subsequent story of the Transfiguration (Mark 9.2–8) is intended as the divine confirmation of Peter's statement.[12] Mark here elaborates his christological concern. It is certainly striking that this is the only passage in which, through Peter as the spokesman for the disciples, the title Christ is accepted (with a command to silence, 8.30) by Jesus; nowhere else is this primitive Christian title read back into the words and sayings of Jesus.[13] It is noteworthy that the title is completely missing in Q. This can no more be accidental than

[11] On the fragmentary nature of the Marcan pericope, see *ibid.*, p. 278 (ET: p. 259). To be sure, he finds in Matt. 16.17ff. the missing response by Jesus to the (Easter-) confession Peter has been stimulated to make. I find this unacceptable, however, since it requires giving up the two-source theory as a working hypothesis, and it does so at a crucial theological point. Against Bultmann's thesis see, *inter alia*, Georg Strecker, *Der Weg der Gerechtigkeit* (FRLANT 82), 1962, pp. 201f. (with bibliography).

[12] Cf. Hans-Jürgen Ebeling, *Das Messiasgeheimnis und die Botschaft des Marcus-Evangelisten*, (BZNW 19), 1939, p. 205 (with bibliography).

[13] The sole exception within the synoptic tradition is Mark 9.41, in which Jesus is made to speak of Χριστοῦ εἶναι. First of all, it is clear on the basis of the history of tradition that the more original reading ἐν ὀνόματί μου (still attested by ℵ D W Θ it vg etc. – cf. the apparatus in Tischendorf's *editio octava* – and already suggested by 9.39) has been secondarily expanded in the sense of primitive Christian baptismal language by the expression ἐν ὀνόματι, ὅτι Χριστοῦ

the equally noteworthy fact that the title 'Christ' appears in only two other passages in Mark (14.61; 15.32), both times on the lips of Jesus' opponents.[14] But the opponents in these instances take up the Jewish concept of the Messiah, which refers to a political, this-worldly, eschatological figure.[15] May not the title 'Christ' in the scene at Caesarea Philippi perhaps also have been understood along the lines of the traditional Jewish messianic hope? If so, of course, a pre-Easter tradition must be presumed to lie behind the present form of the pericope; Peter must have seen Jesus as the future Messiah; and we must take account of and establish the case for a Christianizing of the political, this-worldly title 'Messiah' by appropriate elaborations in details and by the revising of the story itself. For it is beyond dispute that the evangelist himself wishes the title 'Christ' in the present form of the pericope to be understood in the sense of the post-Easter confession.[16]

The question of a possible pre-Easter *Sitz* posed by the title

---

ἐστε. It cannot be shown that this insertion came after the redaction of Mark. Furthermore, however, the anarthrous Χριστός, which occurs only here in Mark, is not an acceptance of the title in a true sense so much as a unique designation in Mark! On the passage see Erich Klostermann, *Markus* (HNT), 1936[3], p. 95; Bultmann, *Syn. Trad.*, pp. 152f. (ET: pp. 142f.); W. L. Knox, *The Sources of the Synoptic Gospels* I, 1953, *ad loc.*: 'the worst system of verbal association'.

[14] We also must not forget the fact pointed out years ago by Bousset (*Kyrios Christos*, 1921[2], p. 3): 'The entire gospel tradition (including the Gospel of John) never uses a title, but only the proper name ὁ Ἰησοῦς for Jesus in simple narrative. It never speaks of Christ, the Son of David, the Son of God, or the Son of Man, but simply of "Jesus".' Note 1 lists the following exceptions: Matt. 11.2; 16.21 and 1.1, 18; Mark 1.1.

[15] On the basis of the history of the tradition I should judge that both Mark 14.61 and 15.32 are secondary and presumably inserted by the evangelist. They serve to document for the whole world the Jews' rejection of Jesus as the Christ; furthermore, such inserted material, like that of the hearing before the Sanhedrin, must be connected with older traditions. Mark, in allowing the Χριστός-title to be used in scorn by Jesus' opponents, consciously leaves open the conceptual ambiguity – whether the title is meant in the Jewish or Christian sense. Neither passage may be used in further argumentation.

[16] This is rightly used as the point of departure in Ernst Haenchen's *redaktionsgeschichtlich* study of Mark 8.27–9.1 in *NovTest* 6 (1963), pp. 81–109. Haenchen, like Bultmann, views the pericope as a post-Easter formulation.

'Christ' in the Caesarea Philippi pericope is also raised by Jesus'
word to Peter as recorded in Mark 8.33: ὕπαγε ὀπίσω μου, σατανᾶ,
ὅτι οὐ φρονεῖς τὰ τοῦ θεοῦ ἀλλὰ τὰ τῶν ἀνθρώπων. The difficulty that
immediately following the messianic confession the association
between Peter and Satan (however it is to be interpreted) is
established, and that this association is maintained and transmitted in spite of the indubitable fact that the first resurrection
appearance is granted to Peter is frequently treated much too
lightly in the exposition of the pericope.[17] Naturally we must
not dismiss *a priori* the possibility that behind this text lies a deposit of Hellenistic anti-Petrine polemic and that rivalries for
hegemony in the primitive church are reflected here.[18] But the
intimate connection with the messianic confession fits ill with
this explanation even in the Matthean form of the pericope,
which is even more blunt than the Marcan form; Luke alone
removes the anti-Petrine invective.[19] In the case of a saying that
rebukes Peter as sharply as this one does one must deal as
thoroughly as possible with the probability of historical authenticity before minimizing the difficulty by assuming a relocation
of the saying during the period of rivalries within the church.
The Satan-saying must be explained by a blunder striking at

[17] It should be noted in passing that the Satan-saying creates no difficulties
for those who hold Mark 8.27–33 to be a unity and view it as the report of an
historical event. Those who accept the predictions of the passion as authentic
logia of Jesus will see the Satan-saying as the appropriate response by Jesus to
Peter's opposing his suffering. See, e.g., Ernst Lohmeyer, *Das Evangelium des
Markus*, 1959[5], pp. 168ff.

[18] Bultmann, *Syn. Trad.*, p. 277 (ET: p. 258). Günther Klein has
elaborated this line of argument in his treatment of the story of Peter's
denial in *ZThK* 58 (1961), pp. 285–328.

[19] Matthew inserts the undoubtedly post-Easter saying about Peter as the
Rock into 16.17ff.; this is intended primarily as Jesus' answer, solemnly
introduced with 'Blessed . . .', to Peter's confession. But Matthew's taking
up (16.20) of the command to silence, which in this context is quite unnecessary, clearly reflects the priority of the Marcan text. Hence even
though the first passion-prediction and Peter's defence ἵλεώς σοι, κύριε
occur as new inserted elements, the Satan-saying is none the less substantially
sharper and more severe, because it practically nullifies the macarism. Luke,
on the other hand, has here simply eliminated (as he so often does) material
derogatory to the apostles and skilfully appended the saying about bearing
the cross directly to the prediction of the passion.

the heart of the faith, which theoretically could certainly be located as easily after Easter as before it. To locate it after Easter one would have to make an anti-Petrine group responsible for the saying; this would create the difficulty, however, that in Matt. 16.17–19 a saying is secondarily inserted into the Caesarea Philippi pericope which sets forth not only the resurrection-appearance to Peter but also the claim to hegemony in the church of the Peter-group, while only shortly thereafter (in 16.23) an anti-Petrine saying of the rival group is preserved! Hence if one judges the sayings directed to Peter (Matt. 16.17–19 and 16.23 = Mark 8.33) as reflections of rivalries in the primitive church he finds himself in the dilemma of having to accept the view that in this pericope, central for Matthew, pointedly pro- and anti-Petrine statements are combined and harmonized. It is not convincing, of course, to argue on the basis of the Matthean text, although we must not assume that the first evangelist naïvely took over the Marcan concept and merely elaborated it. I have chosen to examine the Matthean redaction only in order to point up the difficulty in Mark, where the tradition of a saying like 8.33b from the first Christian generation is taken up; this saying obviously created difficulties for the historical and theological *Tendenz* of that period. Sayings like Mark 8.33b could be retained in such periods only because they pointed back to an event that was still too well-known to be passed over. Here too one must be subject – *mutatis mutandis* – to Bengel's rule: *lectio difficilior probabilior*. In my opinion the same applies to Peter's denial (which is not here under discussion), though of course only to its facticity, not to the whole pericope, which has doubtless been completely revised and retouched with secondary materials.[20] Yet such observations and comments still do not

[20] It is painful to me to have to differ in the judgment of Peter's denial with both Bultmann, *Syn. Trad.*, p. 290 (ET: p. 269; cf. also *Erg.-Heft*, 1962, p. 43) and Klein (see above, note 18). Both see in the story of Peter's denial a post-Easter legend and set over against it the old and materially parallel tradition, preserved in Luke 22.31f., of the inerrancy in matters of faith which characterizes Peter above all the disciples. It is not to be doubted that Luke 22.31 belongs to an old tradition. This is indicated even in the address, 'Simon' (on this see my remarks in *ThR* 25 [1959], p. 196). The question

provide evidence for the authenticity of the 'messianic' confession and the Satan-saying in the life of Jesus. They have only
opened up this possibility and posed the question: Is the missing
answer to Peter's confession to be found in Jesus' Satan-saying?
And does the original cause of the Satan-saying lie in the pro-
vocative title, 'Messiah'?

III.   *Analysis of the Caesarea Philippi Pericope in the History of the Tradition*

1. In Mark 8.27 and Matt. 16.13 the story is given a setting:
Jesus comes with his disciples into the villages which belong to
the region of Caesarea Philippi. The reference is to the region
around the southern slopes of Mount Hermon, the Hellenistic
colony of *Πανιάς*, not far from the source of the Jordan. Josephus
also called the city itself *Πανεάς*.[21] Because of the reference to a
region lying considerably to the north and peopled by Gentiles
(though not to the exclusion of Jews[22]) this setting is often viewed

---

here is merely whether Luke 22.31 puts in our possession such overwhelming
evidence of Peter's inerrancy that all synoptic utterances which put Peter in
a negative light can be disclosed to be secondary and tendentious formulations. I am compelled to answer this question in the negative, since I cannot
accord the Lucan saying historical priority over *both* the Satan-saying and
Peter's denial. For Luke 22.31f. refers back to Peter's first Easter-confession;
materially, therefore, it is a *vaticinium ex eventu* (cf. Dibelius, *Formgeschichte*,
1957[3], p.201 [ET: p.200]). The promise – especially if we exclude the
ἐπιστρέψας (22.32b) as a secondary Lucan gloss in anticipation of the denial
(so, rightly, Bultmann, p.288 [ET: p.267] and Klein, p.302) – is not incompatible with the pre-Easter errors and missteps of Peter, the disciples'
spokesman. Furthermore, Klein has rightly seen that the denial is rooted
badly in the context of the passion-story, and the treatment of Luke 22.31f.
is only one argument – though admittedly an important one – in his essay.

21 Cf. also Jos. *Antiq.* xviii. 28: *Πανεάδα τὴν πρὸς ταῖς πηγαῖς τοῦ Ἰορδάνου
κατασκευάσας ὀνομάζει Καισάρειαν*; hence he speaks of the city itself in terms of
the region. The founding of *Καισάρεια* occurred early in Philip's reign, 3/2
BC; cf. Schürer II §23, n.416 (cf. ET: II. 1, p.133, n.339). Agrippa II re-
named the city *Νερωνίας* in Nero's honour: Jos. *Antiq.* xx. 211. Cf. G. Hölscher
in Pauly-Wissowa xviii.2 (1949), 594–600 (art. *Πανιάς*).

22 On the Jewish-Christian Ebionites, cf. Epiphanius, *Haer.* 30. 18.
On Eusebius' remarks on an early Christian relief in Caesarea as a memorial
of the healing of the woman with an issue of blood (*HE* VII.18.2) cf. W.
Weber in *Festgabe für Adolf Deissmann*, 1927, pp.38f.

as a guarantee of the story's authenticity.[23] Bultmann has suggested that Mark 8.27a be attached to the preceding pericope (the healing of the blind man of Bethsaida) as its conclusion, and points to the analogy of the pericope of the Syrophenician woman (7.24–31), where the story begins with the setting (v. 24) and also ends (v. 31) the same way.[24] But if 7.31 is attached to the pericope of the Canaanite woman the following section (the healing of the deaf and dumb man, 7.32ff.) would be left without any indication of place, at either the introduction or the conclusion. This would be unique in the entire synoptic tradition. Hence one may not set aside the localizing of the pericope by removing 8.27a and pointing to the preceding passage.

In the case of a story like that of Peter's confession the tradition has no interest in a setting as such. Possibly it has replaced a location in *time* in the case of the Marcan text and Luke has eliminated the notice because it seemed to exceed the geographical bounds of his *vita Jesu*. Then Mark ascertained the time of the dialogue from the various sojourns of the itinerant prophets and gave a framework, albeit a rather imprecise one, to the tradition. Here in Mark 8.27 the dialogue occurs ἐν τῇ ὁδῷ, i.e. along the road towards Caesarea Philippi. This is probably a characteristically Marcan place description – which, however, in itself says nothing either for or against its reliability. A certain difficulty is created by the naming of Caesarea Philippi for those who see in the pericope a reflection of the Easter events, in so far as they do not wish to localize the first resurrection appearance in that northerly region (for which in any case there is really no evidence).[25] On the other hand, it is illegitimate, in view of the

---

[23] Karl Ludwig Schmidt, *Der Rahmen der Geschichte Jesu*, 1919, pp. 215ff.

[24] *ZNW* (1919/20), p. 169; *Syn. Trad.*, p. 68 (ET: p. 64).

[25] That it did not take place in Jerusalem itself is quite probable. But if the region around Caesarea Philippi were really connected historically with this event there would have to be more evidence of it in the tradition. It would be going too far to deduce the existence of a Jewish-Christian community in Caesarea Philippi (or Panias) in the middle of the first century on the basis of the citation from Epiphanius (note 22, above) and further to deduce a local tradition on which the community might then have provided itself with a Petrine claim.

questionable nature of *all* place notices in the synoptic pericopes to base the historicity of passages on those individual elements[26] that do not fit the usual categories.[27]

2. Jesus takes the initiative in the dialogue and asks his disciples what men think of him. This in itself is striking. Does he not know that himself? Do the disciples know better than he? Wrede and Bultmann see a secondary stylistic form in Jesus' asking the opening question.[28] Mundle would dissipate this form-critical observation by appeal to the Socratic dialogue.[29] Of course Socrates may not be used to weaken the force of form-critical observations. Yet we may be permitted to ask whether these form-critical observations establish so binding a law for the synoptic tradition as to provide a fixed criterion of authenticity. And to this question, in my opinion, we must answer No. For only in the case of a question used in *exposition* – say, in the con-troversy-discourses – is it legitimate to point to a redactional technique of a secondary nature, not in the case of *a question which forms a component of a unit of tradition*.[30] The question in Mark 8.27b, therefore, could be original, if one accepts the view that here the evangelist has completely reworked the tradition he received and introduced into his christological theme, by the insertion and omission of material, something important and well-known to the community. Only if one were forced to view

[26] In any event, it is somewhat suspicious that the introductions of Mark 7.31f. and 8.22 correspond so pervasively:

8.22 ἔρχονται	7.31 ἐξελθών
φέρουσιν	φέρουσιν
καὶ παρακαλοῦσιν	καὶ παρακαλοῦσιν

[27] Cf. the careful investigation of the place notices in Ebeling, *Messiasge-heimnis*, pp. 210ff.; Ebeling also views Mark 8.27a as a redactional introduction.

[28] Wrede, *Messiasgeheimnis*, pp. 238f.; Bultmann, *Syn. Trad.*, p. 276 (ET: p. 257).

[29] *ZNW* 21 (1922), pp. 308f.; on this, see Bultmann, *Syn. Trad.*, p. 276, n. 1 (ET: p. 257, n. 5); against Mundle see also H. J. Ebeling, *op. cit.*, p. 214, n. 4.

[30] We may point, e.g., to Jesus' question in the pericope about the healing on the Sabbath in Mark 3.4, where it is doubtless an integral part of the story, not exposition. Jesus does not ask to *find* out something; he asks to *point* out something.

the pericope (8.27–33) as an original unity, in fixed form, would the introductory question prove to be *expository* and thus to bear the stamp of the secondary. Whether this is in fact the case, however, can be shown only by an investigation of what follows. At this point we may merely affirm the unity of vv. 27b–29a, quite apart from the question of whether it is primary or secondary tradition, pre-Easter or post-Easter argumentation.

The disciples' answer to Jesus' question is that the people view him as John the Baptist, or as Elijah, or as one of the prophets – and Matthew adds, as Jeremiah (16.14).[31] The difficulties occasioned by these particular names are well-known and need not be discussed here. But we may point out that finding here an intentional christological tendency (which might have determined the selection) creates difficulties of its own. These difficulties, however, are also not of a kind to create an immediate presumption of authenticity. It is more probable that a precursor-dogma has left its mark in the text, as in John 1.19ff.

3. As for the wider context, it may suffice for the moment to concentrate on v. 29b, where the question is directed to the disciples as a group and Peter as their spokesman answers, σὺ εἶ ὁ Χριστός. According to the Marcan portrayal this is supposed to be the first appearance of the messianic faith within the esoteric group of the disciples. In Mark Jesus' answer is not introduced by a macarism addressed to Peter, as in Matt. 16.17; but even in Mark Peter's confession is confirmed by the story of the Transfiguration and especially by the divine voice (9.7), even though the title itself is modified.

The understanding of the confession offered by the disciples' spokesman is completely dependent upon the question of its origin; it makes no real difference whether it rests on pre-Easter tradition or is simply a post-Easter creation. The Χριστός-title

---

[31] The difficulty created by the selection of John the Baptist, Elijah, and some one of the prophets was felt as early as Matthew. The Matthean conception then presumably led to the interpolation in 5 Ezra 2.17f., the only passage in which Jeremiah appears (alongside Isaiah) as an eschatological figure. It is possible that the names and other formulations are consciously intended to portray groping conjecture. The foolishness of what the ἄνθρωποι say provides the stage-setting for Peter's answer in v. 29b.

does not in itself afford a means of determining its precise content. A pre-Easter tradition would require as the only possible meaning of the answer: 'Thou art the *Messiah*' – and the messianic title could only be conceived of as the current Jewish qualification of the coming Ruler.[32] On the other hand, the acceptance of the view that the title involves a reading-back of the post-Easter confession of the primitive church requires that it be understood as a Christianized title, familiar to us but, from the *religionsgeschichtlich* point of view, then quite new.

These alternatives are posed very sharply as soon as one takes into account all the possible, well-attested pre-Easter messianic conceptions. If one takes seriously the possibility that Mark 8.29b is authentic, then he must agree with our suggestion that what is intended here is the Jewish Messiah and that Jesus is recognized as the Messiah of the future. We may assume here that the association of the concepts 'Messiah' and 'Son of Man' was first made in the primitive church, and we can largely omit the controversy over the Son of Man, which has recently been renewed in any case.[33] If in pre-Christian thought the conceptions of the Messiah and the Son of Man are not only stamped with differing genealogies but are also competing eschatological

[32] This is rightly emphasized by J. Héring, *Le royaume de Dieu et sa venue* (1937), 1959[2], pp. 51ff. See also Oscar Cullmann, *Petrus, Jünger, Apostel, Martyrer* (1952), 1960[2], pp. 200f. (ET: pp. 179f.); his *Der Staat im NT*, 1956, p. 18 (ET: p. 18); and his *Christologie des NT*, 1957, pp. 122ff. (ET: pp. 122ff.); W. Grundmann, *Das Evangelium n. Mk*, 1959, p. 168. Cf. also Ferdinand Hahn, *Christologische Hoheitstitel* (FRLANT 83, 1963), pp. 174f. That the danger of a 'misunderstanding' of the title in the Jewish sense was also felt in the early church is shown by the elaboration of the title carried over from Matt. into the Marcan MSS. ℵ W φ etc.: ὁ υἱὸς τοῦ θεοῦ (τοῦ ζῶντος).

[33] Only Eth En provides an exception with respect to the association of the concepts of the Messiah and the Son of Man; but even here the interpretation is disputed. It is also significant that there is no evidence for an association of the conceptions of Messiah or Son of Man with the concept of the suffering Servant of God in Judaism. On the controversy, see: Philipp Vielhauer, 'Gottesreich und Menschensohn', *Festschrift für Günther Dehn*, 1957, pp. 51–79; H. E. Tödt, *Der Menschensohn in den Synopt. Evangelien*, 1959, esp. Excursus, pp. 298–315 (ET: pp. 329–47); Eduard Schweizer, 'Der Menschensohn', *ZNW* 50 (1959), pp. 185–209; and his 'The Son of Man', *JBL* 79 (1960), pp. 119–29; Hahn, *op. cit., passim*; Vielhauer, 'Jesus und der Menschensohn', *ZThK* 60 (1963), pp. 133–77.

figures, the question immediately arises concerning the Χριστός-title in Peter's confession: Does a suffering, dying, and resurrected Messiah exist in Jewish thought? Further: Is the differentiation in the Qumran texts between a priestly and a royal Messiah significant for the understanding of the Petrine Χριστός-title?

Both questions are to be answered in the negative.[34] Although one must be very careful about systematizing the Jewish conceptions of the Messiah, because quite different expressions crop up with differences of time, place, kind of community, etc., and also because older biblical conceptions were constantly being taken up anew and reinterpreted, we still cannot assert that at the time of Jesus the concept 'Messiah' was a 'form' of the hope of a redeemer, a hope that could be 'filled with the most widely varying content'.[35] There are rather clear constant factors which impose both positive and negative limits on messianic concepts,[36] so long as one concentrates on the single concept 'Messiah' and does not include various redeemer-figures in it. The varieties of things in the secondary literature that are subsumed under pre-Christian understandings of the concept 'Messiah' serve in many ways to mystify rather than to provide clarification of that concept.

One 'positive' constant is the prophetic promise of the 'Anointed King of Israel' who will establish a Kingdom whose Rule is permanent.[37] Charismatic traits are also attributed to this Messiah-King: He is endowed with a 'Spirit', he exercises authority vicariously for Yahweh on earth, and he intercedes for the rights of the poor.[38] Furthermore, in spite of the recurrent

[34] See, on both questions, Excursuses I and IV in Hahn (*op. cit.*, pp. 54ff., 231ff.) and Günther Klein in *RGG*[3] IV, 906f. (with bibliography).

[35] Cullmann, *Christologie*, pp. 111f. (ET: pp. 111f.).

[36] Cullmann himself rightly adds that *the* messianic type which came to prevail was 'that which we roughly designate "political Messiah" or simply the "Jewish Messiah" ' (*ibid.*, p. 112 [ET: p. 112]).

[37] On the anointing of the King in Israel see Martin Noth, 'Amt und Berufung im AT' (*Bonner Akadem. Reden*, 19, 1958 = *Gesammelte Studien zum AT*, 1960², pp. 309ff.); Gerhard von Rad, *Theologie des AT* I, 1957, pp. 304ff. (ET: pp. 306ff.); II, 1960, pp. 125ff. (ET: pp. 112ff.). For the oldest messianic predictions in the OT see esp. Isa. 8.23–9.6; 11.1–9; Micah. 5.1–3.

[38] Cf. esp. Isa. 11.2–5.

disorder in the post-exilic period, the view continues to be held[39] that the messianic king is to come from the Davidic dynasty and hence is to be the 'Son of David'. A persistent 'negative' constant is that there is no association of a dogma of suffering with the Messiah-King: indeed, in conjunction with the hope of the this-worldly kingdom there can hardly be any. The Messiah is not the 'suffering Just One'. What is retained, at least for the concept of the Messiah in the Judaism of Jesus' time, is the OT expectation of the Anointed King of Israel.[40] One need only cite in this connection the fourteenth petition of the *Shemoneh Esreh* and Ps. Sol. 17,[41] in which the nationalistic messianic hope of Israel is expressed.

A reduplication of the Messiah-figure which is traceable from the time of Zechariah has now been more clearly brought to our attention in the Qumran texts. If Zech.4.1ff. speaks of two messianic bringers of salvation, the Davidic Zerubbabel and the Zadokite Joshua, the Qumran texts speak of the Messiah of Aaron and the Messiah of Israel, i.e., a priestly Messiah and a political Messiah – a conception found also in the Testaments of the Twelve Patriarchs.[42] At Qumran the eschatological 'Prophet' also appears, in addition to the two Messiahs. It cannot be shown, however, that the 'priestly' Messiah influenced the

[39] Cf. Jer. 22.24–30. It is noteworthy that in Ezekiel and all of deutero-Isaiah there is no Messiah-king; in deutero-Isaiah the Servant of God appears instead. On the designation of King Cyrus of Persia as Messiah in Isa. 45.1 cf. von Rad, *op. cit.*, II, pp. 258f. (ET: pp. 243f.) and n. 16.

[40] This is unanimously emphasized by Cullmann, *Christologie*, p. 117 (ET: p. 117); R. Meyer, 'Messias', *RGG*[3] IV, 904ff.; and Hahn, *Hoheitstitel*, pp. 156ff.

[41] The texts in German translation are given in P. Riessler, *Altjüdisches Schrifttum ausserhalb der Bibel*, 1928, pp. 9f.; 897ff.; the Hebrew text is given in Karl Georg Kuhn, *Achtzehngebet und Vaterunser und der Reim*, 1950. (ET of the Psalms of Solomon by G. B. Gray in R. H. Charles, *Pseudepigrapha*, pp. 625–52; of the *Shemoneh 'Esreh* in F. C. Grant, *Ancient Judaism and the NT*, pp. 45ff.)

[42] G. R. Beasley-Murray first turned his attention to the Test. XII with respect to the conception of the Messiah in *JTS* 48 (1947), pp. 1–12. His theses then were given further support by the finds at Qumran: Millar Burrows, 'The Messiahs of Aaron and Israel', *ATR* 34 (1952), p. 204; K. G. Kuhn, *NTS* 1 (1954/55), pp. 168ff. and *RGG*[3] V, 747f.; Kurt Schubert in *Judaica* 12 (1956), pp. 24ff.

Christian Christos-concept in any essential way[43] (except for the letter to the Hebrews), nor can it be established that here any vicarious, expiatory role is associated with the Messiah. The result of our investigation thus far, then, is: The pre-Easter concept of the Messiah designates the this-worldly, national Ruler, charismatically endowed, who establishes an enduring Kingdom and restores Israel.

If one expects in his exegetical, historical-critical work always to contribute in a fresh and radical way to the understanding of history and of the texts he must naturally above all be bold enough to take up anew questions which seem to have been long since completely settled. One such question is: Why must the association of the motif of suffering with the Jewish concept of the Messiah necessarily have been made only *after* Easter in the primitive church simply because one does not find it in the literature of Judaism? Must we exclude the possibility that Jesus himself set forth this association on the basis of passages like Isa. 49.7, with reference to the coming Kingdom of God, and that this association perhaps arose first *in nuce* in his own proclamation and was then merely rendered explicit and materially stronger by the community on the basis of the cross? Naturally it is no proof of one's scholarly freedom from bias to deny to Jesus any theological innovation and to ascribe everything 'creative' solely to the post- rather than the pre-Easter community. Theoretically the possibility cannot be excluded that a new conception of the Messiah might have been present even in the teaching of Jesus, one which by inference interpreted and corrected the Jewish tradition on the basis of the inbreaking βασιλεία τοῦ θεοῦ. Such a theoretical possibility, however, can only be raised to the status of an hypothesis or even of a thesis if the evidence supporting it can be found unambiguously in the various sources and strata of the synoptic gospels. And this has not heretofore been possible.[44]

[43] This thesis is held by G. Friedrich, 'Beobachtungen zur messianischen Hohepriestererwartung in den Synoptikern', *ZThK* 53 (1956), pp. 265–311. *Per contra*, cf. Günther Klein in *RGG*[3], IV, 906f.; J. Gnilka, 'Die Erwartung des messianischen Hohenpriesters in den Sektenschriften von Qumran und im NT', *RQ* 7 (1960), pp. 395ff.

[44] On this theme, see also the remarks below, pp. 189ff.

Hence as far as Peter's confession σὺ εἶ ὁ Χριστός is concerned, the following alternatives seem to be established as the only possible ones: *Either* Simon, as spokesman for the disciples, saw Jesus as the this-worldly messianic Ruler *or* we must recognize in the passage the post-Easter confession of the community, projected back into a setting in the lifetime of Jesus, in which the Χριστός-title used by Peter had become completely disassociated from the Jewish concept of the Messiah. On historical grounds neither possibility can be excluded. The exegete must therefore try to make his decision on the basis of the history of the tradition and the whole of the synoptic teaching.

4. Can *Jesus' answer* to Peter's confession still be understood and, if so, can it bring about a clarification of these alternatives? If we restrict ourselves to the Marcan text, omitting the special problem of the Matthean form of the pericope, we note that what immediately follows (8.30) in the command to silence is an attitude that is capable of quite different interpretations: in conservative circles it is interpreted as a confirmation by Jesus of Peter's confession, while in historical-critical exegesis since Wrede it has been increasingly recognized as characteristic Marcan redaction. If the Χριστός-confession is rooted historically in the life of Jesus, the command to silence cannot be Jesus' answer to it; it cannot be an implied Yes which for tactical purposes was put off into the post-Easter period. If Peter's confession arose after Easter, however, the command to silence is all the more clearly secondary Marcan reflection.

This is followed in Mark 8.31 by the first passion prediction and by the striking shift from the Christos-title in Peter's confession to the title 'Son of Man' in the words of Jesus. In the present Marcan text the identity of the two titles is presupposed; yet at the same time Peter's attitude shows clearly that they are fundamentally different concepts. The self-revelation of Jesus in the text refers explicitly only to his role as Son of Man and serves – in connection with the divine δεῖ – to proclaim his death on the cross *and* the resurrection. In Mark 14.61f. the terms Χριστός and υἱὸς τοῦ ἀνθρώπου are also associated. In this case we have a secondary stratum of tradition[45] in which the material unity of the two concepts has already become self-evident, but behind it lies the oldest type of Son of Man title, which refers to the *coming* Son of Man. This secondary passage in the passion story makes it clear that the connection between Mark 8.31 – the Son of Man is to suffer and rise again – and Peter's Χριστός-confession (8.29b) is literarily late and theologically impure. Actually we do not have to prove all over again[46] that all three passion predictions are *vaticinia ex eventu*. They are intended to overcome the scandal of the cross by means of a clear prediction made by the Son of God, to legitimize the event of the cross soteriologically as willed by God and thus to remove it from the sphere of Fate and the powers of this world – in short, to proclaim it as God's Victory.[47] It should of course be noted that the *vaticinium* is inserted at *this* point and that it remains here in all the synoptics, connected with Peter's confession. We shall return to this matter later.

But if Mark 8.31 is a post-Easter saying, how do things stand with the connection between the following verses (32–33a) and the passion-prediction? Are they automatically to be designated as also secondary? On the basis of Peter's reaction in 8.32, this must be affirmed. Stylistically Peter's reaction creates an extremely awkward impression: it picks up the ἐπιτιμᾶν of v. 30,[48] which recurs immediately in v. 33a; but this verb ordinarily carries quite a different *nuance*, and at a very early stage it must have provided the occasion for the assimilation of the text to the Matthean version. The whole picture of Peter's reaction must consequently have been created by the evangelist to provide a transition between the passion-prediction and the (already existing) formulation of the Satan-saying.

[45] Cf. above, note 15.

[46] We adduce the remarks, not yet confuted, in Wrede, *Messiasgeheimnis*, pp. 82–92; Julius Wellhausen, *Einleitung in die drei ersten Evangelien*, 1911², pp. 79–82; Rudolf Bultmann, 'Die Frage nach der Echtheit von Mt 16, 17–19', *ThBl* 20 (1941), pp. 287f.; and *Theologie des NT*, p. 30 (ET: p. 29).

[47] On this theme, cf. Dinkler, 'Kreuzzeichen und Kreuz', *JAC* 5(1962), pp. 93–112.

[48] As early as Mark 3.12 the verb ἐπιτιμᾶν appears as a reaction to the demons' confession. On ἐπιστρέφειν cf. Mark 5.30.

The introduction to Jesus' answer to Peter, which follows in v.33a, is connected only by purely external logic. Again the connection is stylistically awkward. Why the emphasis on the fact that Jesus turned to the disciples? Apparently because of the introductory words in v. 32: καὶ προσλαβόμενος ὁ Πέτρος αὐτόν κτλ. Is the intent to represent Peter's answer as heard by all the disciples? Or are the disciples, who sympathize with their spokesman, supposed to be included in Jesus' rejection? It is highly probable that a secondary connection with the context is present here, one that is reflected even within v.33a. The concluding answer of Jesus, which is given directly, is not really a solemn 'threat' and has no rabbinic parallels.[49] We need not enter here into the question of just *how* Peter is thought of as connected with Satan. His unreasonable request is called 'Satanic', i.e. it is a 'Satanic intention' or a 'temptation'; it is simultaneously interpreted as a φρονεῖν τὰ τῶν ἀνθρώπων. Expressions involving the antithesis φρονεῖν τὰ τοῦ θεοῦ/τὰ τῶν ἀνθρώπων do not occur elsewhere in the synoptic tradition, though they are well attested in the rabbinic literature.[50] Unless it is purely accidental, the use of οἱ ἄνθρωποι could be explained as the taking up of the same phrase from v.27b, which would then provide a framework.[51] In the context of that period the expression φρονεῖν τὰ τῶν ἀνθρώπων would imply opposition to the Passion, the attempt to prevent the sacrifice of the cross, while the phrase τὰ τοῦ θεοῦ would imply the acceptance of what had been proclaimed for the first time about the Son of Man (=Christ) in the prediction of 8.31. But if this first announcement of the Passion and both of those that follow are secondary, post-Easter *vaticinia*, whereas the Satan-saying goes back to an historically attested rebuke to Peter as the spokesman for the disciples – to what can the φρονεῖν be related?

[49] Cf. Morton Smith, *Tannaitic Parallels to the Gospels* (*JBL* Monograph Series, vi, 1951), p.30 and n. 100 on p.44.

[50] Bill. I, p. 748.

[51] J. Sundwall, *Die Zusammensetzung des Markusevangeliums* (Acta Acad. Aboensis, ix), 1934, p.55; Günther Bornkamm, 'Enderwartung und Kirche im Matthäusevangelium', in Bornkamm-Barth-Held, *Überlieferung und Auslegung im Matthäusevangelium*, 1961², p.43 (ET: p.46).

The analysis provides the obvious answer: Since the command to silence is Marcan and the announcement of the Passion a post-Easter *vaticinium*, the Satan-saying (along with the phrase, φρονεῖν τὰ τῶν ἀνθρώπων) must relate to Peter's Messianic confession.[52] So Mark 8.29 and 8.33 belong together. The historical character of the messianic confession is strengthened by the Satan-saying, which can hardly be located anywhere except in

[52] This thesis has already been set forth in various forms and based on differing grounds; yet it has been neither generally accepted nor seriously confuted. Johannes Weiss, in *Das älteste Evangelium*, 1903, pp. 235ff., seems to have been the first to mention the connection between Peter's confession and the Satan-saying. But Weiss' views are too strictly determined by his opposition to Wrede's *Messiasgeheimnis*; furthermore, he is not yet ready for a really radical criticism, and he is still trapped in the *Ur-Markus* hypothesis. In the final analysis, he defends the pericope on psychological grounds after having mentioned (p. 238) as a possibility a reconstruction of the old tradition consisting basically of the following items: Mark 8.27b, 29, 33b. As a further basis for rejection he emphasizes the original connection between the Transfiguration and Peter's confession.

Without giving any literary analysis, A. Merx, *Die Evangelien des Markus und Lukas*, 1905, pp. 88ff. vigorously defends the thesis that the Satan-saying is related to the messianic confession because the declarations of the passion neutralize the concept 'Messiah'. He sees in the Matthean arrangement of the pericope, with the inclusion of Matt. 16.17–19, 'an interpolation which completely breaks through and even destroys the original context of the passage' (p. 91).

In this regard mention should also be made of Wellhausen, who in his *Einleitung in die drei ersten Evangelien* (1905, 1911[2]) – esp. in the second ed., pp. 70f. and 80ff. – strongly emphasized (without literary analysis) Jesus' rejection of the Jewish concept of the Messiah held by Peter.

E. Wendling, *Die Entstehung des Mk-Evangeliums*, 1908, pp. 113–19 has taken up the thesis mentioned (but rejected) by Johannes Weiss and offered a variant of it. He reconstructs the original text as follows: (v. 29b) ἀποκριθεὶς ὁ Πέτρος λέγει αὐτῷ· σὺ εἶ ὁ Χριστός. (v. 30a) καὶ ἐπετίμησεν . . . (v. 33) Πέτρῳ καὶ λέγει· ὕπαγε ὀπίσω μου, σατανᾶ . . . (vv. 36, 37; 9.2). Wendling's analysis of the sources, largely carried out without any very perceptive criteria, and his often impossible reconstructions of a primitive Marcan item are perhaps the chief reasons why the analysis of Mark 8.27ff. was also neglected and left undiscussed. In any case Arnold Meyer, 'Die Entstehung des Markus-Evangeliums', *Festgabe für Adolf Jülicher*, 1927, pp. 35–60, seems not to have recognized it in his defence of a connection between Peter's confession and the Satan-saying. However, he apparently does not understand the Χριστός title in the Jewish sense and relates Jesus' rebuke only to Peter's interference with what rightly belongs to God.

In 1934 J. Sundwall (see above, note 51), in conscious dependence on

the pre-Easter tradition; the confession itself is thus interpreted
as Jewish, this-worldly, and triumphally intended. Jesus explicitly rejects Peter's unreasonable request that he be the promised Messiah; he condemns it as Satanic, merely human
thought, opposed to God. The parallel phrase, τὰ τοῦ θεοῦ, then,
does not refer to the portrait of the suffering, dying, and rising
'Son of Man' but to the imminent βασιλεία τοῦ θεοῦ and the
μετάνοια which is now necessary once and for all.

Has this analysis resulted in the uncovering of an old element
of tradition? As far as Mark 8.29b and 33b are concerned, the
answer must be Yes. As for the rest, however, though we can
note seams and a certain amount of overlapping, we cannot
speak with assurance of old tradition. Of course 8.30, 31f. are
secondary, post-Easter insertions; the topographical introduction (v.27a) must also be judged secondary if we are to avoid the
ever present danger of historicizing theological tendencies and
then using them as historical evidence. The question to the
disciples in v.27b and the subsequent answers given by 'men'
(v.28), as well as v.33a all seem to be redactional creations.
Hence we must not boldly speak of a 'biographical apothegm'
including (with Ferdinand Hahn) vv.27a–29b, 33. Our counter-
hypothesis is that a fragment consisting of Peter's Messianic confession and the Satan-saying lies behind the pericope. The tradition has been so over-laid by interpretive post-Easter redaction
as to render more precise analysis and form-critical description
impossible. As a fragment of tradition, however, these two
verses, like the secondary inclusion of this old material in a post-
Easter context, provide evidence of first-rank importance for the
question of Jesus' stance on the messianic expectations then current; they also indicate a dramatic turning-point, in so far as

---

Wendling, put forth a reconstruction (p.55) that recognized in principle
the connection between Peter's confession and the Satan-saying, but it was
untenable both materially and philologically.

Finally, Hahn, *op. cit.*, pp.226–30 has set forth an independent and
extensive analysis of the Caesarea Philippi pericope that rests on real fam-
iliarity with the history of research on the matter; he is in partial agreement
with what I suggest here. He speaks of a 'biographical apothegm' consisting
of Mark 8.27a . . . 29b . . . 33.

Jesus' No to the messianic chimera destroyed the this-worldly illusions of many 'disciples' and pointed instead to the Kingdom of *God*.

IV. *The Rejected Messianic Office*

If our understanding of the connection between the messianic confession and the Satan-saying is correct, we must conclude that the rejection of the role of Messiah has also left traces behind in other passages. It must suffice here to set forth in summary fashion several indications that in spite of the thorough-going kerygmatic revision of the 'history' of the Synoptic tradition the traces of such a rejection are still recognizable, even though taken individually they cannot in the nature of the case be conclusive.

1. Jesus' eschatological proclamation of the *imminence of the Kingdom of God* is characterized, particularly in the oldest elements of the tradition, by an emphasis on the Kingdom itself and silence about the one who proclaims the message. The summary of Jesus' proclamation, formulated in Marcan terms in 1.15, with its twofold emphasis, ἤγγικεν ἡ βασιλεία τοῦ θεοῦ—μετανοεῖτε, still reflects the original correlation of proclamation and demand. But the secondary inclusion of the primitive Christian kerygma is equally clear in the addition, καὶ πιστεύετε ἐν τῷ εὐαγγελίῳ, which anachronistically makes Jesus Christ as the object of faith the content of Jesus' proclamation.[53] The tendency to replace the βασιλεία τοῦ θεοῦ by βασιλεία μου (sc. Χριστοῦ: Matt. 16.28) or the υἱὸς τοῦ ἀνθρώπου (Matt. 16.28 vs. Mark 9.1) or the υἱὸς Δαυίδ (Matt. 21.9 vs. Mark 11.9f.) shows the same shift from the event to the person. Because Jesus did not reflect on or speak about his soteriological or *heilsgeschichtlich* titles but assumed completely the prophetic burden of eschatological proclamation the Kingdom comes radically to the fore. On the other hand, because the Easter faith did not have at its disposal any honorific titles

---

[53] A comparison of Mark 1.15 with Matt. 10.7 and Luke 10.9ff. shows that the demand for faith in the gospel is a Marcan addition. Furthermore, Mark 1.1 fixes the meaning of the concept εὐαγγέλιον as the Good News which has Christ as its content. εὐαγγέλιον τοῦ θεοῦ (1.14) is a *gen. auct.* For the absolute use of εὐαγγέλιον cf. further: 8.35; 10.29f.; 13.10; 14.9.

legitimized by Jesus himself it necessarily took up a large number of overlapping and even contradictory predicates. If Jesus had accepted a Χριστός-confession, understood in the Christian sense, and merely imposed a command to silence on it (until after Easter), the theological struggle for adequate predicates would be completely unintelligible.

2. The *Passion-story* in the Synoptics reflects a clear ambiguity: It is intended, on the one hand, to prove (be*weisen*) by its details and the use of scriptural proof that Jesus is the promised Messiah but, on the other, to reject (ab*weisen*) the concept of the political Messiah. The incompatibility of these theological tendencies has never been overcome; it mirrors the dilemma of post-Easter reflection, which must defend the innocence of the Crucified One and at the same time assert Jesus' christological claims. But this brings clearly into focus in the oldest part of the gospel corpus the serious difficulty inherent in the title 'Messiah' itself.

3. We have already noted that the Χριστός-title is completely missing in Q. Now the enigmatic saying about the 'men of violence', which has retained its sharpness in spite of subsequent revisions, is present there; its authenticity is beyond question.[54] In its Matthean form (11.12f.) it speaks of the Kingdom of God, which has been promised in the law and the prophets until John.[55] From the time of John it has suffered violence. This cannot be meant in a good sense – as many church fathers and even Luther understood it, as if only men of violence could gain the kingdom of heaven – since the verbs βιάζειν and ἁρπάζειν are never used in a good sense but only in the sense of what ought not to be.[56] Hence the meaning here can only be that men –

---

[54] Ernst Käsemann, in *ZThK* 51(1954), p.149 (= *Exeget. Versuche* I, p.210 [ET: *Essays*, p.42]). He rightly points to the fact that the positive evaluation of John the Baptist, who belongs with Jesus to the new era and is set over against the time of the prophets, speaks in favour of authenticity.

[55] Even though Matt. is responsible for such secondary elements as associating the saying with other sayings of John and adding the reference to Mark 3.22, which reverses the two halves of the saying, it is beyond question that the Matthean form is more primitive than Luke 16.16f.

[56] Cf. Schrenk in *TWNT* I, pp.608ff. (ET: pp.609–14) and the bibliography cited there, including patristic bibliography; also G. W. Lampe, *A Patristic Greek Lexicon*, 1961–68, s.v.

wrongly – seek to force the Kingdom of God, to bring it about by force; and the meaning of the saying is probably that this is inappropriate, that men are to wait and to watch but not to use force. Of course, this says nothing negative about the title 'Messiah'; but it does represent a criticism of the identification of 'messianic kingdom' and 'Reign of God' and thus provides evidence of the problematic inherent in the title 'Messiah/Christ'.[57] Luke, however, in his own way, gives us the earliest interpretation of the saying. He no longer speaks of a criticism of a wrong conception of the βασιλεία τοῦ θεοῦ (as in Matt.), but of εὐαγγελίζεσθαι; and both the middle form of the verb and the insertion of πᾶς now serve to indicate the Gentile mission.

4. Mark 8.33, ὕπαγε ὀπίσω μου, σατανᾶ suggests a closer look at the third temptation (Matt. 4.8–10; cf. Luke 4.5–8), since here the same word appears[58] in a context in which worldly power plays a key part. It can hardly be disputed that the pericope, which comes from Q, is formulated along the lines of the Haggada and comes from the Palestinian community.[59] This

---

[57] Two interpretations are possible. The reference to the use of force by impatient, fanatical adherents of God's Kingdom is more probable than a reference to God's Kingdom suffering violence at the hands of hostile powers, in the sense of persecution. Rabbinic parallels in particular support the former interpretation: Bill. I, pp. 598ff.; H. Scholander in *ZNW* 13(1912), pp. 172ff.

It may suffice here to discuss the question of the Zealots very briefly. We exclude it because a special study would be required to do it justice, in view of the widespread thesis, most recently set forth (following others) by Cullmann, *Staat*, pp. 8ff. (ET: pp. 8–23) and *Christologie*, pp. 124f. (ET: pp. 123f.), that Peter's messianic confession must be understood in the context of Jesus' running battle with the Zealot movement, to which we may with more or less probability assign (from his disciples) Judas Iscariot, the sons of Zebedee, Simon the Zealot, and Simon Barjona (= Peter). On the question of the Zealots, see William R. Farmer, *Maccabees, Zealots and Josephus*, 1956; Bertil Gärtner, *Die rätselhaften Termini Nazoräer und Iskarioth*, 1957; M. Hengel, *Die Zeloten. Untersuchungen zur jüdischen Freiheitsbewegung . . .*, 1961; Hahn, *op. cit.*, pp. 154ff.

[58] In 𝕏 D it syr^{eur} even 4.10 is assimilated to Matt. 16.23 and ὕπαγε ὀπίσω μου, σατανᾶ is given instead of the better attested shorter form ὕπαγε σατανᾶ. The same MSS. also insert the words secondarily into Luke 4.8. It is to be noted that there is here no otherwise attested 'formula'.

[59] On the imitation of Haggada cf. A. Meyer in *Festgabe für H. Blümner*, Zürich, 1914, pp. 434–68.

temptation was either created on the basis of Mark 8.32f. and the fact, not yet forgotten, of its connection with Peter's misguided 'Messianic' suggestion or else it rests on a legendary variant of it.[60]

5. Bultmann has given extensive treatment to the Johannine variant of the Marcan form of Peter's confession in John 6.66–70 and commented on the Johannine elaboration of the more primitive Synoptic form.[61] The agreements and disagreements between John and Mark 8.27–33 are such as to suggest that they should be more thoroughly investigated, for the sake of both the question of the connection between Peter's confession and the Satan-saying and the opening up of the possibility that this tradition is historical.

One striking fact is immediately evident: In the Johannine material the title used by Peter in his confession is not ὁ Χριστός — Messiah, but rather ὁ ἅγιος τοῦ θεοῦ.[62] That is all the more striking in that this title never appears elsewhere in the Fourth Gospel, while a positive use of משיחא, transcribed as Μεσσίας, occurs in 1.41 and 4.25. Of course these two passages might also reflect a sensitivity towards Jewish modes of thought.[63] It would seem to me to be going too far, however, to erect a bridge to the demonic confession in Mark 1.24, where the confession reads, οἶδά σε τίς εἶ, ὁ ἅγιος τοῦ θεοῦ, and interpret the verb (ἐγνώκαμεν John 6.69) as the tertium comparationis.[64]

Another surprising fact emerges from comparing the two pas-

---

[60] The interpretation of the story of the Temptation is highly disputed. Bultmann, *Syn. Trad.*⁴, pp. 273f. (ET: pp. 255f.) rejects any messianic reference even for the third temptation. Dibelius, *Formgeschichte*³, p. 274 (ET: p. 274) says of the whole pericope in Matt. and Luke, 'The conversation itself, however, is concerned with the question of Messiahship.' Cf. also J. Schniewind, *Matthäus* (NTD) pp. 29f; Hahn, *Hoheitstitel*, pp. 175f.

[61] Bultmann, *Das Evangelium des Johannes*, 1962¹⁷, pp. 343ff.

[62] Cf. also C. H. Dodd, *Historical Tradition in the Fourth Gospel*, Cambridge, 1963, p. 219. On the title: *TWNT* I, p. 102 (ET: pp. 101f.).

[63] The narrative context of Andrew's communication to Simon (1.41) does not exclude the not yet Christianized concept of the Messiah, especially since the woman of Samaria in 4.25 makes known her 'pre-faith' in the 'Messiah who is coming, who is called Christ'.

[64] Dodd, *op. cit.*, seems to imply this.

sages: Jesus does not give a Yes or No answer to the confession –
which of course is not to be expected, in view of the position of
this section in the Fourth Gospel as a whole – but points instead
to the traitor within the circle of the Twelve: καὶ ἐξ ὑμῶν εἷς
διάβολός ἐστιν (6.70). In place of the Satan-saying addressed to
Peter the text stigmatizes Judas as a 'devil'.[65] This is presumably
a correction necessitated by the redaction of traditional material
in which the inserted passion-prediction, Mark 8.31 (along with
v. 32), was still lacking.

A further item of note is that many disciples ἀπῆλθον εἰς τὰ
ὀπίσω (6.66); they refuse to become disciples. This is noteworthy
not so much because of the use of ὀπίσω – this is common in
various contexts[66] – but because of the fact of the alienation of
some, a crisis within the circle of the disciples. It is, to be sure,
portrayed in the text as a consequence of the 'hard saying', and
Bultmann includes it in 6.6off., which he relocates as originally
following 8.30–40.[67] But quite apart from these *redaktionsgeschichtlich* questions it remains evident that the σκανδαλίζειν (6.61)
arises primarily in response to the Revealer's address and leads
to the crisis, the division among the disciples, where the Revealer points to the cross and thus shatters the merely human
ideal of the triumphant Son of God. Of course it is not impossible that this should be understood as the author's paradoxical
elaboration of the consequence and theological transcending of
Peter's false messianic conception as it is reported in Mark
8.29–33. This cannot be rejected out of hand, even though the
sequences of thought, especially in the context of 8.30–40 and
6.60–65, are so characteristically Johannine that they need not
be explained as reflecting the unevenness caused by a source
which the author had to reinterpret.

But apart from this question the fact remains that some kind

---

[65] Cf. Bultmann, *op. cit.*, p. 346, n. 1. On the correction of the Satan-saying
in the Judas/devil saying, see further C. Kingsley Barrett, *The Gospel according
to St John*, London, 1958, p. 254; R. H. Lightfoot, *St John's Gospel*, Oxford,
1956, p. 170.

[66] Cf. *TWNT* V, pp. 289ff. (Seesemann) (ET: pp. 289ff.).

[67] Bultmann, *op. cit.*, pp. 214ff.; and his 'Johannesevangelium', *RGG*³ III,
84off.

of historical relationship must exist between Mark 8.27–33 and
the tradition taken up and reworked in John 6.66–70. This relationship can hardly rest on the use of the Gospel of Mark by
John, for there would have been no reason to change the Χριστός
confession of Mark 8.29 into an expression foreign to the Fourth
Gospel, even if he were presumed to have read 'Μεσσίας'. Hence
we may assume, with Hahn, that even in the tradition used by
John the Messiah/Christ-confession was unacceptable and was
replaced by ὁ ἅγιος τοῦ θεοῦ, 'the expression used for the eschatological Prophet'.[68] In this case, different strata of tradition lie behind the pericope in the Second and the Fourth Gospels, but
both still reflect the unacceptability of the Messiah-title and
especially the sharp rebuke of Peter in the Satan-saying. Hence
it is permissible to find in the Johannine passage a genuine confirmation of the fact that Peter's messianic confession and the
Satan-saying originally belonged together, even though the messianic office rejected by Jesus can only be deduced from the controversies which are now glossed over in the text.

V.   *The Christianizing of the Title 'Messiah'*

It has become more and more widely recognized since Wrede
that Jesus did not understand himself as the Messiah, that he had
no 'messianic self-consciousness', and that he lived a non-
messianic life.[69] We may now add: It is very probable that Jesus
rejected both the role and the title of Messiah for himself. But
now a further question necessarily arises: How could it come
about that in spite of Jesus' rejection of it this title came to be
accepted and Christianized? For as the struggle in the primitive
church after Easter for an adequate honorific title for Jesus, the
Crucified and Risen One, is clear, and as the variety of such

---

[68] Hahn, *op. cit.*, p. 228, n. 4. R. H. Lightfoot, *op. cit.*, p. 170 also sees in
Mark 8.29 'the more primitive form of his confession'.

[69] Günther Bornkamm, *Jesus von Nazareth*, 1956, p. 158 (ET: p. 172), in-
sists, to be sure, that one ought not to speak of a 'non-messianic' history of
Jesus before the Passion. But apparently he conceives of 'messianic' here
in the broader sense and not in the limited and specific Jewish sense.

titles shows that the historical Jesus did not tolerate the title 'Messiah' simply imposing a restriction of silence on its use during his lifetime, it becomes all the more surprising that this title came to be used and later even became dominant.

The basis for the Christianizing of the title can be seen in the inscription on the cross, ὁ βασιλεὺς τῶν Ἰουδαίων, which is handed down by the synoptists in almost the same form as in John (Mark 15.26; Matt. 27.38; Luke 23.38; John 19.19).[70] Here we encounter the difficulty (for our interpretation) that widespread doubt exists about the hearing before Pilate and the predicate 'Messiah' found in it (Mark 15.2; Matt. 27.11; Luke 23.3; cf. also John 18.33) because Jesus' answer to Pilate's question, σὺ λέγεις, which is to be understood affirmatively, renders it suspect.[71] Because the title in the hearing before Pilate is secondary, however, it does not necessarily follow that the inscription on the cross is also inauthentic. On the contrary, the formulation of these words, which is Roman and contemptuous of the Jews,

---

[70] The historicity of the inscription on the cross is contested by Bultmann, *Syn. Trad.*, p. 293 (ET: p. 272; cf. also *Erg.-Heft*, 1962, p. 44), but it is strongly affirmed in many quarters: Martin Dibelius, 'Das historische Problem der Leidensgeschichte', *ZNW* 30 (1931), p. 200 (= *Botschaft und Geschichte*, I, p. 256) and his *Jesus*, 1960³, pp. 79, 115 (ET: pp. 95, 138); Hans Lietzmann, *Der Prozess Jesu* (SAB 1931, p. 320 = *Kleine Schriften*, II, p. 261) and *Geschichte der Alten Kirche* I, pp. 50f.; more recently esp. by Paul Winter, *On the Trial of Jesus*, 1961, pp. 107ff.; Nils A. Dahl, 'Der gekreuzigte Messias', *Der historische Jesus und der kerygmatische Christus*, 1960, pp. 189f.

In any case, as far as the substance of the charge is concerned Bultmann holds 'that Jesus was crucified by the Romans, i.e., that he died the death of a political criminal. This death can hardly be understood as the internally necessitated consequence of his ministry; it happened rather because of a misunderstanding of his ministry as a political one' ('Das Verhältnis der urchristlichen Christusbotschaft zum historischen Jesus' [SAH, 1960], 12 [ET in Braaten and Harrisville, *Historical Jesus . . .*, p. 24]).

The inscription on the cross was viewed as the basis for the taking over of the title 'Christ' as early as Clarence T. Craig, 'The Problem of the Messiahship of Jesus', *NT Studies*, ed. by E. P. Booth, New York/Nashville, 1942, pp. 95ff.; and Dahl, *op. cit.*

[71] Bultmann, *loc. cit.*, begins his criticism of the historicity of the inscription on the cross esp. with Pilate's question in Mark 15.2. In my view too this is secondary, even in so far as the title appearing here is concerned. But there must be some basis for the widespread use of the βασιλεύς-title in Mark 15.1–20, and in my opinion it is to be found in 15.26.

speaks very strongly for their historicity.[72] A Christian invention
would surely have chosen the title Χριστός, or at least not left it
out. The primitive church would hardly have designated Jesus
as 'King of the *Jews*', either, though perhaps as βασιλεὺς 'Ισραήλ,
since 'Ιουδαῖος refers to political and sociological contexts and
was first used by non-Jews and then taken over by diaspora
Jews, whereas 'Ισραήλ remained a self-designation with sacral
overtones.[73] It is also along these very lines that the contemptuous phrase used by Jesus' opponents at the cross is formulated
(Mark 15.32): ὁ Χριστὸς ὁ βασιλεὺς 'Ισραήλ. On the basis of the
authentic title used on the cross the title 'βασιλεύς' then became
the focal point of the concept 'Messiah'.

Because the One who died on the cross was raised by God and
revealed as God's Son the event of the cross was itself the act of
God and the title on the cross was God's ἐπιγραφή. Hence Jesus
of Nazareth was the 'anointed King' – naturally both 'anointed'
and 'King' in a completely new sense, established by God himself. The positive understanding of the cross which arose from
the Easter faith thus led to the acceptance of the title 'Messiah' in
this transformed sense and brought about the Christianizing of
the Jewish this-worldly messianic title. From the political Messiah arose the eschatological Christ; what did not get included
in the word was the triumphant victory of the Anointed One, of
course victorious through his death on the cross.

The pre-Easter traditions of the life of Jesus preserved in the
primitive church now demanded an interpretation based on
history. The kerygma of the crucified and risen 'Anointed One'
and 'Son of Man' corrected the period *before* the eschatological
event of the revelation of salvation. Both the course of events at
the time of the Passion and the proclamation of Jesus himself
were reconceived and modified on the basis of the confession of

[72] By the 'historicity' of the title I mean the authenticity of those words
which reflect the *causa poenae*, the αἰτία. This is not to assert that the bringing
of a formal charge such as is reported in the NT in Mark 15.25; Matt. 27.37;
Luke 23.38; and John 19.19 is assured. For this there are no parallels of any
kind in contemporary sources.
[73] Cf. K. G. Kuhn in *TWNT* III, pp. 36off. (ET: pp. 359–69) and
Dinkler in *Festschrift für G. Dehn* (1957), p. 83, n. 7.

the Easter-faith. The story of Peter's confession and the Satan-saying in the form in which they had originally been handed down were now unintelligible, so they were 'Christianized', i.e., taken over into the realm of the Easter-truth. Of course this happened in such a way as to leave the corrections clearly visible. Indeed, even in the Marcan text the messianic confession of Peter is met with the command to silence (8.30) and then the Messiah/Christ-title is interpreted by means of the passion prediction, i.e., corrected 'historically' (8.31), but in this form it is not affirmed by Peter. The position of the first passion prediction, which remains attached to the messianic confession in all the synoptics, thus shows clearly that at this point the church needed a commentary. This was necessary as long as the background of the Jewish concept of the Messiah still showed through in the title Χριστός.[74] Consequently, the present form of the pericope containing Peter's confession at Caesarea Philippi is the result and not, so to speak, the cause of the post-Easter association of materially different and conflicting conceptions of the Messiah and the Son of Man. For the cause lay in the event of the cross itself and in the possibility of interpreting the title on the cross, with its proclamation of the *causa poenae*, from the standpoint of the Easter victory.

The question may still be asked whether the groundwork for the association of the motif of suffering and the concept of the Messiah was not already laid in Jesus' teaching of humility and discipleship as a 'bearing of the cross'.[75] In support of this contention one might adduce the fact that Peter's confession and

[74] Similarly, Hahn, *op. cit.*, pp. 174f.

[75] Eduard Schweizer, *Erniedrigung und Erhöhung bei Jesus und seinen Nachfolgern*, Zürich, 1955; Schweizer defends in this monograph, undoubtedly important for systematic theology, a connection between the motifs of discipleship and suffering. But he seems to me to oversimplify when, without engaging in an appropriate analysis, he judges key exegetical issues like Jesus' use of 'Son of Man' or the original meaning of 'bearing the cross' by saying that Bultmann's theses on the question of the Son of Man or my interpretation of Mark 8.34 'cannot be sustained' (pp. 12, 14, n. 40; ET: cf. pp. 16–19). This is the place at which the ground for Schweizer's view must be laid and hence a counter-thesis confuted. On the question of the extent to which in pre-Christian times traits of deutero-Isaiah's Servant of God were

the Satan-saying are immediately followed (surely not accidentally) by the saying about self-denial and bearing one's cross, while the negative answer to Peter gives way to positive instructions to all the disciples. The words attested by both Mark (8.34; cf. Matt. 16.24; Luke 9.23) and Q (Matt. 10.38; Luke 14.27) go back to an authentic saying of Jesus, the oldest form of which is preserved in the Q-tradition and here in the Lucan form (as a whole). I showed in an earlier essay, also dedicated to Bultmann,[76] that originally the logion did not speak of the $\sigma\tau\alpha\nu\rho\acute{o}s$ and did not use the figure of the necessity of suffering and instead demanded $\lambda\alpha\mu\beta\acute{a}\nu\epsilon\iota\nu$ $\tau\grave{o}$ $\sigma\eta\mu\epsilon\hat{\iota}o\nu$, i.e., repentance and sealing. It should further be observed that in the Marcan tradition an original $\check{\epsilon}\rho\chi\epsilon\sigma\theta\alpha\iota$ $\grave{o}\pi\acute{\iota}\sigma\omega$ $\mu o\nu$ (preserved in Luke 14.27) has been replaced by $\mathring{a}\kappa o\lambda o\nu\theta\epsilon\hat{\iota}\nu$, which can only be explained on the basis of the expression $\check{\epsilon}\rho\chi\epsilon\sigma\theta\alpha\iota$ $\grave{o}\pi\acute{\iota}\sigma\omega$ $\mu o\nu$ in the Satan-saying, which necessitated the use of a different verb. But this fact shows that 8.34 is only secondarily attached by the evangelist to the confession of Peter and the Satan-saying and that it is actually a subsequent 'Christianizing' of the concept of the Messiah. The necessity of suffering is thus not to be anchored as a *topos* in Jesus' proclamation of the Kingdom of God and the urgency of repentance.

As far as the notion of suffering and dying in Jesus' understanding of his own vocation is concerned, two theoretical possibilities are conceivable, both of which are actually represented in exegetical history: (1) Jesus could gradually, step by step, have come to the realization that his conflict with the religious leaders of the people would lead to a crisis in which, outwardly at least, he would be vanquished. (2) Jesus could have held the theological conviction that the eschatological Prophet of the imminent Kingdom of God would have to suffer and die, either as the

---

carried over to the Messiah, see, most recently, M. Rese in $\mathcal{Z}ThK$ 60(1963), pp. 21ff., in critical opposition to Joachim Jeremias, '$\pi\alpha\hat{\iota}s$ $\theta\epsilon o\hat{v}$', *TWNT* V, pp. 676–98 (ET: pp. 677–700; also *The Servant of God* [SBT 20], 1965[2], pp. 45–79).

[76] 'Jesu Wort vom Kreuztragen', *Neutestamentliche Studien für R. Bultmann* (BZNW 21, 1954) 1957[2], pp. 110–29.

Righteous One suffering for his people, as a ransom for many
(as Mark 10.45 says of the Son of Man), or for the sake of the
self-sacrifice required by God in unconditional obedience.

In the former case the motif of suffering would have the
character of a gradually developing insight, based on experience
and eventually mounting to complete certainty, of the possibility
of a 'tragic' issue; Jesus' concern was that his disciples not be
mistaken about him and hence about the truth of his message.
In the latter case the motif of suffering would be a firm prophetic knowledge (based perhaps on Isa. 53 or Ps. 22) *prior* to any
specific experience;[77] Jesus' concern was to convince his disciples
of it and to correct, by instructing them in the divinely-willed
necessity of the act of redemption, their triumphal understanding of his mission, an understanding rooted in the Jewish
messianic tradition and hence opposed to the notion of suffering.

The synoptic gospels contain traces of both possibilities and
associate them somewhat naïvely: On the one hand, the necessity of suffering is not a gradually dawning insight on Jesus' part,
but a firm knowledge, fixed from the outset, of a thoroughly
theological and dogmatic character. As early as the controversy
over fasting (Mark 2), in fact, at least in the understanding of
the evangelist, there is a prediction of Jesus' death: the disciples
will fast when the Bridegroom has been taken from them (2.20).
On the other hand, Mark also passes on pre-Marcan traditions
according to which Jesus instructs his disciples about the necessity of his suffering only from one particular moment on (a
moment originally fixed late in his career but gradually becoming earlier and earlier), intending not to be understood by them.
The pericope in Caesarea Philippi is a very pregnant example!
One may also – as Hans von Soden used to do – distinguish between a *dogmatic* and a *pragmatic* suffering motif; but if he does,
he must grant, as Mark 8.27–33 itself shows, that pedagogical
motifs have crowded into the pragmatic conception as well.
What is really important for the question of whether or not Jesus
himself may possibly have corrected the current messianic con-

[77] So, e.g., H. W. Wolff, *Jesaja 53 im Urchristentum* (1950) 1952³; cf. also
the criticism by Ernst Käsemann in *VuF* 1949/50, 1952, pp. 200ff.

ception is the dogmatic rather than the pragmatic line. And here we must not allow the fact to pass unnoticed that in our synoptic gospels, in spite of the extensive pedagogical elaboration of the suffering-motif in conjunction with the Son of Man, the teaching itself – at least until Easter – seems to have remained completely foreign to the disciples. It is also noteworthy that the proclamation of the βασιλεία τοῦ θεοῦ is nowhere connected with an exposition of the motif of suffering, that a genuine *dogmatic* of suffering, so to speak, is absent, in spite of the announcements of the suffering. Our pericope is a clear illustration of the way in which the paradox of suffering is set forth as a simple fact side by side with Peter's confession of Jesus as Χριστός.

But such a combination is historically unthinkable. Either Jesus' knowledge of his suffering arose pragmatically, in which case it could not be used pedagogically; or it was dogmatic in nature, in which case it could not have remained completely foreign to his disciples until the crucifixion and, in its theological significance, incomprehensible. And if one or the other possibility had a point of departure in Jesus' proclamation, yet it would still be an inexplicable riddle that in the whole tradition incorporated in Q not a single saying on the theme of Jesus' suffering is either quoted or reflected.[78] We are forced to admit that Jesus neither took over the suffering-motif into his proclamation of the Reign of God nor taught an 'indirect Christology' himself.[79] Neither pragmatic nor dogmatic factors 'Christian-

---

[78] Naturally, this statement is intended with respect to the authentic tradition, not the canonical gospels, and it presupposes the results of the essay noted in n. 76, above.

[79] The concept of an 'indirect Christology', introduced, to the best of my knowledge, by Hans Conzelmann in his article 'Jesus Christus', *RGG*[3] III, p. 631 and in 'Zur Methode der Leben-Jesu-Forschung', *ZThK*, Beiheft 1, 1959, pp. 4–14 (ET in Braaten and Harrisville, *Historical Jesus*, pp. 54–68) is not a happy one, since it permits the inclusion of a post-Easter 'doctrine' in the proclamation of Jesus. This certainly preserves the 'continuity' between the two, but it inappropriately detaches Jesus' 'consciousness' of his mission and his authority from the conceptions current in contemporary Judaism. We do not doubt, of course, that Jesus saw his ministry, in word and deed, as an eschatological sign, that 'he understood himself as an eschatological phenomenon, as it were' (Bultmann, 'Das Verhältnis . . .', p. 16; ET in Braaten and Harrisville, *Historical Jesus*, . . ., p. 29). But to speak of an

ized' the Messiah-concept, but an event, an act of God in the event of the cross and the resurrection, laid the foundation for such a transformation.

The result of our investigation, then, is this:

1. The Caesarea-pericope, in its Marcan form, is the post-Easter reworking of a tradition that goes back to the lifetime of Jesus, a tradition, revised on the basis of the saving event of the cross and resurrection, that revealed Jesus as the Anointed One of God. The original tradition attests the connection of Peter's confession of Jesus as the future Messiah with an explicit answer on the part of Jesus, namely, the Satan-saying. According to this saying Jesus rejected the role of Messiah, and with the rejection of this role and this title he laid upon the primitive community the necessity of finding an adequate title for him.

2. The truth of the Christian confession that Jesus is the Christ does not rest on some kind of affirmation (covered over by the command to silence) by the historical Jesus of Peter's confession; it is an enduring truth based on the Easter-faith, which is an answer to the saving act of God in the cross.

3. The consequence of this is the establishing of a continuity between the proclamation of Jesus and the kerygma of the primitive church (i.e. in eschatology and the ethics borne by it). This may be differentiated – as the continuity of the thing and its meaning – but as far as pre-Easter messianology and post-Easter Christology are concerned, a change has occurred. This is not to be explained as a direct or indirect Christianizing of the Jewish Messiah-concept which can be traced back to Jesus; it is rooted *solely in the act of God*, which revealed itself to faith on Good Friday and Easter in the person of Jesus of Nazareth, who originally shunned all the traditional honorific predicates.

'indirect Christology' seems dangerous to me, since in Jesus' mission and authority the accent falls completely on the Reign of God, not on an indirect 'Christ' implied by it. Are not the bridges built here in the service of 'continuity' too massive? Is not the judgment of E. Heitsch, 'Die Aporie des historischen Jesus als Problem theologischer Hermeneutik', *ZThK* 53 (1956), pp. 196–210, closer to the truth of the matter, though admittedly more radical and certainly more provocatively stated?

4. This essay began with two statements by Martin Buber. The first, 'To claim to be the Messiah is fundamentally incompatible with Messiahship', is also valid for a critical-historical judgment of Jesus' stance on the messianic question. But for that very reason the 'first-ness' which Buber ascribes to him in the second statement is inappropriate for Jesus. For he specifically did not intend to be 'Messiah', and the title was first ascribed to him when the possibility of misunderstanding was eliminated by Christian reflection, in subsuming it under the dogmatic category of the Son of Man.

The essay has also become a critique of several of Bultmann's judgments on matters of the history of tradition and redaction; I could – and can – attest my gratitude to him only by such a 'critical' investigation. The result is, to be sure, along the lines of what he himself demanded in his Heidelberg Academy essay,[80] namely, that faith in the Christ-kerygma be kept separate from an ingeniously created continuity with the kerygma of Jesus. Jesus' proclamation is directed towards the Realm of God, not towards the person of the One who proclaims it. But the primitive church, on the basis of its understanding of the unity between the person of the Exalted Christ and the historical Jesus, did not hesitate to make its Christ-kerygma into the content of Jesus' proclamation and thus to allow its title 'Messiah' to be Christianized by Jesus himself.

[80] Bultmann, 'Das Verhältnis . . .', p. 17 (ET in Braaten and Harrisville, *Historical Jesus* . . ., p. 30).

8

The Risen Lord and the Earthly Jesus
Matthew 28.16–20*

Günther Bornkamm

I

THE concluding scene of the gospel of Matthew is simultaneously both more and less than an Easter-story. It is a continuation, to be sure, of the series of Easter-stories which precede it: the finding of the empty tomb (28.1–8), elaborated by the appearing of the Risen One to the women (28.9f.)[1] and the clumsy apologetic legend of the chief priests' deceit (28.11–15).[2] A rather effective contrast with this story, which relates the evil and ineffectual enmity of the Jewish opponents, is provided by the concluding scene, the appearing of the Risen Lord to the Eleven, which eventuates in Jesus' claim to full authority and in the Great Commission. Clearly the description of the situation in 28.16 corresponds to the angelic word in 28.7 and to Jesus' parallel saying in 28.10, even though there has been no real preparation in the gospel for the place description in the last scene, for the mountain, or for the reference to Jesus' instructions. Matthew 28.16ff. unquestionably belongs to the old (if still somewhat

---

* Translated from *Zeit und Geschichte*, pp. 171–91.

[1] Cf. R. Bultmann, *Die Geschichte der synoptischen Tradition*, 1958³, p. 313 (ET: p. 288); H. von Campenhausen, *Der Ablauf der Osterereignisse und das leere Grab*, SAH, 1958², p. 28.

[2] On the inconcinnities of this text see von Campenhausen, *op. cit.*, pp. 28ff.

isolated and fragmentary) tradition of Galilean appearances, and it is to be classed with that type of Easter-account which is centred in the Risen Lord's commissioning of the disciples (like Luke 24.44–49; Acts 1.4–8; John 20.19–23).[3]

Yet it is obvious that the text no longer reflects any interest in the details of the mere isolated event and that the historical framework is just barely indicated, not to say abolished completely.[4] The 'mountain' is not a concrete geographical datum; it is rather a typical site of revelation, as in numerous other Matthean passages (cf. 5.1; 15.29; 17.1), even though one must not immediately jump to the conclusion that it is a counterpart of Sinai. The appearance itself is not discussed at all;[5] it is rather presupposed in the expression καὶ ἰδόντες αὐτὸν προσεκύνησαν, οἱ δὲ ἐδίστασαν (28.17). This is in itself sufficient reason for not designating the whole scene as an appearance-story.[6] In the text there is not a single word about the nature and circumstances of the appearance and the disappearance of the Risen Lord, nor is anything said about the disciples' fear or joy or their recognizing the Lord.[7] All the more worthy of note, therefore, is the occurrence of the motif of doubt in 28.17, which is to be understood on the basis of the problems faced by the later community.[8] It is well-known that this motif shows up repeatedly in Easter-texts. Yet the disciples' doubt is overcome in various different ways in these texts: in Luke 24.41, the Risen Lord allows himself to be given food; in John 20.24ff., Doubting Thomas is permitted to

---

[3] Cf. Bultmann, op. cit., pp. 312ff. (ET: pp. 288–91).

[4] Cf. M. Dibelius, Die Formgeschichte des Evangeliums, 1963[4], p. 285 (ET: From Tradition to Gospel, p. 283).

[5] Contrast the Transfiguration account, Matt. 17.1ff. par.

[6] Vs. E. Lohmeyer, 'Mir ist gegeben all Gewalt', In memoriam E. Lohmeyer, 1951, pp. 26f. K. Stendahl, in Peake's Commentary, 1962, p. 798, also speaks of a 'glorious epiphany'. Dibelius, op. cit., p. 91 (ET: p. 94), rightly says of epiphany-stories: 'The epiphany in the miracle is for its own sake.' This is just what cannot be said of Matt. 28.16ff.

[7] Contrast John 20.16, 20; Luke 24.25ff., 31ff.

[8] This is lucidly demonstrated in O. Michel, 'Der Abschluss des Matthäus-Evangeliums', EvTh 10 (1950/51), pp. 16ff. Cf. also G. Barth in Bornkamm Barth Held, 'Das Gesetzverständnis des Evangelisten Matthäus', Überlieferung und Auslegung im Matthäus-Evangelium, 1963[3], pp. 123f. (ET: pp. 131ff.).

touch Jesus' wounds; in Mark 16.14ff., the Risen Lord appears once more to the hitherto unbelieving disciples. In Matt. 28.16ff., the situation is quite different. Here the question of the basis of the Easter certainty and the overcoming of doubt is answered by reference to the word of the Exalted Jesus alone; rational confirmation is dispensed with.[9] Clearly this answer is given with the later community in view, since for them the mere ὅραμα of the first disciples cannot and should not suffice; because it cannot, they are directed all the more to the full authority of, and the commission given by, the Risen Lord.

How centrally Matthew is concerned with the later community is also shown by the fact that nothing more is said about the Eleven, about the overcoming of doubt and about their faith and their confession, just as nothing is said about the departure and ascension of the Risen Lord. The scene relates completely to the present, which is to continue until the consummation; even Jesus' words, Matt. 28.18–20, are not, properly speaking, a farewell discourse.[10] The extremely abbreviated narrative of vv. 16f. serves only to introduce and prepare the way for these verses. They provide an impressive ending, not only to this scene, but also to the gospel of Matthew as a whole.

II

The words of the Risen Lord (Matt. 28.18–20) have been rightly designated as a key text and a kind of summary of the whole gospel of Matthew.[11] As we shall show, a very complex tradition is embedded in them, though this complex tradition has at the same time been given a unique interpretation. The grouping of the sayings is obvious: (1) the word about the full authority of the Risen Lord (v. 18b); (2) his commission to the

[9] So, rightly, Michel, *art. cit.*, pp. 17ff., who properly points to John 20.29; so also Barth, *op. cit.*, p. 124 (ET: pp. 132f.).

[10] Against J. Munck, *Aux sources de la tradition chrétienne, Mélanges Goguel*, 1950, p. 165, and Stendahl, *op. cit.*, p. 798.

[11] Michel, *art. cit.*, p. 21; G. Schille, 'Bemerkungen zur Formgeschichte des Evangeliums. II: Das Evangelium des Matthäus als Katechismus', *NTS* 4(1957/58), p. 113; E. P. Blair, *Jesus in the Gospel of Matthew*, 1960, p. 45.

disciples (vv. 19,20a); (3) the promise of his presence (v. 20b).
Obviously, the internal coherence of all three words[12] is highly
significant. This can be seen even in the concatenation of
phrases: πᾶσα ἐξουσία (v. 18) – πάντα τὰ ἔθνη (v. 19) – πάντα ὅσα
ἐνετειλάμην (v. 20a) – πάσας τὰς ἡμέρας (v. 20b).

The three sayings were certainly not a free formulation of the
evangelist. Rather they came to him from the tradition, as is
evident from the parallels to v. 18b (cf. 11.27; John 3.35) and
v. 20 (cf. 18.20) and from the formal character of the baptismal
command in v. 19. It is less certain whether Matthew or the pre-
Matthean tradition first united the three *logia*. The former is
more probable,[13] since there are no comparable parallels to
Matt. 28.18–20 as a whole. Moreover, connecting diverse sayings
and forming a unitary discourse out of them is particularly
characteristic of the technique of composition so masterfully
practised by this evangelist.

More important for a basic understanding of the text as a
whole is the question as to whether or not Matthew made use of
a current pattern in his composition. M. Dibelius in this regard
points to the association of self-recommendation and the call to
proclamation in Hellenistic-gnostic revelatory discourses (*Offen-
barungsreden*).[14] Yet the expression ἐδόθη μοι πᾶσα ἐξουσία ἐν
οὐρανῷ καὶ ἐπὶ γῆς (v. 18) does not, as in Matt. 11.27,[15] describe the
qualification of the Revealer; it describes rather the enthronement as Lord of heaven and earth, which is here (as often) connected directly with the resurrection, or, to put it more exactly,
equated with it.[16] There is some justification, therefore, for finding in Matt. 28.18–20, as some have, this well-known pattern,

---

[12] The well attested οὖν (v. 19) is missing in several MSS. But it is at least
consistent with the sense of the passage. καὶ ἰδού also attests this inner coherence.

[13] So Michel, *art. cit.*, p. 20; Barth, *op. cit.*, p. 124, n. 3 (ET: p. 133, n. 2);
per contra, G. Strecker, *Der Weg der Gerechtigkeit* (FRLANT 82), 1962, pp. 210f.

[14] *Formgeschichte*, pp. 282ff. (ET: pp. 283ff.).

[15] πάντα μοι παρεδόθη ὑπὸ τοῦ πατρός μου, καὶ οὐδεὶς ἐπιγινώσκει τὸν υἱὸν εἰ μὴ ὁ
πατήρ, οὐδὲ τὸν πατέρα τις ἐπιγινώσκει εἰ μὴ ὁ υἱὸς καὶ ᾧ ἐὰν βούληται ὁ υἱὸς ἀποκαλύψαι.

[16] There is no room in Matthew for a special act of ascension and exaltation such as we find in the Lucan and Johannine Easter stories.

which lies behind numerous early Christian hymns and confessions.[17] The motifs that ordinarily belong to the enthronement
of a new Ruler include the granting of full authority, the presentation and proclamation before the world of the one exalted as
Ruler, and his recognition by the peoples and powers. And there
are, in fact, many echoes in our text of this christological conceptual pattern, especially in the word of universal ἐξουσία in
v. 18 and also in the motif of the nations (v. 19a), though the
ὄνομα-concept of the baptismal formula (v. 19b) hardly belongs
to it.

But it is immediately obvious how severely the traditional
pattern has been shattered and transformed in the Matthean
text. One must not overlook the fact that it is a far cry from the
word of full authority in 28.18 to the known primitive Christian
hymns and confessions. The exaltation of the Risen Jesus to
Lordship is not expressly stated, however clearly the text presupposes it. It has become a part of Jesus' own claim and is to
be proclaimed as his full authority in heaven and earth. Nor is
any christological honorific title used. One might perhaps think
of the concept of the Son of Man, since the first word is possibly
formed in dependence on the Son of Man saying in Dan. 7.14:
'And ἐξουσία was given to him and all the nations and tribes of
earth and all glory, that they should serve him; and his ἐξουσία
is an everlasting ἐξουσία which shall not be taken away, and his
kingdom (is an everlasting kingdom) which shall not be destroyed.'* Yet in spite of the echoes of Dan. 7, the Son of Man
title should not be imported too quickly from this source into
Matt. 28, and the fundamental difference between the two texts
should not be overlooked, if for no other reason than that
the use of this particular title would imply the concept of the
Parousia. But Matt. 28 does not speak of the Parousia, but of
the Lordship of the Risen Jesus over heaven and earth until the

---

[17] Cf. Michel, *art. cit.*, pp. 22f; F. Hahn, *Das Verständnis der Mission im
NT*, 1963, pp. 52ff. (ET: pp. 63–7).

* καὶ ἐδόθη αὐτῷ ἐξουσία, καὶ πάντα τὰ ἔθνη τῆς γῆς κατὰ γένη καὶ πᾶσα δόξα αὐτῷ
λατρεύουσα· καὶ ἡ ἐξουσία αὐτοῦ ἐξουσία αἰώνιος, ἥτις οὐ μὴ ἀρθῇ, καὶ ἡ βασιλεία αὐτοῦ,
ἥτις οὐ μὴ φθαρῇ.

consummation of the world.[18] Nor do the honorific titles κύριος
(Phil. 2) or υἱός (Heb. 1) occur. Matthew 28.18 is completely
lacking in apocalyptic or mythological details. Nothing is said
of the homage of angels (Heb. 1.6ff.) or of the acclamation of
peoples and cosmic powers (Phil. 2.10f.; cf. also I Tim. 3.16).
Verse 18 is rather primarily and exclusively centred in the concept of ἐξουσία. In the gospel of Matthew, however, this concept
has already been used, always to designate the full authority of
the earthly Jesus in relationship to his teaching (7.29), his act
of healing (8.9), his word of forgiveness (9.6, 8), etc. The motif
of full authority as such does not serve to distinguish the risen
from the earthly Jesus; on the contrary, it binds them together.
Thus it is the earthly Jesus who says in Matt. 11.27, Πάντα μοι
παρεδόθη ὑπὸ τοῦ πατρός μου, which serves, as in Matt. 28, to
ground the claim for Jesus' teaching, just as in both passages the
recognition of his full authority is demonstrated by the obedience
of the disciples (μαθεῖν 11.29 – μαθητεύειν 28.19). So the only new
thing in Matt. 28 is the universal extension of his ἐξουσία over
heaven and earth.[19]

III

The commission itself, Matt. 28.19,20a, is not only palpably
the focal point of the group of sayings; it also bears a completely
Matthean stamp in both language and content.[20] Yet here too
we must not overlook the degree to which the evangelist is pre-
supposing and using traditional material, even though he does so
critically and with his own special emphasis. We have already
said above that this concluding pericope as a whole is to be
understood as a definite type of Easter-story, in which the ap-

---

[18] So, rightly, H. E. Tödt, *Der Menschensohn in der synoptischen Überlieferung*,
1959, p. 261 (ET: pp. 287f.) (vs. Schniewind and Lohmeyer); cf. also Hahn,
Mission, p. 55 (ET: p. 66).

[19] So, rightly, Strecker, *op. cit.*, pp. 211f.

[20] On the pericope as a whole, see G. D. Kilpatrick, *The Origins of the
Gospel according to St Matthew*, 1946, pp. 48f.; Barth, *op. cit.*, p. 123, n. 1 (ET:
p. 131, n. 1); Strecker, *op. cit.*, p. 209. The following are characteristic of
Matthean style (28.19f.): the pleonastic use of πορεύεσθαι, οὖν, μαθητεύειν, τηρεῖν,
πάντα, ἐντέλλεσθαι, καὶ ἰδού, συντέλεια τοῦ αἰῶνος.

pearances and the commission of the Risen Jesus are associated.[21]
We may assert with confidence that the command to baptize
and the baptismal formula also belong to this type of story in the
form in which they occur here. Yet this is not yet an adequate
characterization of the Matthean tradition, which we have already identified in the structure of the text as a whole and which
we must now consider more specifically in connection with the
commission itself. To be precise, what is unique about our text
is not only the association of appearance and mission but also the
association of exaltation and the mission to all nations.

The two motifs do not, however, belong together originally or
universally. The *logion* in Mark 13.10 (Matt. 24.14) 'The gospel
must first be preached to all nations' is related neither to the
resurrection nor to the exaltation of Jesus as Kyrios. Jeremias
finds the original form of the *logion* in Matt. 24.14[22] and connects it with Rev. 14.6f. in his interpretation of it: He denies that
Mark 13.10 (and 14.9) refers to the mission of the disciples, i.e., to
human preaching. The original reference of Mark 13.10 (Matt.
24.14) is rather to the consummation of all things, the Last
Judgment, and the 'angelic proclamation of God's final act'.[23]
But this can hardly be right. The use of fixed missionary terminology (κηρύσσειν, τὸ εὐαγγέλιον, πάντα τὰ ἔθνη) and the fact that in the
synoptic *logion* (unlike Rev. 14.6f.) no angel is mentioned speak
against this view.[24] Yet it is quite permissible to think that in

[21] See above, p. 203.
[22] Cf. J. Jeremias, *Jesu Verheissung für die Völker*, 1959², pp. 19f. (ET: pp.
22f.); *per contra*, rightly, Hahn, *Mission*, pp. 59f., 104f. (ET: pp. 70f., 120f.).
[23] Jeremias, *op. cit.*, p. 20 (ET: p. 23).
[24] For a more precise discussion, see F. Hahn, *Mission*, pp. 60f. (ET: pp.
71f.). To be sure, I do not find convincing his assertion that εὐαγγέλιον αἰώνιον
in Rev. 14.6f. means *the* Gospel, not *a* gospel (p. 47, n. 1; ET: p. 57, n. 4).
Naturally, in 14.6f., as in 10.7, what is meant is not 'just any divine message'
but rather the bringing to pass of God's ultimate mystery, the fulfilling of his
eschatological counsel of salvation, proclaimed by the prophets. But this does
not justify the equating of εὐαγγέλιον in Rev. 14.6f. with τὸ εὐαγγέλιον in Mark
13.10. The apocalyptist's vision anticipates an eschatological event, while
the proclamation of the gospel in the sense of the synoptic *logion* occurs before
the End. Of course Hahn does not deny this (though it speaks against his
understanding of Rev. 14.6f.). Moreover he rightly asserts that Rev. 14.6
*ex*cludes, not *in*cludes, a mission among the nations (p. 47; ET: pp. 57f.).

Hellenistic-Jewish Christianity the apocalyptic pledge of Rev. 14.6f., which certainly does not speak of a mission carried out by men, is redeemed by the world-mission of the disciples. The apocalyptic origin of the motif is still visible in the fact that Mark and Matthew insert the saying into the synoptic Apocalypse, even though the resulting conception of the saying bursts the bounds of the apocalyptic conceptual pattern. For it is beyond dispute that πρῶτον implies nothing less than 'first . . . before'[25] and inserts the observable epoch of the world-mission between the present and the Parousia.[26] It is significant that Matthew reproduces the saying without the typically apocalyptic concepts πρῶτον and δεῖ,[27] while Luke has completely eliminated it.[28]

It is important to note that Matthew in ch. 28 takes over the motif of the mission to the nations and co-ordinates it with and subordinates it to the concept of exaltation. This motif is also widespread apart from this association. Just as the great conception of the universal mission to all nations, of which we have just spoken, presupposes and expresses the delay of the Parousia, so the christological concept of the enthronement of Jesus as Kyrios has obviously contributed decisively to the extreme relativizing of the expectation of the Parousia of the Son of Man in the primitive Palestinian church. Nothing could be more inappropriate than calling the Kyrios-faith a kind of substitute by which the later community hoped to transcend its disappointed hopes. Rather the positive power of this belief in the exalted Kyrios and his present Lordship, which had already arisen early in primitive Hellenistic Christianity, prevented the delay of the Parousia from becoming a catastrophe for primitive Christianity, even though, as may be seen particularly in Paul,

[25] Cf. W. G. Kümmel, *Verheissung und Erfüllung*, 1953², p. 77 (ET: p. 84); Hahn, *Mission*, p. 62, n. 2 (ET: p. 73, n. 5).

[26] Cf. E. Grässer, *Das Problem der Parusieverzögerung in den synoptischen Evangelien und in der Apostelgeschichte*, 1957, p. 159, and H. Conzelmann, 'Geschichte und Eschaton nach Mk 13', *ZNW* 50 (1950), pp. 218f.

[27] Cf. Hahn, *Mission*, p. 104 (ET: p. 121).

[28] The πρῶτον is now dated; (in Acts) the universal proclamation of the gospel has become a reality in the present age. Cf. H. Conzelmann, *Die Mitte der Zeit*, 1964⁵, p. 109 (ET: *The Theology of St Luke*, pp. 127f.).

the Kyrios-faith and the expectation of the Parousia in the near future could be very closely associated. The beginnings of this Kyrios-faith are surely to be found, in spite of the accretion of layers of tradition, in the movement which is still more or less recognizable in the book of Acts, the 'Hellenists'. Apart from this movement (which early encountered persecution), particularly their attitude towards the Temple and the Law, which differed from that of the Jerusalem community, the new communities which they established (Antioch!), and their mission, in which the obligations of the Law were not imposed – apart from all this Paul and his work would be unthinkable. But more than this, this new christological conception, unaffected by all kinds of modifications and variations in details, made 'history' in the truest sense of the word.

Yet it is not immediately and universally to be found in association with the thought of the mission to the nations. Generally and indeed primarily the exaltation and Lordship of Christ over the world meant the conquest of the powers of the world[29] – a motif that could be elaborated in various ways: in the acclamation of all earthly, heavenly, and subterrestrial powers (Phil. 2.9ff.), in Christ's Lordship over the living and the dead (Rom. 14.9), in the redemption of the visible and invisible All (Col. 1.19f.; 2.9ff.), in the 'gathering up' of the All in Christ as the Head (Eph. 1.10, etc.), in the homage of the angels (Heb. 1.6ff.), in the victorious epiphany and proclamation of Christ in the heavenly and earthly spheres (I Tim. 3.16), in the liberating message to the spirits of the dead held ἐν φυλακῇ (I Peter 3.19).[30]

Nowhere in any of these passages is the motif *eo ipso* of the disciples' mission to the nations connected with the exaltation of Christ. And yet it is clear that the commission to the whole world given to the disciples and apostles could be and had actually been immediately connected with the mythically (and not his-

[29] Note the significance which Ps. 110.1 (in the Greek text, which alone contains the honorific title Kyrios) came to have in the development of Christology; cf. F. Hahn, *Christologische Hoheitstitel* (FRLANT 83), 1963, Exkurs II, pp. 126ff. and *passim*.

[30] On this, see R. Bultmann, 'Bekenntnis- und Liedfragmente in I Petr', *In honorem Antonii Fridrichsen sexagenarii* (CN 11), 1947, pp. 4f.

torically) conceived exaltation and epiphany of the Kyrios before the world. It is from this connection that the fixed if multiform sermonic type grew which N. A. Dahl has appropriately designated as 'pattern of revelation' (*Revelationsschema*).[31] In this pattern apocalyptic ideas and concepts are taken up and transformed in the service of an exaltation- and epiphany-Christology; it speaks of the mystery (i.e., God's eschatological plan of salvation)[32] which was once hidden and is now revealed. In this form the pattern is well-known on the basis of Col. 1.26f.; Eph. 3.4-7, 8-11 and the secondary doxology with which Romans concludes (16.25ff.). It is also richly attested in other early Christian literature in widely varying forms (without the concepts of 'mystery' and 'hiddenness').[33] It is known and used as early as Paul (I Cor. 2.6ff.). But he is not its creator. This is shown by the fact that he uses it himself in a fragmentary form, with corrections obviously directed against the gnostic heretics in Corinth.[34] From this we may conclude that these heretical teachers used the pattern in their own proclamation, although in a sense which differs from Paul's usage. What is characteristic for the concept as such is not so much a primary interest in the question of the historical *locus* and content of revelation as a concern with the question, 'Who can mediate revelation?' or 'How can I participate in the benefits of salvation?'[35] Thus it is not accidental that in the context of this pattern numerous concepts crop up which relate to proclamation and the authorized proclaimer: λόγος τοῦ θεοῦ (Col. 1.25), καταγγέλλειν, διδάσκειν (Col. 1.28), εὐαγγελίζεσθαι (Eph. 3.8), εὐαγγέλιον, κήρυγμα (Rom. 16.25), κῆρυξ, ἀπόστολος, διδάσκαλος (II Tim. 1.11; cf. Titus 1.3); cf. also I Peter 1.12; I John 1.3; Ignatius, Magn 6.1. It thus becomes com-

---

[31] N. A. Dahl, 'Formgeschichtliche Beobachtungen zur Christusverkündigung in der Gemeindepredigt', *Neutestamentliche Studien für R. Bultmann* (BZNW 21), 1957[2], pp. 3ff.

[32] Cf. G. Bornkamm, art. μυστήριον, *TWNT* IV, pp. 809ff. (ET: pp. 802-28), esp. pp. 825ff. (ET: pp. 817ff.).

[33] Passages cited in Dahl, *op. cit.*, p. 5.

[34] On this and what follows cf. D. Lührmann, *Das Offenbarungsverständnis bei Paulus und in den paulinischen Gemeinden* (unpubl. diss., Heidelberg, 1964), pp. 97-121.

[35] So formulated by Lührmann, *op. cit.*, p. 107.

prehensible that in this very conceptual environment such deutero-Pauline concepts as the apostolic office and the church as the bearer and mediator of revelation to the world were developed (Col. and Eph.)[36] and so were the teachings of the Pastorals about the called and legitimized apostle and the παραθήκη which comes from him. How familiar Paul himself was with such teachings is shown by his apostolic description of himself as οἰκονόμος μυστηρίων (I Cor. 4.1) and by the fact that in I Cor. 2.13 he not only formally equates his pneumatic qualifications with those of his opponents but even sets himself as a pneumatic over against them; here he practises the charisma of distinguishing the spirits (I Cor. 12.10), just as he does, in fact, throughout I and II Cor.[37]

IV

It would obviously be impermissible to project all of these concepts and ideas back into the background of Matt. 28. But on the basis of the partially highly developed and variously differentiated concepts of Hellenistic theology, the roots of which in any case go back to or even before Paul, we are justified in examining Hellenistic Christianity, which was also a distinctive component of Matthew's thought. What we must keep firmly in mind here is the close connection between the Kyrios-faith and a specific understanding of prophecy and charisma, a connection which undoubtedly was made in the earliest days of Christianity. Here it is characteristic of the early Christian prophet that he is accompanied by charismatic signs and brings about wonders in the name of the Exalted Jesus. Such signs and wonders are, e.g., enumerated in detail in the inauthentic conclusion to Mark (16.15ff.),[38] and directly connected to the sending

[36] On this, see Lührmann, *ibid.*; he also rightly shows how far the concept in this environment goes beyond apocalyptic in the direction of gnosticism (pp. 107ff.).

[37] Evidence for this is provided, in my opinion, by the expression πνευματικοῖς πνευματικὰ (taking both as neuters) συγκρίνοντες in I Cor. 2.13.

[38] Casting out demons, speaking in tongues, taking up snakes, drinking poison with impunity, healing (16.17f.) – here promised to all believers but also confirmatory signs given by the Kyrios to the apostles in their proclamation (16.20).

of the disciples into all the world, the proclamation of the gospel to every creature, the promise to the baptized, and the promise of the Kyrios' presence with the disciples.[39] Many details make it clear how strongly this picture of the apostle as a charismatic dominates the presentation in the book of Acts and, in a specially concentrated way, dominates those parts of that presentation which are concerned with the Hellenists, with Antioch and the mission under Paul and Barnabas that went out from there. As early as Acts 6.3,5 it is noted that 'the Seven' are men full of the Spirit, of faith, and of wisdom;[40] Stephen, full of grace and power, accomplishes signs and wonders (6.8), just as Philip does (8.6f., 13). Barnabas and Paul, sent out by the Holy Spirit through Christian prophets (13.1–3), proclaim Jesus as Kyrios in Cyprus and Asia Minor and accomplish signs and wonders in his Name (13.6–12; 14.3, 8ff.), in order to convert the heathen from idols to the living God (14.15a; cf. 13.12).[41] There are

[39] Michel (*art. cit.*, pp. 20f.) rightly holds the view that Mark 16.15–18 contain older material; that the expression ἐν τῷ ὀνόματί μου in vv. 17b, 18 is to be understood (unlike the same expression in Matt. 28.19) charismatically, not liturgically; and that Mark 16.15–18 is not to be viewed as a mere echo of Matt. 28.16ff. Yet he consistently brings the two texts into too close proximity. Actually both combine the missionary commission and sayings about baptism and the presence of the Kyrios in one composite discourse. Hence Mark 16.15–18 may have been formulated not as a free composition but in dependence upon Matt. 28.18–20. (Hahn, *Mission*, pp. 53f. [ET: pp. 64f.] considers it an independent and comparatively ancient witness.) But what is decisive is the fact that Mark 16.5ff. moves completely within the realm of popular conceptions and lays its entire emphasis on the apostles' miracles, on which Matthew is specifically (and characteristically) silent (see below).

[40] Cf. also Barnabas (11.23) and the prophet Agabus (11.27f.).

[41] Hahn believes that all these passages involve traditional material of Antiochene provenance (*Mission*, pp. 50ff. [ET: pp. 61ff.]) and adduces in support the unique and varied use of εὐαγγελίζεσθαι (see pp. 50f., n. 4 [ET: p. 61, n. 2]). This is not the place to discuss the extent to which this thesis is correct. In essence it could be. The fact that these elements also fit Luke's theology and his portrait of the apostolic age does not disprove it. In any case Luke no longer knows of any theological difference between the Hellenists and the Jerusalem community. The emergence of the Kyrios-faith and its significance for the Gentile mission in its opposition to the primitive church's observing of the Law is thus only rather unsatisfactorily observable on the basis of the book of Acts.

strong indications that Matthew is familiar with and presupposes such a Hellenistic Christianity. He certainly never rejects it *in toto*. To some extent, in fact, as a Hellenistic Jewish Christian, he is a representative of it. How truly this is the case is shown – to mention only a few particularly clear indices of it – by the inclusion of all of Mark in his own gospel; by his use of the honorific christological title Kyrios, which considerably exceeds the Marcan usage; and not least by the Hellenistic traditions which are presupposed in and reflected by Matt. 28.16–20.[42]

Yet this 'Hellenistic' character must not under any circumstances mislead us into making Matthew simply a Gentile Christian.[43] Matthew will be much more properly understood when one recognizes that he is engaged in a war on two fronts, against Pharisaic Judaism on the one hand,[44] and against a Hellenistic Christianity in which under the sign of the Kyrios-faith the Law had lost its validity and saving significance, on the other. In this essay we are concerned only with the second aspect of this warfare, with Matthew's impassioned opposition to the preaching and mission of the Hellenists who reject the Law. Matthew 5.17–20 is a programmatic expression of his opposition to any abrogation of the Law;[45] it even goes so far as to use the decidedly Jewish-Christian *logion* about the jot and tittle (5.18), for which the evangelist provides a christological introduction (5.17), which he directs against Hellenistic teachers in the community (5.19) and which, together with the comprehensive thematic formulation in 5.20, he places just before the Antitheses. There is a close correspondence between the polemic section of the

[42] R. Bultmann, *Die Geschichte der synoptischen Tradition*, p. 313 (ET: p. 289) rightly characterizes them, along with Luke 24.44ff. and the Johannine accounts, as 'quite late formulations of Hellenistic Christianity (though perhaps in part also formulations of Hellenistic Jewish-Christianity)'.

[43] This thesis has been recently put forth by G. Strecker in his book, otherwise useful in many ways, *Der Weg der Gerechtigkeit*, 1962. Against this, see the excellent work of R. Hummel, *Die Auseinandersetzung zwischen Kirche und Judenchristentum im Matthäus-Evangelium*, 1963, esp. pp. 26ff. (completed before Strecker's book was published).

[44] Naturally, the Pharisaism of the years after the destruction of Jerusalem. On this see the book by Hummel cited in the preceding note.

[45] On this, see G. Barth, *op. cit.*, pp. 6off. (ET: pp. 64–8).

introduction to the Sermon on the Mount and the Sermon's no
less polemic conclusion. Already present in Q for Matthew's use
were the concatenation of *logia* about the Tree and its Fruits
which we may deduce from the Sermon on the Plain (Luke 6.43–
49), the short saying about those who say 'Lord, Lord' (not yet
pointed towards the Last Judgment), and the concluding parables about hearing and doing. Matthew is the first to make of
all this an effective unity, a warning about false prophets and
an extended description of the Last Judgment (7.15–23). Those
who say 'Lord, Lord' are now the false prophets who boast before
the Judge of the earth of the charismatic deeds they have accomplished 'in the Name' of Jesus (προφητεύειν, δαιμόνια ἐκβάλλειν,
δυνάμεις ποιεῖν) and who are rejected as workers of ἀνομία because
they have not done the will of the Father. So too it is only in the
Matthean text of the synoptic apocalypse that the characteristics of the false prophets (24.10ff.) include concepts which are
typical of his battle against antinomians (ψευδοπροφῆται, πλανεῖν,
ἀνομία against ἀγάπη, σκανδαλίζεσθαι).[46]

V

It is highly instructive to place Matt. 28.18–20 as well in the
context of these passages. Certainly this concluding pericope is
not *expressis verbis* polemical. And yet its unique features become
really comprehensible only against this background. The exaltation and full authority of Jesus as Kyrios and the sending of the
disciples into all the world, to be sure, form a unity here just as
much as they do in the comparable Hellenistic texts. But characteristically in Matthew there is no mention of the imparting of
the Spirit nor of the signs and wonders which one otherwise
encounters everywhere in the parallel texts. It is also to be noted
that we find no trace here of those concepts which are well-
known in the other mission passages: ἀποστέλλειν, κηρύσσειν, εὐαγγέλιον, εὐαγγελίζεσθαι, μάρτυς, etc. Nor is there any hint of the
proclamation that the Basileia is drawing near.

[46] On Matt. 7.15ff. and 24.16ff. see *ibid.*; on the overall characteristics
of the antinomians, see *ibid.*, pp. 149ff. (ET: pp. 159–64).

In all of these features the instructions given the disciples by the earthly Jesus in Matt. 10 stand considerably closer to the other mission texts[47] than to the words of the Risen Jesus. The missionary address in Matt. 10 is not yet, to be sure, universal in extent; it is confined to Israel (10.5f.). From this arises the striking fact that Matthew assigns to the pericopes of Jesus' pre-Easter activity those very features which in Hellenistic thought characterize the post-Easter mission. In the period before Easter Jesus is in a real sense the Messiah of Israel, and the time of his presence and ministry is a time of salvation for Israel. Yet since his rejection as Israel's king this time is past. From now on, after his death, his resurrection, and his exaltation, he is the Kyrios and Judge of all peoples.[48]

However strongly Matthew shares in this, the christological thought of the Hellenists, the interpretation he gives to this belief is different. This is expressed not only negatively, in his elimination of all charismatic elements in the commission of Matt. 28.19f., but also positively, in the term μαθητεύειν,[49] which is selected by him and peculiar to him, and in the content of the commission as he defines it.

[47] Both post- and pre-Easter (Mark 6.7; 3.14; Luke 9.1).

[48] On this understanding of the periods of *Heilsgeschichte* see G. Bornkamm, 'Enderwartung und Kirche im Matthäus-Evangelium', *Überlieferung und Auslegung im Matthäus-Evangelium*, 1963³, pp. 30f. (ET: pp. 33f.) and especially Hummel, *op. cit.*, pp. 141f. Hummel rightly asserts, 'The exaltation of Jesus is not for Matthew, as for Mark, a heightening of his messianic dignity; it is rather in a certain sense opposed to it. It is a loss for Israel. The kerygma of Jesus' exaltation is at the same time a message, though not a final message, of judgment on Judaism' (p. 142). Hahn, *Mission*, pp. 103ff. (ET: pp. 120–8) wishes to arrange the particularistic understanding of mission in Matt. 10 with the universalistic understanding in Matt. 28 not in terms of chronological sequence but rather as two concentric circles (p. 111 [ET: pp. 127f.]). Similarly, Barth, *op. cit.*, p. 94, n. 2 (ET: p. 100, n. 4). This would be an expression of the Pauline πρῶτον 'Ιουδαίοις, a motif which is also important for Matthew. To some degree, to be sure, this is correct: the mission to Israel is certainly not for Matthew something now definitively ended, and ch. 10 in Matthew's view is supposed to include directions which are still valid in many respects for the present. Yet this express limiting of the missionary enterprise to Israel is now no longer valid for the situation of the Matthean church. Israel's prerogative has been removed by the exaltation, and the christological status of Jesus is now different.

[49] Cf. Matt. 28.19; 13.52; 27.57. Elsewhere in the NT only in Rev. 14.21.

It is well-known how significant the theme of discipleship
(*Jüngerschaft*) is in Matthew. The whole Matthean understanding
of discipleship (*Nachfolge*), indeed essentially his whole understanding of the church, is embraced by the concept of the disciple
(*Jünger*). Οἱ μαθηταί is *the* specific ecclesiological concept of the
evangelist.[50] But μαθητής is already in Jewish thought a correlative concept of διδάσκαλος. In Matthew, however, it is characteristic of discipleship that it is defined in terms of being called by
Jesus to follow him (*in die Nachfolge*); it proves itself by obedience,
humility, and readiness to suffer, and it signifies not a transitory
stage but an enduring relationship to Jesus. The disciple never
becomes a rabbi (διδάσκαλος), a father, a leader (23.8ff.). The
corresponding verb μαθητεύειν, which comes originally from the
relationship to the earthly Jesus, is apparently used to make it
clear that this very same relationship is also now, after the Resurrection, permanently binding.

Matthew does not say this in opposition to the Kyrios-faith.
As a matter of fact, it is he, as we have said, who goes far beyond
Mark in the use of the Kyrios-title and who consistently changes
the wording when Mark openly follows the tradition in allowing
the disciples to address Jesus as διδάσκαλε or ῥαββί.[51] Wherever
one encounters the designation ὁ διδάσκαλος in Matthew, it is
never used by a disciple in addressing Jesus (with the single –
and significant – exception of Judas Iscariot: 26.25, 49). The
Pharisees and their friends say 'your teacher' (9.11; 17.24), while
the disciples use 'the Teacher' in speaking to the Jews but generally address Jesus himself as 'Lord'. What is the significance of
this for Matt. 28.16ff., where to be sure the concept of the Kyrios
does not occur but is unmistakably presupposed? The answer
is beyond doubt: *Here* the emphasis lies in the fact that this very
Kyrios is the Teacher whose teaching remains obligatory. That
teaching had shown him to be the fully authoritative Lord

---

[50] Bornkamm, 'Enderwartung', pp. 37f., 39f. (ET: pp. 40f., 42ff.). The
assertion that this concept contained an historicizing tendency and was
reserved for the Twelve (so Strecker, *op. cit.*, pp. 192f.) stands the matter on
its head.

[51] Texts in Bornkamm, 'Enderwartung', p. 38 (ET: p. 41).

(*Herr*) even during his earthly ministry (7.29; cf. also 11.27ff.);
it should now be understood that the Exalted Jesus is the same
Jesus who was διδάσκων during his earthly life.

VI

Thus the essence of the church, which from now on is to include
all peoples, is characterized.[52] In 16.18 the evangelist uses for the
church the concept of the ἐκκλησία (οἰκοδομήσω μου τὴν ἐκκλησίαν).
But, as W. Schrage has shown,[53] this concept arose in Hellenistic-
Jewish Christianity; it is by no means a satisfactory designation
to say that it is the LXX equivalent of קהל יהוה. Rather it
contains from the very beginning of its use a programmatic
element, namely a decision opposing the synagogue as the place
of the Jewish religion of Law and tradition. For in the synagogue
Moses is proclaimed (Acts 15.21). In other words, the concept
ἐκκλησία is, from the time it is first used, a counter-concept to the
cult and the observance of the Law; it could only have been
coined where faith in the Kyrios who is present through the
Spirit was determinative, where the Law had no more validity
as *nota ecclesiae* and hence where the way of the Gospel was first
really open to the Gentiles. It is all the more remarkable that
in Matt. 16.18 the concept of the ἐκκλησία is used, not merely
casually but with a great deal of emphasis, even though in Matt.
5.17–20, among other places, the evangelist so energetically
opposes the ἀνομία of a Hellenistic theology.[54] In Matt. 16.18,
however, he does not use it in an antinomian sense; he uses it
rather in connection with the installation of Peter as the
foundation-rock of the church and the possessor of the power of
the keys, which here in all probability designates his authority in

---

[52] So, rightly, Strecker, *op. cit.*, p.212, vs. E. Lohmeyer's assertion (*Matthäus*, pp.424f.) that prospective disciples were being sent forth in 'splendid
eschatological uncertainty'.

[53] W. Schrage, 'Ekklesia und Synagoge', *ZThK* 60 (1963), pp.178ff.

[54] *Ibid.*, p.201. Earlier pointed out by R. Bultmann, *Die Geschichte der
synoptischen Tradition*, pp.146f. (ET: pp.138ff.); E. Käsemann, 'Die Anfänge
christlicher Theologie', *ZThK* 57 (1960), pp.165f. (ET: *NT Questions of
Today*, p.85).

matters of tradition and doctrine.[55] It is certainly not proper to say that the mere taking over of the concept of the ἐκκλησία by Matthew betrays a polemical intention. The whole *logion*, which surely comes from pre-Matthean tradition, reflects nothing of this. Moreover, such factors as language and content point back to old Palestinian Jewish-Christian tradition. Nevertheless it would be inadvisable in this instance to set 'Palestinian Jewish-Christian' and 'Hellenistic Jewish-Christian' over against one another as alternatives. Whatever Aramaic equivalent one may postulate as lying behind ἐκκλησία, in its present Greek form the *logion* can hardly be ascribed without further ado to the primitive Palestinian community, since in any event it makes use of this Jewish-Hellenistic concept and hence to this extent has an anachronistic and idealized character: it ascribes to Peter a permanent teaching authority for the church as a whole, to last until the final Judgment, just as it promises permanence to the post-Easter[56] church (οὐ κατισχύσουσιν αὐτῆς). Further, in this saying the Torah is not simply said to be binding; it rather designates with the words 'binding' and 'loosing' a form of Christian teaching which is to stand under the authority of Peter, according to which he is to decide in the community what is prohibited and what is permitted. All of this militates against the view that the origin of the *logion* in its present form is to be sought in the earliest Jerusalem community, where all of this, particularly this position for Peter, is historically hardly conceivable. This saying presupposes the resurrection, the delayed Parousia, the Hellenistic concept of the ἐκκλησία and its energetic correction in the direction of a renewed assertion of the obligatory nature of the commandments. But all this means that Matt. 16.18f. reflects the entrance of Jewish-Christian tradition into Hellenistic Christianity and that it manifests an outspoken critical tendency towards all charismatic movements, which are here already presupposed.[57]

[55] Cf. H. von Campenhausen, *Kirchliches Amt und geistliche Vollmacht in den ersten drei Jahrhunderten* (BhTh 14, 1963²), p. 141; Hummel, *op. cit.*, pp. 59ff.
[56] Note the futures: οἰκοδομήσω, δώσω, ἔσται.
[57] If the question is asked when and where the concepts in Matt. 16.18f.

Historically, then, this is the context into which the commission in Matt. 28.19 should probably be placed. Probably we must also conceive of the specifically Matthean ecclesiological term μαθητεύειν as an energetic corrective to the understanding of the ἐκκλησία which was represented in the Hellenistic world and associated with the Kyrios-faith, the Gentile mission, and charismatic and prophetic Christian movements. To repeat: Matthew does not simply contest any of this. Faith in the Kyrios is unambiguously emphasized in the ἐξουσία-saying, just as it has been throughout the gospel, while prophecy plays an essential role in the community and in Matthew's thought in particular (5.12; 10.41; 23.24; cf. also 10.20), which accounts for the emphasis on distinguishing true from false prophecy (7.15; 24.4ff., 10ff.). The commissioning, 28.19, also demonstrates the ἐξουσία of the Kyrios, here in conjunction with the granting of full authority to the disciples (cf. also 10.1, 7f.).[58] And the mission

---

were first preached we must remain content with suppositions. But whatever antecedents there may have been for these concepts and for the *logion* itself, we must grant that the formulation and validity of this tradition presuppose the sharp conflict between Peter and Paul in Antioch and Paul's departure from the (hitherto purely) Hellenistic community. Only after these events could the conceptions arise which were thus invested with Petrine authority. On the significance for the church of the conflict in Gal. 2.11ff. and of the fact that at that time it was Peter, not Paul, who won out in the sphere of Hellenistic Christianity, cf. E. Haenchen, *Apostelgeschichte*, 1961[13], pp.461ff. The two texts, Gal. 2.11ff. and Matt. 16.18f., ought not to be brought into too close proximity, for by Matthew's time neither the question of circumcision nor that of table-fellowship between Jews and Gentiles any longer played any role whatever. On Peter's teaching authority, cf. Hummel, *op. cit.*, pp. 59ff.

[58] How strictly, especially for Matthew, the calling and sending of the disciples belong in intimate connection with the messianic work of Christ is shown as early as the introduction to the gospel, in the sequence of pericopes in 4.12–17 and 4.18–22. Already in these passages the world-wide mission in the sense of Matt. 28 is set forth: Jesus moves into 'Galilee of the Gentiles' (4.15) and appoints the disciples 'fishers of men' (4.19). It is also significant for Matthew's Christology and for his understanding of the sending of the disciples that the comprehensive expression τὰ ἔργα τοῦ Χριστοῦ is used to characterize (looking back upon the accounts of what immediately precedes) the Messiah of the Word (chs. 5–7), of the Act (chs. 8–9), and of Mission (ch. 10). On the understanding of 11.2, cf. H. J. Held, 'Matthäus als Interpret der Wundergeschichten', *Überlieferung und Auslegung im Matthäus-Evangelium*, 1963[3], pp. 237ff. (ET: pp. 249–53).

to all nations fulfils the promise of the earthly Jesus (24.14). Now
its hour has come. The validity of all this is presupposed. Hence
Matthew is all the more concerned with the rule of life for the
church into which the nations are to be called.

This concern is expressed even in the fact that Matt. 28.19
speaks of baptism before teaching. (In Did. 7.1 instruction precedes baptism.) Matthew 28.18ff. is thus primarily directed
towards the life of the church itself, not missionary praxis. So if
one is looking for Matthew's special intention he will not direct
his attention primarily towards the command to baptize, which
ordinarily and understandably, on account of its unique triadic
form, has attracted the greatest historical and theological interest. In all probability, this command belongs to the liturgical
tradition already presupposed by the evangelist.[59]

In this connection the specifically Matthean conception of
the second participial phrase διδάσκοντες αὐτοὺς τηρεῖν πάντα ὅσα
ἐνετειλάμην ὑμῖν is all the more important. Two things in this formulation are to be noted above everything else: (1) the fact that
Jesus' message as a whole is conceived as the *command* of Jesus,
and (2) the fact that it is spoken of in *terms of the past*: 'which I
have commanded you'. As a comparison with other texts shows,
neither fact is self-explanatory. In Luke 24.47 Jesus' message to
all nations is described as the forgiveness of sins in Jesus' name;
in Acts 1.8 the promise is given the disciples that they are to be
witnesses of the Resurrected One; Mark 16.15 speaks of the
gospel which shall be proclaimed to all creatures (cf. also Mark
13.10; 14.9; Matt.24.14); the content of the commission in John
20.21ff. is the sending of the disciples, their being equipped for
their task with the Holy Spirit, and their full authority to forgive
or retain sins. All these and similar expressions are avoided in

[59] It is well-known that the triadic formula is unique in the NT and
points to a relatively late period; the older baptismal formulas consist of a
single member (I Cor. 1.13, 15; Acts 2.38; 8.16; 10.48; 19.5). Yet the triadic
formula should not be understood as completely without preparatory prece-
dent (I Cor. 12.4ff.; II Cor. 13.13; II Cor. 1.21f.) nor as simply the baptismal
practice of the community represented by Matthew. It is attested by Did. 7.1,
3 and Justin, I Apol. 61. 3, 11, 13. Hence the view that it is a later interpolation is untenable.

Matt. 28.19f., and the commands of Jesus are here and only here made in the most concentrated form possible into the content of the disciples' commission to all peoples.

The preterite ἐνετειλάμην is no less characteristic. Elsewhere the sending of the messengers and the empowering of them with the Spirit are demonstrated in the proclamation of the *present* word of the Exalted Jesus. The exalted Lord or even the Spirit himself speaks through the prophets (cf. Acts 13.2); hence apostles and prophets belong as close together as possible (Rev. 18.20; Eph. 2.20; 3.5; 4.11; I Cor. 12.28), and both are, according to Eph. 2.20, the foundation of the church. Even in Matthew the prophets are sent directly by the Lord (23.24; 10.40f.). Hence the letters of Revelation characteristically close, 'He who has an ear, let him hear what the Spirit *says* to the churches' (2.7, 11, 17, etc.). Similarly, in the gospel of John the activity of the Paraclete is spoken of in these terms: 'Whatever he hears he will speak, and he will declare to you the things that are to come . . .' (16.13ff.), even though his revelations are at the same time to be reminders of what Jesus said (14.26). This, however, does not change the fact that the future word of the Spirit after Jesus' departure from the earth is different from the word of the earthly Jesus (14.25f.; 16.12ff.), nor that it is the Paraclete who first leads into all truth, even though he 'does not take it from himself'. Only against this background can the special emphasis be understood which Matthew lays upon the expression, 'which I *have commanded* you', i.e., upon the emphatic conception of Jesus' words as exclusively commands and upon the retrospective reference to the teaching of the earthly Jesus. But this means that the Risen and Exalted One makes the word of the earthly Jesus obligatory upon the church on earth for all time until the end of the world. *Here* is the focal point, often overlooked,[60] of

---

[60] I cite as an example only H. Grass, *Ostergeschehen und Osterberichte*, 1962[2]: 'The Word of the risen, exalted Lord in Matt. 28.18–20 contains within itself its permanent kerygmatic significance: It proclaims that Christ has all power in heaven and on earth, it calls to missionary service and promises his Presence until the end of the world' (p. 283). It is immediately obvious that this is a good description of the Hellenistic outlook but that it misses the specifically Matthean point.

the entire Matthean text, expressed even in the author's peculiar
formulation of the commission: μαθητεύσατε πάντα τὰ ἔθνη.

The content of these 'commands' of Jesus cannot be anything
but his call to the righteousness which exceeds that of the scribes
and Pharisees, the righteousness without which no one may
enter the Kingdom of Heaven. And what this implies is the Will
of God, proclaimed in the Law and the Prophets, realized and
authoritatively set forth in Jesus' teaching, and summed up in
the love-commandment.[61] The concept of a *nova lex* would be
completely inappropriate here. It would contradict the concept
of 'fulfilment',[62] the thoroughly conservative tendency in both
the traditional material and the theology of the first evangelist,
and the undeniable fact that in his gospel he builds a Christian
halacha on the basis of the Law, shared with Judaism, and moves
towards a Christian concept of tradition.[63] Even the not incon-
siderable critique of the letter of the Law (the third, fifth, and
sixth antitheses, the criticism of the legal prescriptions for sacrifice and ritual purity) remains subordinate in Matthew to the
saying in 5.18f., just as the love-commandment is a critical
exegetical principle (9.13; 12.7; 23.23) and even the basic content of the Law itself (7.12).

The net result of this portrayal of the various elements in
Matthew's theology is very complex. The gospel clearly stands
in a close relationship with Pharisaic Judaism – a relationship of
both dependence and antithesis – and it has unquestionably preserved essential traditions of the primitive Palestinian community. But the distinctive elements of primitive Hellenistic
Christianity are no less clear.[64] But the two are not simply fused
in an eclectic fashion; they are rather woven into a unity, though

[61] 5.17–20 and the antitheses, which follow immediately; 7.12; 22.34ff.;
9.13; 12.7; etc.

[62] πληροῦν = to bring to realization. Cf. Barth, *op. cit.*, pp. 64f. (ET: p.
69); Strecker, *op. cit.*, p. 147.

[63] Hummel (*op. cit.*, pp. 56ff.) has shown this in illuminating fashion. Cf.
also his analysis of the Matthean *Streitgespräche* (pp. 36ff.) in contrast to
Mark's christologically grounded freedom from the Law (pp. 53ff.).

[64] Hence it becomes comprehensible that two fundamentally different
portrayals of Matthean theology could be published almost simultaneously, as
in the books by Strecker (1962) and Hummel (1963).

not without tensions. The unity created is such that the elements
of the one sometimes serve as critic and corrector of the other.
To cite one example, not only the Jesus-tradition but also the
specific Christology of Hellenistic Christianity enable Matthew
to carry on his attack on Pharisaic Judaism and to break through
the theological bounds of the Palestinian community. The reverse, however, is also true: The close connection between Torah
and Christology – the Law and the Scriptures as the basic
legitimizing factors for Jesus' Messiahship, but at the same time
Jesus' call to righteousness and discipleship as the fulfilling of the
Law and the prophets – now serves as a strict and decisive corrective of a Hellenistic Christianity which has been loosed from
those roots, and of its Kyrios-faith and its understanding of
apostleship, prophecy, the church, and the church's mission as
well.[65]

VII

That the evangelist Matthew, in spite of this contrary critical
tendency, may be looked upon as a representative of Hellenistic-
Jewish Christianity is, in conclusion, further confirmed by the
fact that he energetically opposes the traditional Jewish understanding of the People of God. Proof of this, in my opinion, is
given by the very first sentence in the gospel and the genealogy
which that sentence serves to introduce, though this fact has not
yet, so far as I can tell, been satisfactorily taken into account. It

[65] There are many terminological points of contact between the gospel of
Matthew and the Johannine writings (cf. Grass, *op. cit.*, p.291): μαθηταί is
the preferred usage, as in John; ἀκολουθεῖν is a central concept in both (Matt.
4.20, 22; 8.19, 22f.; 10.38; 19.27f.; etc.; John 8.12; 10.4f., 27; 12.26; etc.);
on Matt. 28.20a, τηρεῖν πάντα ὅσα ἐνετειλάμην ὑμῖν, cf. John 13.34; 14.15, 21,
26; 15.10, 20; I John 2.3f.; 3.23f. On Matt.28.20b cf. John 14.16. We cannot
decide here the extent to which in both cases an older terminology or a
language developed later lies behind the texts. At the same time, the substantial difference is undeniable: just as the uniquely Johannine concept of
the Revealer is lacking in Matthew, so the specifically Matthean association
between Law and Christology is lacking in John. The ἐγὼ δὲ λέγω ὑμῖν of the
Antitheses of the Sermon on the Mount is not interchangeable with the
Johannine ἐγώ εἰμι. Similarly, the expression 'all that I have commanded you'
has quite a different sense from the exclusively Johannine 'my commandments', an expression stamped by the revelation-Christology of John.

is well-known that this genealogy leads back through David to
Abraham in three groups of fourteen members (1.1f.). Why? It
is certainly beyond question that here the Messiah is supposed to
be portrayed as the scion of David, a designation with which the
title 'Son of David', common in Matthew (ten times), is fully
consistent. The following pericope, 1.18–25, also belongs in the
closest possible connection with this section. For the following
pericope, as K. Stendahl has convincingly shown,[66] is by no
means a birth-story to be interpreted analogously to the Lucan
birth-stories; it is only 'the large footnote to the crucial point in
the genealogy'.[67] It shows how miraculously Jesus Christ was
implanted into the Davidic family tree by God. At the same time,
it serves to introduce his name, Jesus, to provide the basis for it,
and hence to set forth its significance as Ἐμμανουήλ (v.23; Isa.
7.14). But this does not yet adequately explain the express
emphasis on Jesus Christ's Abrahamic sonship. This is not (as is
repeatedly asserted) common Jewish tradition, if for no other
reason than that Abrahamic sonship is characteristic of Israel as
a whole and of each individual Israelite. For the Messiah it is so
self-evident that it is never mentioned by itself as one of his
characteristics. Yet the introduction and the construction of
Matt. 1.1–17 require us to take the Abrahamic sonship no less
seriously than the Davidic.

Behind the scribal learning which the genealogy betrays and
which Matthew equally presupposes and represents, one must
conclude, is a theology for which Abrahamic sonship *eo ipso* no
longer characterizes the People of God and guarantees to it
participation in the Blessing and the Promise. All the more
emphatically it is now said, with Christ exclusively in view: *He*
is the son of David and of Abraham. It cannot be doubted that
such conceptions point to Hellenistic-Jewish Christianity, just as
the genealogy also gives both the names and the sequence of the
LXX. The larger context fits exactly into the same framework:
the unambiguously Hellenistic background appears as early as

[66] K. Stendahl, 'Quis et unde? An Analysis of Matt. 1–2', *Judentum, Urchristentum, Kirche* (*Festschrift J. Jeremias*, BZNW 26, 1950), pp. 94ff.
[67] *Ibid.*, p. 102.

1.18–25 with the virgin birth motif, grounded in the citation from Isa. 7.14 (Matt. 1.23), taken (with insignificant differences) from the LXX, and the clear dependence in the whole context on the Jewish-Hellenistic Moses-legend, which continues as far as 2.23.[68] The story of the Magi, inserted in 2.1–2 but surely originally independent,[69] points proleptically to the expansion of the concept of the People of God to include all peoples. This expansion is already presupposed in Matt. 1.21, where the name Jesus is not so much translated as elaborated: αὐτὸς γὰρ σώσει τὸν λαὸν αὐτοῦ (!) ἀπὸ τῶν ἁμαρτιῶν αὐτῶν.[70] This can hardly be taken to mean the Jewish people in the context of the first gospel; rather it should be taken in the larger sense of the people (λαός) redeemed by Jesus, just as the concept ἔθνος (21.43) means the new people of God, who 'produce the fruits of the Kingdom of God'.[71] Thus 'his people' in 1.21 prepares the way for the term 'my church' in 16.18. If this interpretation is correct, then it follows that as early as Matt. 1–2, in the motif of the Abrahamic sonship of the Messiah as in the understanding of the People of God who belong to him, Hellenistic-Jewish Christian concepts are already at work, concepts which Paul could take up and use, though in a completely different direction. From the *one* universal heir of the promise to Abraham and through him alone blessing and Abrahamic sonship are given to all peoples (Gal. 3.16, 29).

In Matthew's view, to be sure, this is true only under the condition that all peoples, baptized in accordance with the instructions of the Risen Jesus, hold to the commands of the earthly Jesus (28.19f.) and, having become disciples, walk in the 'way of righteousness' (21.32; 5.6; 5.20; 6.33; etc.) just as the earthly Jesus in his baptism fulfilled 'all righteousness' (3.15ff.). 'All the nations' will be judged by no other criterion than this obedience (Matt. 25.31ff.).

[68] On this, cf. Strecker, *op. cit.*, pp. 52ff.

[69] For an analysis, cf. F. Hahn, *Christologische Hoheitstitel*, pp. 277f.

[70] It is uncertain whether a conscious allusion to Ps. 130 (129). 8 is involved here. In spite of the divergences in wording it is not impossible.

[71] Cf. F. Hahn, *Mission*, pp. 108f. (ET: p. 125).

Here too we see confirmation of the fact that for Matthew the
question of the Gentiles' title to salvation, still so burning an
issue for Paul, is no longer a problem. That understanding of the
People of God which includes the Gentile peoples as well – an
understanding vigorously opposed in Hellenistic-Jewish Christian circles – is now simply presupposed and beyond dispute. But
all the more decisive for Matthew is the question of the rule of
life for the church founded by the Risen and Exalted Lord. This
is the reason, as we have shown, that he connects the Hellenistic
concept of mission and the Hellenistic Kyrios-faith so closely
with the obligations imposed by the commands of the earthly
Jesus. But it is also the reason that in Matt. 28 he does not simply
repeat the charge of the earthly Jesus to proclaim the nearness of
the Kingdom of God (10.7). For the church between the
resurrection and the coming Judgment is asked whether or not
it finds the way into the future Basileia and walks in obedience.
The Exalted Jesus, who sets forth with authority the commands
of the earthly Jesus for the church until the end of the world, and
who makes them obligatory, gives to that church the pledge of
his presence (28.20b), so that the gospel ends with the 'Immanuel' with which it began (1.23).

It would be a rewarding study to compare Matthew and Paul
from this point of view. But that would exceed the limits of this
essay. Within the limits prescribed only this much may be said:
both presuppose to a very high degree a common acceptance of
the Kyrios-faith and the understanding of the church and its
mission which generally characterized Hellenistic Christianity.
Both share, though in quite differing ways, an opposition to
Hellenistic antinomianism and enthusiasm. There are, to be
sure, radical differences between them: in their understanding
of the Law, in their thought on the relationship between the
Exalted and the earthly Jesus, and in the understanding of
δικαιοσύνη. It hardly needs to be said that Matthew could never
have spoken of Christ as the end of the Law or of the justification of the ungodly, just as Paul could never have spoken of the
necessity of the Law, valid to the last jot and tittle, for salvation.
It should also be clear that Paul's reflections on the fact that

the Law declares all, Jews and Gentiles, guilty without distinction are completely foreign to Matthew, just as the concept of δικαιοσύνη enables him almost consciously to hold in abeyance the question of the assurance of salvation. According to Paul, however, this question cannot and must not be held in abeyance; it is answered in his thought by the doctrine of justification by faith not works.[72] Hence he carries on his battle against enthusiasts on the basis of this fundamental message, whereas Matthew appeals back to obedience and discipleship, obeying and following the earthly Jesus. Both at any rate are agreed, each in his own way, that the eschatological tension of the Christian life must not be destroyed. It is for this reason that they neither find a common meeting-ground in nor allow for the harmonization of, say, what the synergistic expression in James calls 'faith and works' (James 2.20ff.).

[72] On this, see R. Bultmann, '*ΔΙΚΑΙΟΣΥΝΗ ΘΕΟΥ*', *JBL* 83 (1964), pp. 12–16.

9

The Mother of Wisdom

*Hans Conzelmann**

I

THE search for the antecedents of the Johannine Logos led the
scholar to whom this volume is dedicated on the trail of 'Wisdom'.[1] He did not derive the Logos from Wisdom directly – to
put it mythically: he did not view the Logos as the child of
Wisdom[2] – but he characterized the two as siblings, shoots from
one mythical root,[3] which, however, had not yet been found.[4] In
spite of diligent searching since that time, this situation still ob-
tains.[5] Egypt,[6] Canaan,[7] Babylonia,[8] and Persia[9] have all been

---

* Translated from *Zeit und Geschichte*, pp. 225–34. (Minor revisions made
in consultation with the author – tr.)

[1] Rudolf Bultmann, 'Der religionsgeschichtliche Hintergrund des Prologs
zum Johannesevangelium', *EUCHARISTERION: (Festschrift für H. Gunkel)*
(FRLANT 36) II, 1923, p. 3ff.

[2] So Philo, *De fug.* 109.

[3] Bultmann, *Das Evangelium des Johannes*, 1941 (1957²), p. 8, n. 9.

[4] *Ibid.*, n. 10: 'The attempt to trace the myth back to one definite origin
has not yet been successful.'

[5] For a survey, see Ulrich Wilckens, *Weisheit und Torheit*, 1959, pp. 193ff.;
G. Fohrer and U. Wilckens, art. 'σοφία', *TWNT* VII, pp. 465ff., esp. 490f.

[6] Richard Reitzenstein, *Zwei religionsgeschichtliche Fragen*, 1901, pp. 104ff.;
W. L. Knox, 'The Divine Wisdom', *JTS* 38(1937), pp. 230ff. Helmer Ringgren, in *Word and Wisdom*, 1947, pp. 143ff. draws attention to Isis but rejects
Egyptian provenance. The Isis thesis is modified in J. Pascher, *'Η βασιλικὴ
ὁδός*, 1931 who reconstructs (on a Philonic basis) a mystery closely related
to the Isis-mystery (Plutarch, Apuleius!); cf. Antonie Wlosok, *Laktanz und
die philosophische Gnosis* (Abh. d. Heidelb. Akad. d. Wiss., phil.-hist. Kl.,
1960.2), p. 95, n. 103.

[7] The Semitic goddess of heaven and of love: G. Boström, *Proverbia-
Studien*, 1935. A Canaanite goddess of wisdom: William Foxwell Albright,

suggested as the place of origin of the concept. All the hypotheses about its derivation have failed to receive decisive confirmation. The disturbing thing about them is that the mythical origin of 'Wisdom' is even today a matter of dispute: The figure is a typical personification, an hypostatizing[10] of the verbal concept 'Wisdom'.[11] Some scholars, however, deny the necessity of finding an 'origin' of the concept, since what is involved is merely a poetical form of expression.[12] Still others combine various explanations.[13]

'The Goddess of Life and Wisdom', *AJSL* 36(1919–20), pp.258ff. and his *From the Stone Age to Christianity*, 1946[2], pp.367–71. An originally Canaanite text lies behind Prov.8f. Against this view: Georg Fohrer, *TWNT* VII, p. 491, n.180. In the Baal-epic, to which Albright points, Wisdom does not possess personality. Those who hold to other views of the derivation of Wisdom also find the Ishtar/Anath motif intermingled here (so Knox).

[8] Albright (see the previous note): The Babylonian Siduri Sabitu is called 'goddess of wisdom, genius of life'. In the Words of Ahikar, Wisdom is the bearer of the power of Shamash. But these are not really analogous.

[9] Richard Reitzenstein, *Das mandäische Buch des Herrn der Grösse und die Evangelienüberlieferung*, SAH 1919, Abh.12, pp.46ff.; W. Bousset and H. Gressmann, *Die Religion des Judentums* (HNT 21) 1926[3], p.520. The Persian thesis is attractive, since it eliminates the simple alternative, *either* goddess *or* hypostasis. (Note that in Persian religion concepts are personified.) The Spenta Armaiti, which appears as σοφία, in Plutarch, *De Iside et Osiride* (Moralia V, 370a), is particularly close. In this case, however, the mythical-erotic component remains unexplained.

[10] So Ringgren. The view that Wisdom is the apotheosis of an abstract concept is widespread. Egypt: Adolf Erman, *Die Religion der Ägypter*, 1934, p.57; Ringgren, *op. cit.*, pp.9ff.; Siegfried Moren, *Ägyptische Religion*, 1960, pp.31, 6off., 117ff. Greece: Martin Nilsson, *Geschichte der griechischen Religion*, I[2], 1955, pp.812ff. Rome: K. Latte, *Römische Religionsgeschichte*, 1960, pp. 233ff., 300ff.

[11] In Egypt the personified Maat (order, truth, etc.) is especially noteworthy. Maat is honoured in the cult. But as a personification she has no genuine myth; see Erman, *op. cit.*, p.57 (Ringgren, *op. cit.*, p.52, takes a different view).

[12] B. Gemser, *Sprüche Salomos*, 1963[2], pp.48f. Cf. Theognis, *Eleg.* I, 1135ff.: 'Hope is the only (see note 36 below) benign god among men; the others have forsaken men and gone to Olympus. Faith, the great goddess, has departed from men, and so has Prudence; the Graces, too, my friend, have left the earth' ['Ελπὶς ἐν ἀνθρώποισι μόνη θεὸς ἐσθλὴ ἔνεστιν, ἄλλοι δ' Οὔλυμπόν <δ'> ἐκπρολιπόντες ἔβαν· ὤιχετο μὲν Πίστις, μεγάλη θεός, ὤιχετο δ' ἀνδρῶν Σωφροσύνη, Χάριτές τ', ὦ φίλε, γῆν ἔλιπον].

[13] H. Becker, *Die Reden des Johannesevangeliums und der Stil der gnostischen Offenbarungsrede*, 1956, p.42; cf. also p.46.

The statements made by or about Wisdom actually do reflect so many shades of meaning that every attempted explanation can be supported by some texts.[14] The denial of any mythical derivation, to be sure, leaves entirely too many statements unexplained. Apart from the postulate of mythical origin neither the most important Wisdom-songs[15] as a whole nor the widespread concatenations of individual motifs can be explained. Wisdom appears not only as an hypostasis but also as a Person.[16] Ulrich Wilckens speaks expressly of a 'coherent Wisdom-myth' as background.[17] Unfortunately for this view the myth as a whole is attested only in late texts.[18] Wilckens explains this by saying that in the early period it was domesticated, adapted from Judaism. Later, especially in Hellenistic Judaism, the mythological traits came more freely to the fore. But this thesis hardly corresponds to the data in the texts, and furthermore such a development itself requires explanation. If any progress is to be made we must distinguish more sharply than is customary between mythical material and reflective mythology as a current form of theology and then re-examine the extant materials once more from this point of view. There are two difficulties to be faced in such a re-examination: the diversity of the materials to be compared and the variety of statements about Wisdom itself. Her realm is both the cosmos and the whole of humanity (or only one people). She *exists* from the primordial beginning, but in a hidden form, so that she must be *sought*. But

[14] Tomas Arvedson, *Das Mysterium Christi*, 1937, p. 166. Boström, *op. cit.*, p. 12, n. 46: 'Naturally we are not speaking here of the origin of the Wisdom-figure. What must be emphasized is merely that in all probability foreign influence is to be discerned in certain traits of that figure.'

[15] These are the well-known ones, esp. Prov. 8.22ff. and Sir. 24.3ff.

[16] W. Schencke, *Die Chokma (Sophia) in der jüdischen Hypostasen-spekulation*, 1913, p. 24 (on Prov. 8); most recently, the works of Wilckens cited above (note 5), esp. *Weisheit und Torheit*, p. 194. Only one ought not to speak of a 'gnostic' myth (against Fohrer, *op. cit.*, p. 490). For the gnosticizing of the motif is a late stage in the development. Fohrer's clear distinction between Wisdom and Primal Man is very important.

[17] *TWNT* VII, p. 508.

[18] Especially among the Barbelo-gnostics and in the Valentinian system. Wilckens gives all the necessary proof-texts.

she is also *created* by God at the beginning of his 'ways'; she appears, and hence must be *recognized* and honoured. She is the syzygy of God, and, again, she is alone.[19] Especially bewildering is the variety in Wisdom's sexual aspects: She is Wife, Mother, Beloved, Virgin; i.e., Isis, Ishtar, Aphrodite and Psyche, Demeter and Kore.[20]

No precise derivation can be given in this kind of syncretism. For mixing of motifs is the essence of this figure. She is a splendid example of a richly attested type of God which exists only in a 'syncretistic' form.[21] It is consequently methodologically impossible to look for the ancestry of one Goddess, 'Wisdom', and her myth. On the contrary, one must look for one *genuine* goddess with her myth and then for the mythical revision of it in (pre-Hellenistic and) Hellenistic syncretism. This latter stratum is what we find in the texts.

The goddess who was most widely honoured and who united the various aspects named above in herself in a way no other goddess did, who was identified with other gods and goddesses

[19] For hiddenness, see Bar. 3.15ff. and Job 28.12, 23, which follow the OT version of the '$\pi o\lambda\lambda\dot{a}$ $\tau\dot{a}$ $\delta\epsilon\iota\nu\dot{a}$'. (Translator's note: the reference is to lines 332–5 in Sophocles' *Antigone*; the verses read

Wonders are many; yet than Man
None more wonderful is there known.

[Cited from the verse translation by R. C. Trevelyan, Cambridge, 1939.]

For Wisdom as creature and consort: Prov. 8.22ff. Sexual partner also in Prov. 9.1ff.; Sir. 14.22ff.; 15.2ff.; 51.13ff. On Wisdom, see *TWNT* VII, p.499; on Philo, *ibid.*, pp.501f. The sexual reference is also evident in the Ahikar tradition; see A. Cowley, *Aramaic Papyri*, 1923, 'The Words of Ahikar', col. VI. 92–VII. 95.

[20] Wife: Sir. 15.2; 51.13ff.; see G. Hölscher, *Das Buch Hiob*, 1937, pp. 65f. Sister: Prov. 7.4 = Bride, Wisd. 8.2. Beloved: Prov. 8.26ff.; Sir. 15.2; Wisd. 6.12ff. Mother (of the world, of the Logos): Philo *De ebr.* 30; *De fug.* 109. Virgin-wife-mother: Philo *De cher.* 48ff.

In extra-canonical material: Wisdom is the Bride mentioned in the *Acts of Thomas* 6f., where traits of the Mother-motif are also evident; see Günther Bornkamm, *Mythos und Legende in den apokryphen Thomasakten*, 1933, pp.82ff. She is the 'excellent One', the speaker in the thirty-third Ode of Solomon, where she appears simultaneously as Virgin and male Revealer, i.e., as Kore/Isis and as Horus or Thoth/Hermes. On the fusion of Mother and Son, Daughter and Spouse, see Arvedson, *op. cit.*, p.167; Plut. *Is. Osir.* 372e, f.

[21] Arvedson, *op. cit.*, p.166.

and hence represents syncretism itself, is Isis, who was simultaneously Egyptian, Syrian (Ishtar/Astarte/Anath), and Greek;
Mother, Virgin, irate Mother-in-law (Aphrodite) and perse-
cuted Beloved (Psyche, Io). The equating of her with other gods
actually belongs to the fixed forms of praise to the 'many-named'
Isis.[22]

That Judaism also participated in the theology of this Isis-
type is shown by the Wisdom-song in Sir. 24.3ff., which is regularly cited but which has not yet been genuinely analysed along
religionsgeschichtlich lines.[23]

II

Sirach 24.3ff. is an especially clear example of the adapta-
bility of the Wisdom-myth to Jewish thought; this is obviously
beyond dispute. At the end Wisdom is identified with the
Torah.[24] The style used in the appropriation, however, becomes
clear only when one observes that the unity of the present passage has been formed from heterogeneous elements. Verses
3–6(7) are nothing but a hymn to Isis, taken up almost literally
and retouched lightly at only one or two points.[25] A simple
reading shows the polytheistic import:[26]

[22] 'Many-named' is a fixed predicate of Isis in many texts. Equated names
are given in, e.g., Pap. Oxy. XI. 1380.

[23] The connection with Isis was seen by Reitzenstein and Knox. But they
provide no real analysis.

[24] Wilckens, *Weisheit*, pp. 166ff.

[25] The texts are given in W. Peek, *Der Isishymnus von Andros und verwandte
Texte*, 1930 (cited according to the location in which they were found: Cyme,
Andros, etc.); R. Harder, *Karpokrates von Chalkis und die memphitische Isis-
propaganda*, APAW, phil.-hist. Kl. 14, 1943; Pap. Oxy. XI. 1380; *SEG* VIII,
1937, pp. 548–51 (hymns of Isidore); Kore Kosmu (Nock-Festugière, IV).
Egyptological commentary: D. Müller, *Ägypten und die griech. Isis-Aretalogien*,
(AAL 53.1), 1961. On the religio-political situation: Knox, *op. cit.*, p. 236.
The following should also be noted: Apul. *Metamorph.* XI; Ael. Arist. *In
Sarapim* 17 (on this, see A. Höfler, *Der Sarapishymnus des Ailios Aristeides*, 1935).
The material in ancient novels has not yet been evaluated; on the role of
Isis in this material see R. Merkelbach, *Roman und Mysterium in der Antike*,
1962 (Amor and Psyche: pp. 1ff.). It is not yet recognized that Isis is also
disguised in the story of Joseph and Asenath.

[26] This would have been seen long ago if scholars had not been misled by
chimerical 'reminiscences' of the OT. On the polytheistic background of
Prov. 8.22ff. see Wilckens, *Weisheit*, pp. 183f.

I came forth from the mouth of the Most High,
  and covered the earth like a mist.
I dwelt in high places,
  and my throne was in a pillar of cloud.
Alone I have made the circuit of the vault of heaven
  and have walked in the depths of the abyss.
In the waves of the sea, in the whole earth,
  and in every people and nation I have gotten a
    possession (see n. 43).
Among all these I sought a resting place . . .

(Sir.24.3–7, RSV)*

There is nothing specifically Jewish in this text.[27] On the contrary, non-Jewish statements abound: Wisdom goes forth from the mouth of God. This comes from Egyptian theogony and cosmogony.[28] The mist rises to heaven. Subsequently Sophia/

---

* ἐγὼ ἀπὸ στόματος ὑψίστου ἐξῆλθον καὶ ὡς ὁ μ ί χ λ η κατεκαλύψα γ ῆ ν. ἐγὼ ἐν ὑψηλοῖς κατεσκήνωσα, καὶ ὁ θ ρ ό ν ο ς μου ἐν στύλῳ νεφέλης· γῦρον οὐρανοῦ ἐκύκλωσα μ ό ν η καὶ ἐν βάθει ἀ β ύ σ σ ω ν περιεπάτησα· ἐν κύμασιν θ α λ ά σ σ η ς καὶ ἐν π ά σ ῃ τ ῇ γ ῇ καὶ ἐν παντὶ λαῷ καὶ ἔθνει ἐκτησάμην. μετὰ τούτων πάντων ἀνάπαυσιν ἐζήτησα . . .

[27] The first person is characteristic of the Wisdom-songs, just as it is of the Isis-aretalogies.

One may see a reminiscence of Gen. 1.2 in the word ὀμίχλη; but the word does not occur in the text. ἄβυσσος occurs in Gen. 1, but embedded in a different (and moreover quite non-Jewish) world-view. ὕψιστος may have been written by the redactor (cf. vv. 2, 23), but this is a typical expression of the syncretistic situation, and in any case the word is a catchword in the aretalogies (Cyrene 7; Isidore III [*SEG* 550] 1). 'Pillar of cloud' may well be a retouching occasioned by Exodus. But not a word of the text recalls the history of Israel. Furthermore, the pillar here is cosmic. So the motif is not of biblical origin.

[28] The Jewish concept would be that Wisdom was *created* (vv. 9ff.; Prov. 8.22ff.). Egypt: Hymn of Creation, Gressmann, *Altorientalische Texte*, pp. 1ff. (ET in Pritchard, *Ancient Near Eastern Texts*, pp. 6f.): The Almighty inseminates himself and spews out Shu (air) and Tefnut (mist); cf. the cosmogony of Heliopolis, Morenz, *op. cit.*, pp. 170f.; H. Kees, *Religionsgeschichtliche Lesebuch* 10, p. 12. In any case, Isis is not the oldest daughter. But in the aretalogy 'the eldest' is a fixed predicate: Cyme 5 (with a secondary variant; see Harder, *op. cit.*, pp. 20, 37f.); Anubis-hymn from Chios 8, Peek, *op. cit.*, p. 139; Andros pp. 14f. (*ibid.*, pp. 34f.). One must remember that the

Isis reigns on a pillar of cloud, i.e. in heaven. The underlying
conception of the world is the antithesis between 'above' and
'below'.[29] Especially striking is the next phrase: 'Alone I have
made the circuit of the vault of heaven.' This brings to mind
Plutarch, *Is. Osir.* 372–3: the primal God *abides*, i.e. symbolically,
He is Being (*das Sein*). Isis is movement. This is represented
mythically in our text as walking the circuit of the world.[30] This
means: Isis creates the Cosmos[31] and consequently rules it.[32] Although the conception of the circuit of the heaven and the earth
is general and widespread,[33] in Egypt it is particularly closely
interwoven with the picture of the world (*Weltbild*) and the myth
of the gods. The circuit traversed includes both the upper and

---

divine names and predicates are interchangeable and the myth infinitely
variable (Merkelbach, *op. cit.*, p.67). Osiris and Isis are portrayed as the
first gods in Plutarch, *Is. Osir.* 377a. They are cosmogonic principles; cf.
ibid., 372f. Note Dittenb. *Syll.* III³, 1133: Ἴσιδι Τύχηι Πρωτογενείαι.

The only comparable passage in the OT, Deut. 8.3, may itself reflect
Egyptian influence; see H. Brunner in *VT* 8(1958), pp.428f. For 'vapour'
see Wisd.7.25. Plut. *Is. Osir.* 367a: Horus is strengthened ἀναθυμιάσεσι καὶ
ὁμίχλαις καὶ νέφεσι. Other OT passages to be noted include Ps.33.6, a passage
also evidencing Egyptian colouring (see Hans-Joachim Krauss, *Die Psalmen*, I,
1960, pp.263f.) and Isa.11.4.

[29] This pillar has nothing to do with the seven pillars of the House of
Wisdom. It is Egyptian. My colleague S. Schott informs me as follows: 'The
Crown Goddess of Lower Egypt often sits in the "basket" (phonogram nb. t,
so that it may also be transcribed as Mistress) of the Crown Goddess on a
papyrus stalk. Like the vulture in Upper Egypt, the cobra also serves as a
heavenly goddess, so that the papyrus grows up to heaven and supports it.
Hence in the Temple (for the Temple as a copy of the world, see Bonnet in
Reallexikon, p.787) pillars under the roof (the roof = Heaven, with stars
on the under side) are often formed as stalks (pillars) of papyrus.' See also
the illustrations in G. Roeder, *Die ägyptischen Götterwelt*, 1959, p.203, fig.
30; plates 10, 11. Horus on the papyrus stalk: G. Roeder, *Kulte und Orakel
im alten Ägypten*, 1960, pp.351f. (figs. 52f.).

[30] In the framework of the Egyptian world-view, the ascent to Heaven
and the descent to 'Hell'.

[31] We may ignore here the question of whether or not in Prov.8.22ff.
Wisdom is Creator.

[32] Nepthys, the sister of Isis, is the Mistress of the upper and lower world.
In Plutarch *Is. Osir.* 368e the hegemony is divided between them (and Isis'
realm is the upper world).

[33] Job 22.14 – Egyptian influence is clear.

the lower world: 'And in the depths . . .'[34] Unity-in-tension[35]
is superbly set forth even in the style.

The cardinal point in the exposition is the remarkable μόνη.[36]

[34] Adolf Erman, *Die Literatur der alten Ägypter*, 1923, p.366 (ET: p.295):
(Harakhti) 'Who traverses heaven and passes through the underworld.'
Kees, *op. cit.*, p.12: (Ptah) 'Thy feet are on the earth, Thy head in the
heavens . . . cloudy vapours . . . the circle encompassing the two shores
of heaven . . . the exhalation of air . . .' Pantheistically, Kees, pp. 16f.:
(Osiris) 'Lo, Thou art the Moon on high . . . But Thou art also the Nile
. . . I found Thy majesty also as King of the underworld . . . Thou art
on high in heaven, but Thou rulest on earth as well, and the world beyond
is subject to Thee forever and ever' (Plut. *Is. Osir.* 368c).

[35] Plut. *Is. Osir.* 382; Isis is the *complexio oppositorum*.

[36] μόνη is a technical term and motif in Isis-theology, in varied forms.
Mythical use in Pap. Oxy. XI. 1380. 186–189. The common use is in the
sense of the μόνος-θεός-predicate, i.e., with an emphasis on God's *Rule*. In
this usage the cosmological components may become either more or less
prominent. With Wisd. 7.27, 'Though she is only One, she can do all things'
(μία δὲ οὖσα πάντα δύναται), cf. Cyrene 4: 'I am Isis, sole ruler for ever, and
I oversee the ends of the sea and the earth; I have authority, and though I
am but One I oversee them' ('Εγὼ τύραννος Εἶσις αἰῶνος μόνη πόντου τε καὶ γῆς
τέρμονάς τ' ἐπιβλέπω καὶ σκῆπτρ' ἔχουσα καὶ μί' οὖσ' ἐπιβλέπω; Peek, *op. cit.*, p.130
conjectures ἐπικρατῶ). Isidore I (*SEG* 548). 23f.: 'For Thou alone art all the
other goddesses named by the nations' (ὅτι μούνη εἶ σὺ ἄπασαι αἱ ὑπὸ τῶν ἐθνῶν
ὀνομαζόμεναι θεαὶ ἄλλαι).

The Egyptians call her θιοῦσις, *ta-wat*. The commentary notes: aeg. *ta-wat*,
unica, cf. *CIL* X. 3800: 'to Thee, Isis, one goddess who art all things' (*te tibi,
una quae es omnia dea Isis*). Ael. Arist. XLV (*In Sarapim*) 17: '(Wisdom) who
alone shows to men the relationship with the gods . . .' (ἡ μόνη τὴν πρὸς θεοὺς
συγγένειαν ἀνθρώποις δείκνυσι). On the pre-history of the motif in Greek thought,
cf. the anonymous tragic fragment 503 (Nauck, 937): 'For Fate alone among
gods and men is not ruled, but she herself rules' (μόνη γὰρ ἐν θεοῖσιν οὐ δεσπόζεται
μοῖρ' οὐδ' ἐν ἀνθρώποισιν, ἀλλ' αὐτὴ κρατεῖ). For Isis and Osiris together, see Kore
Kosmu 68. The nicest proof-text would be Apul. *Metam.* XI.2.5: 'Thou
whose feminine light illuminates the walls of every city, whose moist heat
nourishes the joyful seeds, Thou who dost direct Thy ever-changing light
along the courses of the sun . . .' (*ista luce feminea conlustrans cuncta moenia
et udis ignibus nutriens laeta semina et solis ambagibus dispensans incerta lumina* . . .)
– that is, it would be a good proof-text if we could, with P. Valette (*Apulée*,
ed. by S. Robertson, tr. by P. Valette, Paris, 1956), conceive *solis ambagibus*
as 'lonely' courses. Lucretius I. 21: '(Venus) . . . since Thou alone dost
govern the universe' (*quae quoniam rerum naturam sola gubernas*).

The μόνη-motif appears in gnostic transformation in the *hybris* of Sophia,
who wishes to exercise her creative powers *alone*: see the writing on the
Essence of the Archons (H.-M. Schenke, *TLZ* 83 [1958], cols. 661ff.), 142.5ff.;
the *Apocryphon of John* IV, 36.16ff.; Hippolytus *Ref.* VI.30.6 (cf. Hans Jonas,
The Gnostic Religion, 1963², p.182, n.11); Cairo Pap. I.114.15ff.

The meaning of this predicate is: She is Sovereign, Overseer of
the world and its order.[37] Since she has traversed the All, she
knows all and can provide instruction about it.[38]

It would be superfluous to cite texts about Isis and the Sea:
she is above all the Sea-goddess.[39]

The circuit is completed: Isis is demonstrated to be the
Sovereign over all the regions of the world and also Sovereign
of the stars[40] in their courses and of Fate. Isis as Sovereign over
Fate – an Egyptian motif – has become a part of the Greek
aretalogies.[41] This concept provides the basis for the Isis-
mystery, in which the initiate repeats the circuit of the world.[42]

[37] Cf. the preceding note. Isidore III (*SEG* 550) 24ff. on the joining of
cosmology and historical government: 'Thou dost both rule (see below) in
heaven on high, among the immortals, and mount the chariots of the swift-
running sun and traverse the world completely, looking down and observing
(cf. Cyrene 4ff.) the awful works of ungodly and godly men . . .' (ἢ καὶ ἐν
οὐρανῶι ὕψι μετ' ἀθανάτοισι δικάζεις, ἢ καὶ ἠελίου ὠκυδρόμου ἅρματα βᾶσα, κόσμον ἅπαν
διάγουσα, κατοπτεύουσα ἄπλητα ἔργ' ἀνδρῶν ἀσεβῶν τε καὶ εὐσεβέων καθορῶσα).
Anubis-hymn from Chios (Peek, *op. cit.*, p. 139) 8–10; Pap. Oxy. XI.1380.
120ff.

[38] Wisd. 7.12ff. Isis is derived from εἰδέναι, Plut. *Is. Osir.* 351f.

[39] Cyme 15, 39, 49; Apul. *Metam.* XI.5.1. In the nature of the case the
Greek influence here is particularly strong. Isis becomes the protector of
sea travel (*navigium Isidis*! Apul. *Metam.* XI!); see Müller, *op. cit.*, 41, 61.
Isis becomes Aphrodite, born on the sea, in the Anubis-hymn 5f. The motif
of Io's sea journey is transferred to Isis; see Merkelbach, *op. cit.*, pp. 65ff.

[40] She is Sirius (Müller, *op. cit.*, pp. 33ff.). Cyme 12-14 = Ios 9–11: 'I
divided earth from heaven. I set forth the paths of the stars. I established
the course of the sun and moon . . .' ('Εγὼ ἐχώρισα γῆν ἀπ' οὐρανοῦ. 'Εγὼ ἄστρων
ὁδοὺς ἔδειξα. 'Εγὼ ἡλίου καὶ σελήνης πορείαν συνέταξα [Ios; Cyme = -μην]). Müller,
op. cit., 39: This is 'a part of the work of Creation'.

[41] Müller, *op. cit.*, pp. 71ff.; Erman, *Literatur*, pp. 187ff. (ET: pp. 140ff.)
of Osiris (18th Dynasty): 'The heaven and its stars obey him and the great
gates open unto him.' Cyme 46f.: 'Whatever I determine, this too will be
performed for me; all things obey me' (Ὁ ἂν ἐμοὶ δόξηω, τοῦτο καὶ τελεῖται(ι). 'Εμοὶ
πάντ' ἐπείκει [this last phrase is attested as an Egyptian expression, see Müller,
op. cit., pp. 71f.]). Cyme 55f.: 'I conquer Fate. Fate hearkens to me' ('Εγὼ τὸ
ἱμαρμένον νικῶ. 'Εμοῦ τὸ εἱμαρμένον ἀκούει). Cyrene 15: 'Nothing ever came into
being without me. Nor do stars traverse the same path apart from my commands . . .' ('Εμοῦ δὲ χωρὶς γείνετ' οὐδὲν πώποτε. Οὐδ' ἄστρα γὰρ φοιτῶσι τὴν αὐτὴν
ὁδόν, ἄν μὴ ἐξ ἐμοῦ λάβωσιν ἐντολ[ὰς . . .]). An honorific formulation is found in
Apul. *Metam.* XI.25.3; cf. also Isis as Fortuna with vision (*vis-à-vis* the sight-
less), *ibid.*, XI.15.2f. In the context the 'mystical' sense is clear.

[42] Apuleius. Cf. the famous 'symbol', XI.23.8: 'I have come to the boun-

In the conception taken over by Sirach the thought of Fate is
not worked out expressly, but to the informed it is clear in the
use of μόνη.

Verse 6 connects the goddess' rule in the Cosmos with that
over mankind.[43] This corresponds to the theme with which the
aretalogy opens: 'I am Isis, Mistress of every land' (Cyme 3a —
Ios 2a).[44] Cyme 40 also belongs here: 'No one is honoured without my knowledge.'[45] Sirach 24.11f. corresponds to this passage.

This is all of the Isis-text of which the reconstruction is certain. Perhaps one may also add the next phrase, 'Among all
these I sought a resting place . . .† (Smend: a residence)':
Isis' journey is concluded. The non-mythical meaning would be:
She has found the place where she is honoured.[46] This is a con-

---

dary of death and trod upon the threshold of Proserpina; I have journeyed
through all the elements and returned . . .' (*Accessi confinium mortis et calcato
Proserpinae limine per omnia vectus elemente remeavi*). See Martin Dibelius, *Botschaft und Geschichte*, II, 1956, pp. 30ff. Transposed into cosmological philosophy the circuit means: 'I am all that has been and is and will be' (ἐγώ εἰμι πᾶν
τὸ γεγονὸς καὶ ὂν καὶ ἐσόμενον [Plut. *Is. Osir.* 354c]).

[43] Similarly, Isidore III (*SEG* 550) 24ff.; see above. The ἐκτησάμην is
difficult. But 'gain', 'subdue' (Ryssel in Kautsch) give a meaningful sense
for Isis, the 'Ruler'. Schencke, *op. cit.*, p. 29, n. 8 reads ἡγησάμην, 'I was Ruler',
following the Syriac, which amounts to the same thing. Fritzsche *ad loc.*
considers ἐκτησάμην a mistranslation of קנה, 'gain', 'create', and reads ἔκτισα,
'I created'; cf. Prov. 8.22. On this catchword cf. Pap. Oxy. XI. 1380. 280,
284 (σὺ ἔκτισας . . .); Cyme 51; on Soconopis, who dwells in the same
temple as Isis, see Isidore II (*SEG* 549) 11f.: 'Creator of both earth and the
starry heaven and all rivers . . .' (κτίστης καὶ γαίης τε καὶ οὐρανοῦ ἀστερόεντος καὶ
ποταμῶν πάντων . . .).

[44] Εἶσις ἐγώ εἰμι ἡ τύραννος πάσης χώρας. Cf. Andros 7–9; Cyrene 4; Pap.
Oxy. XI. 1380. 24: 'Lady of every country' ([κυ]ρείαν πάσης χώρας); *SEG*
548.2f.; 551.8; Anubis-hymn 9. Plut. *Is. Osir.* 355e of Osiris: 'Lord of all'
and 'great and beneficent king' (ὁ πάντων κύριος and μέγας βασιλεὺς εὐεργέτης).
SEG 551 shows the connection with the Egyptian idea of kingship; Müller,
op. cit., p. 20.

[45] Οὐθεὶς δοξάζεται ἄνευ τῆς ἐμῆς γνώμης. Müller, *op. cit.*, pp. 69ff.; Höfler, *op.
cit.*, p. 50.

† μετὰ τούτων πάντων ἀνάπαυσιν ἐζήτησα.

[46] ἀνάπαυσις is an Isis- and a Wisdom-motif. Wisdom promises rest; hence
she has found rest herself: Sir. 51.27; Matt. 11.25ff. The initiate arrives 'at
the harbour of rest' (*ad portum quietis*), Apul. *Metam.* XI.151. Other disguised
forms of the motif: *Acts of Thomas* 42 (harsh in the context – see Bornkamm,
op. cit., pp. 34f.); the background of the motif of the sojourning People of

clusion that gives good sense. One need not postulate that a curse on Wisdom on account of her dwelling in Israel has broken off.[47]

III

In Sirach the 'Egyptian' part of the song is followed by a Jewish part: Wisdom finds her dwelling-place in Israel. It is a further step in the adaptation when, after the close of the song, Wisdom is identified with the Torah.[48] In this second part, too, close analysis yields some further results. In substance it is a new Wisdom-hymn, which can exist by itself. It also begins with the creation of Wisdom in the 'beginning', – cf. Prov. 8.22. The association with the Isis-hymn has brought about the scheme, Rule in the Cosmos/Rule among men (namely, among those who honour her).[49]

However clearly this part (or this hymn) may be Jewish, the scheme as such is taken over from early material, namely, the aretalogies. And it can be traced back very far in Egypt, even in this specific form, in which in the second or 'historical' part the theme of the Law, of Justice, comes dominantly to the fore.[50]

God (Ernst Käsemann, *Das wandernde Gottesvolk*, 1938). There is nothing comparable in the Isis-aretalogies, but the motif occurs in the Isis-myth, especially if one finds Psyche and Io disguised forms of the goddess. A parallel exists in the primal man/revealer of the Pseudo-Clementines: 'For the true prophet also, from the beginning of the world and through the course of time, speeds towards rest' (*nam et ipse verus propheta ab initio mundi per saeculum currens festinat ad requiem*; *Recog.* 11.22).

[47] Flight belongs to only one of the several variants. How variable the motifs are may be shown by a comparison of the Greek and Hebrew texts of Prov. 8: In 8.31 Wisdom acts upon earth; according to the LXX, she is in heaven. Arvedson, surely wrongly, *op. cit.*, p.159, n.1, holds that the LXX is original. In Egypt: 'When the sun-god (Re, the "Master of Maat") is angry with a land, he drives Maat out' (after Morenz, *op. cit.*, p.137).

[48] Did the whole hymn exist before Sirach? If so, there are three stages in its appropriation.

[49] As we have shown above, this is implicit even in the first part; now it comes thematically to the fore.

[50] Erman, *Literatur*, pp.187ff. (ET: pp.140ff.; Hymn to Osiris, 18th Dynasty): 'He it is that hath the noble *ka* in Busiris' (his dwelling-place; see below). The text goes on to describe his position among the gods: 'The firmament and its stars hearken unto him . . . Offering is made to him . . . He

The traditional fixed form of the scheme is obviously preserved in the Hellenistic, syncretistic epoch, especially in the aretalogies. It provides the only clue for recognizing any articulation in them (if not formally, at least as far as content is concerned) As far as form is concerned, both groups of statements are woven together and repeated in a variety of ways. Efforts at further elaboration of the formal construction have uniformly proved unsuccessful.[51]

For comparative purposes the following motifs may be mentioned: In the aretalogy Isis is portrayed in the introduction as the giver of the Law.[52] This is then developed in a variety of ways. The viewpoint is unified around the concepts of Right, Truth, Order, i.e. Maat.[53] The cult, among other things, be-

---

that put the fear of him in all lands (see above), to the intent that they might make mention of his name . . . He that established *right* throughout the Two River-banks . . .' Then Isis, in mourning, appears: '. . . that traversed this land mourning, and took no rest until she found him.'

[51] The question naturally arises, whether different conceptions of the aretalogy have been more or less mechanically interwoven. Peek, *op. cit.*, pp. 158f., objects to this view that in any case it is no longer possible to isolate any of the sources. So also Harder, *op. cit.*, p. 33, n. 2: A compilation would produce no such effects. What is involved is a deliberate Egyptian 'serial' style. The construction of the Carpocrates-hymn (Harder, *op. cit.*, pp. 8, 18) is clearer. A. J. Festugière, 'À propos des arétalogies d'Isis', *HThR* 42 (1949), pp. 209ff. (esp. pp. 220ff.), finds three themes (A, B¹, B², C) in which C is inserted between B¹ and B²: A. Nature of the deity (Cyme 3–11). B. Omnipotence (12–14, 39ff). C. εὑρήματα (15–38). This is supposedly the pattern of the Greek hymn to the gods. But he must admit that there are other interpolations and dislocations in the Isis-aretalogy. And even for Greek hymns (esp. Cleanthes' *Hymn to Zeus*) there is no binding principle for *form*.

[52] Cyme 4 = Ios 3: 'I have established a law for men and ordained ordinances which no one can set aside' ('Ἐγὼ νόμον ἀνθρώποις ἐθέμην καὶ ἐνομοθέτησα ἃ οὐθεὶς δύναται μεταθεῖναι); Müller, *op. cit.*, p. 26.

[53] Cyme 16: 'I have made Right strong ('Ἐγὼ τὸ δίκαιον ἰσχυρὸν ἐποίησα); 28f.: 'I have made Right stronger than gold or silver. I have ordained that what is true be accounted good ('Ἐγὼ τὸ δίκαιον ἰσχυρότερον χρυσίου καὶ ἀργυρίου ἐποίησα. 'Ἐγὼ τὸ ἀληθὲς καλὸν ἐνομο[θέ]τησα νομίζε[σ]θαι). *SEG* 548.4ff.: 'While Thou gavest life (see below) to all men and also good order, Thou didst introduce ordinances so that a degree of righteousness might come to pass.' (ὄφρ' ἀναδοίης ἀνθρώποισι βίον τε καὶ εὐνομίην τε ἅπασι, καὶ θεσμοὺς κατέδειξας, ἵν' εὐδικίη τις ὑπάρχη). Pap. Oxy. XI. 1380.204: Isis gave νόμιμα. She is expressly called Δικαιοσύνη in Plut. *Is. Osir.* 352b; cf. Kore Kosmu 67; Dittenb. *Syll.*

longs to the orders: Isis lives in Bubastis (Cyme 11, etc).[54] She reveals the worship.[55]

IV

It may be profitable to point out an unjustly overlooked text, namely Aelius Aristides XLV (*In Sarapim*) 17.* It is striking because in a remarkable way it has penetrated its environment:[56] '. . . she adorns our soul by Wisdom, which alone shows to men their kinship with the gods and by which we differ from other mortals [or living things],[57] which also gave to men even the conception of their gods and devised sacred rites and festivals and all due honours;[58] it also taught and established laws and civil life,[59] and all skills; it gave the distinguishing of false things from true[60] – so to speak, it created human life.'[61] Cosmology is absent here. The speaker is concerned with the soul. But here too the relationship between Isis and Sophia is the key to the interpretation.

The materials now permit us, with more assurance than was

III³,1131. Müller, *op. cit.*, pp. 42ff. Examples for δικ- and the like could easily be multiplied. Harder, *op. cit.*, p. 27, comments on Cyme 28f. that this use of ἀληθής goes beyond the Greek concept of truth. He points to the *Corpus Hermeticum*.

[54] Andros 1ff.; cf. Sir. 24.10.

[55] This too is a fixed item: Cyme 10f., 22ff.; Andros 94ff.; Sir. 39.1ff.; Wisd. 7f.

* τὴν μὲν ψυχὴν σοφίᾳ κοσμῶν [ἡμῶν], ἣ μόνη τὴν πρός θεοὺς συγγένειαν ἀνθρώποις δείκνυσι καὶ ᾗ τῶν ἄλλων θνητῶν [ἢ ζῴων] διαφέρομεν, ἣ θεῶν τε αὐτῶν ἔννοιαν ἔδωκεν ἀνθρώποις καὶ ἱερὰ καὶ τελετὰς καὶ τιμὰς πάσας εὗρεν. ἔτι δὲ νόμους καὶ πολιτείαν, καὶ μηχανήματα πάντα καὶ τέχνας πάσας ἐδίδαξε καὶ κατεστήσατο, καὶ ψευδοῦς καὶ ἀληθοῦς ἔδωκε διάγνωσιν, ὡς δ' εἰπεῖν, ἐποίησε τὸν βίον.

[56] Like the passage on the Logos in Wisd. 18.14ff.; see A. Adam, *Die Psalmen des Thomas und das Perlenlied als Zeugnisse vorchristlicher Gnosis*, 1959, pp. 31f. Cf. also the material in Kore Kosmu (see above). On Ael. Arist., cf. Höfler, *op. cit.*, p. 50: In this section Sophia displaces Sarapis. 'Quite possibly the whole section with its three-part outline has been taken over.'

[57] Cf. Plato, *Prot.* 322a/b. This is not a true parallel. It falls short at the crucial point.

[58] A fixed *topos* in the aretalogies. Müller, *op. cit.*, pp. 22ff., 26ff., 31, 35ff., 49f.

[59] *Ibid.*, pp. 51f., 72f.

[60] Cyme 29. Müller, *op. cit.*, p. 53. See note 53 above.

[61] *SEG* 548.4–6; 549.3.

formerly the case, to explain as an Isis-text a papyrus fragment which E. Heitsch discovered to be such.[62] Here too the pattern sketched above is decisive, even as an outline for the presentation.[63] Now the fragment from Sirach may also be used as a source for the history of the veneration of Isis.

These texts seem to me to show that personified Wisdom belongs not to a stage of the *myth* but rather to *mythology*. Its predecessor is the syncretistic goddess which is most widely known under the name of Isis. The task now before us is to pose the analogous question for the genealogy of the Logos.

[62] First in *Mus. Helv.* 17(1960), pp. 185–8; now in E. Heitsch, *Die griechischen Dichterfragmente der röm. Kaiserzeit*, I² 1963, no. 48. The reservations of A. Wifstrand in *Gnomon* 35 (1963), pp. 465ff. are not relevant to the extant material (even though his elaborative suggestions are quite convincing).

[63] Cf. the depersonalizing of Isis in the poem of Mesomedes (Peek 145). Peek 147: 'Isis is more a cosmic potency than a representation of a divine being.'

II

THEOLOGY AND PHILOSOPHY

10

Time and Word[1]

*Gerhard Ebeling**

IT ACCORDS with academic tradition that in a 'concert' of the faculties at the university theology is assigned either the prelude or the finale, depending on the circumstances. In the university as it actually exists today this is, admittedly, justified only because we do not know what else to do. How else should one reach agreement about precedence, or who else should have the first or last word? Not that theology is really expected to provide it. No one is expected to do so. Our time is so much a captive of time that we have no first or last word at our disposal. True, because it represents another time, theology does seem to raise a claim not bound to the present time. Hence it is allowed the opening or the closing word, as long as it is around at all – not without irony, since what qualifies it for the task is precisely its deficient insight into the impossibility of such a word. And this is the best place to accommodate theology anyhow. Instead of in the middle of the other faculties, it is placed at the periphery, as a peculiar borderline case of the university.

To be sure, our concert, which has had the general theme, 'The Problem of Time in the Twentieth Century', and is now to be concluded with a final contribution, did not create the impression of a programme so well unified and organized that one

[1] Presented on February 25, 1964, at the University of Zürich as part of a faculty lecture series on 'The Problem of Time in the Twentieth Century'. The whole series is published by the Francke Verlag in Bern.

* Translated from *Zeit und Geschichte*, pp. 341–56.

could expect from the closing number a convincing conclusion of the whole. The variety of presentations (which was confusing rather than anything else) was not an accident; it was an expression of the destiny of our time. If anything has become clear, it is that the understandable longing for a finally clarifying summary of what has been learned cannot be satisfied. Our time is obviously not ripe for such a comprehensive word about time.

But even if one is free of the arrogant presumption of saying a final word, the theologian who is determined to address himself to the common theme – to pose to himself the problem of time in the twentieth century – finds it difficult to know how to do it. What would *his* theme on this theme be, or what would be the specifically theological contribution to the problem of time in the twentieth century?

It is characteristic of the diversity with which the problem of time is posed in the particular disciplines that the specific formulation of theme for some of them is almost automatic, whereas for the others finding the relevant theme requires considerable effort. This does not mean that in the one case the problem of time is really solved already and in the other case it is not really acute. Nor is the different degree of self-evidence in formulating the problem determined simply by the accidental situation of the particular branches of scholarship. It is determined above all by the peculiar aspect of each discipline which determines in advance to what extent the many dimensions of the problem of time are consciously reduced or, on the contrary, amplified. It is a sober fact, unrelated to the debates between faculties, that theology has to work with an especially oppressive variety of aspects in the problem of time. Hence our formulation of the problem here already leads us into the moot character of the problem of time itself.

One might try to escape the difficulty by choosing a historical sub-theme. In the context of the text-tradition which has immediate theological relevance – the biblical and church-historical – the sources for the problem of time are unusually abundant. Even in terms of general human history, it is incontestable that determining their meaning is still a relevant concern. Augustine suffices as an illustrative example. Yet a historical contribution would only indirectly do justice to the question of the problem of time in the twentieth century. It would do so to the extent, but also within the limits, that its interpretive meeting with the self-understanding of another time contains and advances, but also relativizes and calls into question, the problematics of our own time.

For that reason it might seem better to report on the problem of time in the theology of the twentieth century. There is no lack of material. But even in that case one would remain within a historical frame of reference so long as one did not push forward to one's own critical judgment and decide whether the way in which contemporary theology has discussed the problem of time gives expression to our twentieth-century problem of time at all, and if so, to what extent. After all, it could be the case that theology, in spite of all its discussion on the theme of time, has not addressed the problem of time in its own time, having gone into it at most with apologetic interest, without having made an authentic contribution to it. If one wishes to enter the conversation about the problem of time in the twentieth century as a theologian, one will of course have to start with the problem as one finds it in contemporary theology – in which, incidentally, our twentieth-century problem of time is very sharply delineated, as we shall see. But if the aim of the lecture is to work out precisely this point, then it is advisable to have the conception of the theme itself indicate the direction in which to take the problem of time in the twentieth century for a more exact theological formulation, rather than to create the impression of giving a simple report.

'Time and Word' is an attempt to give such a direction. It might have an adverse effect. The formulation, after all, does not seem to be recognizable as explicitly theological. It appears to enter into competition with questions in linguistics and literature. Or it arouses the suspicion of an intention to reminisce about our common undertaking, to catch transient time with a transient word. Words about time – what good are they? What prevents agreement about time? Why does time elude the word? What compels us none the less to speak about time?

If one were to understand the theme thus, some not insignificant perspectives of a general kind would result. Conversely, if stamped with a theological intention, the theme, 'Time and Word', appears specialized and abstract – in contradiction to the express assurance that the problem of time in the twentieth century would be posed, and at the same time in contradiction to the essence of theology. For if theology understands itself rightly, it owes to its time the word it has to say – that is, it lets time be the forum for its word. In spite of declining a claim to make a concluding statement, the theological contribution should not wish to disregard what the other faculties have to say on the matter. It cannot escape giving an account in these broader terms, at least tacitly. Whether it at least points the direction for this task with the formulation, 'Time and Word', (even if it does not satisfy the task itself; that would be too large an undertaking in the framework of a lecture anyhow), and what this theme really means, must become apparent in what follows. It would already be a great gain if at the end we should have a question which has an opening effect, rather than a conclusive answer.

We begin, as already indicated, with some remarks about the main knots of the work on the problem of time in the theology of the twentieth century. A brief preliminary agreement about the usage of the word 'time' is requisite for that purpose. Some of you may already have been offended at the apparently chameleonic use in my introductory remarks when I stated that our time is so much a captive of time, or that one should not address the problem of time in disregard of the problem of time of one's own time. The impression of a confusing fluctuation arises from the juxtaposition of time as such and a definite time, abstract and concrete time, formal time and time filled with content, mathematico-physical and historical time, measurable and experienced time, objective time and the time of consciousness, or however one may designate the two fundamentally differing ways of using the word 'time' and, correspondingly, of speaking of the problem of time. Only the distinction is too difficult for

the pairs of catchwords mentioned to be a unity among themselves or for them to be able to fix the distinction even approximately satisfactorily.

To be sure, the right to a distinction is provided already by
our common theme, 'The Problem of Time in the Twentieth
Century', or, as we could also say: 'The Problem of Time in Our
Time'. Yet this double occurrence of the term cannot be identified simply with the distinction in meaning indicated by the
catchwords before. After all, 'our time', that is, the experienced,
concrete, content-determined, qualitatively special time is also
abstractable, quantifiable, chronologically measurable. And the
expression, 'problem of time', points accordingly in both directions of meaning too. A major problem lies precisely in their
relation. In spite of that fact, we must accept this distinction,
though still imprecise, when it comes to view as different perspectives on the question in the natural sciences and the humanities: as quantitative and qualitative conceptions of time, as
mathematically determined and historically determined time.
Like the humanities, theology too considers time with a view to
how it becomes a problem in man's relation to it.

This point of view makes the problem of time in the theology
of our century acute under three major aspects, which are
designated by the labels 'eternity', 'eschatology', and 'history'.
As themes deeply rooted in tradition they have all fallen into a
crisis in the present spiritual situation, a crisis of which the problem of time is a point of convergence. So the circles of questions
are closely intertwined, but first they must be sketched separately.

The thought of eternity signalizes most visibly – so one might
think – the place where theology's concern clashes with the
modern understanding of reality. 'Only existence in space and
time is existence', as Feuerbach formulates what was self-
evident to post-Idealist man who had left Hegelian philosophy
behind him as the 'last place of refuge', the 'last rational support
of theology'.[2] Eternity as an epitome of the perfections of God

---

[2] *Vorläufige Thesen zur Reform der Philosophie* (1842), in: L. Feuerbach,
Sämtl. Werke, new edition by W. Bolin and Fr. Jodl, 2nd ed. II (1959),
pp. 232 and 239.

and the sustaining ground of all theological statements about the eternal Word, which creates time and everything temporal and towards the end of the time enters temporality by becoming man in order to give men a part in eternal life – all this is now placed into question, from root to crown, by the fact that time itself takes the place of God and declares the creator of time to be a product of time. God too is subject to time, as is everything else. And precisely with this recognition he has *had* his time, he is dead.

This annihilation of eternity through time is a symptom of the estrangement of modernity from the Western metaphysical tradition formed out of the Greek and Christian heritage, an estrangement which we shall not here analyse historically. Nietzsche calls this process an erasing of the whole horizon, an unleashing of the earth from its sun.[3] Rightly so. Time and eternity did after all traditionally belong together as dialectically related determinations – eternity as the horizon of time, time as sustained by eternity. To be sure, the distortion into something trivial and therewith unintelligible was also based upon the tradition, which contained the notion of eternity as simply a continuation of time or, in the sense of timelessness, as the negation of time. In both cases, to take time seriously one had to negate eternity.

In the theology of recent decades, by contrast, three paths have been struck, if one may schematize matters. The one, which indirectly had the strongest effect even though it was only a short transition, was the affirmation of the infinite qualitative difference between time and eternity; they were opposites which – like the balance in a clock – alternately posited and cancelled themselves. This conception is found in the early dialectical theology of Karl Barth. Eternity as the negation, as the judgment of time, allows no tranquillity in time; and time as the negation of eternity forbids every claim to possess eternity. Thus out of the crisis itself theology acquires the explosive material for radicalizing the crisis; out of the insight into the fact that theological discourse cannot be manipulated or managed it acquires

[3] *Fröhliche Wissenschaft*, p. 125 (ET: p. 125).

a new dynamics of theological discourse; out of the inculcation of temporality, it can afford eternity again as the Wholly Other.

A second way opened, less dramatically, in historical-exegetical work. As a consequence of turning away from Idealism and culture-Protestantism there was a sharper awareness of the deep tensions which were at the very roots of the synthesis of Christianity and the ancient world. By setting it off against the Greek metaphysical thinking which regarded time as the moving image of immovable eternity and therefore as the sphere of ontological deficiency, of mere becoming instead of unchangeable being,[4] scholars worked out the distinctiveness of the biblical understanding of time.

The peculiar structure of the Hebrew language itself points to the profound difference from the Greek.[5] Instead of the three tenses which Indo-Germanic languages have – past, present, and future – Hebrew knows only a temporal bi-polarity, which it is even misleading to designate by terms from our grammatical thinking. Instead of objectively grasped succession within the empty continuum of time there is the distinction based upon whether one is speaking of something in its finished state or in its taking place. Time is experienced here not on the basis of its formal duration but on the basis of the beginning and end of the period of ripening, of growing to maturity. Time is therefore always concrete time – time of weeping and laughing, time of need or time of salvation. Thus the apparently deficient and inexact temporal structure of the language is just what gives dominance to a structure of reality that possesses the character of event. 'For everything there is a season and a time for every matter under heaven.'[6] The world is temporally ordered by God. Its preservation is the maintenance of the difference of times: 'While the earth remains, seedtime and harvest, cold and heat, summer and winter, day and night, shall not cease.'[7] God counts therefore as

[4] Cf. Plato, *Tim.* 37a 6ff.

[5] Cf. T. Boman, *Das hebräische Denken im Vergleich mit dem griechischen* (1952[2]), pp. 104ff. (ET: pp. 123–83). M. Kartagener, *Zur Struktur der hebräischen Sprache* (Stud. Gen. 15), 1962, pp. 31–9.

[6] Eccles. 3.1ff.

[7] Gen. 1.22.

the Lord of time; so far is he from being considered in opposition to time that the OT does not know 'eternity' as a concept opposed to that of 'time'. What is usually translated as 'eternal' and 'eternity' is a many-sided vocable for time. It is related to God and comes to about this: God has time unlimitedly and is in sovereign control of time in allotting times. God's eternity is not timelessness, but fulness of time and authority over time.

Although in the NT, by contrast, the understanding of time is considerably displaced in consequence of Jewish apocalyptic, and although the question which was quite at the periphery in the OT – namely, what will happen after death and after the time of this world – now becomes determinative, still the temporal relation in the thought of eternity is preserved. The favourite interpretive pattern today places the NT conception of time as a linear one over against the Greek cyclical conception, in which what is called time is only a limited piece of the unending duration of God.[8] As important as is the element of the irreversible direction of time which is included in it, the formalizing pattern does distort into a successive relation what, according to biblical thinking, aims at a concrete temporal determination on the part of God. That eternal life according to the NT is understood at least partially as a qualification of this temporal life, and in any case is opened up through the word in time as time-determining word, contradicts an objectification of it into a succession.

Still these remarks provide only a quite incomplete circumscription of the set of historical and exegetical problems relating to the understanding of time, because eschatology, of which we shall speak presently, was excluded. There is a third way which recent theology took in order to come to terms with the atheistic interpretation of time; it sought to make the biblical and exegetical insights on time and eternity systematically and theologically fruitful. But the great weight of the previously mentioned themes, which grew like an avalanche, has not yet allowed it to enjoy any special growth. In the Ritschlian school there was a

[8] O. Cullmann, *Christus und die Zeit. Die urchristliche Zeit- und Geschichtsauffassung*, 1948[2] (revised ET: 1962, 1964).

recognition of the need to think through anew theologically the relation of time and eternity, a task to be done by critical revision of the amalgamation of the biblical with the metaphysical tradition and in view of the historical character of revelation. A statement of Wilhelm Herrmann can make that clear: 'To the true mystic God is the Eternal as opposed to the temporal; . . . to us God is not the Eternal itself, which inspires us and humbles us; he is the Power who rules both the eternal and the temporal, and who brings us, men who live in time, to a life in the Eternal. . . . It is not in the Eternal itself that we find the God who turns to us with abundant help; it is in that process in time which makes a life in the Eternal possible for us.'[9] Instead of thus including the Greek concept of eternity in theology and instead of simply excluding the ontological problem from theology, one should approach the theme of God and time in such a way that all speaking of God is interpreted in view of its temporal meaning. Classical Christian dogmatics could provide points of contact for that, precisely in its metaphysically grasped doctrine of God, if one maintains the point of view which interprets the material temporally: God as the presence that makes present, whose predestination is the presence of the future, whose judgment is the presence of the past, whose word is the presence of the present. It looks as though the problems of God and time, temporarily suppressed by the theme of eschatology, are coming to the fore again; and only with that resurgence does theology's entrance upon the problem of time in the twentieth century reach a decisive stage.

Just as the metaphysical understanding of time threatens to undo theology under the catchword 'eternity', so does the mythical understanding of time under the catchword 'eschatology'. Statements about the future are of themselves subject to the objection that they do not take the future seriously as future to the extent that they are not either limited to what is scientifically calculable or understood expressly as prognostic or utopian. Portrayals of the end, like those of the very beginning, are pro-

[9] W. Herrmann, *Der Verkehr des Christen mit Gott, im Anschluß an Luther dargestellt*, 1903[4], pp. 162f. (ET: pp. 196f.).

jections of cosmological views into mythical time, which in distinction from historical time not only eludes observability and the principle of the analogy of experience but to a certain degree also lords it over the time of history itself, making one indifferent or blind towards it. The fact that the biblical statements about the beginning and end not only contain indications of anti-mythical tendencies but also try to provide a chronological connection with datable history – in a certain sense to make the first and last periods of time historical – has not exactly attenuated the conflict with historical thinking, as is well known. Losing battles fought against prehistorical research are a tragi-comic chapter of the history of theology. And to want to re-pristinate the apocalyptic visions of the future as a kind of anticipatory reportage only provokes an even stronger offence at the mythological material which receives especially rich treatment here. Basically, these things have been clear for a long time. That they throw up so much dust once again in the theology of our century is on the one hand humiliating, yet on the other hand based upon a new situation.

If one considers that in ecclesiastical dogmatics the doctrine of the last things was long treated peripherally as a last chapter which harmonized and systematized the biblical material, and that this shrinkage of eschatology made really rapid progress in more recent theology, then nothing is more surprising than the fact that eschatology became a main theological theme in our century. Two very different factors worked together. The first one, again, was historical exegesis, which, using the method of comparative history of religion, made known more clearly than previously the weight of the apocalyptical element in primitive Christianity. Even in Jesus himself, it was believed, one could show the determinative role of an immediate apocalyptic expectation, contrary to Ritschl's religio-ethical interpretation of the proclamation of the Kingdom of God. That seemed to have catastrophic consequences. Even the person of Jesus, the nineteenth century's refuge from the dogmatic Christ, became something alien, precisely as he was historically reconstructed. Still more: What was now shown to be the core of primitive Christi-

anity was not something one could take over. It had been refuted
by the fact that the parousia did not take place. The history of
the church and of dogma becomes an attempt to come to terms
with this fact. The pioneers of this view neither intended to re-
store the original Christian eschatology – 'consistent eschatology'
as its inner self-dissolution was called – nor did they think they
might have to give up the Christian faith altogether. Indeed its
most significant representative, Albert Schweitzer, became a
saint of our century.

Since then the judgment of the historical and exegetical
material has changed considerably. But prior to this change another factor came upon the scene. Early dialectical theology,
which through Rudolf Bultmann was in fact in a personal union
with the *religionsgeschichtlich* school and the great tradition of
historical-critical study of the Bible, saw in the collapse of the
historical Jesus as a support of faith a confirmation of itself and
its rejection of Ritschlian theology and historicism. Moreover,
against the background of its own experience of time, it felt itself addressed by the seriousness and the force of eschatological
self-understanding. Its difference from the early Christian
futurist expectation was at first overrun by an interpretation
which turned that expectation into an expression of the general
structures of temporality. Time as such is eschatological – as
allotted time, which drives in an irreversible pattern towards an
end which, as the future that awakens anxiety or hope, determines existence, qualifies every time as a time of decision, an
eschatological moment, and on that account makes both uniqueness – and in so far finality – and transitoriness characteristics of
temporality. The primary experiential basis of this understanding of the eschatological is, to be sure, the fact that death
hangs over our being (*Sein zum Tode*) – or what, in the ecclesiastical doctrine of the last things, is inserted as an individual
aspect into an eschatology whose thrust is that of a universal
history. Yet experiential indications of the problem of eschatology can also be drawn from an analysis of the course of history
as a whole; for example, the element of the irreversibility of the
development of mankind and of an increasing interdependence,

universalizing and acceleration of events[10] – just as, conversely, the universal-historical way of looking at events and the philosophy of history arose as a secularization of eschatological thinking.

With all of this we have, to be sure, established only the condition of the possibility of eschatology or, stated unguardedly, only a 'natural' eschatology. Yet what makes the concern of theology in a specific sense eschatological is neither the structure of time as such, which we have sketched, nor again the apocalyptic imagery, which as such is not peculiar and essential to Christian faith. What is decisive is rather a new understanding of time which contradicts that 'natural' eschatology and its apocalyptic version and bursts its basic understanding by the fact that the eschatological future, though it does not disappear, changes its meaning under the claim of an apparently paradoxical eschatological perfect. All statements of faith about Jesus – his messianic titles as much as the affirmation of his resurrection from the dead – have this character of an eschatological perfect. That means that the turn from the old aeon to the new which is expected at the end of this time, from the time of sin to the time of salvation, already exists: 'If any one is in Christ, he is a new creation; the old has passed away, behold, the new has come.'[11] 'Behold, now is the acceptable time; behold, now is the day of salvation.'[12]

That does not exclude the relation to the future. After all, man still must die, the world still must pass away. What is new is the freedom for this future, which is at the same time freedom from this future. This freedom does not grow out of the future. For what makes one unfree over against the future is precisely the flight into the future, that is, the flight from time. Time which drives men to flee to the future is the past which is not mastered, not made present. The new time as freedom for the future grows out of the freedom from the past. Hence, with

[10] G. Krüger, *Geschichte und Tradition* (Lebendige Wissenschaft 12), 1948. Now in: G. Krüger, *Freiheit und Weltverwaltung, Aufsätze zur Philosophie der Geschichte* (1958), pp. 71ff.

[11] II Cor. 5.17.

[12] II Cor. 6.2.

reference to sin and death, Paul interprets salvation in Christ as
the eschatological perfect, temporally as freedom *from* the past,
which now includes precisely freedom *for* one's own past, and as
freedom *for* the future, which rightly understood is, at the same
time, freedom *from* the future. For faith, as a transposition into
God's presence which makes things present, leaves the past and
future to the Lord of time.

This new eschatological understanding of time was combined
very early with the traditional futurist eschatology by a pattern
for the chronology of the history of salvation. With this the viewpoint of a formal time-continuum won the upper hand – an
event with immense consequences. It could be shown that the
traditional understanding of the church and the traditional
structure of dogmatics are rooted in an understanding of time
which blunts the radical change in the eschatological understanding of time, which was inaugurated by the appearance of
Jesus, by successive additions of eschatological stages upon one
another in the following sense: the eschatological future has indeed begun; but it extends now from the perfect of the event of
Christ over the present of the church to the future of eschatology.
This pattern has the great advantage of a comprehensive and
understandable order and is so familiar to us that a critique of
it is not welcome. Today too there are zealous efforts to reinstate
it theologically. But it imperils the Christian faith's understanding of time. Of course, to set against it the slogan of a present
eschatology is likewise dubious, in so far as the eschatological
qualification of the present moment as a time of decision ignores
the problem of the extension of life and the world into the future
and thereby eliminates the hope disclosed in Christian faith and
the anxiety that accompanies faith, the 'already' and 'not yet'
which are always together.

The fact that the material understanding of eschatology is at
stake in the understanding of time is apparent from the following: the traditional understanding of eschatology eventuates
finally in a cancellation of the theology of the cross. One thinks
one knows what salvation, or resurrection, or eternal life is,
whether one then holds to it or denies it precisely as so thought.

The glory of the end receives its colours from the contrast to suffering. But if sacrifice is the language of love, should it be contradicted at the end with the language of triumph? Should not love rather have the last word and should not eschatological joy be the voice of *that* freedom which perfected itself on the cross?

What has been said on 'eternity' and 'eschatology' has already touched the third catchword under which the problem of time today confronts theology: history. Next to the metaphysical and the mythical it is now the historical understanding of time that demands we come to terms with it. That may be surprising after it has been shown to be an ally against the metaphysical and mythical understandings of time. At any rate we have always used historical research to gain new approaches for grasping theologically the problem of time. Is it not inconsistent to subject the historical understanding of time to a critique now also? What is at issue here is not the necessity of the historical-critical method and its conscientious application in the area of theology. Nor are we now discussing what kinds of tasks the omnivorous power of the historical presents for theology. The solidarity of theology with the world that today has become radically historical must, however, be proved precisely at that point where out of historical thinking itself the problem arises how to understand history at all. How are happening and understanding related to each other? What really happens in this relation? And what does it have to do with that which, during the time of history, stands in question?

Instead of starting just anywhere in the broad hermeneutical problem that cuts in here – a problem which is a common concern of all faculties – we take the innermost theological aspect as a point of departure. Time proved to be the real theme underlying eternity and eschatology, with regard to what in time stands in question, or more exactly: *how* time stands in question. Eternity and eschatology do not mean turning away from time; they are, as contrapuntal determinations of time, ways of understanding time. Theology, therefore, has to do with eternity and eschatology as something historically encountered. But how do eternity and eschaton come towards us historically, so that within time the debatability of time comes to issue? Not as timeless experience of eternity, nor as an apocalyptic view of eschatological history. Or more correctly: in so far as it does also come in such a way, then only as veiled forms of word-experience. Eternity and eschaton happen as word. Eternity, theologically understood, is God's lordship of time getting linguistically expressed in the Word of God. Eschatology, theologically understood, is Jesus' understanding of time[13] getting linguistically expressed in the gospel. Precisely because the concern of the Christian faith is the right relation to time, it lives from the word, and only *thus* does it live in active loving and patient hoping.

The fact that on this account the concern of theology is the word which has been committed to the church's proclamation is something that everyone knows even without closer insight into what is all involved in the matter – the vocable 'proclamation', which has become anaemic, and the model of the usual Sunday sermon in church do not exactly give it a clear representation. But this much is none the less clear, to the outsider probably more than to the church-member: that simply for this reason the relation of word and time must become a central problem for theology. And that can be seen in a double respect. The word is obviously threatened by time. The word of faith reaches us from far away. To be sure, it has been relayed in an unbroken transmission through the centuries down into the present. But in order not to let it become tradition, but rather to have it again and again as spring water clear and fresh, we must go back to the scripture in which its original form was fixed. Yet we must do so in such a way that out of the past there emerges a present, out of the word become text, a text again becomes word. Theology has to do with the relation of word and time in such a way that it is situated in the basic hermeneutical difference between the time of the text and the time of the interpreter as the time of the present word. But – and this is the second aspect of word and time – it is a question whether that endeavour can succeed, or

[13] On this cf. E. Fuchs, 'Das Zeitverständnis Jesu', in: *Zur Frage nach dem historischen Jesus* (1960), pp. 304ff. (ET: pp. 104–66).

whether time is not faster than the word which emerges from the text only through translation. Is not such a word, as soon as it does take place, already behind other things rather than ahead of them, as it should be? Obsolete instead of, according to its claim, possessing – probably not modernity but – that renovating newness to which the NT owes this, its eschatological, name?

The criterion for whether the word succeeds as what, theologically judged, it should be is its power in reference to time, not in the sense of a translation spanning time, nor again in the sense of a race with time, but in the sense of creative authority over time. In concourse with the word the final aim is for authority to occur. Therefore empty words are the epitome of nullity. Authority, however, has a temporal sense. That word is authoritative which is timely, that is, which affects the situation in such a way that it is the very thing which first brings one into the situation by its illuminating and changing the situation. The situation which the authoritative word creates and which can only be created through the word in the first place is freedom in relation to time, that is to say, not a situation of the violation of time, and the enslavement through time, but a situation of freedom for time and even of freedom through time, specifically, through the time which is authoritatively announced in the word.

In spite of all its limited correctness the historical understanding of time proves short-winded in the fact that it posits ascertained time absolutely as the unquestionable element of history. But is not time itself what is really in question in time? Is not the real happening in time hence the debatability of time itself? Does not a word-happening in which the debatability of time comes to issue hence take place on the basis of the happening of time? Does that not give an indication how in history happening and understanding are finally related to each other? Is not time, understood as historical time, essentially the *problem* of time, that is, time which calls forth the word and word which calls forth time? Should not the theme, 'Time and Word', far from being a special theological theme, indicate what there is to think about in the problem of time as such for everyone who poses it?

That would be the question which I said at the beginning might stand at the end in place of a conclusive answer. But for a question really to have an opening effect one must allow one-self to be carried along by it to see where it leads. We shall at least attempt to do that in three steps.

The first step is for us to consider time's connection with language. Without claim to originality let us recall something well known. Man is not simply in time as are all other temporal things, whose mode of being is not determined by the experience of time even though man does chronologically fix and causally explain their being as successive being. Man by contrast is in time through being related to time, that is, through being in time in such a way that he is simultaneously outside the present moment. He remembers the past; he transports himself into the future. To him, accordingly, what is no longer and not yet present is present. And he knows of his present only in such a way that he puts himself at a distance from his present, that he is, as it were, present outside of himself. Therefore, his temporal relation is, on the one side, superiority to time. He is not locked in the immediate present but can elevate himself above it. On the other side, it contains a bondage to time. The past or the future takes him captive and does not allow him to be present. Thus time really becomes virulent as its modes get confused with each other. Time becomes problematic only when it has lapsed from a succession into a mixture. Therefore time is always *experienced* only as *problematic*, more specifically as the problematical character of man in his world, as the question of the right distinction of times and of gaining true contemporaneity with oneself.

This eruption of a successively ordered being-in-time into a problem-laden concourse with time is identical with the emergence of language. Without going into the difficult borderline questions and the questions of detail which are touched upon by this statement, we can ascertain clearly that language and the experience of time originate together. The debatability of time is experienced as the claim of time and as being placed in question by time, as being sustained and being let down in an infinite variety of linguistic relations. Only through language do the past and future become present and the present gain the depth-dimension of past and future. Language's relation to time is rooted much more deeply than in the fact that we can fill out or even kill time with talking. Language always comes from linguistically experienced time and is challenged to fulfil the claim of time, but also to resist the claim of time. For abstract time is time made speechless. Concrete time, as time *for* something, is time which is meaningful, taken cognizance of in the context of language, though again and again bursting that context; it is time which cannot be mastered linguistically, and makes us speechless. The dimensions of linguistically experienced time pull man *in infinitum* and make the finite inexhaustible and limitless.

The second step concerns the temporality of the word. Word, in its original sense, is not a vocable but the unity of meaning which discourse has in the temporally structured sentence or at least in the temporal intention of an exclamation. The word is therefore basically a verb. The atrophy of temporality is the decay of language symptomatic of the dissolution of the humane. The language of juvenile gangsters in New York knows only the use of the present. Conversely, the wealth of language depends on the history gathered in it. Yet all this is after all only the consequence of the word-happening that takes place temporally. Word-happening is, strictly taken, a tautology. For this reason, to interpret always means to consider the whence and whither (*Herkunft und Hinkunft*) [14] of the word, to look for the situation from which it has sprung, and to open oneself to the situation which springs from it. To understand the word as a happening guards against deprecatingly isolating it as *only* a word but also against overestimating the expressed word in contrast to the deed that speaks for itself or to the silent listening for what is unexpressed. The emphasis on the event-character of the word underlines furthermore the peculiar double aspect of the conservability of the word through scripture, or even through a re-

[14] With this formulation I am taking over with appreciation a suggestion of my colleague, Emil Staiger.

cording of the voice, and the non-conservability of word-responsibility. The differentiation of time which is concretized in the differences in time among human beings – for everyone's time comes differently – will not tolerate the uniform word but calls for the word which wastes itself in the unique. Time changes the unchanged word. And in some cases the same word can be said to another time only by being said differently. After all, it is not always time for the word. And when it is time for the word, the word is not always at our disposal. The word depends on permission, freedom, authority for the word.[15]

With the third step we come to the decisive relation of time and word: the temporal power of the word. The formulation intentionally leaves undecided what remains to be decided in time: whether the word carries out the power of time or exercises such a power over time that it liberates us from the power of time. This either-or could be developed in many variations. We shall thrust immediately to the theological version of it. The word which subjects us to the power of time we call the word of the law. It more or less takes care that externally and, if need be, with compulsion, the necessary thing happens at the right time. The date calendar is a familiar symbol of the temporal character of the word of the law, though occasions for joy are not absent from it either. To be sure, it is at the same time a symbol in which we are made clearly aware of the curse of the law: being delivered to the demands of time, whose power does not let us have any more time, as well as being powerless over against the accusation of time lost, opportunity missed, life misspent. On the other hand, the word which creates freedom in relation to time we call the word of the gospel. It empowers one to let the burden of what is not past be forgiven and the unavailable future be controlled by its own lord; to be engaged with the present; to recognize what is timely; to be contemporaneous with oneself; and to let liberating love count as the standard of time allotted to one. As the word of the Lord of time it makes those under this lordship lords of time who are free for serving in time.

[15] On the concept of 'freedom for the word', cf. E. Fuchs, *Zur Frage nach dem historischen Jesus* (1960), pp. 271ff., 296ff. (ET: pp. 76–83, 98–103).

If we look back once more to the three foci of the problem of time in the theology of our time, we can state simply how time and word belong together.

History is the time which, as allotted, is to be answered for.
Eschatology is the time which, as fulfilled, is to be proclaimed.
Eternity is the time which, as perfected, is to be affirmed.

II

The Hermeneutical Problem[1]

*Ernst Fuchs**

I. *Introduction and Literature*

EXEGESIS, as we theologians say, or interpretation of texts written in a foreign language or perhaps in poetry, ends in an appropriation of the text. We may use the word 'translation' for this process. Translation is something like an appropriating repetition of the text under new linguistic conditions. In some way a poet too can be said to be translating. Does he not translate what he wants to say into a text? What then is translation? This question provides a preliminary circumscription of the whole range of questions involved in the hermeneutical problem, which always arises where linguistic material is linguistically translated.

To put the question into a modern form: Into what does one really translate? If I myself am to translate, I should probably have to say: into my own language. Translating something into a foreign language comes about only as a second step. But what is one's 'own' language? Perhaps that language in which words come to me effortlessly, of themselves, as they do in one's mother tongue. That is the reason why it is difficult to learn a foreign language. The problem of appropriating a language does not consist in learning new words – languages are learned from

[1] Revision of a lecture given at Marburg on August 1, 1963, before a French group on a vacation course in German studies which included Franz Kafka.

* Translated from *Zeit und Geschichte*, pp. 357–66.

mothers. For there is something like a spirit that is peculiar to every language – French, for example. We speak of classics of literature. Now, the classics are 'classic' if they have given expression to the linguistic spirit of their nation or several nations so purely that a nation or nations recognize themselves in their classical linguistic works. But we notice that the spirit of language changes with the time in which we live, also and precisely through the literature it creates. Why are the modern languages becoming more like each other? In part certainly as a consequence of the structure we might call 'the' modern literature, as it is demarcated for example by the Nobel prize. But it is due even more to the phenomenon of the world press. Newspapers dictate even to language. Through this historical process our languages as languages, if they are not in fact ruined, become increasingly scantier, poorer, more superficial and like one another. This is what we are resisting. And thus it happens that problem-poets, such as Franz Kafka, achieve world rank in the literature of the world. Kafka knows of the dictum, 'You cannot escape from yourself!' He asks: 'Who then still has anything to say at all?' We are posing the same question when we ask: 'Into what shall we translate great texts from the past if our own language is threatening to go lost on us modern men? Or can the very process of translating produce language for us? Or give us language as a gift?' Now, this is the very question which holds the hermeneutical problem in suspense. So much as preliminary observation.

In this lecture I should like to report on what is happening in my discipline. In Protestant and Catholic theology a whole literature has grown up about the hermeneutical problem. It is occupied especially with the work of the Marburg theologian, Rudolf Bultmann. Bultmann has become known to the intellectual world through the catchword of 'demythologizing'. He set himself the task of demythologizing the NT's way of speaking, which was still tied to mythical conceptions, in order to make the concern of the NT intelligible in the modern horizon of a scientific understanding of the world, without in the process losing what the NT has to say. Should we perhaps rewrite the

NT foundation documents? On the contrary, Bultmann says; and this is very much in contrast to liberal theology which thought it could save the core of content if it dispensed with everything else, with the framework of presentation. For that would mean to ignore many statements of the NT as archaic, that is, practically to eliminate them (so, for example, the statements about God as father, about man as sinner). Bultmann rejects such elimination. He demands interpretation instead: Let the texts stand! But if interpretation is the task, we are faced with the hermeneutical problem, that is, the question of what translation will be relevant to us. Where does that take us? Catholic theology, which always admitted that it interpreted the Bible, understood this task somewhat better than Protestant theology, which strangely was more rigidly bound to its doctrines. In America too people are more open to the problem than we in Germany; more and more theologians there are undertaking hermeneutical investigations.

The best way to make the whole range of the hermeneutical problem clear is with a few important titles from the *literature*. I mention the following:

Gotthold Hasenhüttl, *Der Glaubensvollzug. Eine Begegnung mit Rudolf Bultmann aus katholischem Glaubensverständnis*. With a foreword by Bultmann.[2] Bultmann emphasizes differences between Hasenhüttl and himself only in the understanding of the church.

Schubert M. Ogden, *Christ Without Myth. A Study Based on the Theology of Rudolf Bultmann*.[3] A critical discussion, as significant as it is sympathetic, with Bultmann on the latter's 'structural inconsistency'.

Bultmann's own most important contribution is the German translation of his Gifford Lectures of 1955,[4] after Bultmann in 1950 had already published a programmatic article on 'The Problem of Hermeneutics'.[5]

---

[2] *Koinonia* (Beiträge zur ökumenischen Spiritualität und Theologie I) (1963).
[3] New York, 1961.
[4] *History and Eschatology* (1957). German transl. by Eva Krafft, *Geschichte und Eschatologie* (1958, 1964²).
[5] *ZThK* 47 (1950), pp. 47–69 (= *Glauben und Verstehen* II [1961³], pp. 211–35 [ET: pp. 234–61]).

Demythologizing, interpretation, history and eschatology, the problem of hermeneutics – these catchwords refer to a single context, to a research effort of historical but also philosophical character. Bultmann's theology thus contains a philosophical component too – this is the very thing about him that people in the homeland of the Reformation took amiss. I mention the following:

Martin Heidegger, *Sein und Zeit*.[6] Bultmann critically adopted much, though not all, of this book; especially the basic distinction between authentic and inauthentic existence, which Bultmann understood dialectically and assigned to faith and sin.

Hans-Georg Gadamer, *Wahrheit und Methode*, 1960. Gadamer places truth and method in direct opposition; he rightly wishes to call attention to the snare of positivistic research, above all that of 'protocol', and he discusses the problems created by Heidegger on the basis of the general task of understanding by adducing for comparison the phenomenon of play.

Besides Friedrich Gogarten the following have been the main participants from among the theologians:

Gerhard Ebeling, *Wort und Glaube*[7] and *Das Wesen des christlichen Glaubens*,[8] in addition to *Theologie und Verkündigung*.[9]

Ernst Fuchs, *Hermeneutik*,[10] an attempt to bring the hermeneutical problem back into the dimension of language with the aid of the phenomenon of 'empathy' as the foundation of all understanding. The book does not develop its intention in a systematic way. It is a presentation revolving around central exegetical points and taking into account Bultmann's and Heidegger's work. In addition there are two volumes of collected works.[11]

---

[6] First ed. 1927, 1962[10]. – Cf. on this question the English article by E. Dinkler, 'Martin Heidegger', in: *Christianity and the Existentialists*, ed. Carl Michalson (1956).

[7] Collected articles with important contributions to the theme, especially to the historical-critical method, 1962[2] (ET: 1963 = German 1960[1]).

[8] A Zürich lecture series for students from all faculties in the winter semester 1958–59 (1959); now also as Siebenstern-Taschenbuch (1964).

[9] HUTh 1, 1963[2].

[10] 1954, 1963[3] with a supplement.

[11] E. Fuchs, *Zum hermeneutischen Problem in der Theologie* (= Ges. Aufs. I

Eberhard Jüngel, *Paulus und Jesus*.[12] Jüngel is concerned especially with the phenomenon of the parable in Jesus and with the structure of analogy.[13]

We see that the work within theology pertains first to the continuing significance of the historical-critical method but, beyond that, mainly to the question of the connection between 'truth and method', as Gadamer says. If Bultmann as a scientific exegete asks about the relevant concepts for interpreting the NT, the philosopher asks about the relevant concepts for every possible self-understanding of man. The result of this is Bultmann's concept of 'existential interpretation', in which he takes up the anthropological question of the philosopher. Behind it stands the insight into a 'pre-understanding' which concretely asks: What can be a point of orientation for man today if neither a mythical nor a natural-scientific world-view can answer his existential question about himself?

Thus the hermeneutical problem has grown far beyond the special concerns of understanding philosophical or other texts from the past. If we evade the issue, we are threatened with the destruction of spirit as well as of language in an increasingly tyrannical positivism – whose sign is calculus, pure calculation. This is the very threat that Kafka saw. Spirit never settles accounts. It speaks, if it is not silent, only among its own kind. That can hardly be remedied through a lecture unless the questions have grasped us.

II. *Results*

1. Bultmann is also to be thanked for the previously mentioned participation of young Catholic and American theologians in the reflection on hermeneutics. This reflection has set the decisive tasks for other systematicians too besides Gerhard

---

[1959]), and by the same author, *Zur Frage nach dem historischen Jesus* (=Ges. Aufs. II [1960]) (ET: 1964).

[12] HUTh 2, 1964[2].

[13] *Zum Ursprung der Analogie bei Parmenides und Heraklit* (1964). Further: 'Die Möglichkeit theologischer Anthropologie auf dem Grunde der Analogie', *EvTh* 22 (1962), pp. 535–57.

Ebeling. True, Karl Barth did not take part, although he too in his way entered the discussion with philosophy. For example, he worked on the problem of analogy and he enriched it with his christological contribution. A student of his and Bultmann's, Heinrich Ott,[14] sought to correct Barth, but in my judgment he has not yet advanced the problem itself. Helmut Gollwitzer tried to formulate at least the phenomenon of existence theologically,[15] but his thinking is still partly under the influence of Cartesian presuppositions, of which he (like others) accuses his partners in discussion. On this point we should indeed move ahead. For we *all* know something of the fact that Luther, for example, understood the *extra nos* not in a Cartesian way but as a *nos extra nos esse*, because Luther as an exegete was protected against the modern separation between subject and 'object' in the sense of the question about the reality of the external world. God is in no sense an 'object'. And our concept of object should certainly be able to conform to this. The controversial question, in other words, is precisely that of the 'how' (how God 'is' and how man 'is') and not of the 'that'! Similarly the question of the 'who' in this 'cause' of 'existence in the relation between God and man' seems to me to be more 'with it' than the stubborn question of the 'what' (who or what anyone 'is'); and particularly those people who appeal to the OT in our discussion ought to agree with this. The 'late' Heidegger does after all want to direct us theologians back to our own 'cause'. So our discussion remains in the charge of exegetes.

2. Between theology and philosophy too there arose an unforeseen debate in 1927 which is difficult to comprehend because it has remained unclear how far Heidegger has moved from his book *Sein und Zeit*. Is he as far from it as Bultmann was when he made theological use of the distinction between authentic and unauthentic existence? According to Bultmann the centre of hermeneutical reflection, then as now, is the question how man can, and how he should today, understand himself.

[14] Heinrich Ott, *Denken und Sein: Der Weg Martin Heideggers und der Weg der Theologie* (1959).

[15] *Die Existenz Gottes im Bekenntnis des Glaubens* (1963) (ET: 1965).

Theology certainly cannot wish to solve this question alone. For no one will concede without more ado that he can exist as himself only in faith. But the Christian message of faith does direct itself to every man. So it must aim to make itself understandable to every man. Therefore the central question, then as now, is whether there are 'structures' which are, so to speak, ontologically constitutive for the being of man. *Here* is the seat of the hermeneutical problem, even if it was occasioned by the dilemmas of historical exegesis which gave rise to the question of the possibility of 'demythologizing'. The early philosophy of Heidegger (similarly and yet differently, that of Karl Jaspers) answered the question of the structures of human existence with the *'existentialia'*. Did we find in them the relevant concepts for interpreting the biblical statements about human existence – were they, say, 'anthropological' leading concepts, or better, leading phenomena?

3. Theology itself made a contribution in this matter to philosophical work. Bultmann, following *Sein und Zeit*, spoke of the 'self-understanding' of man. Self-understanding is not simply the same as self-consciousness although our self-understanding must be a conscious one if we want to speak of it as self-understanding. From Descartes' *cogito me cogitare* one arrives at an ego-consciousness rather than a self-consciousness. The ego-consciousness is notably constant. One can feel that one is now the same as 'formerly'. But surely self-consciousness consists, does it not, of a correlation to the 'self', as Kierkegaard showed with psychological means? What does that mean? In the ego-consciousness a *question* is hidden under the mask of self-consciousness, the question of the 'self'. If we now move to the answer, to self-understanding, then we shall have to say: In self-understanding it is precisely the 'self' that is at stake! 'Am' I what I am in my self-understanding? Can it be that I 'understand' myself as a sinner even though I do not at all feel myself as a sinner? The same question moved Luther too. And if it should turn out that, contrary to my consciousness, I understand myself only as a sinner, how and when do I become aware of it, that is, of my true self-understanding? Can I perhaps understand myself as a

sinner only after I am no longer stuck in sin? But where am I then? Then, what if I 'objectify' myself as sinner because I am free of myself as sinner? Do self-understanding and self-consciousness perhaps coincide only in faith? If so, the question of the self-understanding we can achieve is indeed not answerable without faith, although as a question it can hardly be dismissed in the horizon of an analysis of self-understanding. It is equally obvious that our ego is a dialectical quantity, in spite of Descartes. The question remains: When am I myself? Kierkegaard asked that question, as had Fichte also.

I am not unacquainted with the fact that some people want to exclude Kierkegaard from a theological discussion because they do not consider him morally qualified for it. If this pharisaic premise gains ground, we should not be surprised that genuine theological discussion among us threatens more and more to die out. In the NT things proceed differently. There existential questions are not only allowed but even encouraged. To be without problems in theology is certainly not the mark of honest faith but of supreme arrogance, which is very dangerous because it seems to move about with such self-assurance.

4. So the *explicit* question of the 'self' is asked only when one has arrived in the area where one must discuss the 'self-understanding' which is at first, perhaps on account of sin, different from self-consciousness. Even on the basis of conscience the possible and normally imperilled self-understanding awakens in an individual man the question of his 'authenticity', and that very thing is also Kafka's question: How do I get into the 'castle'? 'Dear friend', one young man asks another in a humorous book (in Hungarian the location is in Paris), 'have you too missed your life?' Everyone *can* only exist as the one he 'is'. Actually I exist only by adopting my existence as my existence. In practice that will usually require self-sacrifice. The believer is precisely the one who gives himself up, Bultmann thinks. Only thus does love take place, Kierkegaard knows. If unbelief must misunderstand this existence as an existence in nothing, faith understands itself as existence in God 'before' God. And thus this faith approaches nihilism itself. Only thus does it correspond to our

'post-Christian' era (the problem occupies a book by Gabriel Vahanian, *The Death of God: The Culture of Our Post-Christian Era*,[16] which is highly valued by Bultmann). In spite of that, faith is not really a partner of nihilism. – Whether it is possible to understand God's own existence ontologically, or better: analogically, as Ogden,[17] following his teacher Charles Hartshorne, maintains, is a question I shall not treat here, although I am sceptical; this question has to be studied more closely first.

III. *New Questions*

Another constitutive element appears to me not to have been considered in Bultmann's description of human existentiality. What is responsible for this is an ambiguity in Heidegger's book, *Sein und Zeit*, which allowed the book to be understood as a 'transcendental' analysis of human being (whereas the phenomenon of 'existence' actually bursts every transcendental horizon). I mean the fact that human existence is connected with *language*. Nature does not speak, though man does. To be sure, one can doubt whether we ourselves are today 'on the way to language', in spite of this title of a collection of essays of Heidegger.[18] At any rate an independent metaphysical essence should not be ascribed to language. But language is a constituent part of the essence of man. Only man can, for example, produce a linguistic work of art.

What appears in language as language? Not only a giving of names (which Plato too emphasizes in his dialogue *Cratylus*), certainly not only information, but a special power of understanding, of giving to understand, in which someone gives himself to another to be understood (Friedrich Gogarten). This can

[16] 1961.

[17] Schubert M. Ogden, 'Bultmann's Demythologizing and Hartshorne's Dipolar Theism', in: *Process and Divinity: Essays in Honor of Charles Hartshorne* (1963). Also in German: 'Zur Frage der "richtigen" Philosophie', *ZThK* 61 (1964), pp. 103–24. Cf. on this R. Bultmann, 'Zur Frage einer "philosophischen Theologie"', in: *Einsichten: Gerhard Krüger z. 60. Geburtstag* (1962), pp. 36–8.

[18] Martin Heidegger, *Unterwegs zur Sprache* (1959).

happen in a completely indirect way. When my sister recently delivered to me from the estate of my mother the first dress I wore as a baby, this modest item had very much to say to me because I knew that at the time, as a result of a virulent illness, I was literally carried by my parents between life and death. Thus language unites us in understanding beyond time and death. And yet what is understood is precisely that which at one time did find words and at a given time presses towards finding words again. And that is what is 'to be' understood, not only the understanding, but that which grants the word or grants itself as word and which sometimes needs expression as little as understanding does because language no longer is only an instrument but a power that lets its essence happen. Language does something. It *lets* man *into* his own, whether into a history or into a concourse with nature that brings forth a world. And thus language has the spirit that fits itself into its world (W. v. Humboldt). But the spirit is concentrated in language. Language is not really invented; it is found. And for that reason we have to answer for our language (everyone for his own!) in our existence. So it can very well happen that we really have nothing to say to one another and that others, even such as no longer live among us, have much more, and more important things, to say than our so-called fellow man. The current talk about the 'claim' of our neighbour on us seems to me to be quite unclear. Presumably we are far more urgently challenged by what challenges us in common, namely, language; so that the question is what we have 'to say' to each other. Informatory talking does not really say anything, and will not say anything until listening is deepened to become a new and necessary hearing. Christian proclamation at any rate does not wish to inform us about things but to let what is new to hear be heard.

In this context I have called 'freedom for the word' the *existentiale* that in my judgment is the most important. Whether we really exist is shown by freedom for the word. It is missing in fact if, for example, one evades the confession of his faith. Whether it is missing in the genuine question I will leave open. If one sticks to this *existentiale*, then what we commonly call 'anthropology' in theology becomes a doctrine of language (Ebeling says occasionally: a school of language). Theology must then be the 'doctrine of the language of faith' because it has assumed a hermeneutical character. But this definition of theology does on its part correspond to tradition completely. Was not Christian theology at its high points always a theology of the word? Was not Jesus' own proclamation as parable always a 'language-event' (parables of the treasure in the field, of the precious pearl, of the lost son)? Do such parables wish to show something distant which one can only approach or approximate by means of analogous conceptions? Does the Kingdom of God hover behind the clouds? Or is it not the case that Jesus was in a position to make use of the Kingdom of God in the way that language makes use of the very thing that lets us into our own existence? Does not the Kingdom of God, including the Johannine statements, provide the possibility for something like rebirth? Or for the present? If the Johannine Jesus goes 'to the Father', does he not go precisely into the present, which the poet, death, distorts for us? And if the Kingdom of God *creates* a present, does it not burn so strongly that man, just as he is, must be shielded against this fire? The 'near' God could at that time obviously be proclaimed only in a parable, only indirectly. Was Kafka talking about things far-fetched? Did he not rather give a compassionate portrayal of what is closest to us?

Those are more or less the questions which are treated by Ebeling and me as the content of the hermeneutical problem because we think that the texts must translate us before we can translate them. If our texts – for example, the NT – by and large have become sources for historical-critical analysis, data in the dimension not of existence but of assembling some conceptions 'about' God, man, and all sorts of happenings, then the question for us is whether we can regain the texts as texts of proclamation. All texts can become mere sources of research because they were language. But they should now and then speak again. How does one make them talk, indeed bring out *their* word? If we remain sovereign over them, the texts remain merely sources for things like the historical-critical method of interpretation. But if they become sovereign over us, they have again become texts of proclamation, even though in a new situation. The hermeneutical event could consist of the knowledge that, precisely because God wishes to say to us what he once said to other people, a distinction can no longer be made between 'constants' and 'variables'. God does not state (*aussagen*) himself; he awards (*zusprechen*) himself. Surely it is the case, is it not, that what corresponds theologically to the formally initiated dialectic of our human existence leading to authenticity and inauthenticity is only the one inescapable Word of God which does what it says.

12

Dietrich Bonhoeffer and Rudolf Bultmann

*Gerhard Krause**

A WIDELY espoused thesis, which prejudges some decisive questions, contests any substantive relation between Bonhoeffer's testamentary demand for a non-religious interpretation of biblical concepts and Bultmann's programme of demythologization. This essay undertakes to investigate the correctness of that thesis in connection with the current state of theological concern with the work of Bonhoeffer. This question, one part of a larger complex of problems, is restricted to (1) a sketch of the most important literature and (2) an examination of the direct utterances of Bonhoeffer himself regarding the theme. This is in line with the double intention of this investigation: to hold open for investigators a door whose untimely closing would distort Bonhoeffer's word and effect for our time, and to commend to our attention the voice of the sources of the intellectual honesty represented by Bonhoeffer himself, because this voice is still the most reliable protection against arbitrary interpretations. The presupposition, which I shall not explicate here, is as follows: the dominant constant in Bonhoeffer's thinking was the question of Christ for today; it was pursued from various approaches but always in view of the relation between church and world, and it placed before him, from his earliest publications on, the task of a non-religious interpretation,[1] although it was formulated thus only in the last year of his life.

1. No one recognized more quickly and acutely than Karl

* Translated from *Zeit und Geschichte*, pp. 439–60.
[1] For the writings of Dietrich Bonhoeffer the usual abbreviations are used:

Barth the set of problems which the edition of Bonhoeffer's previously unpublished work presented. His attempt to choke the
problems in embryo seemed to be justified because he was the
very one who, sooner than anyone else, had pointed to the fundamental significance of most of the writings of Bonhoeffer. He had
done so in the *Church Dogmatics* with a praise[2] that he otherwise
seldom gives, which for that reason was especially impressive, in
spite of the criticism of Bonhoeffer that it also contained. At
least in part we can understand why Barth declined to take up
Bonhoeffer's critical questions and attacks against Barth's earlier
theology[3] if we remember the very close friendship between Barth

---

SC   *Sanctorum Communio*, 1960[3] (ET: 1963).
AS   *Akt und Sein*, 1956 (ET: 1961).
SF   *Schöpfung und Fall*, 1933 (ET: 1959).
N   *Nachfolge*, 1937 (ET: 1959[2]).
E   *Ethik*, ed. by E. Bethge, 1953 (ET: 1955).
R   *Dein Reich komme*, ed. by E. Bethge (Furche-Bücherei 146), 1957.
WE   *Widerstand und Ergebung*, ed. by E. Bethge, 1955[5] (ET: *Letters and Papers
       from Prison*, 1967[3]).
GS   *Gesammelte Schriften*, ed. by E. Bethge, 1958–1961 (four volumes to
       date). Partial ET: *No Rusty Swords*, 1965; *The Way To Freedom*, 1966;
       Christology = *Christ the Centre*, 1966. Also the volumes with works about
       Bonhoeffer:
MW   *Die mündige Welt*, Vols. I–IV, 1955–1963.

[2] As early as 1945 Barth acknowledged Bonhoeffer's lectures, *Creation and
Fall*, with reference to the explanation of Gen. 1.26f. as 'an important advance'
and 'an advance in getting close to the text' (*KD* III, 1, pp. 218f. [ET: pp.
194f.]); in 1951 Bonhoeffer's *Ethics* is praised on account of its 'concern with
the dogmatic context' and as 'brilliant' (*KD* III, 4, p. 2 [ET: p. 4]); in 1955
he calls *The Cost of Discipleship* 'by far the best' that has been written about
the summons to discipleship. Barth would almost like to take it 'as a long
quotation' into the course of his own remarks (*KD* IV, 2, p. 604 [ET: pp.
533f.]) and in several places adopts Bonhoeffer's terminology of an opposition
between 'cheap and costly grace' (*KD* IV, 1, p. 74 [ET: p. 70]; IV, 2, pp.
571, 626 [ET: pp. 505, 553]); *Sanctorum Communio* not only is presented as
more 'instructive, stimulating, illuminating, really "edifying"' . . . than all
sorts of famous things that have since been written on the problem of the
church' but also makes Barth himself concerned about being able to maintain on his part the high level reached by Bonhoeffer at that time (*KD* IV,
2, p. 725 [ET: p. 641]).

[3] Barth does not mention Bonhoeffer's habilitation thesis, *AS*, at all. In it
one finds the most detailed and as yet unsurpassed critique of Barth and
dialectical theology, as R. Prenter ('Dietrich Bonhoeffer und Karl Barths

and Bonhoeffer since 1931, a friendship which was determinative for Bonhoeffer's development. For, in spite of the partners' 'structural difficulties in understanding each other',[4] this friendship not only was 'not a very lucky one'[5] but, so far as outsiders can judge, led them into the sphere of that charisma which 'is not jealous'.

To be sure, even this provides only a partial understanding of Barth's quite different judgment, in content as well as method, about Bonhoeffer's conception of a non-religious interpretation. His letter to W. Herrenbrück of December 21, 1952, concerning the person and work of Bonhoeffer – a letter which had wide circulation and influence – was a spirited and loving 'attempt to understand him'.[6] But despite the twice-emphasized intention not to blunt the 'sting' of the letters from prison, a threefold wall is erected out of the difficulties of interpretation which have 'long since' existed and exist 'now also'. (*a*) Bonhoeffer was personally an 'impulsive, visionary thinker', whose vigorously asserted insights never seemed to be final. One always had to grant him the possibility that 'he would express himself some other time . . . still more clearly and concisely, perhaps even take it back, perhaps advance further', so that Barth always read him with the question 'whether, viewed from some angle or another, he might not be right'. (*b*) The situation of the prison cell forced him to think with a 'picture from memory'; the books of Barth and (Barth does not mention this) of Bultmann were not available. (*c*) Formally the prison letters contain 'enigmatic expressions', intuitions of something which 'did not stand tangibly before his own eyes', and they certainly have not left behind 'anything tangible' for us.

Offenbarungspositivismus', *MW* III, 1960, pp. 36ff.) and H. Gollwitzer (*Die Existenz Gottes im Bekenntnis des Glaubens*, 1963, pp. 9, 98, 125, 149, 180 [ET: pp. 15, 123, 157, 186, 223]) confirm.

[4] Thus W. Fürst, 'Motive der theologischen Arbeit Dietrich Bonhoeffers', in *Hören und Handeln, Festschrift für Ernst Wolf*, 1962, p. 136.

[5] Thus E. Bethge, 'The Challenge of Dietrich Bonhoeffer's Life and Theology', in: *The Chicago Theological Seminary Register*, Vol. II, Feb. 1961, No. 2, 7.

[6] Published in *EvTh* 15 (1955), pp. 243–5 and *MW* I, 1955, pp. 121ff.

What could have been the intention of these lightning impressions which suddenly disclosed so many sympathetic negatives about Bonhoeffer's work? Certainly the 'primarily psychological'[7] reference to the instability of Bonhoeffer's insights would not be true of the work he himself edited, which Barth praised with such emphasis, although it would affect the prison letters. The entirely correct stress on the provisional character of the technique and style of the letters would not induce one to inquire into their legitimate context in the earlier works; in fact it discredits them. The second part of the letter shows the reason. The difficulties of interpretation which he mentioned do not prevent Barth's knowing, with astounding definiteness, what Bonhoeffer's relation to Bultmann is. In a significant alteration of Bonhoeffer's terminology Barth speaks consistently only of his 'programme of an unreligious speaking'. This, he says, is in 'distinction to the "demythologizing" of a spiritually unsettling kind' and does not point 'in the direction of existentialism, pre-understanding, etc.', since Bonhoeffer certainly 'made no bones about substituting "other words" to circumscribe the kerygma – in other words, doing what Bultmann practically is aiming for'. Bonhoeffer could not have meant any more 'than a warning against all Christian gobbledygook, against all unreflective reciting of biblical and traditional pictures, forms of speech, combinations of concepts'. It is useless to 'search for a profundity' that he did not display, and 'probably did not think through himself'. Barth sees only one direct relation between Bonhoeffer and Bultmann (he means it humorously, but it quickly became an effective *cliché*): both belong to the 'melancholy theology of the north-German plain', which is 'Lutheran', but which has not yet 'victoriously demonstrated' that the one and last word is to be sought in this direction.

This tendency of contemporary theologians to draw caricatures and to trivialize (*bagatellisieren*)[8] is all right, sometimes even

---

[7] Thus H. Schmidt, 'Das Kreuz der Wirklichkeit', *MW* IV, 1963, p. 79.

[8] The last expression is in G. Ebeling, 'Die "nicht-religiöse Interpretation biblischer Begriffe"', *ZThK* 52 (1955), p. 298 (the article is reprinted in

desirable, as long as one smiles about it; but by supplying super-ficial interpreters of Bonhoeffer with arguments, it became dangerous. The arguments which are here still hidden under imponderables and clever phraseology Barth later brought into the debate with desirable clarity. The one argument recom-mends a study of the Bonhoeffer who speaks clearly and distinctly in his earlier writings, 'instead of' succumbing to the temptation to read one's own wishes into the catchwords on the shaky ground of the letters.[9] The reason why the sound exegetical rule which says that obscure texts should be interpreted by clear ones is not recommended is explained by Barth's antipathy for taking up the theme of non-religious interpretation at all. The reason for this is given in 1959 by one of the famous small-print and incisive digressions in the *Church Dogmatics*.[10] Rarely has there been, Barth says, 'a discussion so empty as the discussion about the so-called religious and the so-called non-religious language'. There is after all only the one human, mundane lan-guage; even what is called 'religious' language is primarily al-ways non-religious, and both kinds are equally near to, and far from, the word of the Christian congregation. The congregation can speak its word, down to the very foundation, only in a worldly way, it cannot escape secularity or flee to it from a non-existent sacred language 'in order perchance to make itself better and more easily understandable there'. This rigorous declaration that a language problem for theology and the church does not exist costs Barth something. He must pay for it by a sovereign ignoring of linguistic studies which assert the contrary of his thesis about the primary worldliness of language; by

---

MW II, 1956, pp. 12–73 and in the volume: G. Ebeling, *Wort und Glaube*, 1960, pp. 90–160 [ET: pp. 98–161]). In what way Bonhoeffer on his part also sought to understand Barth geographically and historically is shown by the words from the year 1932/33 quoted by J. Glenthøj, 'Dietrich Bonhoeffer und die Ökumene' (*MW* II, p. 200): 'Barth does not come out of the trenches but from a small Swiss village pulpit.'

[9] Orally communicated by Ernst Wolf 1956: *MW* II, p. 5.

[10] *KD* IV, 3, p. 841 (ET: p. 735). Barth does not mention Bonhoeffer here, but H. Diem too refers the section to the 'non-religious interpretation of religious concepts' (*Theologie als kirchliche Wissenschaft*. III. *Die Kirche und ihre Praxis*, 1963, p. 86).

ignoring the responsibility which is committed to faith and is therefore also to be reflected upon theologically – the responsibility to be intelligible in ecclesiastical speaking; and by ignoring the fact that Bonhoeffer was not in the first place concerned with finding a more effective language for preaching the gospel but with the decidedly theological and dogmatic work of explicitly 're-interpreting' (*'Uminterpretation'*)[11] the main biblical concepts, on the basis of the centre of faith and in the direction of the goal of faith, that Christ is the Lord of the religion-less. If one wishes to see the 'spiritually unsettling' element of the letters of Bonhoeffer in his having traffic with ghosts in prison, that would have to be made credible on a somewhat broader foundation. If it is supposed to be only the 'rejection of the phraseological,'[12] his intense struggle for a moral principle so self-evident as this would remain incomprehensible. He would have nothing new to say to us in that case. If Bonhoeffer wrote in 1944 that Barth 'gave no concrete directions for the non-religious interpretation of theological concepts, neither in dogmatics nor in ethics',[13] one has to add in 1964: Nor does he wish to do so, for – this is the premise of the statements cited – Bonhoeffer cannot and dare not have meant anything even remotely similar to Bultmann.

2. A substantial or explicit agreement with this judgment prevented several works about Bonhoeffer, which in their own way were of high quality, from making important independent contributions to a more exact clarification of our theme and a more precise understanding of what is distinct in Bonhoeffer. Thus we are left only with suggestions, which do not determine the understanding of the whole Bonhoeffer, when H. Schlingensiepen quite rightly observes that he brings 'the genuine concern of liberalism . . . to an astonishing fulfilment',[14] when R.

[11] *WE*, p. 185 (ET: *Letters and Papers from Prison*, pp. 156f.)

[12] *WE*, p. 174 (ET: p. 149).

[13] *WE*, p. 219 (ET: p. 181).

[14] H. Schlingensiepen, 'Zum Vermächtnis Dietrich Bonhoeffers', *EvTh* 13 (1953), pp. 97–106 (reprinted in *MW* I, pp. 102ff.); see *EvTh* 13, p. 105: 'What is involved is neither a "point of contact (*Anknüpfungspunkt*)" nor something like it, such as Bultmann's "pre-understanding".'

Grunow correctly notes that he disregards almost completely 'a discussion with literary-critical research and the question of demythologizing',[15] and when W. Fürst rightly asks whether he should have 'questioned Barth's putting the gospel in the first rank, as he himself also did in his own way, as a method of proclamation'.[16] An exact examination of these insights would have laid bare the foundations of Bonhoeffer's thinking and could have provided a more convincing definition of its real relation to the thinking of Bultmann than global assertions of complete discontinuity between them.

G. Harbsmeier is the only one thus far to have made 'the "non-religious interpretation of biblical concepts" in Bonhoeffer and demythologizing' the object of a detailed discussion.[17] To carry out his intention of 'not having the heritage of Bonhoeffer transferred into a "genus" in which it loses its own illuminating power',[18] Harbsmeier constructs a conception of hermeneutics regarding which one does not know whether it is supposed to be that of Bonhoeffer or of Harbsmeier himself. Hermeneutics is not, as with Bultmann, what it was for the Reformation and for criticism; that is, it is not the science of understanding subject matter which from the very start takes into account the revelation confronting us in history and word, and the person addressed in view of this actual encounter. Rather it is an 'exalted art', a 'discussion of the hermeneutical principle and the method to be applied', occupied only with 'bare (*bloss*)' difficulties in a 'Hellenic' understanding. '*No* hermeneutic, as necessary as this might be in its own place, can extricate' one from the anxiety impelling Bonhoeffer through the world's coming of age. There

[15] R. Grunow, 'Dietrich Bonhoeffers Schriftauslegung', *EvTh* 15 (1955), pp. 200ff. (reprinted in *MW* I). *EvTh* 15, p. 204: With Bonhoeffer's demand of a non-religious interpretation 'Bultmann's demand for demythologizing is superseded, indeed – may we so express it? – downright obsolete'. Recently Grunow makes more exact distinctions in the foreword to *MW* IV, pp. 13ff.

[16] W. Fürst, *op. cit.*, p. 147.

[17] G. Harbsmeier, 'Die "nicht-religiöse Interpretation biblischer Begriffe" bei Bonhoeffer und die Entmythologisierung', *MW* II, pp. 74–91, reprinted in: *Antwort, Festschrift für Karl Barth*, 1956, pp. 545–61.

[18] G. Harbsmeier, *op. cit.*, p. 90.

exists a fundamental 'divergence in hermeneutics on both sides'; one finds in Bonhoeffer 'nothing of that distance between reflection and execution, nothing of a "thinking of thinking", of a cleft intentionally kept open between an existentialist theology and an existential proclamation; he does not press 'at all towards the problem "faith (!) and understanding"', his question lies 'on a plane entirely different from that of Bultmann'; the basis of his question is 'essentially deeper', he has 'an entirely different interest', for he does not take as 'the basis of all further considerations' the distinction between existentialist and existential, ontological and ontic, which is fundamental for Bultmann.[19] If it is already surprising that the distinctiveness of Bonhoeffer is formulated by means of such a distortion of the hermeneutics of Bultmann, Harbsmeier presents us with further riddles when he ascribes to Bonhoeffer (without documentation or documentability), as though he were a Barthian, a 'downright instinctive, theological aversion' towards Bultmann's hermeneutics, without critically examining this aversion on the basis of his insight, expressed almost simultaneously, that 'the simple aversion towards hermeneutic considerations in Bultmann is, of course, not sufficient warrant for letting the problem lie and going one's own way'.[20] Harbsmeier sees the categorical difference between Bonhoeffer and Bultmann in the way they are related to wisdom and theology, which are opposed to each other as doing (*Vollzug*) and thinking. Non-religious interpretation is a matter of wisdom, demythologizing a matter of theology.[21] Even if one disregards the problems involved in this concept of wisdom[22] as well as the fact that this exaggeration (otherwise carefully avoided by Harbsmeier[23]), which results in an exclusive opposition to Bonhoeffer's theology, puts charisma into an ivory tower and raises

[19] *Ibid.*, pp. 75–9.

[20] *Ibid.*, p. 75, cf. p. 88. The second quotation from: G. Harbsmeier, 'Was ist Freiheit?' *EvTh* 15 (1955), p. 486.

[21] *MW* II, pp. 90f.

[22] On this see H. Diem, *op. cit.*, pp. 31ff. (in opposition to H. Schlier).

[23] G. Harbsmeier, 'Was ist Freiheit?' *EvTh* 15 (1955), pp. 482ff., where this same distinction between wisdom and theology is applied to Barth and Bultmann, whom he does not at all see in an objective opposition.

a taboo against theological questioning, one still is left with the problem that Harbsmeier ignores a fact painfully evident on all sides; namely, that for the hermeneutical foundations of a non-religious interpretation Bonhoeffer in his letters does not once employ his considerations in a first-order way – that is, 'in the act (*Vollzug*)', but only in reflections about the act, indeed, precisely in a 'thinking of thinking'. In the process Harbsmeier indirectly proves the inadequacy of his categories of distinction too. To understand Bonhoeffer's concept of 'man come of age', for whose sake a non-religious interpretation is demanded, Harbsmeier refers to the concern that comes from having to be inescapably responsible for oneself.[24] It seems to me that he has, quite in the sense of Bonhoeffer, done what he wanted us to believe Bonhoeffer meant quite differently: without loss of substance he has interpreted Bonhoeffer existentialistically, in the best sense.

The fact that a widely influential expert and advocate of the hermeneutics of Bultmann, as G. Harbsmeier[25] is, confirmed Barth's claim of a diametrical opposition between Bonhoeffer and Bultmann could not remain without its consequences. Not only did R. Prenter, with explicit appeal to Harbsmeier, now take his earlier and more questionable judgment about Bultmann into his Bonhoeffer interpretation and conclude that Bonhoeffer agreed 'essentially with the intentions of Barth and not with those of Bultmann';[26] the first German exposition of the

[24] *MW* II, pp. 79f.

[25] Cf. the references to literature in G. Bornkamm, 'Die Theologie Rudolf Bultmanns in der neueren Diskussion', *ThR* 29 (1963), p. 38.

[26] R. Prenter, 'Dietrich Bonhoeffer und Karl Barths Offenbarungspositivismus', *MW* III, p. 21, and also the whole section from p. 17, where one finds the truly 'enigmatic' sentences: 'The Word of God, which through the religionless interpretation is placed into relation to the mature, worldly life as such, does not first need to be made understandable through any "translation" . . . This is what takes place in the religious interpretation. For the biblical concepts . . . already – without "translation" – take their meaning, which makes them understandable, from God's being precisely for the world.' I hope Prenter will pardon me if in reading his sentences I must think of the famous missionaries Ziegenbalg, Egede, Stach, and others, sent out from Denmark, who accomplished significant translations, and if I ask myself what they would probably have done with such theology. – On

whole theology of Bonhoeffer, which was done by H. Müller and is distinguished by its methodological clarity and strictness, also appeals to Schlingensiepen and Harbsmeier[27] in regard to the non-religious interpretation. These latter had exempted Bonhoeffer's demand from theological and hermeneutical critique. Müller now, in several dialectical operations, strips the demand first of the character of 'interpretation', then that of 'worldly speaking', in order to deposit it finally as 'non-religious doing' and as 'preaching'. This doing and preaching, however, does not aim to make the gospel understandable but, under waiver of immanent meaning and purpose, remains in the to-and-fro of dialectical formulas, which – at the best – dissolves Christ for the religion less into pure inwardness.[28] It is worth pondering that it was not Bultmann but Müller's Bonhoeffer-interpretation 'in opposition to Bultmann' which led to a dissolution of the church into the world, in contradiction to Bonhoeffer.

It is of still greater consequence and a constant reminder for critical self-examination that even E. Bethge, the best expert and the highly respected literary executor of Bonhoeffer, has entrusted himself on this question almost entirely to the lead of Barth and Harbsmeier. True, he does assure us that, contrary to Barth's recommendation, he does not wish 'to let the case of the later Bonhoeffer lie and become "worrisome",'[29] and for an article on Bonhoeffer in the *Encyclopedia Britannica* he did plan to include the sentence (rejected by the editors as unintelligible): 'His fragmentary "non-religious interpretation" programme is under discussion together with Bultmann's demythologisation.'[30]

Prenter's earlier statements about Bultmann's programme of demythologizing see G. Bornkamm, *op. cit.*, p. 57.

[27] H. Müller, *Von der Kirche zur Welt* (1961), p. 548 n. 1129, and p. 554 n. 1184.

[28] *Ibid.*, pp. 400–21. cf. p. 356: 'The connection of the *theologia crucis* with immanent optimism thus seems to us the new way which Bonhoeffer opens for us in the last letters.' H. Pfeifer attributes it to this clear misunderstanding of the statements of Bonhoeffer about the world come of age when Müller 'does not know what to do with Bonhoeffer's demand for a religionless interpretation of biblical concepts' (*EvTh* 24 [1964], p. 52).

[29] E. Bethge, foreword to *MW* II, p. 5.

[30] E. Bethge, 'The Challenge . . .', p. 26.

But otherwise almost all of his statements are pervaded by a concern lest Bonhoeffer be misunderstood along the lines of that hermeneutics which Barth had abjured and Harbsmeier had confirmed. The programme of the Tegel letters does not come from 'concerns of exegesis and interpretation . . ., which one has at his writing table', 'does not use a process of subtraction to make acceptable what can, if need be, pass the toll gate of modern man', 'a new connecting of vocables cannot be meant'. Bethge sets 'the opening of splendid halls in hermeneutics and the tour through its secrets of interpretation' over against 'the honest hermeneutics which does not make everything else dependent on it'. The otherwise excellent lecture in Chicago, which was an introduction to Bonhoeffer, puts it even more sharply in English: 'Bultmann's interpretation is undressing and redressing existence-understanding; Bonhoeffer, with his worldly interpretation, means more than hermeneutic, language, vocabulary, terminology, translation.'[31] In a repetition of Harbsmeier's idea the opposition between Bonhoeffer and Bultmann is inculcated again and again, summarized in the sentence: 'It appears that Bonhoeffer's non-religious interpretation, if acknowledged and accepted, is somewhat more explosive for the substance and structure of our present church than that of Bultmann's existential interpretation.'[32] With consistent logic Bethge praises H. Müller's 'important separation of the non-religious

---

[31] The quotations are from: E. Bethge, 'Dietrich Bonhoeffer, Person und Werk', *EvTh* 15 (1955), p. 158 (reprinted in *MW* I); 'Dietrich Bonhoeffer, der Mensch und sein Zeugnis', *Kirche in der Zeit*, X (1955), Offprint col. 6 (reprinted in *MW* II, p. 100); afterword to *R*, p. 38; foreword to *GS* IV, p. 8; 'The Challenge . . .', p. 36.

[32] 'The Challenge . . .', p. 37. There we read on p. 36: 'Bultmann's problem is that of faith and understanding. This problem is not to be found in Bonhoeffer's letters. Where Bultmann is worried about how the modern man might comprehend, there Bonhoeffer is troubled about the man come of age without any religion. The hindrance with Bonhoeffer is not just misunderstanding, but God's absence and hiddenness . . . Second, Bonhoeffer's accusation of liberalism might mean the obvious distinction which Bultmann draws between appearance and essence. The mythological facts stand for something else behind. But resurrection for Bonhoeffer is not a clothing for something else behind. It is the *extra nos* itself, *pro nobis*, and not a signal only for another reality.'

interpretation from the academic question of hermeneutic'.[33]
Here the 'aversion', once granted in the Bonhoeffer research,
has grown into a whole complex, with regard to which one can
only ask in astonishment who in the world ever championed this
distorted picture of hermeneutics against which the understanding of Bonhoeffer has to be secured at the cost of having his
vigorous demand actually not say 'anything tangible' any more.

K. Wilkens sums up the result of these efforts about Bonhoeffer thus – again by appeal to Harbsmeier: 'In view of the whole
body of Bonhoeffer's writings it is striking how surprisingly un-
touched it was by any of the problems of understanding, . . .
that Bonhoeffer was really uninterested in questions of understanding and of language from the beginning.'[34] Little is gained
with such generalizations, especially since the documentation
cited is not even concerned with the problem of understanding.[35]

[33] E. Bethge, 'Besprechung: Hanfried Müller, *Von der Kirche zur Welt*',
MW IV, p. 173. – E. Hübner has also misunderstood H. Müller's intention
on this point, among other things, when he writes: 'In thus defining the
formula on the basis of the christological-soteriological centre of the New
Testament, he succeeds in relating Bonhoeffer's apparently contradictory
statement against Bultmann to it' ('Eine marxistische Bonhoeffer-Interpretation', *Kirche in der Zeit*, XVI [1961], p. 380).

[34] K. Wilkens, 'Die Frage Dietrich Bonhoeffers und unsere Antwort'.
VuF 1958/59, 1962, pp. 160, 163.

[35] The Bonhoeffer texts adduced by Wilkens, *op. cit.*, p. 160 n. 10 and p.
163 treat – significantly for what is here meant by 'problems of understanding'
– of the clarity of the word God speaks (*N*, pp. 140f. [ET: pp. 187f.]), of the
unbreakably literal validity of the peace-command (*GS* I, p. 216), of making
judgments about God's word (*SF*⁴, pp. 84ff. [ET: pp. 684]), of Jesus' speaking
with the Pharisees without being bound 'to the law of logical alternatives'
(*E*, pp. 136ff. [ET: pp. 151–61]), of the unity of hearing and doing demanded in the letter of James (*E*, pp. 151f. [ET: pp. 168f.]), of the 'concretion' of the will of God in deeds (*E*, p. 221 n. 1 [ET: p. 252, n. 1], of the
self-evidence of morality (*E*, p. 204 [ET: p. 231]). How inadequately Wilkens
understood the issue is shown by the last two pieces of 'documentation':
Bonhoeffer writes of creating a new decalogue in proclamation in which the
content of the commandments would be 'better demonstrable', although they
would not be based upon the proclamation (*GS* I, p. 64), and that naturally
demands 'interpretation'. The lecture, 'Vergegenwärtigung neutestament-
licher Texte' (*GS* III, pp. 303ff.), shows on the whole Bonhoeffer's split at
that time between Barthian theology and liberal-idealistic hermeneutics
('Making present means . . . "discovering" the eternal doctrine, or the
universal ethical norm, or the myth which the Holy Scripture contains, and

To work out the hermeneutics of Bonhoeffer one would have to take the trouble to trace the roots of his thought structures in the Berlin theology and the general spiritual situation of the twenties and follow them, in connection with Bonhoeffer's own development, in their very diverse modifications by dialectical theology. Presumably Bonhoeffer's own understanding of 'interpretation' could be significantly clarified by such work. Whether the 'hermeneutics of wisdom', which Harbsmeier expects, will then come to light no one at present probably knows.[36] Contrary to Wilkens, however, we do know that he not only carried out the task which he had undertaken earlier, of a 'genuine theological formation of concepts' in order to 'understand, in terms of social philosophy and sociology, the structure of the reality of a church of Christ given in the revelation in Christ', but also provided an even more fundamental formulation: 'To examine the relation between theology and philosophy with respect to the use of general philosophical thought forms in the sphere of theology.' So he demanded later, in view of 'the changed ethical problems . . ., a changed terminology'.[37] We know that his lectures on Gen. 1–3 are a paradigmatic attempt 'to translate the picture language of the magical world into the new picture language of the technological world' and to do so 'always under the presupposition that there as well as here *we* are the ones meant'. In other words, he already attempts an existentialist interpretation of the myths without knowing Bultmann's terminology.[38] We know too that, especially in the lectures on

---

then it means applying this universal to the present', p. 309); if it is cited as a whole, Wilkens ought to have seen that it also treats of the necessity of interpretation, of translation and of theological criteria for the language of proclamation!

[36] G. Harbsmeier, *MW* II, p. 91. – For a close examination of the hermeneutics of Bonhoeffer one must also take into account his paper on pneumatic and historical exegesis which was presented in R. Seeberg's seminar. I learned of its existence through E. Bethge, who kindly called my attention to it.

[37] *AS*, p. 9 (ET: p. 12); *SC*, p. 14 (ET: p. 20); cf. E. Bethge: 'He uses sociology for interpreting the shapes of this pretentious and mysterious body, the church' ('The Challenge . . .', p. 8); *GS*III, p. 538; *E*, p. 173 (ET: p. 194).

[38] *SF*, p. 43 (4th ed. pp. 58f.) (ET: pp. 45f.).

Christology and in *Discipleship*, he considers the question of transcendence valid only as the question of existence, and 'knowledge' as valid only when 'not separated . . . from existence', and that he considers this an 'ontological' problem.[39] Finally, we know that efforts with the theological problem of language do not begin in the prison letters and poems but in *Sanctorum Communio*.[40] What is 'surprising' here, to use Wilken's language, is only that a considerable number of Bonhoeffer interpreters think they can ignore and deny this line of thought simply because 'what should not be cannot be', or because no relationship at all can be conceded between the theological intentions of Bonhoeffer and of Bultmann. This line has only been indicated here but is in fact a very firm line in Bonhoeffer. It certainly does not constitute everything that he has to say, but it is indispensable for a correct understanding of his demand for a non-religious interpretation.

3. Has Barth's prospective warning turned out to be right? Hardly! Even the important studies which try to interpret Bonhoeffer's concept of the church, his ethics, his thinking on history, and his new theory of a secret discipline on the basis of a unified interpretation of his whole work, and which provisionally disregard clarifying the non-religious interpretation and defining his relation to Bultmann, are intended only as preliminary work for this decisive problem.[41] What speaks even more clearly against the correctness of Barth's warning is the existence of another direction of research which sees Bonhoeffer's programme as having a general, though not unproblematic, connection with Bultmann's programme of demythologizing.

[39] *GS* III, pp. 170–5 (ET: *Christ the Center*, pp. 31–37); *N*, p. 8 (ET: p. 43).
[40] *SC*, p. 42 (ET: p. 46) and elsewhere.
[41] H. Chr. von Hase, 'Begriff und Wirklichkeit der Kirche in der Theologie Dietrich Bonhoeffers', *EvTh* 15 (1955), pp. 164–84 (reprinted in *MW* I); O. Hammelsbeck, 'Zu Bonhoeffers Gedanken über die mündig gewordene Welt', *EvTh* 15 (1955), pp. 184–99 (reprinted in *MW* I); G. Meuss, 'Arkandisziplin und Weltlichkeit bei Dietrich Bonhoeffer', *MW* III, pp. 68–115; J. Moltmann, *Herrschaft Christi und soziale Wirklichkeit nach Dietrich Bonhoeffer* (ThEx 71), 1959, and 'Die Wirklichkeit der Welt und Gottes konkretes Gebot nach Dietrich Bonhoeffer', *MW* III, pp. 42–67; E. Wolf, 'Das Letzte und das Vorletzte', *MW* IV, pp. 17–32.

G. Ebeling in 1955 was the first to examine 'the non-religious interpretation of biblical concepts'[42] in a large systematic study. He did so in a methodical and critical way that takes full account of the source material from the late Bonhoeffer and with a view to getting at its presuppositions in the thinking of Bonhoeffer (Christology, intellectual honesty, concern with the task of proclamation); and he analysed the special sources of the concept (theological interpretation of the contemporary situation, concept of religion, contrasts between Christian faith and religion). According to content a 'religious' interpretation is defined as legalistic; a non-religious one 'distinguishes law and gospel'. The task recognized and posed by Bonhoeffer aimed at a kind of spiritual interpretation of the law which was to relate the Christ-reality (as the reality of God suffering in this world) to the reality of the religionless man in such a way that they would verify each other as law and gospel.[43] Regarding our particular question Ebeling comes to the conclusion that Bonhoeffer 'does indeed come into close proximity to Bultmann'. A definition of the relation of the two which 'in no way' equates 'Bonhoeffer with Bultmann' in detail and seeks 'the real differences' at the right place would have to take account of the fact that: (*a*) in the prison letters Bonhoeffer 'mistakes the express intention of Bultmann', (*b*) 'non-religious interpretation means . . . *eo ipso* the liberation of the biblical message from . . . mythological misunderstanding', (*c*) Bonhoeffer plans 'to go a decisive step further than Bultmann – and only therewith to proceed really theologically' by wishing to interpret not only mythological concepts but all religious ones whatever.[44] In his article

[42] See above, note 8.

[43] *ZThK* 52 (1955), pp. 341, 355ff. I must forgo entering into a criticism of Ebeling's use of the concepts of law and gospel which have recently been brought forward by J. Moltmann (ThEx 71 [1959], p. 40 n. 43: '. . . not an application of the dogma of law and gospel . . .') and, following him, K. Wilkens in more detail (*op. cit.*, pp. 161–4); but I am convinced that a thorough examination of the truth and error in them would dislodge the categorial foundations of the whole present theological conversation, which would certainly also benefit an understanding of Bonhoeffer. On that account it is better not to operate at the periphery with these objections.

[44] *ZThK* 52 (1955), pp. 338–40.

'Hermeneutics'[45] G. Ebeling observes, in connection with a presentation of the outlines for a hermeneutics presented after the First World War: 'In a similar way D. Bonhoeffer's idea of a "non-religious interpretation of biblical concepts" connects the hermeneutical problem with the fundamental historical changes in understanding reality.'

As early as 1958, quite independently of the controversy of Harbsmeier and Ebeling, A. D. Müller named in one breath 'the most stimulating attempts in interpretation . . . that have moved us in recent times: Bultmann's and Bonhoeffer's.[46] In 1961 his further research resulted decisively in a report in which he had worked through almost all the writings of Bonhoeffer and the most important contributions to the discussion. The report brought three convincingly grounded conclusions: (a) Bonhoeffer's demand doubtless intends 'to be understood as fundamentally theological';[47] (b) Bonhoeffer's leading concepts must be critically appropriated;[48] (c) non-religious interpretation is the consequence 'of a basic theological position carried through from the first literary beginnings on'.[49] Müller was the first after Ebeling and Bethge[50] to say what every unbiased student of the

[45] The article 'Hermeneutik' in: *RGG*[3] III, 257.

[46] A. D. Müller, 'Die Sprache als Problem der praktischen Theologie', in: *Das Problem der Sprache in Theologie und Kirche. Referate vom Deutschen Evangelischen Theologentag* 1958 *in Berlin*, ed. by W. Schneemelcher (1959), p. 108.

[47] A. D. Müller, 'Dietrich Bonhoeffer's Prinzip der weltlichen Interpretation und Verkündigung des Evangeliums', *ThLZ* 86 (1961), col. 723.

[48] In the concept of 'being of age' one must make a 'distinction between the claim to be, and really being, of age', in order to avoid mere 'rhetoric about being of age' (*ibid.*, cols. 738f.). Bonhoeffer's intellectualistic understanding of religion must be supplemented by showing the theological and anthropological reality of religion (cols. 739–42). In agreement with this, M. Stallmann, *Die biblische Geschichte im Unterricht* (1963), pp. 247f. n. 71, expands the reasons and consequences of this critique.

[49] *Op. cit.*, col. 723. Also: 'The "enigmatic character" of the prison letters, to which Karl Barth referred, thus loses its absolute and its confusing meaning . . . The only correct interpretation would be one which did not understand it as a break with the earlier views but as an accentuation and illumination of what was meant there, including rather than excluding, and confirming rather than cancelling, these views' (col. 735).

[50] In the Chicago lectures, unfortunately hardly known in Germany, E. Bethge had allowed that Bonhoeffer's accusation of liberalism 'does not explicitly strike Bultmann's intention' ('The Challenge . . .', p. 36).

material notices: that Bonhoeffer's statements in his letters 'certainly do not do justice' to Bultmann. These 'characteristically ambiguous' notes are, however, helpful for understanding Bonhoeffer's intention in so far as it maintains that mythological concepts 'must remain standing'. In that case 'interpretation' would indeed be superfluous; yet Bonhoeffer emphatically desires interpretation. Müller finds the way out of this dilemma by means of his well-known concept of 'unconditional realism', which seems to me, in spite of its consistency, not to accord with Bonhoeffer's concern entirely.[51]

In other countries Bonhoeffer's demand for a non-religious interpretation was seen from the very beginning in close connection with the whole renewal of theology in Germany in the post-war period. W. Hamilton understands it as a challenge of Barth, Bultmann, and Tillich,[52] J. Godsey understands it as different from them and from R. Niebuhr because its point of departure is in the concrete church.[53] By contrast, R. G. Smith[54] and J. A. T. Robinson[55] place Bonhoeffer in the same line as Bultmann and Tillich, whom they view, in spite of some criticism in details, as participants in the general effort to overcome a metaphysical and religious picture of the world. J. Glenthøj too looks for the difference between Bonhoeffer and Bultmann on the basis of a more embracing common concern.[56] In view of the dubious fact that Bonhoeffer has become innocuous in Germany, one can seek the reason for his influence in other countries, where it extends far beyond theological circles, in several factors. It was not only his pioneer services for the ecumenical movement, but also the fact that people there exposed themselves to his pleas on behalf of heretics and Catholics, liberals and anony-

[51] *Op. cit.*, cols. 729f.

[52] W. Hamilton, 'A Secular Theology for a World Come of Age', *Theology Today* (1962). – On the whole section cf. J. A. Phillips, 'Die Bedeutung des Lebens und Werkes Dietrich Bonhoeffers für britische und amerikanische Theologen', *MW* IV, pp. 152–69.

[53] J. Godsey, *Theology of Dietrich Bonhoeffer* (1960).

[54] R. G. Smith, *The New Man* (1956).

[55] J. A. T. Robinson, *Honest to God* (1963).

[56] *Op. cit.*, *MW* II, p. 200.

mous Christians, and to his attacks against repristination. They did not categorically ban him from the circle of hermeneutical questions nor did they use his letters as cheap ammunition in a battle against Bultmann. Finally, they did not try to put onto an orthodox track the work of the man who demanded of every sermon that it go 'up to the limits of heresy';[57] on an orthodox track, even as a preacher of wisdom or edification or repentance, he obviously starts neither the world nor the church moving, not even if one wrests from him a blessing upon Marxist totalitarianism.

A last argument, and henceforth one not to be overlooked, against the correctness of Barth's warning was given by Bultmann himself in his article, 'Der Gottesgedanke und der moderne Mensch'.[58] Without reference to Bonhoeffer's problematical statements about him in the prison letters Bultmann here documents an agreement with the larger intention of these letters. Characteristically he shows this agreement without using the terminology 'non-religious interpretation' and 'demythologizing' and he does not extend it to his own projects for carrying out this intention. Bultmann agrees with Bonhoeffer (as with other philosophers and theologians) that 'Christianity itself was a decisive factor in shaping the secularization of the world', that 'with the loss of a relation to the transcendent the certainty of man's knowledge of himself has also been lost'; he agrees with him further in understanding revelation as an action of God, 'which is not visible to the objectifying thinking of reason and . . . affects the existence of man' and leads Christian faith into a battle against the ideologizing of religion; finally he agrees with this conclusion: 'Now that the God above the world has become the God beyond the world, today's task is to find God in the midst of the world, in the present.'[59] In summary: Bultmann agrees with Bonhoeffer in the recognition of the historical and theological causes for the necessity and structure of a new concept of God. Bultmann did not intend to make any contribution

[57] Foreword to GS IV, p. 10.
[58] ZThK 60 (1963), pp. 337–48.
[59] Ibid., pp. 338–43.

to the Bonhoeffer-research; indirectly, however, he did do that by his affirmative reception of the points mentioned from the (detailed) programme of Bonhoeffer. For if beside the sources one wishes to ask the theologians adduced by Bonhoeffer for clarification of his intention how they understand the issue, then certainly Bultmann's understanding of, and reference to, the prison letters is as helpful a signal for research as Barth's not understanding them and his warning about them.

II

In 1944, by the two attempts in his letters to clarify his intention regarding a non-religious interpretation in the form of a debate with Bultmann's article, 'New Testament and Mythology', Bonhoeffer tied all future clarification of the question closely together with his relation to the theology of Bultmann. Since both passages in the letters[60] pose a series of difficulties not soluble by themselves, an examination of the almost twenty-year history of his discussion with the theology of Bultmann offers some assistance. The main stages of this history are already visible. If the discussion were to disclose a directional constant; if those letters could be made understandable as the terminal point of a recognizable line, this would simultaneously provide a further proof against the interpretation of Bonhoeffer by his 'fragments'. Even a glance into the pertinent texts shows that Bultmann is never cited as an exegete but only as his systematic thoughts relate to problems of theological principle. Since Bonhoeffer was occupied with these problems predominantly in the early and late periods, and less during the years of struggle, 1934–39, Bultmann's name is missing in the middle period of his activity.

1. In the years between his promotion and his habilitation (1927–30) Bonhoeffer, through his own critical discussion with their work, took over decisive material from the inaugurators of dialectical theology and reworked it very independently. He was also incisive enough to notice significant differences among them. In his *Sanctorum Communio*, when he attempted a non-religious in-

60 *WE*, pp. 183, 220f. (ET: *Letters and Papers from Prison*, pp. 156, 181f.).

terpretation as a way of working out the 'social intention of all
basic Christian concepts', he appealed to sentences out of Bultmann's book on Jesus which asserted a unity between love of
God and love of neighbour in the act of faith-obedience.[61] This
was in full agreement with Bultmann but in opposition to
Barth's definition of neighbour-love, which in Bonhoeffer's opinion unjustifiably reduced the concrete neighbour to indifference.
Some sentences in *Akt und Sein* – the habilitation thesis in which
Bonhoeffer is concerned with the 'interpretation' of religion, the
'mode of being' and the 'understanding of existence' on the part
of church members, where he also pleads for 'the necessity of a
certain formal "pre-understanding"'[62] – stand in close connection with this affirmation of Bultmann's theological understanding of the 'concrete' Thou. In them Bonhoeffer agrees with
Bultmann's derivation of dialectic 'from the historical character
of existence' and summarizes his view quite correctly: 'Man in
the historical situation poses, or "is", the question to which God
in freedom gives his answer, and in history the only way to speak
about this answer is dialectically.'[63]

In developing 'a theological doctrine of man's self-understanding in its connection with "being placed into truth" by
revelation', Bonhoeffer in many ways acknowledges that Bultmann (as also Gogarten) is concerned with 'relieving man in the
"concrete situation" of "historical being" of his control over
himself'.[64] Yet even so he decisively criticizes the inadequacy of
other categories used by Bultmann for interpreting existence. If
one tries to present Bonhoeffer's view on our topic without regard to the correctness of his understanding of the authors he
adduces, or to the inner logic of his own thoughts, two complexes
of questions result, though they overlap. First, he criticizes (with
K. Löwith) Bultmann's definition of the relation of philosophy
and theology. He says its presupposition lies 'in Bultmann's
assertion, which he does not further support, that "a believer's

[61] *SC*, pp. 7, 118 n. 2 (ET: pp. 13, 226 n. 47).
[62] *AS*, pp. 130f. (ET: p. 174).
[63] *AS*, p. 62 n. 9; cf. p. 102 n. 47 (ET: p. 84 n. 1; cf. p. 135 n. 1).
[64] *AS*, pp. 113, 8, 74 (ET: pp. 148, 11); *GS* III, p. 77.

existence is after all still existence"'. Bonhoeffer contests the unity of existence as well as the thinkability of revelation outside the relation of both to the event of revelation as the free act of God. For 'in the existential event of revelation the existentialist structure of existence too is affected and transformed'. Bonhoeffer means that 'speaking of us is possible only through speaking of God' and he sees Bultmann's well-known converse proposition 'as a questionable failure to recognize that faith can be directed only and exclusively to God' – and in any case it is in danger of sacrificing 'the concern of a genuine faith in God, namely, to be able to assert the being of God outside the self'.[65]

Secondly, Bonhoeffer establishes 'the danger of a concept of existence gained apart from revelation' through a critique of the concept of 'possibility' in Bultmann's anthropology. This concept was suggested 'to Bultmann obviously by Heidegger's existentialist-ontological analysis of existence'. It defines man's being as an able-to-be and appears to deny 'the idea of man-at-the-limit and that of the man of infinite possibilities'. In so doing, it mistakes the reality of man under revelation to the extent that with respect to grace and sin 'to be possible' means 'to be actually in it' already, existentialistically as well as existentially. Thus the concept of a decision of faith is also 'no existentialist nor existential possibility of my existence'. Because this concept is so far 'from an understanding' of revelation 'as pure act', it is 'finally irrelevant for theology'.[66]

Now, Bonhoeffer himself wishes to get away from understanding it as pure act and to preserve the continuity between the whole self and the new existence of the believer. Thus he has to make a reservation (formally quite like his 1944 claim to overcome Barth's limits through Bultmann[67]) and to say that whereas Barth was unable to think the new self in unity with the whole empirical self but could think it only 'at the expense of the historical character of man', as a sort of 'heavenly *Doppel-*

[65] *AS*, pp. 54–6 n. 89; pp. 72f.; 23f. (ET: pp. 73–6 n., pp. 96, 32).

[66] *AS*, pp. 75, 74 n. 24 (ET: pp. 99, 98 n. 3); *GS* III, p. 77 (ET: *No Rusty Swords*, p. 63); *AS*, pp. 79; 56 n. 89 (ET: pp. 104, 75).

[67] *WE*, p. 220 (ET: *Letters and Papers*, pp. 181f.).

gänger', Bultmann certainly grasped 'the continuity of the new self with the whole self correctly by his concept of historical being'. What remains to be asked – because it is 'unclear' – is how Bultmann thinks the continuity of the new self as a believing self if it is 'constituted only by that conscious act of decision for Christ'. Significantly, the task which results for Bonhoeffer from this contradiction remains (probably without Bonhoeffer's having noticed it clearly) within the intention of Bultmann's theology, terminologically and in content. 'If a discontinuous new self is not to be assumed, everything would depend upon connecting the being of this new self with the concept of existence. That, however, seems to us possible only through the idea of the church.'[68]

Though it does not do full justice to Barth, Bultmann, and Heidegger[69] and though it does not, so far as I can see, ultimately penetrate the relation of believing and thinking, Bonhoeffer's incisive analysis of the problems seeks an independent way, by learning critically from Bultmann and delimiting itself from him. A disagreement arises only on the basis of an acknowledged agreement about the uncontrollability of revelation and about man's historical being under it. To historical man the question of the unity of being existentially affected by revelation and of the continuity between the self when believing and the self before believing presents itself as an explicit task for theological reflection. The disagreement, which arises only upon this acknowledged agreement, does not contest the usability of general concepts in theology on the whole, but it does contest their fitness for grasping the reality of man and the phenomena of faith from case to case; or rather, it tries to show this unfitness theologically. Consensus and dissensus are to be found – though

---

[68] *AS*, p. 79; cf. earlier pp. 76ff. (ET: p. 105, cf. pp. 101–4).

[69] H. Müller, *op. cit.*, p. 467 n. 354, correctly calls Heidegger's presentation in *AS* 'twilight-like'; cf. also J. Moltmann, ThEx 71, pp. 25ff. W. Pannenberg, 'Akt und Sein im Mittelalter', *KuD* 7 (1961), pp. 197ff., shows that Bonhoeffer's 'stylizing' of recent theology as transcendental philosophy and ontology and his concepts of act and being, which are dependent upon R. Seeberg's definition of the opposition between reality and possibility, are forced.

Bonhoeffer does not use the term – in the horizon of the hermeneutical problems that are indispensable within theology. It should be noted that Bonhoeffer nowhere characterizes the theology of Bultmann with the uncouth word 'anthropocentric', as is becoming usual today in reference to the texts mentioned.[70]

2. Only after a ten-year silence concerning our question on the part of the sources does Bonhoeffer in an essay on 'Die Geschichte und das Gute', written in the midst of his conspiratorial activity, appeal to two passages from Bultmann's recently published commentary on John.[71] In both cases Bonhoeffer accepts Bultmann's theological interpretation of the Johannine concept of life. His use and esteem of the commentary on John can be shown elsewhere also.[72]

All the other (four) references to Bultmann on the part of Bonhoeffer concern Bultmann's 1941 article, 'New Testament and Mythology'. Although they have been treated in detail several times, they must be considered here in their inner connection.

In a letter to Ernst Wolf of March 24, 1942, which unfortunately was delivered incomplete, Bonhoeffer expresses 'great joy' over Bultmann's article. He was impressed 'again and again by the intellectual honesty of his works'. Bonhoeffer calls it 'arrogance' when pastors of the Confessing Church in Berlin, aroused under the aegis of O. Dilschneider, spoke abusively of Bultmann 'in a rather silly way' and did nothing but protest. This action showed a lack of understanding of the issue and is 'a real shame for the Confessing Church'.[73] If this note which, so

[70] Thus J. Moltmann, ThEx 71, p. 25 and E. Bethge, 'The Challenge', p. 36.

[71] *E*, pp. 169f. (ET: p. 189); 6th ed. pp. 231f. The second quotation from Bultmann's commentary on John is interesting also because Bultmann's observation there (p. 308) – that the promised life stands 'beyond human possibilities' – was capable of showing Bonhoeffer that his youthful polemic against Bultmann's concept of possibility misses the heart of the matter; and this polemic now no longer appears.

[72] *GS* III, p. 46. Bonhoeffer's work on the commentary on John can also be noticed in his meditations on Johannine texts (*GS* IV, pp. 480–504).

[73] *GS* III, pp. 45f. – Dilschneider's quite confusing reaction at the time to

far as I know, has thus far been mentioned only by E. Bethge[74] shows essentially the 'aristocratic Christian . . . who seemed to jump ahead of a person in the most diverse dimensions' (as K. Barth aptly formulates),[75] then the letter of July 25, 1942, written to *my brother Winfrid* in the hospital at Marburg substantiates a criticism of Bultmann too.[76] As the most detailed up to now of the known letters of Bonhoeffer concerning Bultmann's article on demythologizing from the period of his freedom, when he still had the text available, it will have to provide the norm for understanding the relevant prison letters, whose exact sense is less clear. What has remained from Bonhoeffer's early period is the familiar juxtaposition of Yes and No to Bultmann: he welcomes, but he also criticizes; he rejoices in the intellectual honesty which mentions by name the liberalism only suppressed in theology, church, and himself, and recommends that it be critically transcended; indeed, he desires a clear discussion with Bultmann and he detests and (only too much) fears the 'pharisaism of faith . . . on the part of many brethren' which supplants such dis-

---

Bultmann's programme of demythologizing is found in his article: 'Mythos? Gedanken über ein Thema unserer Zeit', *DtPfrBl* 46 (1942), pp. 153f.

[74] E. Bethge, 'The Challenge . . .', p. 36.

[75] In the above-mentioned letter to W. Herrenbrück: *EvTh* 15 (1955), p. 243.

[76] The letter, which heretofore has been printed only by E. Bethge in his foreword to the German edition of J. A. T. Robinson's *Honest to God* (p. 17) – unfortunately with a mistake that quite distorts the meaning – reads as follows in the pertinent section:

'. . . Now on Bultmann: I belong to those who have welcomed his writing; not because I agree with it, I regret the double approach in it (the argument from John 1.14 and from the radio should not be mixed together, though I do consider the second one an argument too – only the separation should be clearer), and to that extent I am probably still a disciple of Harnack. Put crudely: B. let the cat out of the bag, not only for himself but for very many (the liberal cat out of the confessional bag), and I am glad of that. He has dared to say what many suppress in themselves (I include myself) without having overcome it. He has done service to intellectual honesty by that. The pharisaism of faith, which by contrast is now proclaimed by many brethren, is fatal to me. Now talk and answer must be admitted. I would like to talk with B. about it and expose myself to the draught of air that comes from him. But then the window has to be closed again. Otherwise susceptible people catch cold. – If you see B. give him my greetings . . . tell him that I would like to see him and how I see things . . .'

cussion; but he would also like to protect 'the susceptible'. His criticism is directed only against the 'double approach' in Bultmann. With the 'argument based on the radio' Bonhoeffer lifts out one of the many examples that Bultmann had mentioned[77] as illustrating the irreconcilability of the mythical picture of the world with the modern scientific one. With the 'argument based on John 1.14' he can only be referring to Bultmann's pointed citation of this text at the conclusion of his article. In this citation Jesus, the Word of God, proclaimer and church are summarily characterized in the paradox of their worldly and eschatological character in the following way. 'All these are phenomena subject to historical, sociological, and psychological observation, yet for faith they are all of them eschatological phenomena . . . The transcendence of God is not as in myth reduced to immanence. Instead, we have the paradox of a transcendent God present and active in history: "The Word became flesh".'[78] Anyone who surveys Bonhoeffer's whole work cannot overlook the fact that here his general theme, which he worked through intensively in many ways, is heard in a concise formulation. This general theme is: sociological observation and reality of faith, transcendence and immanence of God, Christ and the Church – existing together ambiguously in the historical man Jesus, in whom God is active and present, known and asserted by faith and for faith. On the basis of his own theology Bonhoeffer had to welcome Bultmann's writing. He does not oppose the doubleness of the arguments; rather, he considers both of them legitimate. But he wishes a clearer separation. Since the outline and content of Bultmann's essay in actual fact does not lack clarity on this point, one can scarcely avoid the conclusion that Bonhoeffer no longer took the time to check his judgment against the text itself. This way out, which is never completely satisfying, does not, however, alter anything in the unambiguous facts, that (*a*) in tenor and principles the motives affirming Bult-

---

[77] R. Bultmann, *Offenbarung und Heilsgeschehen* (BevTh 7), 1941, pp. 30f. (reprinted as 'Neues Testament und Mythologie' in *KuM* I [1954³], p. 18 [ET: p. 5]).

[78] *Ibid.*, p. 69 (*KuM* I, p. 48 [ET: p. 44]).

mann are predominant and (b) the later accusations of liberalism are not yet raised against Bultmann; rather, Bonhoeffer
affirms the need to challenge the untranscended liberalism and
undertakes to do so with an appeal to his having been a disciple
of Harnack.

Between this letter and those written two years later from
prison lie not only Bonhoeffer's continued work on the *Ethik*, in
which the clarification of the horizon and structure of his demand for a non-religious interpretation of biblical concepts is
already marked out, but also thoughts and conversations about
Bultmann's programme of demythologizing, which modified his
judgment about it.[79] If one wishes to understand the two letters
of May 5 and June 8, 1944,[80] cautiously, in view of the situation
of their composition, but yet as the relevant working through of
Bonhoeffer's earlier views expressed in greater freedom and
clarity, the result is this: Bonhoeffer sketches his demand for a
non-religious interpretation of biblical concepts in pointed discussion with Bultmann's project for demythologizing, and he
sees an affinity between them as over against all other theological
programmes. Like Bultmann he defines the present task of
theology as interpretation, in opposition to conservative repristination and to 'Barth's boundary'. Like him he wishes to
accept and transcend the concerns of liberal theology. No opposition exists in this definition of the task, though there is one in
regard to its execution. (a) As to scope: Bonhoeffer wishes to
include not only mythological concepts (as does Bultmann) but
all religious concepts (like God, faith, etc.) which in principle
are inseparable from the mythological and are equally problematic. Today this opposition can be regarded as resolved, on
the one hand because of Bonhoeffer's concept of 'religion' which
almost everyone has declared inadequate and on the other hand

[79] Unfortunately evidence is still lacking on the question whether Bonhoeffer, during his tense political activity, was even able to become acquainted
with the debate in the periodicals that began as early as 1942, above all
Bultmann's answer to H. Thielicke (*DtPfrBl* 47 [1943], pp. 3f. = *KuM* I,
pp. 221–6).

[80] *WE*, pp. 183–5, 215–21 (ET: *Letters and Papers from Prison*, pp. 155–7,
177–82).

because of Bultmann's most recent inclusion of the concept of God in his reflections on interpretation. (*b*) As to the criteria of interpretation: Bonhoeffer, wrongly recalling it, considers Bultmann's conception ('not selection or subtraction')[81] liberal to the extent that it might try to select an 'essence' of Christianity by eliminating mythological elements and thus curtail the gospel. This criticism appears untenable when compared with the way things actually are in Bultmann. What is tenable, however, is Bonhoeffer's positive intention not to lose 'the cause (*Sache*) itself' by a theological interpretation oriented upon the Pauline understanding of the law. He clearly marked the Scylla of 'sliding away from the cause' and the Charybdis which is 'that even the biblical terminology cannot be used without danger'[82] – and even here there is no substantive opposition to Bultmann today, even though Bonhoeffer believed at the time that he had to note one at this point. Though he recognized it with rare decisiveness, he was no longer able to carry out this task of working out theological criteria for a contemporary interpretation of the gospel, with which he hoped 'to be able to perform a service for the future of the church'.[83] Anyone who devotes himself to such a task, mindful of Bonhoeffer's heritage and certainly mindful also of the freedom to be responsible towards time and history, which Bultmann has always taught, will not be able to do it simply and solely in opposition to the work of Bultmann, at least not if he is following Bonhoeffer.

[81] So the first heading in Bultmann's development of the task: *Offenbarung und Heilsgeschehen*, p. 34 (= *KuM* I, p. 21 [ET: p. 9]).

[82] *E*, pp. 173f. (ET: pp. 193f.).

[83] *WE*, p. 262 (ET: *Letters and Papers*, p. 211).

13

The Debt and Responsibility of Theology

*Friedrich Gogarten**

WHAT IS probably expected under the theme of the debt and
responsibility of theology is a discussion of what theology as a
science owes to the world. What it does owe the world is to provide the world with a correct knowledge of the content which
theology knows and for which theology bears responsibility. The
world is to know this and know it correctly – which is to say, the
conception people have of the content of theological knowledge
should correspond to what it actually is. It might be considered
self-evident that what theology studies is Christianity, and more
specifically Christianity as the revelation of God, that is, as the
reality in which salvation for man and his world is present. But
as soon as this self-evident statement is put into words, the deep
and very real problems contained in the question of theology's
debt and responsibility become apparent.

For about a generation – in other words, since the radical
collapse of our whole spiritual life in the first world war –
theology has been wrestling with a recognition of something
which has made it more and more questionable for theology to
understand its subject matter as something that can be objectively grasped, such as 'Christianity' would be. The kind of
idea behind this, and what it means, may become clearer if I
say that it is remarkably similar to the one which has raised entirely new questions for contemporary physics. In physics this

* Translated from *Zeit und Geschichte*, pp. 461–5.

idea, as Heisenberg has formulated it, says that modern natural science, unlike science even in the nineteenth century, no longer deals with nature 'as an orderly course of things in space and time', in the understanding of which one can 'in principle, if not in practice, disregard man and his intrusion into nature'. Modern science's field of vision contains above all the network of relations between man and nature, of contexts in which we as corporeal living beings are dependent parts of nature and simultaneously, as men, objectify it for our thinking and dealing. Natural science is no longer the observer of nature. Accordingly, the object of research, as Heisenberg says, is 'no longer nature in itself but nature as exposed to human questioning'.[1]

This same idea came to theology almost at the same time as to physics, though independently and in a quite different way; and it has presented theology with entirely new questions. Indeed, we must say that what is involved is an entirely new kind of questioning about what theology deals with. This is what is meant when I say that theology can no longer self-evidently consider Christianity its subject matter as it did for two centuries prior to the time of the first world war. Natural science, especially atomic physics, no longer investigates nature in itself but 'nature as exposed to human questioning', as Heisenberg's statement puts it; so too the reality with which theology is concerned and of which it is to have knowledge can no longer be, as was previously thought, a salvation present in and for itself in the Christianity which one can objectively ascertain and see in history. Natural science no longer stands before nature as an observer, but recognizes itself as part of the interplay between man and nature, 'in the midst of which science stands from the very beginning'. So too it is no longer possible for theology, after once acknowledging this idea, to believe it can recognize the revelation of God and the reality of the salvation of man and his world in this historically and objectively presented Christianity. The same thing happens to theology as to natural science. As science recognizes itself as part of the interplay between man

[1] 'Das Naturbild der heutigen Physik', in: *Die Künste im technischen Zeitalter* (1954), pp. 43ff.

and nature, so theology must recognize itself as part of the inter-play between man and his salvation (*Heil*) or loss (*Unheil*), in the midst of which theology stands from the very beginning. As the laws of nature for natural science 'no longer treat of the elementary particles in themselves but of our knowledge of the elementary particles', so the knowledge of theology does not concern the salvation and loss of man as something present in and by itself, but concerns our knowledge of it, or more exactly, our being affected by it. According to the nature of this reality, there is no way of having knowledge of, or being affected by, the reality of salvation and loss except in faith or in unfaith. And finally: if man encounters himself in natural science because its study no longer relates to nature in itself but to nature as given to human questioning, there is an especially high degree of human self-encounter in theology.

It is very impressive when a scientist like Heisenberg, taking the situation of modern science as a point of departure, thinks that an attempt to explore the now dislodged foundations of our spiritual world leads to the impression that it is probably not an oversimplification to say that for the first time in the course of history man now faces only himself. That is, I think, true for theology with special decisiveness. And one must ask whether it is not only this special decisiveness which makes it possible for man to face the truth of himself alone, and here that means, in complete exclusion of everything else.

In natural science man encounters himself because what he studies is nature as exposed to human questioning, yet he meets himself there only as one occupied with nature. So it is with the other sciences, depending on what they are occupied with and what they are asking for. In theology, on the other hand, man encounters himself as one occupied with nothing but himself, and he is asking about himself. He is not asking about himself so as to involve some other factor also, as is the case, for example, in medicine or psychology. That would still be a question about something other than himself. This question, then, in which man asks only about himself, in which he has become a question for himself, can have no other sense than this: he is asking whether he, *man*, whether he *as* man, is whole (*heil*) or not. We might also say this is the question of his essence. Whenever it is asked, this question has already been dislodged, it has been roused by man's dis-essence. Dis-essence is essence that has been perverted, changed into its negative, just as (for example) dishonour, or shame, is honour that has been perverted, transformed into its negative. If we call the essence of man his salvation (*Heil*), his dis-essence is his loss (*Unheil*). Thus the man in whom this question about himself alone has once become vocal must decide between his essence and his dis-essence, between his salvation and his loss.

But we have not yet stated the real aspect of man's becoming a question to himself which is essential for theology's knowledge and questioning. This becomes clear only when we recognize that in such a questioning man is not really the questioner but the questioned. Since in this extreme sense he is asking only about himself, he is only repeating a question that is put to him. He perceives this question about himself as coming from the ground of his self which is accessible to him only in this way. But once he has perceived it coming from there, he can never again forget it; he remembers it and must repeat it. For this question asks about him; and because it asks only about him, not about this or that other person, he can answer it only with himself, with his essence or his dis-essence. Thus the man who must repeat this question is faced with a decision between his salvation and his loss. He is saved if he is prepared to give himself as an answer to this question; he is lost if he denies himself to the question. In this decision he has to do only with himself since he cannot answer the question with anything but himself.

If it is true that in theology (as we said earlier) man faces himself with a special decisiveness, then it is clear that theology could never summon this decisiveness if it believed it could, or even had to, possess the salvation or loss of man in an objective reality. Theology is capable of this decisiveness only if it recognizes itself as standing with its questions and knowledge in the middle of the interplay, or more correctly put: in the middle of the decision between salvation and loss. Thus the knowledge that theology owes the world concerns our knowledge of the fact that being human in the most extreme sense, in which we can and should ask about it, means facing the inescapable decision between salvation and loss. Or, expressed differently, theology's knowledge relates to man as he, having become a question to himself, faces the decision whether he is ready to give himself as an answer to the ground of his human being, from which the question about himself comes, or whether he withholds himself.

The theology of which we are speaking is not just any theology but Christian theology, and its debt and responsibility is to provide the world with a right knowledge in these matters. If we now add that this knowledge is the knowledge of Jesus of Nazareth as the man in whom salvation is present for men, then what we mean by this statement is a knowledge of the same kind as that of which we were previously speaking. That means first of all that, so far as the humanity of this man is concerned, the knowledge which theology owes the world is not of the same kind as, say, the knowledge which history has of a man. Thus, theology would not be giving to the rest of the world what it owes it, if it communicated only a knowledge of some historical accomplishments of Jesus or of his individual person with its uniqueness and capacities. The knowledge of the man Jesus, which theology owes the world, relates only to the man himself when as himself, apart from accomplishments or individual characteristics, he becomes a question to himself in the most extreme way; that is to say, when the question of salvation or loss – the question which he cannot answer with anything but himself – becomes vocal. The man Jesus of whom theology knows or of whom alone it should know, is the bare, naked man who perceives the question of the salvation or loss of man.

Theology knows that in this bare, naked man, Jesus of Nazareth, salvation is present, or that – as the NT itself says – the crucified is the Christ. But this too is not a knowledge of salvation as an objective reality. Here too everything depends on the fact that it remains a knowledge in the middle of the decision between salvation and loss. For only thus can it be a knowledge in which one has a co-knowledge of what was known by the man who with his naked, bare humanity endured the question of man until he reached the bitterest knowledge of his loss. And only thus – in this co-knowledge of the deepest loss of man which became manifest in this man Jesus of Nazareth – is it possible also to know that the same man brought to light the salvation of man by submitting to the abyss in the question of man and giving himself in answer. Only this double co-knowledge is faith in the crucified man who is the Christ.

If it is in fact true that in all areas of life, and not only in natural science, man faces himself today in a way that was never before the case; and if it is also true that the man who encounters himself is one occupied with something other than himself and one who therefore forgets himself because of his pre-occupation, then it is easy to see how great is the danger today that man will no longer hear the question of himself which is the question of his salvation or loss, and that he will thus fall victim to his dis-essence. But then we shall also understand how great and relevant theology's responsibility is when it owes the world a right knowledge of salvation and loss and of how this has become manifest in Jesus Christ.

14

From the Last Marburg Lecture Course*

Martin Heidegger

IN THIS course of lectures, given in the summer semester of 1928, we set ourselves the task of attempting a discussion with Leibniz. The plan of the course was oriented with reference to the ecstatic Being-in-the-world of man, with a view to the question of Being.

In my first semester at Marburg in 1923–4, I had ventured the corresponding discussion with Descartes that was later included in *Sein und Zeit* (Sections 19–21).

This interpretation (and others) arose from the discernment that in philosophical thinking we are in conversation with the philosophers of earlier times. Such a conversation means something other than the completion of a systematic philosophy by setting forth in historical terms how it has come about. It must not be likened either to that remarkable identity which Hegel succeeded in establishing for the thinking of his own thought and the history of thinking.

The metaphysic developed by Leibniz is, traditionally, an interpretation of the substantiality of substance.

The writing which follows, taken from the above-mentioned lecture course and revised, seeks to show what project Leibniz had in view and what clue he followed, and how these led him to define the Being of entities.

The very word that Leibniz chose to designate the sub-

* Translated from *Zeit und Geschichte*, pp. 491–507, by J. Macquarrie.

stantiality of substance is already characteristic. Substance is a monad. The Greek word μονάς means the simple, unity, the one; and also, the single, the solitary. Leibniz used the word 'monad' only after his metaphysic of substance was already formed, in fact from 1696. What Leibniz intended by 'monad' concentrates, as it were, in itself all the basic significances of the Greek word. The essence of the substance lies in the fact that it is a monad. That which really is, is characterized by the simple unity of the single self-subsistent thing. To anticipate, we may say: A monad is that which unifies, simply, primordially, and in a manner which isolates in advance.

Thus we must bear in mind three things for the adequate definition of the monad.

1. The monads, unities or points are not themselves in need of unification; rather, they are what gives unity. They enable something.

2. The unities, as conferring unity, are themselves primordially unifying and, in a certain way, active. Thus Leibniz designated the points as *vis primitiva, force primitive*, primordially simple force.

3. The conception of the monad has a metaphysical and ontological aim. Therefore Leibniz called the points not mathematical points but *points métaphysiques*, 'metaphysical points' (Gerhardt, vol. IV, p.482; Erdman, p.126). In addition, they are called 'formal atoms', not material; they are not the ultimate elemental particles of ὕλη, *materia*, but the primordial indivisible principle of formation, of *forma* or εἶδος.

Every autonomous entity is constituted as a monad. Leibniz says (G. II, p.262): *ipsum persistens . . . primitivam vim habet.* Every autonomous entity is endued with force.

To understand the metaphysical meaning of the doctrine of monads depends on rightly grasping the concept of *vis primitiva*.

The problem of the substantiality of substance is supposed to get solved in positive terms, and for Leibniz this problem is a problem of unity, of the monad. In terms of this horizon for the problem – the horizon of the positive definition of the unity of substance – everything that is said about force and its metaphysical function must be understood. The character of force is to be thought of in terms of the problem of unity, the problem lying in substantiality. Leibniz marks off his concept of *vis activa*, force, from the scholastic concept of *potentia activa*. According to the usage of the words, *vis activa* and *potentia activa* seem to signify the same. But: *Differt enim vis activa a potentia nuda vulgo scholis cognita, quod potentia activa Scholasticorum, seu facultas, nihil aliud est quam propinqua agendi possibilitas, quae tamen aliena excitatione et velut stimulo indiget, ut in actum transferatur* (G. IV, p. 469). 'For *vis activa* differs from the sheer potency for action, as this is commonly known in the schools, because the scholastic potency for action, or the capacity for realization, is nothing other than the impending possibility of doing something, and this still needs an external stimulus, a spur, as it were, in order for it to pass over into realization.'

The *potentia activa* of the schools is a bare capacity for acting, so that this capacity is very close to acting, but is not yet acting. It is a capacity present-at-hand in something which is itself present-at-hand, but it has not yet come into play.

Sed vis activa actum quendam sive ἐντελέχειαν continet, atque inter facultatem agendi actionemque ipsam media est, et conatum involvit (*ibid.*). 'But *vis activa* includes a certain acting that is already actual, or an entelechy; it is something intermediate between a mere inactive capacity for acting and the acting itself, and it contains in itself a *conatus* or urge.'

Accordingly, the *vis activa* is a certain acting, but not action genuinely realizing itself; it is a capacity, yet not a quiescent capacity. What Leibniz has in mind here, we call a 'tending towards'; better still, in order to express the specific element of action which is somehow already actual, a 'thrusting' or 'thrust'. It is neither a predisposition nor a triggering off, but bringing something (oneself, namely) to the point of acting, applying oneself to oneself (in the sense in which we speak of someone 'applying himself' to some enterprise), sitting close to oneself.

What is characteristic of a thrust is that it spontaneously passes over into acting, not just occasionally but intrinsically. This passing over does not first need a stimulus coming from elsewhere.

The thrust is itself the impulse which, by its very nature, gets set off by itself. The phenomenon of the thrust is characterized by the fact that it brings along spontaneously, as it were, its cause, in the sense of a releasing; the thrust is, as such, already released, yet in such a way that it still remains in a state of tension. It is true that the thrust can be hampered in its thrusting, but even when hampered, it is not the same as a quiescent capacity for action. To be sure, getting rid of the restraint first lets the thrusting become free. The disappearance of a restraint – or, to use a felicitous expression of Max Scheler, the 'de-restraining' – is different from some external cause that comes along additionally. Leibniz says: *atque ita per se ipsam in operationem fertur; nec auxiliis indiget, sed sola sublatione impedimenti* (*ibid.*). To look at a bow in a state of tension illustrates what is meant. The expression 'force' therefore is easily misleading, for the idea is close to that of a quiescent property.

After this clarification of the *vis activa*, as thrust, Leibniz comes to the essential definition: *Et hanc agendi virtutem omni substantiae inesse aio, semperque aliquem ex ea actionem nasci* (*ibid.*, p. 470). 'So this force, I say, inheres in every substance (constitutes its substantiality) and constantly gives birth to a certain acting.' In other words, it is a thrust and is productive. '*Producere*' means: bringing forth something, letting it arise from itself and letting it retain in itself what is given in this way. This holds also for bodily substance. When two bodies are contiguous, the thrust is merely limited and restricted in many ways. This was overlooked by those (the Cartesians) *qui essentiam eius* (*substantiam corporis*) *in sola extensione collocaverunt* (*ibid.*).

Every being has this thrust-character; it is determined in its being as thrusting. This is the basic metaphysical trait of the monad, though admittedly the structure of this thrust is not yet explicitly defined.

But here there is a metaphysical assertion of the greatest importance, and some advance exposition of it must be given now. For this interpretation of what really is must, as a general interpretation, explain also the possibility of the beings as a whole. What does the basic thesis of monadology say about the occurrence together of a plurality of beings in the whole, which is the universe?

If the essence of substance gets interpreted as the monad, and the monad in turn as *vis primitiva*, as thrust, *conatus, nisus prae-existens*, as primordially thrusting and carrying in itself the completely unifying, then, in face of this momentous interpre-tation of the beings, there arise these questions:

1. How far is the thrust, as such, that which primordially and simply unifies?

2. How, on the basis of the monadic character of substance, does one explain unity and connectedness in the universe?

If every being, every monad, thrusts of itself, this means that it brings along what is essential to its being, whither and how it thrusts. All co-thrusting of other monads is intrinsically negative in its possible relation to the single monad. No substance can give to another its thrust, that is to say, what is essential to it. What it can do is merely to restrain or de-restrain, and even in this negative way it always functions only indirectly. The relation of one substance to another is only that of limiting it, and thus of determining it in a negative way.

In this regard, Leibniz says quite plainly: *Apparebit etiam ex nostris meditationibus, substantiam creatam ab alia substantia creata non ipsam vim agendi, sed praeexistentis iam nisus sui, sive virtutis agendi, limites tantummodo ac determinationem accipere*. The *praeexistens nisus* is decisive. Leibniz concludes: *ut alia nunc taceam ad solvendum illud problema difficile, de substantiarum operatione in se invicem, pro-futura.*

N.B. The *vis activa* is also designated ἐντελέχεια with reference to Aristotle (*cf., e.g., Système nouveau*, Section 3). In *La monadologie* (Section 18) may be read the reason for this designation: *car elles ont en elles une certaine perfection* (ἔχουσι τὸ ἐντελές); 'for the monads have in themselves a certain perfection', they somehow carry in themselves a completeness, in so far as each monad, as has been shown, already brings along what is positive in it, and in such a way that this has the possibility of being the universe.

This explanation of ἐντελέχεια does not correspond to Aristotle's real intention. On the other hand, Leibniz claims this term for his monadology in a new signification.

Already in the Renaissance ἐντελέχεια in the Leibnizian sense was translated by *perfectihabia*. The *Monadologie* (Section 48) names Hermolaus Barbarus as the translator. This Hermolaus Barbarus at the time of the Renaissance translated and commented on Aristotle and the Commentary of Themistus (320–90), and he did so with the intention that the Greek Aristotle might come into his own, as against medieval scholasticism. Admittedly his work was attended by great difficulties. The story is told that, in his distress and perplexity over the philosophical signification of the term ἐντελέχεια, he charged the Devil to give him illumination!

We have clarified the concept of *vis activa* only in a general way. (1) *Vis activa* signifies 'thrust'. (2) This thrust-character is supposed to inhere in every substance, *qua* substance. (3) A realization or tendency to fulfilment constantly arises from this thrust.

However, only now do we come to the real metaphysical problematic of substantiality, that is, to the question about the unity of substance as the primary entity. What is not substance, Leibniz calls 'phenomenon', meaning something that flows from substance and is derivative.

The unity of the monad is not the result of putting things together, something subsequent, but is what gives unity in advance. Unity as giving unity is active, *vis activa*; it is thrust, as *primum constitutivum* of the unity of substance. Here is the central problem of monadology, the problem of *thrust* and *substantiality*.

The basic character of this activity has become apparent. It remains obscure how exactly the thrust itself is supposed to be unity-giving. There is a further question of decisive significance: how is the totality of the universe in its connectedness constituted on the basis of the monad that has unity in itself?

First, an incidental matter needs to be considered. Already it has been stressed more than once that we can only come at the metaphysical sense of monadology if we venture a construction of the essential connections and perspectives, and use this as the clue to what was determinative for Leibniz himself when he projected his monadology.

Monadology aims at clearing up the Being of the beings. Thus, a paradigmatic idea of being must have been obtained from somewhere. It has been obtained at the place where something like Being immediately reveals itself to those who are inquiring philosophically. We relate ourselves to beings, become absorbed and lost in them, and are overpowered and made dizzy by them. But we not only relate ourselves to beings – we are at the same time beings ourselves. We are beings, and not just as a matter of indifference but in such a way that our own being lies close to us. Therefore, leaving aside other grounds, the inquirer's own being is always somehow the clue, and this is also the case with the project of monadology – though here, what has got into the initial outlook remains, admittedly, uninterrogated ontologically.

The constant regard to one's own *Dasein*, to the kind of being of one's own ego and how this is constituted, affords Leibniz the model for the unity which he ascribes to every entity. This is clear in many passages. To see clearly the part played by this clue is of decisive importance for understanding the monadology.

De plus, par le moyen de l'âme ou forme, il y a une véritable unité qui répond à ce qu'on appelle 'moi' en nous; ce qui ne sauroit avoir lieu ni dans les machines de l'art, ni dans la simple masse de la matière, quelque organisée qu'elle puisse être; qu'on ne peut considérer que comme une armée ou un troupeau, ou comme un étang plein de poissons, ou comme une montre composée de ressorts et de roues. (Système nouveau, Section 11.)

'Mediated to us by regard to "soul" or "form", there is offered the idea of a true unity, which corresponds to what is called in us the "I". Nothing of the sort is found either in man-made machines, or in material substance as such. So it can be considered only like an army or a flock, or like a pond full of fish, or even like a watch put together from springs and wheels.'

Substantiam ipsam potentia activa et passiva primitivis praeditam, veluti τό Ego vel simile, pro indivisibili seu perfecta monade habeo, non vires illas derivatas quae continue aliae atque aliae reperientur (Letter of June 20, 1703, to de Volder, Cartesian philosopher at the University of Leyden; G. II, p. 251; Buchenau II, p. 325). 'I think of substance itself, if it indeed has primordially a thrust-character, as an indivisible and complete monad, which is comparable to our "I" . . .'

Operae autem pretium est considerare, in hoc principio Actionis pluri-mum inesse intelligibilitatis, quia in eo est analogum aliquod ei quod inest nobis, nempe perceptio et appetitio . . . (June 30, 1704; G. II, p.270; B. II, p.347).

'One may consider further that this principle of action (thrust) is in the highest degree intelligible to us, for in some measure it forms an analogue to what inheres in ourselves, namely, to idea-tion and conation.'

Here particularly is made plain the fact that, first, the analogy to the 'I' is essential, and that, secondly, precisely this origin brings in its train the highest degree of intelligibility.

Ego vero nihil aliud ubique et per omnia pono quam quod in nostra anima in multis casibus admittimus omnes, nempe mutationes internas spontaneas, atque ita uno mentis ictu totam rerum summam exhaurio (1705; G. II, p.276; B. II, p.350).

'However, I presuppose everywhere and in everything only what we all must often enough acknowledge in our souls, that is, inward spontaneous variations, and with this one presupposi-tion of thought, I exhaust the sum of things.'

From self-experience, from the spontaneous variations per-ceptible in the 'I', from thrusting, this idea of being is drawn; and this idea is the only presupposition, i.e. the real content of the metaphysical project.

'Therefore, if we think that the substantial forms (*vis primitiva*) are something analogous to souls, then it must be doubted whether they have been justifiably repudiated' (Leibniz to Bern-ouilli, July 29, 1698; G. III, p.521; B. II, p.366). On this view, the substantial forms are not simply souls, nor are they new things or particles, but they correspond to souls. This is only the starting-point for projecting the basic structure of the monad.

'. . . *et c'est ainsi, qu'en pensant à nous, nous pensons à l'Être, à la substance, au simple ou au composé, à l'immatériel et à Dieu même, en concevant que ce qui est borné en nous, est en lui sans bornes*' (*Monado-logie*, Section 30).

'. . . while thinking in this way on ourselves, we grasp at

the same time the thought of being, substance, the simple and the composite, the immaterial, even God himself, when we represent to ourselves that what in us is found in a limited way is contained in him without limits' (*via eminentiae*).

From where then does Leibniz take his clue for defining the being of beings? Being is explained according to the analogy with soul, life and spirit. The clue is the ego.

The letter to Queen Sophia Charlotte of Prussia, *Lettre touchant ce qui est independent des sens et de la matière* (letter on what lies beyond sense and matter, 1702; G. VI, pp. 499ff.; B. II, pp. 410ff.), also shows that concepts and truth do not stem from the senses, but arise in the 'I' and the understanding.

This letter is of great importance for the problem of how guidelines of inquiry are supplied by the consideration of the self and by self-awareness in general. Leibniz says in the letter: *Cette pensée de* moy, *qui m'apperçois des objets sensibles, et de ma propre action qui en resulte, adjoute quelque chose aux objets des sens. Penser à quelque couleur et considérer qu'on y pense, ce sont deux pensées tres différentes, autant que la couleur même differe de moy qui y pense. Et comme je conçois que d'autres Estres peuvent aussi avoir le droit de dire* moy, *ou qu'on pourroit le dire pour eux, c'est par la que je conçois ce qu'on appelle* la substance *en général, et c'est aussi la considération de moy même, qui me fournit d'autres notions de* métaphysique, *comme de cause, effect, action, similitude etc., et même celles de la* Logique *et de la* Morale (G. VI, p. 502; B. II, p. 414).

'This thought of *my self*, of which I become aware by the objects of sense and by the activity that links me to them, adds something to these objects of sense. It is something quite different, whether I think of a colour or whether at the same time I reflect on this thought, just as the colour itself is different from the "I" that thinks of it. Since I now consider that other beings also may have the right to say "I", or that it might be said for them, it is from this that I understand what is quite generally designated as "substance". Further, it is the consideration of myself that furnishes me with other *metaphysical* concepts, such as cause, effect, action, similarity, etc., and even the basic concepts of *logic* and *morals*.'

L'Estre *même et* la vérité *ne s'apprend pas tout à fait par les sens.* '*Being* itself and *truth* may not be understood from the senses alone.'

Cette conception de l'Estre et de la Vérité *se trouve donc dans ce Moy, et dans l'Entendement plustost que dans les sens externes et dans la perception des objets extérieurs (ibid.,* p.503; B. II, p.415). 'This conception of *being and truth* is found in the "I" and the understanding rather than in the external senses and the perception of external objects.'

As regards the knowledge of being generally, Leibniz says in *Nouveaux Essais* (Book I, Chapter 1, Section 23): *Et je voudrois bien savoir, comment nous pourrions avoir l'idée de l'estre, si nous n'estions des Estres nous mêmes, et ne trouvions ainsi l'estre en nous.* (Cf. Section 21, likewise Section 30 of the *Monadologie*.) 'Here, too, even if by way of misunderstanding, being and subjectivity are brought together. We would not have the idea of being if we were not ourselves beings and found a being in us.'

Certainly, we must be in order to have the idea of being – this is Leibniz's meaning. To express the matter metaphysically, it is precisely our essence that we cannot be what we are without the idea of being. The understanding of being is constitutive for *Dasein.*

But it does not follow from this that we gain the idea of being by retreating into ourselves, as beings.

We are ourselves the source of the idea of being. But this source must be understood as the *transcendence* of the ecstatic *Dasein.* Only on the basis of transcendence can there take place the articulation of the different ways of being. A difficult and ultimate problem is to define the idea of being generally.

Because the understanding of being belongs to the subject as the transcending *Dasein,* the idea of being can be drawn from the subject.

What results from all this? First, that Leibniz – in spite of all his differences from Descartes – retains the self-certainty of the 'I' as the primary certainty, and that, like Descartes, he sees in the 'I', in the *ego cogito,* the dimension from which all basic metaphysical concepts must be drawn. The attempt to solve the problem of being, as the basic problem of metaphysics, is to be made by going back to the subject. Yet, in Leibniz as in his predecessors and followers, this return to the 'I' remains ambiguous, since the 'I' is not grasped in its essential structure and in its specific kind of being.

The way in which the ego functions as a clue is ambiguous in several respects. In relation to the problem of being, the subject is on the one hand the exemplary being, and as a being it furnishes with its being the idea of being. But on the other hand, the subject *is*, as that which understands being. As a being of a definite kind, it has *in* its being an understanding of being, and this is such that 'being' does not mean only the existing *Dasein*.

In spite of the fact that some genuine ontic phenomena are exposed, the concept of the subject itself remains ontologically unclarified.

Thus in Leibniz we are bound to get the impression as if the monadological interpretation of beings were an anthropomorphism, a panpsychism constructed on analogy with the 'I'. But that would be a superficial and arbitrary way of taking it. Leibniz himself tries to establish this analogizing consideration metaphysically: . . . *cum rerum natura sit uniformis nec ab aliis substantiis simplicibus ex quibus totum consistit Universum, nostra infinite differre possit*. 'For, since the nature of things is uniform, our own nature cannot be infinitely far removed from the other simple substances, out of which the whole universe is composed' (letter of June 30, 1704, to de Volder; G. II, p. 270; B. II, p. 347). The general ontological thesis adduced by Leibniz to establish this would, to be sure, still need to be established itself.

Instead of being content with crassly asserting an anthropomorphism, one should rather ask: What structures of one's own *Dasein* are supposed to be relevant for the interpretation of the being of substance? How are these structures modified so that they become appropriate for making intelligible every being and all grades of being?

The central problem which should be taken up again is: How is the thrust which distinguishes substance as such supposed to give unity? How must the thrust itself be defined?

If the thrust, or what is defined as thrusting, in so far as it is something that thrusts, is supposed to give unity, then it must be itself simple and must not have parts, like an aggregate or collection. The *primum constitutivum* (G. II, p. 342) must have an indivisible unity.

Quae res in plura (actu iam existentia) dividi potest, ex pluribus est aggregata, et res quae ex pluribus aggregata est, non est unum nisi mente nec habet realitatem nisi a contentis mutuatam (to de Volder; G. II, p. 267). The divisible has only a derivative content.

Hinc iam inferebam, ergo dantur in rebus unitates indivisibiles, quia alioqui nulla erit in rebus unitas vera, nec realitas non mutuata. Quod est absurdum (ibid.).

La Monade *dont nous parlerons ici, n'est autre chose, qu'une substance simple, qui entre dans les composés;* simple, *c'est à dire, sans parties* (*Monadologie*, Section 1). 'The monad of which we are to speak is nothing but a simple substance, which enters into what is composite. It is simple, i.e. it has no parts.'

But if substance is simply unifying, there must already be a manifold which gets unified by it. Otherwise, the problem of unification would be superfluous and senseless. That which unifies and has unity as its essence must naturally be related to a manifold. Precisely in the monad, as that which simply unifies, there must be a manifold. The essentially unifying monad must, as such, presuppose the possibility of a manifoldness.

The simple unifying thrust must, as a thrusting, at the same time carry in itself a manifold; it must *be* a manifold. Further, the manifold must have the character of thrusting, of the pressed and pushed, of movement generally. The manifold in movement is the variable and the changing. Moreover, that which is pressed in the thrust is the thrust itself. The changing of the thrust, that which changes in the thrusting, is that which gets thrust.

The thrust, as *primum constitutivum*, is said to be simply unifying, and at the same time to be the origin of the variable and its way of being.

'Simply unifying' implies that the unity is not a subsequent one, got by taking collectively something that has been assembled; it is a primordial and organizing unifying. The constitutive principle of the unifying must be prior to that which is subject to the possibility of being unified. That which unifies must be *prior*, it must be reaching out beforehand for something out of which every manifold has already received its unity. The simply unifying must be originally reaching out, and, as reaching out, it must be embracing in advance, so that all manifoldness diversifies itself already in its embrace. As Something which reaches out and embraces, it dominates beforehand, it is *substantia prae-eminens* (to de Volder; G. II, p.252; Schmalenbach II, p.35).

The thrust, *vis primitiva* as the *primum constitutivum* of the primordial unifying, must therefore reach out and embrace. Leibniz expresses the matter thus: *the monad is in its basic essence ideating or re-presenting*.

The inmost metaphysical motive for the monad's representing character is the ontological unifying function of the thrust. This motivation remained concealed from Leibniz himself. But in fact only this can be the motive – we cannot account for it by claiming that as a force the monad is something living, that to the living thing belongs a soul, and that to the soul, in turn, belongs representing. In this form, one would stay with a superficial transference of the mental to beings in general.

Because the thrust is that which originally and simply unifies it must remain 'representing'. To 'represent' is not to be taken here as a special capacity of the soul but is a structure in an ontological sense. Therefore the monad, in its metaphysical essence, is not a soul – rather it is the other way round. *The soul is a possible modification of the monad*. The thrust is not an event that may, on occasion, represent or produce representations; it is essentially representing. The structure of the thrusting event is itself reaching out, ecstatic. The representing is not a pure beholding, but unifies by anticipation into something simple the manifold which it presents to itself. In *Principes de la Nature et de la Grace* (Section 2) Leibniz says: . . . *les actions internes . . . ne peuvent être autre chose que ses* perceptions, (*c'est à dire, les représentations du composé, ou de ce qui est dehors, dans le simple*) . . . To des Bosses, he writes: *Perceptio nihil aliud quam multorum in uno expressio* (G. II, p. 311). And: *Nunquam versatur perceptio circa objectum, in quo non sit aliqua varietas seu multitudo* (*ibid.*, p. 317).

Like 'representing', 'striving' also belongs to the thrust (νόησις – ὄρεξις). Alongside *perceptio* (*repraesentatio*) Leibniz explicitly names a second capacity, *appetitus*. Leibniz has to lay particular stress on *appetitus* only because he himself did not immediately grasp the essence of the *vis activa* in a sufficiently radical way – in spite of the fact that he clearly marked it off from *potentia activa* and *actio*. The force still seems to remain something substantial, a core which then gets endued with representing and striving, while the thrust in itself is a representing striving and a striving representing. In any case, the *appetitus* has a special significance and is not synonymous with the thrust. *Appetitus* means a particular, intrinsic, constitutive moment of thrust, like *perceptio*.

The primordially unifying thrust must be in advance of every possible manifoldness, it must have allowed the possibility of such manifoldness to develop, it must have surpassed and outdistanced it. The thrust must somehow carry manifoldness in itself, and in its thrusting lets it be born in itself. So we must see the essential origin of manifoldness in the thrust as such.

Let us remember again that the thrust which outdistances beforehand is the primordially unifying unity, i.e. the monad is *substantia*. *Substantiae non tota sunt quae contineant partes formaliter, sed res totales quae partiales continent eminenter* (letter to de Volder, January 21, 1704; G. II, p. 263).

The thrust is the nature, i.e. the essence of substance. As a thrust, it is somehow active, but this active principle is always primordially re-presenting (*Principes de la Nature et de la Grace*, Section 2; S. II, p. 122). In the above-quoted letter to de Volder, Leibniz goes on: *Si nihil sua natura activum est, nihil omnino activum erit; quae enim tandem ratio actionis si non in natura rei? Limitationem tamen adjicis*, ut res sua natura activa esse possit, si actio semper se habeat eodem modo. *Sed cum omnis actio mutationem contineat, ergo habemus quae negare videbaris, tendentiam ad mutationem internam, et temporale sequens ex rei natura*. Here it gets plainly said that the activity of the monad is, as a thrust in itself, a thrust towards alteration.

From the ground up, thrust thrusts towards the other, and is a thrust that outdistances itself. This implies that in anything that thrusts, as something thrusting, there arises the manifold. Substance is *successioni obnoxia*, given over to successiveness. Thrust, as thrust, gives itself over to successiveness, not as something other than itself but as something belonging to it. What the thrust seeks to accomplish by thrusting, submits itself to temporal succession. The manifold is not strange to it, but at one with it.

In the thrust lies the tendency to transition from one thing to another. This tendency to transition is what Leibniz intended by *appetitus*. *Appetitus* and *perceptio* are, in the characteristic usage, equiprimordial determinations of the monads. The tendency itself is re-presenting. This means that out of a unity which overtakes it beforehand, it is unifying, unifying the transitions from representing to re-presenting, transitions which have been accomplished and are being accomplished in the thrusting of the thrust. *Imo rem accurate considerando dicendum est nihil in rebus esse nisi substantias simplices et in his perceptionem atque appetitum* (letter to de Volder; G. II, p. 270).

Revera igitur (principium mutationis) est internum omnibus substantiis simplicibus, cum ratio non sit cur uni magis quam alteri, consistitque in progressu perceptionum Monadis cuiusque, nec quicquam ultra habet tota rerum natura (ibid., p. 271).

The *progressus perceptionum* is the original in the monad, the representing tendency to transition, the thrust.

Porro ultra haec progredi et quaerere cur sit in substantiis simplicibus perceptio et appetitus, est quaerere aliquid ultramundanum ut ita dicam, et Deum ad rationes vocare cur aliquid eorum esse voluerit quae a nobis concipiuntur (ibid., p. 270).

The letter to de Volder of January 19, 1706 (first draft) is instructive for the genesis of the teaching on the thrust and the tendency to transition. *Mihi tamen sufficit sumere quod concedi solet, esse quandam vim in percipiente sibi formandi ex prioribus novas perceptiones, quod idem est ac si dicas, ex priore aliqua perceptione sequi interdum novam. Hoc quod agnosci solet alicubi a philosophis veteribus et recentioribus, nempe in voluntariis animae operationibus, id ego semper et ubique locum habere censeo, et omnibus phaenomenis sufficere, magna et uniformitate rerum et simplicitate* (G. II, p. 282 n.; S. II, pp. 54f. n.).

How far is the thrust, as thrust, unifying? To answer this question, we must look into the essential structure of the thrust.

1. The thrust is primordially unifying; this is not dependent on what it unifies and the way this is put together, but unifies by reaching out and embracing, as *perceptio*.

2. This *percipere* is embracing and is directed on a manifold which has already been set up in the thrust and arises from it. The thrust outdistances itself, it is an onrush. This belongs to the monadic structure, which always remains representing.

3. As *progressus perceptionum*, the thrust is thrusting to outdistance itself, it is *appetitus*. The tendency to transition is *tendentia interna ad mutationem*.

The monad, primordially and simply, is unifying in advance, and in such a way that this unifying isolates. The inner possibility of individuation, its essence, lies in the monad as such. Its essence is thrust.

Let us glance at what is said about the substantiality of substance. Substance is that which constitutes the unity of a being. What unifies is thrust, taken as having the characteristics shown above; re-presenting as a tendency to transition and as developing the manifold in itself.

Thrust, as this unifying factor, is the nature of a being. Every monad has its '*propre constitution originale*'. This is conferred with its creation.

What is it that basically determines every monad in this regard? How is individuation itself constituted? Going back to creation is only the dogmatic explanation of the origin of what has been individuated, not the clarification of individuation itself. In what does this consist? To answer this question, we must clear up still further the essence of the monad.

Manifestly, individuation must take place in that which fundamentally constitutes the essence of the monad. What essential character of the thrust-structure makes possible the isolation of the monad and establishes its uniqueness? How far is that which originally unifies something that isolates itself, even in its unifying?

If a moment ago we set aside the connection with creation, this was done only because it dealt with a dogmatic explanation. However, the metaphysical meaning that gets expressed in designating the monad as created is *finitude*. In a formal sense, 'finitude' means the state of being confined. How far can the thrust be confined?

If finitude, as confinedness, belongs to the essence of the thrust, we must define it in terms of the basic trait of the thrust. But this basic trait is unification – the unification that re-presents and outdistances. In this representing unifying, there is an anticipation of the unity towards which the thrust looks, as a representing thrust that tends to transition. In the thrust as representing *appetitus*, there is, as it were, a point to which attention is directed in advance, that unity itself from which the thrust unifies. This vanishing-point, *point de vue*, viewpoint, is constitutive for the thrust.

This vanishing-point, what is represented in advance in it, is also that which in advance regulates all thrusting. This is not impelled from outside, but, as movement that represents, the freely moving is always that which re-presents in advance. *Perceptio* and *appetitus* are determined in their thrusting primarily in terms of the vanishing-point.

But there is something here that up till now has not been explicitly grasped. Something, which in itself is reaching out like a thrust – and in such a way that it is and maintains itself precisely in this reaching out – has in it the possibility of laying hold on itself. In a thrusting towards, that which thrusts always traverses a dimension, i.e. it traverses itself, and is on this account open to itself, and this is in accord with its essential possibility.

Because of this dimensional self-openness, something that thrusts is able expressly to lay hold on itself; thus, as well as outwardly perceiving, it co-presents itself at the same time, so as to perceive itself in addition (*ad*) – so as to *apperceive*. In the *Principes de la Nature et de la Grace*, Section 4 (G. VI, p. 600), Leibniz writes: *Ainsi il est bon de faire distinction entre la* Perception *qui est l'état interieur de la Monade representant les choses externes, et* l'Apperception *qui est la* Conscience, *ou la connaissance reflexive de cet état interieur, laquelle n'est point donnée à toutes les Âmes, ny tousjours à la même Âme* (cf. *Monadologie*, Section 21ff.).

In this viewpoint, in a definite perspective of what is and what is possible, the whole universe, as it were, is brought into view, but in such a way that it is somehow refracted, namely, according to the grade of thrusting of a monad, according to its possibility of unifying itself in its diversity.

This condition of being opened up to itself can occur in varying grades, from complete transparency to insensitivity and giddiness. *Perceptio* and *appetitus* are not lacking to any monad, and with them a certain self-openness (admittedly this is not a co-representing of itself), even if it is only in the lowest degree. Corresponding to it is the particular viewpoint and the possibility of unifying appropriate to it, and this unity is what isolates each monad.

Just to the extent that it unifies – this is its essence – the monad isolates itself. But in the isolating, in the thrust out of the perspective peculiar to it, it unifies the universe represented to it beforehand, only according to its possibility. Thus every monad is itself a *mundus concentratus*. Every thrust in its thrusting concentrates the world – in itself – in its manner.

Because every monad, in a certain way peculiar to it, is the world, to the extent that it presents this, every thrust stands in a *consensus* with the universe. Because of this agreement of every representing thrust with the universe, the monads also stand in a connectedness among themselves. In the idea of the monad as the representing thrust that tends to transition, there is already locked up the fact that the world belongs to it in a perspectival refraction, and that all monads, as unities of thrust, are oriented in advance to the pre-established harmony of the universal All: *harmonia praestabilita*.

However, the *harmonia praestabilita* is, as the basic constitution of the actual world (the *actualia*), that which corresponds to the central monad, God, as that is attained by his thrusting. God's thrust is his will, and the correlate of the divine will is the *optimum*. *Distinguendum enim inter ea, quae Deus potest et quae vult: potest omnia, vult optima. Actualia nihil aliud sunt quam possibilium (omnibus com-*

paratis) optima; possibilia sunt, quae non implicant contradictionem (letter to Bernouilli of February 21, 1699; S. II, p. 11).

In every monad there is a possibility directed to the whole universe. The isolating which in the thrust fulfils itself as unification is thus always essentially an isolation of a being that belongs monadically to the world. The monads are not isolated fragments which yield a universe through their summation. Every monad, as the thrust such as we have characterized it, is, in each case and in its fashion, the universe. The thrust is a representing thrust which in each case represents the world in terms of a point of view. Every monad is a little world, a microcosm. But this last way of speaking does not hit the essential point, in so far as every monad is the world, in the manner that it thrustingly represents the world-whole in its unity, though it does not totally lay hold on it. Thus the universe is, in a manner, multiplied as many times as it has monads; analogously, the same city gets differently represented according to the different situations of a single observer.

From the discussion there may be drawn the illustration which Leibniz often liked to use for characterizing the complete essence of the monad. The monad is a living mirror of the universe.

One of the most essential passages is the one in the letter to de Volder of June 20, 1703 (G. II, pp. 251–2). *Entelechias differre necesse est, seu non esse penitus similes inter se, imo principia esse diversitatis, nam aliae aliter exprimunt universum ad suum quaeque spectandi modum, idque ipsarum officium est ut sint totidem specula vitalia rerum seu totidem Mundi concentrati.* 'The entelechies (monads) must be distinct among themselves, and not wholly like one another. They must (themselves as such) even be the principles of the difference. For each expresses differently the universe, according to its way of seeing (re-presenting). This is their peculiar task, to be so many living mirrors of what is, so many concentrated worlds.'

Several things get expressed in this sentence.

1. The differentiation of the monads is a necessary one, and belongs to their essence. They isolate themselves as they unify, each one unifying in terms of its viewpoint.

2. The monads are therefore themselves the origin of their differences, because of their way of seeing, *perceptio – appetitus*.

3. This unifying setting-forth of the universe, in each case in isolation, is precisely what is an issue for the monad as such in its being (thrust).

4. Each monad is the universe in a concentration. The centre of the concentration is the thrust determined by a viewpoint: *concentrationes universi* (G. II, p. 278).

5. The monad is *speculum vitale* (cf. *Principes de la Nature*, Section 3; *Monadologie*, Sections 63 and 77; and the letter to Remond, G. III, p. 623). A mirror (*speculum*) is a letting-see: *miroir actif indivisible* (G. IV, p. 557; S. I, p. 146), a thrusting, indivisible, simple mirroring. This letting-see comes about in the way of monadic being, where there is accomplished the unveiling of the world. The mirroring is not a rigid portrayal, but itself thrusts as such to new prefigured possibilities of itself. In anticipating the one universe in a viewpoint from which the manifold first becomes visible, it is *simple*.

From this point on, the essence of finite substance may be more clearly grasped, in a respect to which attention has not hitherto been given. Leibniz says in his letter to de Volder of June 20, 1703 (G. II, p. 249): *omnis substantia est activa, et omnis substantia finita est passiva, passionem autem connexa resistentia est.* What is intended here?

As far as the monad is in each case the whole, in *one* point of view, it is finite precisely on account of this co-ordination with the universe. It relates itself to a resistance, to something which it is not, and yet might be. To be sure, the thrust is active, but in all finite thrust, which takes place in a perspective, there is always necessarily the resistant which sets itself against the thrust as such. For in so far as it is thrusting from a particular viewpoint on the whole universe, it is something less. It is modified by its viewpoint. It remains to notice that the thrust, as thrusting, is related to resistance, just because it has the possibility of being the whole universe, but is not. This kind of passivity belongs to the finitude of the thrust, in the sense of what the thrust does not accomplish through its thrusting.

This negative factor, purely as a structural element of the finite thrust, shows the character of what Leibniz understands as *materia prima*. He writes to des Bosses (G. II, p.324): *Materia prima cuilibet Entelechiae est essentialis, neque unquam ab ea separatur, cum eam compleat et sit ipsa potentia passiva totius substantiae completae. Neque enim materia prima in mole seu impenetrabilitate et extensione consistit* . . .

Because of this essential and original passivity, the monad has the inner possibility of *nexus* with the *materia secunda*, with *massa*, with the definitely resistant, in the sense of material mass and weight (cf. the correspondence with the mathematician J. Bernouilli and with the Jesuit des Bosses, who was teacher of philosophy and theology at the Jesuit college in Hildesheim).

This structural element of passivity gives Leibniz a basis for making the connection of the monad with a material body (*materia secunda, massa*) intelligible, and for showing positively why *extensio* cannot constitute the essence of material substance, as Descartes had taught. But we cannot go into these matters here, nor into the further development of the monadology and the metaphysical principles which are connected with it.

15

Philosophical Meditation on the Seventh Chapter of Paul's Epistle to the Romans*

Hans Jonas

IN 1930 I dedicated my first publication, *Augustin und das paulinische Freiheitsproblem*,[1] to Professor Rudolf Bultmann 'in heartfelt gratitude'. The gratitude of the student was later joined by the friendship of maturity and the solace of loyalty. This bond has lasted through a life-time during which many another was broken and irretrievably lost in the dark abyss of our times. But apart from the personal bond which has thus grown through the years, there also stretches from that earliest witness of it to the present occasion a still unredeemed *theoretical* obligation, and I cannot honour the occasion better than by redeeming that obligation at last. What I had obligated myself to was an existential analysis of the Pauline self-experience which finds expression in Rom. 7.7–25. The interpretative history of this chapter in the course of the Pelagian struggle served the study of 1930 as a key to the clarification of Augustine's conception of certain crucial aspects of the Christian life, aspects that meet in the problem of free will. Two considerations determined the choice of just this key. One was the plain historical fact that this text

---

* Translated by the author from a revised version of *Zeit und Geschichte* pp. 557–70.

[1] A second, revised edition was published in 1965, with an introduction by James M. Robinson, and with the present study added as an appendix (Göttingen: Vandenhoeck & Ruprecht).

more than any other happened to serve as the focus and exegetical paradigm of the debate between the combatants themselves; the other was the conviction that this happened by rights, i.e. that the Pauline statements in question are indeed entitled to such a key position. But they are so only if what they express are not contingent but necessary truths.

The statements would be contingent, in the sense here used, if the 'I' speaking about itself were Paul's own empirical person, i.e. if we were dealing with an autobiographical report (of which one part would describe the past, another the present). They would also be contingent if the speaking 'I' were meant to represent a psychological type – such a type of person, e.g., for whom the forbidden, when and because it is forbidden, gains irresistible attraction: widespread as the *fact* may be (but how is irresistibility ascertained?), its generality would be merely empirical and as such admit of exceptions from the rule, which then would also be excepted from the consequences of the rule, such as the need for grace. And again the statements would be contingent if the 'I' were historical mankind (or the people of Israel as its prototype), which 'must' pass successively through the phases 'before the Law' and 'under the Law' in order to reach the phase of Grace 'after the Law': necessary as this sequence might be for the progress of history, the individual's belonging to a particular phase of it would be contingent and, for his perspective, would make the contents of the others inactive – for the post-Pauline Christian, e.g. a matter of mere historical retrospect.

Contrariwise, the statements would be necessary if the speaker were Man as such, so that what is said in this I-form about the failure of the attempted fulfilment of the Law holds for the Christian no less than for the Jew and the pagan, and precisely for this reason constitutes a valid argument for the Christian alternative, even an integral moment in its own inner movement. This last assumption I made and expressed in the study of 1930, without proving it. I rather declared its proof to be a still outstanding task. Now 'proof' can here only mean: explication of the modality of existence where a plight like that described in Rom. 7 is intelligibly at home and is bound to emerge from its radical acting-out. The phenomenologically demonstrated necessity of such a plight in such a life would lend support to the thesis that *it* could be what Paul meant. No proof can go further where in the nature of the case, i.e. according to the condition of all hermeneutics, we work with a hypothesis of empathic understanding.

Plan and draft of such an analysis indeed preceded the publication of the Augustine study and still provide the basis for the present, renewed attempt. It is the attempt at a structural analysis of that mode of human being in which the 'primal sin' spoken of by Paul and Augustine is inevitably committed and constantly renewed. The analysis aims at showing the genuine and dialectical necessity of the structure which here operates – genuine because rooted in the manner of movement of the human will as such, and dialectical because even as necessary it is yet the will's own deed, and thus the self-decreed fate of a freedom delivered up to itself. The philosophical analysis, tracing the necessity back to its existential ground, must show how the operative dialectic, which issues into the experience of insufficiency, in turn springs from the fundamental ontology of man's being. Only on this condition do the Pauline statements have the validity they claim. The essay thus experiments with a specific understanding of those statements, according to which they ought to have such a validity. For the purpose of this experiment we must dare to translate the content of Paul's statements into the language of existential form description – we might say 'translate back into', in so far as our preconception is correct.

We preface the analysis with the passage from the Epistle to the Romans to which it refers. What follows upon the quotation, however, is not an exegesis of the text but a freely philosophical reflection or meditation on the general existential phenomena which by hypothesis may be those that underlie the entire Pauline statement as its premise in the human constitution.

Rom. 7.7–25. (7) What then shall we say? That the law is sin? By no means! Yet, if it had not been for the law, I should not have known sin. I should not have known covetousness, had the law not said 'thou shalt not covet'. (8) But sin, receiving impulse from the commandment, wrought in me all kind of covetousness. For without the law sin is dead, (9) and I once lived without the law: but with the advent of the commandment sin came alive, and I died, (10) and the very commandment given for life proved to be death to me. (11) For sin, taking impulse from the commandment, tricked me and through the commandment killed me. (12) Now the law is holy, and the commandment is holy and just and good: (13) did, then, what is good bring death to me? By no means! Rather it was sin, so that it might come to light as sin, which wrought death in me through the good, so that sin through the very commandment might become sinful beyond measure. (14) For we know that the law is spiritual: but I am carnal, sold under sin. (15) For my own actions are beyond my ken: for not that which I will this I do, but what I hate this I perform. (16) Now if I perform that which I do not will, then I consent to the law and own that it is good. (17) But by that token it is not I any more who acts but the sin which dwells within me. (18) For I know that within me, that is, in my flesh, there dwells no good. For willing what is right is in my power, but doing it is not. (19) For I do not perform the good which I will, but the evil I will not, that I do. . . . (21) So I find in me, who wills to do right, a law by which evil lies close at hand. (22) For I delight in the law of God with the inner man, (23) but I see in my members another law at war with the law of my mind and making me captive to the law of sin which dwells in my members. (24) Wretched man that I am! Who will deliver me from this body of death? (25) Thanks be to God through Jesus Christ our Lord! So then, I of myself serve the law of God with the mind, but the law of sin with the flesh.

Man is that being who not only relates himself to the world in 'intending' acts (*cogitationes*) but in so doing also knows about these acts and therewith about himself as performing them. Thinking is always and simultaneously an 'I think that I think' (*cogito me cogitare*) : thus a being essentially self-related, and 'constitutively' so, because only in and through such self-relation it constitutes itself as an I. This most formal characteristic of 'consciousness' being always self-consciousness, its essential reflexivity, already provides the condition both for the possibility of human freedom and for the correlative necessity of its self-frustration. Both grow from the same root in the same act of realization. Not, it is true, from the innocuous iteration of a neutrally 'representational' *cogito me cogitare* : the *cogito* as mere representational (perceptual) reflection upon itself is not the originative seat of self-consciousness and freedom.

Rather it is the *will* in which the reflexive process relevant for freedom is performed. To the abstract-formal sense of the *cogito me cogitare* (as mere neutral self-awareness), there corresponds in the field of concrete existence the fact that willing likewise says, not only 'I will', but at the same time also 'I will that I will this' (*volo me velle*). Every willing wills itself and has at each moment already chosen itself. The will thus has in itself its own inherent reflexiveness in whose performance it primally constitutes itself as what it is, and by which it is radically distinguished from any mere desire or impulse (*appetitus* of any sort) : impulse, directive as it is, is non-reflective, appetition is not concurrently an *appeto me appetere* as volition is a *volo me velle*. It must be noted that the reflection of the will is itself volitional, the will is at once the wilful positing and affirmation of itself. The formula, therefore, reads not simply *cogito me velle* (after the Cartesian pattern), but *volo me velle*.

Thus understood the will is not just another and particular psychical function among others, classifiable under wishing, desiring, striving, impulse and the like. Nor is it the same as explicit resolve or, in general, anything that appears and disappears, is sometimes present and sometimes absent. The 'will' is *a priori* always there, underlying all single acts of the soul, making it possible for things like 'willing' as well as its opposite – lack or renunciation of will – to occur as special mental phenomena. It precedes any explicit resolve, any particular decision, although it is in itself, in its essential nature, nothing but continuously operative *decision about itself* – that permanent self-determination from which the subject cannot withdraw into the alibi of any neutral, indifferent, 'will-free' state: for the primal decision of will is itself the condition for the possibility of any such state, be it indifference or its opposite.

The 'will' which performs this permanent decision, or rather, which exists as its performance, is thus nothing other than the fundamental mode of being of *Dasein* in general, and the word merely signifies the formal-structural fact that the being of *Dasein* is such that in each of its actualities something or other is its concern, and the final concern in all the variable ones is its own being as the ultimate task of this being itself. In brief, 'will' signifies what Heidegger explicates under the head of 'care'. The formula 'being an issue for itself' circumscribes what we here mean by the reflection of the will.

This activity of the reflection of the will is the primal deed of the self's grounding itself. In its process there is brought about the continual self-constitution of the moral person, which sustains itself through it as the synthesis – at work from moment to moment, but continuously integrating – of the moral self-identification of the ego. Only through this self-constitution in the reflection of interest – be it even in the mode of self-dissembling – can there be an identical subject of possible accountability. All the phenomena of morality – freedom, choice, responsibility, conscience, guilt – are rooted in this primordial reflexiveness. Its *a priori* presence is the ontological basis of freedom.

But how is it to be understood that this selfsame fact also accounts for the necessary failure of freedom, its inevitable ensnarement in itself? Any deduction of 'insufficiency' as culpable and answerable must conceive it as a necessary but none the less self-committed deed of freedom itself, however paradoxical, even absurd this may seem. The (volitional) reflection of the will is the site of freedom: the domain of the will in general is also that of unfreedom: it must therefore be a *mode* of its reflection in which the latter is generated – and an unavoidable mode at that, if the Pauline-Christian insufficiency-thesis is

not to be a mere slander of man (which Nietzsche thought it to
be).

When we first introduced the *cogito me cogitare*, we rejected
its merely 'representational' (perceptual) modality as inadequate for the reflexivity of existence we are dealing with. But
now precisely this objectifying, viewing mode must be considered. Its role too is fundamental for the very possibility of
freedom. For only by objectifying the universe of the other to
the 'world' of objects over against itself, by standing back from
them as a subject, can freedom first create for itself its possible
'space': only from this generic 'distance' does the self enjoy freedom of movement and choice with respect to environing reality.
Now this same objectification which man, as a primordial act of
his being, performs *vis-à-vis* the being outside of him, setting it
over against himself as 'world', extends necessarily and cor-
relatively also to himself: he too becomes a *vis-à-vis* to himself.
In the objectification he steps forth out of an 'original' unity
with the all of being (the 'innocence of the creature') and opens
up an essential distance that is henceforth interposed between
himself and all-that-is. And across this cleavage the ego confronts not only that objectified universe but also itself as one of
whom it can say 'I' – and must say it because, with the isolation
once happened (this 'once' is the imaginary past of the Fall), it
thereafter must hold its own in this apartness for better or for
worse. Thus, along with the objectivation of world, there is already inevitably given the possible, viewing objectivation of
self (which is essentially distinct from the 'reflection of the will')
– and with it also the necessary possibility of that taking distance
from one's self which forsakes the humility of unmediated
creatureliness for the pride of mediacy in the relation to oneself.

Thus the reflection of the will is matched by an equiprimordial self-objectivation in 'intuition' (representation). In
terms of our formula, the relation can be expressed thus: The
volo me velle has in itself the essential possibility of changing into
a *cogito me velle* (*cogito* here taken in the specific sense of object-
thought). In this switch, freedom dispossesses itself: instead of
living within the execution of its self-chosen action, it looks at it

from without as its own observer and so has already become a stranger to it – has at bottom forsaken and betrayed it. Out of the pure futurity of unconditional engagement to which it had committed itself with the action, it has fallen into a 'present' of objectified 'data', in which curiosity finds the secure footing of a beholder against the totally exposed movement of the actor. In such self-objectivation freedom, shrinking from its part, assures itself again of that support of which in the venture of resolution it had just let go. *In concreto*, the objectivation can take a variety of psychological forms. Mostly, it will work with the side-glance of comparison with others (which means that the social sphere, the 'with-one-another', provides the horizon of objectivation, even if only in imagination). At any rate, it always substitutes me the observable actor for the action unconditionally living in the act itself. Shouldn't this be at least one meaning, perhaps the minimal as well as the fundamental meaning, of the Pauline concept of 'self-glorying' in one's work?

This peculiar obduration of temporality in itself, in its immanent performance, or, expressed in the formula chosen above, the inevitable, self-generating alternation from *volo me velle* to *cogito me velle*, can be regarded, so I think, as the trap in the Law that is not only consistent with its holiness but even directly caused by it, since the Law as such enjoins self-consciousness. It is a noble trap for it is nothing but the snare of freedom itself, prepared as well as dared by it, because 'Law' in the highest sense means nothing heteronomous but precisely freedom's demand upon itself. In other words, the dialectics here in force lies beyond the difference of heteronomy and autonomy. For the 'thou shalt not covet' in which Paul epitomizes the meaning of the Law, one might well substitute Kant's idea of duty as opposed to inclination – and the dialectics would remain the same in principle (see below).

However, with the turn from *volo* to *cogito*, from the reflection of the will to self-objectivation, the matter does not rest. A freedom that is in earnest about itself will not stop here; it is on guard against its own tricks and keeps its eyes open. The will in its living reflection will catch up with its own objectivation, find itself out in the appeased anchorage of looking-on and sweep it up in a new resolve that now encompasses this very situation together with the original object: this is thus, on a second plane, restored to its authenticity, and the congealing of the representational 'present' is re-dissolved into the flow of the volitional 'future'. But this new stage of 'reflection', in its temporal performance, will again lapse into objectivation – and so there ensues a ceaseless, self-mirroring back and forth, an elusive but highly real dialectic which is not even separable into successive parts. Driven by its own dialectic, the will modifies itself into the infinite spectrum of its inherent ambiguities, losing itself in it without ever attaining to a univocal condition – unless this, of itself endless, dialectic be halted from somewhere else. About this possibility philosophy has nothing to say.

Let us briefly treat the distinction, just touched upon, between 'heteronomous' and 'autonomous' ethics as it relates to our problem. In the form of heteronomy, especially in the religious context where it was first noted, the dialectic looks as follows: Since faith in the authority of the divine lawgiver (whereon hangs the obligatory force of his commandments) includes faith in his justice, the observation of his commandments *must* go along with the *expectation* of reward and punishment, even if no *wish* for them exists. But the certainty of this very faith, morally necessary as it is, destroys the purity of fulfilling the Law by giving it a utilitarian tinge: it thus protects divine morality and sanctity of the Law at the expense of the possibility of human morality and sanctity of the will. On the other hand, if the certainty of divine consideration of merit, positive and negative, is denied, then the seemingly rescued possibility of human morality is once again destroyed, since the Law of a God who is, if not outright unjust, at least incalculable, capricious, or indifferent – in short, the Law of an amoral God – cannot be holy and so cannot claim any moral authority. Thus fulfilling it cannot be moral either, except by error (lack of clarity) concerning the dubiousness of its source; and error itself, or insufficient reflection, must not be made the condition for morality. This means, then, that the possibility of human morality cannot be rescued at the price of waiving divine morality, any more than the divine can be preserved without perversion of the human; or, more briefly, human morality can no more exist without divine morality than co-exist with it.

So it is under the condition of heteronomy. Kant thought he could evade the dilemma by replacing the divine lawgiver with the self-legislation of reason, that is, by making the moral law autonomous and thereby detached from the idea of reward and punishment. But we have shown above that pure inwardness also procures for itself, through the mirroring of self-objectivation, a kind of self-recompense which (known under the name of vanity) is no less corrupting than the counting on return from outside – possibly more, since it can be enjoyed without delay, in the very performance of the act, whereas the counting on later reward from without demands the strength of a patient, long-sustained faith. In truth, the alternative 'autonomous-heteronomous' is overarched by the more essential alternative of authentic and inauthentic. For, obviously, the antinomy immanent in the act, which we have described, is more fundamental than that deriving from the consideration of transcendent and future facts, and it is common to both the autonomous and the heteronomous positions; it represents the existential antinomy of the moral realm as such, independently of all theories concerning the ground of the moral norm. To put it with utmost brevity, the antinomy means that under the condition of human ambiguity the attempt at holiness of will condemns itself to an unholy will. It is my opinion that this antinomy stands behind the despair of the Pauline self-description.

But why should the slipping into 'objectivation' be necessary? Being a possibility of freedom does not make self-objectivation a necessity. To begin with, the self-objectivation is necessary, indeed morally demanded, *qua* examination of one's own action, which is first of all an examination of one's motives (what Kant called the maxims of the will); and in so far as this examination – the self-exploration of conscience – belongs to morality as such, it is inseparable from the doing of good. In other words, self-objectifying is *eo ipso* given with the fact that morality is reflexive by its nature, and its necessity is itself a moral one, quite apart from its being also a psychological one. For the *homo religiosus* this takes the form of understanding himself from the standpoint of God and asking 'how does my action look to his eyes?' He must try to look at himself through God's eyes: i.e. to turn his own eyes into those of God. The 'before God' becomes thus, of necessity, a 'before myself'. But this substitution can, under the condition of creatureliness, only be maintained if I put in place of the infallibility of the divine gaze, which is denied me, the uttermost distrust of my human gaze. That is to say, for the sake of the good, the self-objectivation must be evil-minded and anticipate all possible wickedness. The distrust must be malicious. The malice of distrust is to know all that is possible, and to suspect that it is actual. In order to be able to know all that is possible, and to miss nothing, the distrust must be inventive in evil. Armed with that inventiveness, the distrust of myself becomes the inevitable price for the absoluteness which I, at one and the same time, ask of myself as an agent and arrogate to myself as a judge, and it must turn into positive self-suspecting. The attitude of distrust which I assume as my own observer *in loco Dei*, with a preconceived partiality *in malam partem*, is the only substitute for the omniscient impartiality of God; it is the sole self-protection against my corruptibility as judge in my own cause – the sole guarantee of my integrity. But it turns against itself. The distrust extends not only to what the observer finds before him, but also to this very observing itself, which again, after all, is an 'acting' of this ambiguous human I that is here meant to play a divine role. And such a distrust cannot help discovering that its own performance is not safe against turning from a critical into a self-enjoying observation, commending itself for being so critical, even merciless . . . Indeed the distrust must discover, if only it is sufficiently radical, that what it thinks, it also endows with reality: that the evil possibilities discovered, i.e. invented, i.e. created by itself, obtain with such discovery already a share in the realization of the will and thus as it were get their money's worth out of it. And it discovers that any purity of the will which may have existed in the naïve state, is lost in the cunning of a

will schooled by distrust itself – in the endlessly opened manifoldness of a soul grown more 'profound' in that school.

But why is the inner temptation irresistible? The question is
hardly distinguishable from the other: Why can one never be
sure not to have succumbed to it? Here lies the deepest mystery
of freedom, and the most difficult to verbalize. It concerns the
relationship of possibility and necessity in matters of freedom; or
rather, freedom's relation to its own possibilities, which is a
peculiar kind of necessity, namely that of a necessary act of freedom. For its description I have nothing at my disposal but
allusions and metaphors.

One might speak of a kind of giddiness of freedom in the
presence of its possibilities. Because those possibilities are left
entirely to its discretion, the giddiness befalls it as soon as it
takes its stand on itself alone and in the sole presence of itself,
i.e. of its own possibilities-to-be. And that giddiness causes it
actually to plunge into every espied possibility of self-variation
and try its taste, so long as this involves no more than the internal
self-interpretative definition of its 'How' and not yet the choice
of external action. Over the latter's 'What' freedom has, of
course, control; but not, paradoxically, over its own 'How', on
which the moral quality of the action depends.[2] Its not having
control over this is the paradoxical result of the power it equally
has over all the alternatives. Not in spite, but because of its unqualified authority over the 'How' of its being, freedom must be
iridescent. As each actual state of it does not simply exist but is
an *ad infinitum* continued product of its subjectively boundless
self-determination (which as such is placed amidst the dizzying
offer of its possibilities), and because this self-entrusted 'How' is

[2] The reader will note that this is the diametrical reverse of the Stoic
position which held that the external domain is outside our power while we
have clearly control over the internal domain. The profoundly significant
meaning of the reversal cannot here be elaborated. The prevalent modern,
counter-classical view of the relation of man's outer and inner power, viz.,
his dominion over things and his impotence over himself, is the end-result of
two largely independent historical developments in the one domain and the
other (that of nature and that of man), whose confluence shaped the modern
situation.

potentially manifold – freedom in each of its concretions is already *actually* many-faced, i.e. ultimately ambiguous.

As entirely left to itself, freedom in its being from moment to moment is its own product, and from this being-entrusted-to-itself no thing-like, unequivocal being, on which it could rest for support, relieves it at any point. Nor does anything protect freedom, fully released to itself as it is in reflection, from the lure of its own possibilities (as the unequivocal biological order did in the state of nature). Giddy with their protean phantasmagoria, it must itself glitter in their changing hues. And since the possibility of spuriousness, without which genuineness would not be that of freedom either, is positively its own, shrewdly self-seductive freedom manages, along with each act of genuineness, somehow to realize the corresponding spuriousness as well. As freedom it enmeshes itself in its possibilities as absolutely self-owned. Thus the self-produced concretion of its How at any moment, ever continued by the unsteady-sovereign reflection of self-concern, is comparable, as regards its critical identifiability, to the iridescence of a mother-of-pearl or an oil-slick on the water: each place seems at first to possess its colour of the spectrum unequivocally; but the slightest change of my location shows me another, and I discover that no place owns any one colour definitively but each already contains them all in itself . . .

Therefore, when in the oscillating reflexivity of the will during the consciously moral act, it happens that freedom is offered the defection into self-objectivation – a possibility inherent in consciousness as such – then it has already made use of it, however concealed: for freedom cannot resist its own possibilities. And this is the true and supreme mode of temptation: not the lure of sense nor outward self-seeking; not calculation of profit or fear of loss; not the charm of the forbidden or whatever else may be the spiritual sweetness of sin – none of these is the ultimate snare, all these one can resist; but this: that freedom, even when successful in abstaining from unethical outward 'work', encounters in the ownmost sphere of its self-grounding this inward possibility of itself which always lies in wait and claims its mental enactment; and the fact that here, within the mind, the mere thought is the act, and the possibility to think it is necessity to think it, and willing not to think it means to have already thought it, and not-having-thought-it may be concealing it, and concealing it may be its most suspicious presence: this labyrinthine structure of subjectivity *per se* makes the self-temptation irresistible to freedom in its helpless dealing with itself. Prior to any explicit counter-resolve, even in the heart of any counter-exertion itself, it has already succumbed to it in some subtle way. For since it is entirely alone with itself and has nothing but itself, it will not pass over any possibility of outwitting itself, if only here too it remains the agent: in being left-to-itself it is tuned to relishing itself and thereby is 'sinful'. If lust is at work here, it is the very non-sensuous, spiritual lusting of the self for itself. All purity of the will stands under this shadow.

Only at the stage of conscious, explicit morality does this temptation to self-objectivation come into play: i.e., precisely when, and not before, freedom in the 'reflection of the will' has come to itself. But that explicitness of morality is brought about by the Law. As the Law through its Ought first makes freedom reflective and thereby morality possible, so through its compulsion to self-scrutiny it creates at the same time the condition for the plight of subjectivity and the perversion of purpose. This is the 'impulsion to sin through the commandment'. But the possibility of the Law in turn rests on the condition of 'knowing' as such, which originates with the primal objectification of the world and the split between self and world that goes with it. Since it is that split which first makes it possible for him who thus can say 'I' to *know* about himself, and thereby generates freedom *and* its inescapable snare at the same time – therefore the myth ascribes the Fall to the eating from the tree of knowledge.

Again, the objectivation of the world is from the first a function of the human being-with-one-another, constituted by it and continuously maintained in its discourse. More specifically, this same discursive collectivity also furnishes the general horizon and the particular references for the self-objectivation as this operates, e.g., in comparison and appraisal and may reach right into the inner recesses of the 'isolated' subject. This is the existential basis for the critical role which the 'cosmos' in the sense of the human-social world plays in the context of the Pauline interpretation of being. This role of the *Miteinander* in the objectifying of self is not to be confused with that of the *man* ('they') in Heidegger's analytic of existence, i.e. with absorption into the anonymity of the many, the taking over by public generality. On the contrary, it is the setting-off of the I from its background, i.e. the attempt at being-oneself in the moral purpose, where the described self-objectivation lurks and does its disturbing work. This of the two is the more central phenomenon and the more profoundly pertinent to the human condition. It is also, admittedly, the rarer phenomenon. Whereas proper will and watchfulness can gain mastery over the one, the other pervades the very exercise of will and watchfulness itself.

If, then, our interpretation is correct, the plight described by Paul is not the individual's submersion into the 'they', but his submersion into the solitary presence of his own conscience; and this plight becomes the greater, the more he withdraws from the 'they' to his self, and the more radically he demands of himself a purity of will. It is a plight, therefore, which the Law produces only when taken seriously, not when practised outwardly. It is the plight, not of superficiality, but of depth, not of the letter but of the spirit, not of legality but of morality.

Jesus, in his critique of 'Pharisaism', had intended to expose the bad 'piety of the Law'. Paul's critique strikes at all piety of the Law. Jesus' critique was intended as a reproof, Paul's as a confession. The former castigates, from without, a false and corrigible attitude; the latter describes, from within, a true and unavoidable experience. Jesus did not summon away from the Law, but called from outward to inward, from blind to seeing, from superficial to serious compliance with the Law. But where that call leads, there the real experience of the Law waits. Thus the Pharisee corrected by Jesus would find himself in the Pauline situation, still unredeemed but cognizant of it: from an inauthentic he would have become an authentic Pharisee. So the

Pauline characterization of the condition 'under the Law', which leaves all caricature and merely empirical typology behind, can be understood as the epitome of an existential concept of 'Pharisaism' (taken in a broad, formalized sense of the word, not bound to the historical case). Accordingly the 'Pharisee' would be man as such *vis-à-vis* the Law whose just claim he strives to satisfy, *as he should*. This means that he would be a 'Pharisee' when at his most serious best; for precisely by assuming the 'holy Law of God' as a personal mandate he exposes himself to the supreme test of man answering for himself – and thereby enters the dimension where alone he can experience the valid defeat of his mere humanity. If he suffers defeat here – this is Paul's logic – then only one road is left to him: that which leads to the cross. 'Pharisee', then, is 'man before Grace' generally, but in earnest 'under the Law' and thus on principle open to the need for Grace, which he will come to feel when he fully realizes the condition of the 'Pharisee'. But such realization can only grow out of the experienced dialectic of the 'condition under the Law' itself, and since this includes the recognized necessity of that dialectic, it is at the same time a recognition of the existential unsurmountability of Pharisaism so understood. According to that understanding, then, existential self-knowledge belongs to the complete wholeness of the Pharisee. In the image drawn of him by Jesus, this is surely not the case.

To Jesus, 'Pharisee' is a party or group name; the Pharisee is an empirically encountered type among others, one faction within the religious variety of his environment, characterized by a specific attitude which Jesus fights because it is wrong and avoidable. He can therefore contrast it with better attitudes of which his environment also offers examples. It has always been debated whether Jesus' typology was empirically fair. But whatever the historical verdict, his was the naïve, popular, as it were visually typified image of Pharisaism; and the 'type' was a polemical caricature: the Pharisee is in the crude sense a hypocrite and demonstrative bigot. The truly pious Jew never had reason to recognize himself in this picture. He could recognize it as the warning against a temptation by which the Torah piety is threatened and to which Jews (and others) have often succumbed, but which they also have time and again successfully withstood. Jesus himself did not have to search far for examples of true piety. He found them in simple, believing women, Samaritans, publicans. Contrasted with them the Pharisee, as the gospel paints him, stands already convicted by the plain standards of popular, moral feeling – which therefore may easily indulge in that sense of superiority in which the roles can become reversed again or the distinctions obliterated.

For Paul, on the other hand, the Pharisee is not a religiously inferior type, as he was for Jesus, but the ultimate position before Grace; and for him it is just the most earnest, most inward striving ('with the inner man') to fulfil the 'holy Law', conceived in its essential demand, that is doomed to that failure which signifies the defeat of man as such – of man who, in the attempt to fulfil the Law, exposed his humanity to the ultimate test and in its pursuit came into his ultimate possibility and impossibility before God. (So it is if one really must push things that far – which of course is open to question.) Jesus thus takes the lowest, Paul the highest mode of Law-piety for his critical object; and that is not just a difference in polemical method, but a difference in the anthropological premise itself. For the highest position comprises all others under itself, and with a verdict on the optimal the lesser is judged *a fortiori*. The lesser, on the other hand, leaves above itself human alternatives still eligible – namely, the non-'pharisaical' – and thus represents a specific corruption, widespread perhaps and typically human, yet capable of rejection and avoidance.

Accordingly, Jesus simply points to the true attitude towards God as the superior alternative and assumes it to be attainable, given genuine human willingness. That he holds that willingness to be more readily found among the poor and oppressed than elsewhere is another matter. But found it is in his view; and so his death on the cross, or generally, the redemption of a mankind, constitutionally sinful, through the suffering and resurrection of a saviour, has no rightful place in Jesus' own message. Men have immediate access to God and to genuine being before him, so long as they hear and heed his call. This statement only reiterates the old, if much-disputed, proposition that Paul's message *about* Jesus as the crucified Christ signifies a decisive step beyond Jesus' own message – a step with which the paths of the old creed and the new really part.

LIST OF ENGLISH WORKS
AND TRANSLATIONS

Albright, W. F., *From the Stone Age to Christianity: Monotheism and the Historical Process*, Baltimore: Johns Hopkins Press, 1957².

Baird, J. A., *The Justice of God in the Teaching of Jesus*, Philadelphia: Westminster Press, and London: SCM Press, 1963.

Barth, Karl, *The Epistle to the Romans*, tr. from the 6th German ed. by Edwyn C. Hoskyns. London and New York: Oxford University Press, 1933, 1957.

Bartsch, Hans-Werner, ed., *Kerygma and Myth*, tr. by R. H. Fuller. Vol. I from *KuM* I–II, London: SPCK, 1953; New York: Harper and Bros., 1954; vol. II from *KuM* III–V, London: SPCK, 1962.

Bauer, Walter, *A Greek–English Lexicon of the New Testament and Other Early Christian Literature*, tr. from the 4th German ed. by W. F. Arndt and F. W. Gingrich. Chicago: University of Chicago Press, and Cambridge: Cambridge University Press, 1957.

Beasley-Murray, G. R., *A Commentary on Mark Thirteen*, London and New York: Macmillan, 1957.
– *Jesus and the Future*, London: Macmillan, and New York: St Martin's Press, 1954.

Black, Matthew, and Rowley, H. H., *Peake's Commentary on the Bible*, London and New York: Nelson, 1962.

Blair, E. P., *Jesus in the Gospel of Matthew*, New York: Abingdon Press, 1960.

Blass, F. W., and Debrunner, A., *A Greek Grammar of the New Testament and Other Early Christian Literature*, tr. and rev. by R. W. Funk. Chicago: Chicago University Press, and Cambridge: Cambridge University Press, 1961.

Boman, Thorleif, *Hebrew Thought Compared with Greek*, tr. by J. L. Moreau. London: SCM Press, and Philadelphia: Westminster Press, 1960.

Bonhoeffer, Dietrich, *Act and Being*, tr. by Bernard Noble. London: Collins, and New York: Harper and Row, 1962.
– *Christology*, tr. from *Gesammelte Schriften* III, pp. 166–242, by J. S. Bowden. London: Collins, 1966. Published as *Christ the Center*, New York: Harper and Row, 1966.

Bonhoeffer—contd

- *The Communion of Saints: a Dogmatic Inquiry into the Sociology of the Church*, tr. by various hands, ed. R. Gregor Smith. London: Collins, and New York: Harper and Row, 1963.
- *The Cost of Discipleship*, tr. by R. H. Fuller. London: SCM Press, and New York: Macmillan, 1959².
- *Creation and Fall: a Theological Interpretation of Genesis 1–3*, tr. J. C. Fletcher. London: SCM Press, and New York: Macmillan, 1959.
- *Dein Reich komme*. See Godsey.
- *Ethics*, tr. by N. Horton Smith. London: SCM Press, and New York: Macmillan, 1955.
- *Letters and Papers from Prison*, tr. from *Widerstand und Ergebung* by R. H. Fuller and others. Rev. and enlarged ed., London: SCM Press, 1967³. Published as *Prisoner for God*, New York: Macmillan, 1967² (with different pagination).
- *No Rusty Swords*, Selections from *Gesammelte Schriften* I–IV, tr. by E. H. Robertson and J. S. Bowden. London: Collins, and New York: Harper and Row, 1965.

Bornkamm, Günther, *Jesus of Nazareth*, tr. by I. and F. McLuskey with J. M. Robinson. New York: Harper and Bros., and London: Hodder and Stoughton, 1960.

Bornkamm, Günther, Barth, Gerhard, and Held, Heinz-Joachim, *Tradition and Interpretation in Matthew*, tr. by Percy Scott. London: SCM Press, and Philadelphia: Westminster Press, 1963.

Braaten, C. E., and Harrisville, R. A., eds., *The Historical Jesus and the Kerygmatic Christ*, New York: Abingdon Press, 1964.

Bultmann, Rudolf, *Essays Philosophical and Theological*, tr. from *Glauben und Verstehen* II by J. C. G. Greig. London: SCM Press, and New York: Macmillan, 1955.
- *Existence and Faith. Shorter Writings of Rudolf Bultmann*. Selected, translated, and introduced by Schubert M. Ogden. New York: Meridian Books, 1960; London: Hodder and Stoughton, 1961.
- *Faith and Understanding*, tr. from *Glauben und Verstehen* I by L. Pettibone Smith. London: SCM Press, and New York: Harper and Row, 1969.
- *History and Eschatology*, Edinburgh: Edinburgh University Press, 1957; New York: Harper and Row, 1962.
- *The History of the Synoptic Tradition*, tr. by John Marsh. Oxford: Blackwell, and New York: Harper and Row, 1963.
- *Jesus and the Word*, tr. from *Jesus* by L. Pettibone Smith and E. H. Lantero, New York and London: Charles Scribner's Sons, 1934, 1958.

– 'The Primitive Christian Kerygma and the Historical Jesus', tr. from *Das Verhältnis der urchristlichen Christusbotschaft zum historischen Jesus* (SAH 1960, Abh. 3), by Braaten and Harrisville, *op. cit.*, pp. 15–42.

– *Theology of the New Testament*, tr. by Kendrick Grobel. 2 vols., New York: Charles Scribner's Sons, and London: SCM Press, 1952, 1955.

Carrington, Philip, *According to Mark: Running Commentary on the Oldest Gospel*, Cambridge and New York: Cambridge University Press, 1960.

Charles, R. H., *The Apocrypha and Pseudepigrapha of the Old Testament*, 2 vols, Oxford: Clarendon Press, 1913.

Cole, R. A., *The Gospel according to St Mark*, London: Tyndale Press, and Grand Rapids, Michigan: Eerdmans, 1957.

Collingwood, R. G., *The Idea of History*, Oxford: Clarendon Press, 1946.

Conzelmann, Hans, *The Theology of St Luke*, tr. from *Die Mitte der Zeit* by Geoffrey Buswell. London: Faber and Faber, and New York: Harper and Bros., 1960.

Cranfield, C. E. B., *The Gospel according to St Mark*, Cambridge: Cambridge University Press, 1959.

Cullmann, Oscar, *Christ and Time*, tr. by Floyd V. Filson. Rev. ed., London: SCM Press, 1962; Philadelphia: Westminster Press, 1964.
– *The Christology of the New Testament*, tr. by S. C. Guthrie and C. A. M. Hall. London: SCM Press, and Philadelphia: Westminster Press, 1963[2].

Dibelius, Martin, *From Tradition to Gospel*, tr. from *Die Formgeschichte des Evangeliums* by B. Lee Woolf. London: Nicholson and Watson, 1934; New York: Charles Scribner's Sons, 1935, 1965.

Dodd, C. H., *The Coming of Christ*, Cambridge: Cambridge University Press, and Toronto: Macmillan, 1951.
– *The Parables of the Kingdom*, London: Nisbet, 1936; New York: Charles Scribner's Sons, 1958.

Doresse, J., *The Secret Books of the Egyptian Gnostics: an Introduction to Gnostic Coptic Manuscripts Discovered at Chenoboskion*, tr. by P. Mairet. New York: Viking Press, 1958; London: Hollis and Carter, 1960.

Dupont-Sommer, A., *The Dead Sea Scrolls: a Preliminary Survey*, tr. by E. M. Rowley. Oxford: Blackwell, 1952.
– *The Essene Writings from Qumran*, tr. by G. Vermès. Oxford: Blackwell, 1961; New York: Meridian Books, 1962.

Ebeling, Gerhard, *The Nature of Faith*, tr. by R. Gregor Smith. London: Collins, 1961; Philadelphia: Muhlenberg, 1962.
– *Word and Faith*, tr. by J. W. Leitch. London: SCM Press, and Philadelphia: Fortress Press, 1963.

Eissfeldt, Otto, *The Old Testament: an Introduction*, tr. from the 3rd German ed. by P. R. Ackroyd. Oxford: Blackwell, and New York: Harper and Row, 1965.

Enslin, Morton Scott, *The Prophet from Nazareth*, New York: McGraw-Hill, 1961.

Erman, Adolf, *The Literature of the Ancient Egyptians. Poems, Narratives, – and Manuals of Instruction from the Third and Second Millennia BC*, tr. by A. M. Blackman. London: Methuen, 1927.

Farmer, W. R., *Maccabees, Zealots and Josephus. An Inquiry into Jewish Nationalism in the Greco-Roman Period*, New York: Columbia University Press, 1956; London: Oxford University Press, 1957.

Fuchs, Ernst, *Studies of the Historical Jesus*, tr. from *Zur Frage nach dem historischen Jesus* by Andrew Scobie. SBT 42. London: SCM Press, and Naperville: Allenson, 1964.

Fuller, R. H., *The Mission and Achievement of Jesus*. SBT 12. London: SCM Press, and Chicago: Allenson, 1954.

Glasson, T. F., *The Second Advent. The Origin of the New Testament Doctrine*, 3rd ed. revised, London: Epworth Press, 1963.

Gloege, Gerhard, *The Day of His Coming. The Man in the Gospels*, tr. from *Aller Tage Tag* by Stanley Rudman. London: SCM Press, 1963.

Godsey, J. D., *Preface to Bonhoeffer: the Man and Two of his Shorter Writings*, Philadelphia: Fortress Press, 1965. (Pages 27–47 = tr. of *Dein Reich Komme*.)

Gogarten, Friedrich, *Demythologizing and History*, tr. by N. Horton Smith. London: SCM Press, and New York: Charles Scribner's Sons, 1955.

Gollwitzer, Helmut, *The Existence of God as Confessed by Faith*, tr. by J. W. Leitch. London: SCM Press, and Philadelphia: Westminster Press, 1965.

Grant, F. C., *Ancient Judaism and the New Testament*, New York: Macmillan, 1959; Edinburgh: Oliver and Boyd, 1960.

Guy, H. A., *The Origin of the Gospel of Mark*, London: Hodder and Stoughton, 1954; New York: Harper and Bros., 1955.

Heidegger, Martin, *Being and Time*, tr. by John Macquarrie and Edward Robinson. London: SCM Press, and New York: Harper and Row, 1962.

Hennecke, Edgar, *New Testament Apocrypha*, tr. by A. J. B. Higgins and others, and ed. by R. McL. Wilson, from the 3rd German ed. by W. Schneemelcher. 2 vols., London: Lutterworth Press, and Philadelphia: Westminster Press, 1963 and 1965.

Jeremias, Joachim, *The Eucharistic Words of Jesus*, tr. from the 3rd German ed. by Norman Perrin. London SCM Press, and New York: Charles Scribner's Sons, 1966.
– *Jesus' Promise to the Nations*, tr. by S. H. Hooke, SBT 24. London: SCM Press, and Naperville: Allenson, 1958.
– *The Parables of Jesus*, rev. ed., tr. from the 6th German ed. by S. H. Hooke. London: SCM Press, and New York: Charles Scribner's Sons, 1963.

Johnson, Sherman E., *A Commentary on the Gospel according to Mark*, London: A. and C. Black, and New York: Harper and Bros., 1960.
– *Jesus in his own Times*, London: A. and C. Black, 1958.

Kant, Immanuel, *The Moral Law or Kant's Groundwork of the Metaphysic of Morals*, tr. by H. J. Paton. London: Hutchinson, 1948.

Käsemann, Ernst, *Essays on New Testament Themes*, tr. from selections from *Exegetische Versuche und Besinnungen* I by W. J. Montague. SBT 41. London: SCM Press, and Naperville: Allenson, 1964.
– *New Testament Questions of Today*, tr. from selections from *Exegetische Versuche und Besinnungen* II by W. J. Montague. London: SCM Press, and Philadelphia: Westminster Press, 1969.

Kidd, B. J., ed., *Documents Illustrative of the Continental Reformation*, Oxford: Clarendon Press, 1911.

Kilpatrick, G. D., *The Origins of the Gospel according to St Matthew*, Oxford: Clarendon Press, 1946.

Kittel, Gerhard, ed., *Theological Dictionary of the New Testament*, tr. by G. W. Bromiley. Grand Rapids, Michigan: Eerdmans, 1964ff.

Kramer, Werner, *Christ, Lord, Son of God*, tr. by Brian Hardy. SBT 50. London: SCM Press, and Naperville: Allenson, 1966.

Kümmel, W. G., *Introduction to the New Testament*, tr. from the 12th German ed. by A. J. Mattill, Jr. Philadelphia: Westminster Press, and London: SCM Press, 1966.
– *Promise and Fulfilment*, tr. by D. M. Barton from the 3rd German ed. SBT 23. London: SCM Press, and Naperville: Allenson, 1957.

Leaney, A. R. C., *A Commentary on the Gospel according to St Luke*, London: A. and C. Black, and New York: Harper and Bros., 1958.

Leeuw, G. van der, *Religion in Essence and Manifestation*, tr. from *Phänomenologie der Religion* by J. E. Turner. London: Allen and Unwin, and New York: Macmillan, 1938.

Liddell, H. G., and Scott, Robert, *A Greek-English Lexicon,* new (9th) ed., rev. and augmented by H. S. Jones, Oxford: Clarendon Press, 1940.

Linnemann, Eta, *The Parables of Jesus; Introduction and Exposition,* tr. by John Sturdy from the 3rd German ed. London: SPCK, and New York: Harper and Row, 1966.

Lövestam, E., *Son and Saviour* (CN 18), Lund: Gleerup, 1961.

Lundström, Gosta, *The Kingdom of God in the Teaching of Jesus. A History of Interpretation from the Last Decades of the Nineteenth Century to the Present Day,* tr. by Joan Bulman. Richmond, Va.: John Knox Press, and Edinburgh: Oliver and Boyd, 1963.

Milik, J. T., *Ten Years of Discovery in the Wilderness of Judaea,* tr. by John Strugnell, SBT 26. London: SCM Press, and Naperville, Allenson, 1959.

Marxsen, Willi, *Mark the Evangelist: Studies on the Redaction History of the Gospel* tr. by James Boyce. New York: Abingdon Press, 1969.

Mowinckel, Sigmund, *He that Cometh,* tr. by G. W. Anderson. Oxford: Blackwell, and New York: Abingdon Press, 1956.

Neville, Graham, *The Advent Hope,* London: Darton, Longman and Todd, 1961.

Nietzsche, F. W., *Joyful Wisdom,* tr. by Thomas Common. New York: Ungar Publishing Co., 1960.

Otto, Rudolf, *The Kingdom of God and the Son of Man. A Study in the History of Religion,* tr. from rev. German ed. by F. V. Filson and B. Lee Woolf. Rev. ed., London: Lutterworth Press, 1943; Boston: Starr King Press, 1957.

Perrin, Norman, *The Kingdom of God in the Teaching of Jesus,* London: SCM Press, and Philadelphia: Westminster Press, 1963.

Pritchard, J. B., *Ancient Near Eastern Texts Relating to the Old Testament,* 2nd ed. corr. and enlarged, Princeton: Princeton University Press, 1955.

Rad, Gerhard von, *Old Testament Theology,* tr. by D. M. G. Stalker. 2 vols., Edinburgh: Oliver and Boyd, and New York: Harper and Row, 1962, 1965.

Rahner, Karl, *Theological Investigations,* tr. by Cornelius Ernst and Karl H. Kruger. Baltimore: Helicon Press, and London: Darton, Longman and Todd, 1961ff.

Richardson, Alan, *An Introduction to the Theology of the New Testament,* London: SCM Press, and New York: Harper and Bros., 1958.

Robinson, James M., *A New Quest of the Historical Jesus*. SBT 25. London: SCM Press, and Naperville: Allenson, 1959.
and Koester, Helmut, *Trajectories through Early Christianity*, Philadelphia: Fortress Press, 1971.

Robinson, John A. T., *Jesus and His Coming*, London: SCM Press, and New York: Abingdon Press, 1957.

Schmithals, Walter, *Paul and James*, tr. by D. M. Barton, SBT 46. London: SCM Press, and Naperville: Allenson, 1965.

Scholem, Gershom, *Major Trends in Jewish Mysticism*, 3rd rev. ed., New York: Schocken Books, 1961.

Schnackenburg, Rudolf, *God's Rule and Kingdom*, tr. by John Murray. Freiburg: Herder and Herder, and London: Nelson, 1963.

Schürer, Emil, *A History of the Jewish People in the Time of Jesus Christ*, tr. J. Macpherson, S. Taylor and P. Christie. 5 parts and index. Edinburgh: T. and T. Clark, reprinted 1898–1900.

Schweitzer, Albert, *The Mysticism of Paul the Apostle*, tr. by W. Montgomery. London: A. and C. Black, 1931, 1953; New York: Holt, 1931, Macmillan, 1955.
– *Paul and his Interpreters*, tr. by W. Montgomery. London: A. and C. Black, 1948; New York: Macmillan, 1956.
– *The Quest of the Historical Jesus*, tr. by W. Montgomery. 3rd ed., London: A. and C. Black, 1956; New York: Macmillan, 1961.

Schweizer, Eduard, *Lordship and Discipleship*, tr. from *Erniedrigung und Erhöhung bei Jesus und seinen Nachfolgern*. SBT 28. London: SCM Press, and Naperville: Allenson, 1960.

Smith, R. Gregor, ed., *World Come of Age*, tr. from selections from *Die Mündige Welt* I–IV by the editor and others. London: Collins, and Philadelphia: Fortress, 1967.

Stendahl, Krister, ed., *The Scrolls and the New Testament*, New York: Harper and Bros., 1957; London: SCM Press, 1958.

Tasker, R. V. G., *The Gospel according to St Matthew*, London: Tyndale Press, and Grand Rapids, Michigan: Eerdmans, 1961.

Taylor, Vincent, *The Gospel according to St Mark*, London: Macmillan, 1952.
– *The Life and Ministry of Jesus*, London: Macmillan, 1954; Nashville: Abingdon Press, 1955.

Teeple, H. M., *The Mosaic Eschatological Prophet*, Philadelphia: Society of Biblical Literature, 1957.

Tillich, Paul, *The Courage to Be*, New Haven and London: Yale University Press, 1952.

Tödt, H. E., *The Son of Man in the Synoptic Tradition*, tr. by D. M. Barton, London: SCM Press, and Philadelphia: Westminster Press, 1965.

INDEX OF MODERN SCHOLARS

INDEX OF REFERENCES

1. OLD TESTAMENT

2. APOCRYPHA AND PSEUDEPIGRAPHA

Testaments of the Twelve Patriarchs

3. QUMRAN

Italic figures indicate references to the book as a whole

4. OTHER JEWISH TEXTS

Philo

Josephus

5. NEW TESTAMENT

6. GNOSTIC WRITINGS AND OTHER NEW TESTAMENT APOCRYPHA

7. CHURCH FATHERS

‡ Anonymous works.

OTHER ANCIENT WRITERS